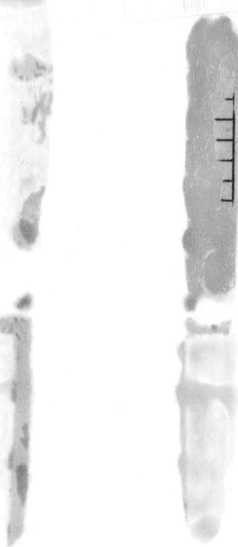

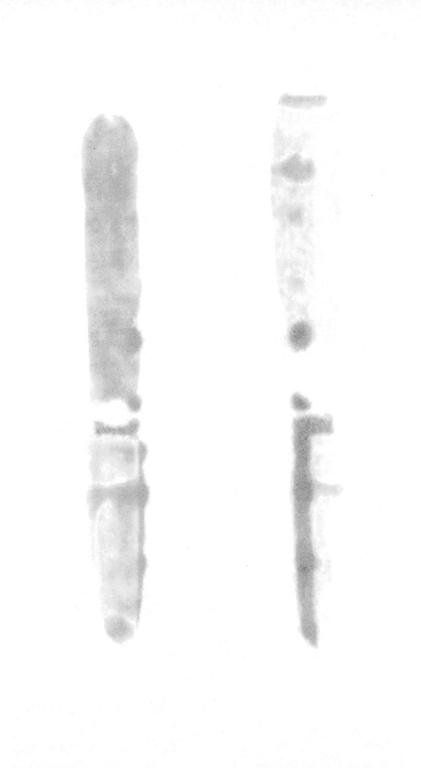

British Drama

By the Same Author

The Development of the Theatre
World Drama
The Theatre and Dramatic Theory

British Drama

Allardyce Nicoll

Revised by J. C. Trewin

Sixth Edition
revised and reset

BARNES & NOBLE
BOOKS
10 East 53d St., New York 10022
(a division of Harper & Row Publishers, Inc.)

First published in Great Britain 1925
by GEORGE G. HARRAP & Co. LTD
182–184 High Holborn, London WC1V 7AX

Second Edition published 1927
Third Edition published 1932
Reprinted: 1944; 1945
Fourth Edition published 1947
Reprinted: 1949; 1951; 1953; 1955; 1958; 1961
Fifth Edition, revised and reset, published 1962
Reprinted: 1964; 1966; 1969; 1973
Sixth Edition, revised and reset, published 1978

Published in the USA 1978 by
HARPER & ROW PUBLISHERS, INC.
BARNES & NOBLE IMPORT DIVISION

ISBN 0–06–495158–8

Set in V.I.P. Palatino
by Western Printing Services, Avonmouth
Printed in Great Britain
by The Pitman Press, Bath
and bound by Western Book Company

Preface

Professor Allardyce Nicoll said in his preface to the fifth revised edition of *British Drama*:

> The title of this book sufficiently indicates its purpose—to provide a general survey of the drama in Great Britain from the earliest times to the present. In this edition the original text has been revised throughout, and extended so as to include reference to the latest dramatic movements of our own time.

I need merely repeat this, adding that I am responsible for the last chapter which deals with the twentieth century. (The bibliography has also been revised to take account of the latest scholarship.) Throughout I have had the wisely discerning professional partnership of Messrs Roy Minton and Simon Colverson to whom this new edition has owed so much. I am also grateful for the valuable help in various matters, textual, pictorial or both, of Wendy Trewin, Dr E. Martin Browne, Mr P. Meredith of the University of Leeds and Mr Stewart Lack.

June 1978   *J.C.T.*

Contents

Illustrations

One
The Beginnings to Shakespeare

Introductory: The Classical Heritage

The mimetic instinct is confined to no single nation; it is universal in its appeal and reveals itself as one of the most primitive of human emotions. The desire of men and women to garb themselves in the semblance of attendants upon a god, even to take upon themselves the god-form in its august majesty; the desire to re-enact the sacred stories, whether of Greek deities or of Jehovah and Christ; the later desire of the peasant to place himself, if but for a fleeting moment, in the position of a courtier, or of the courtier to forget for a time the intrigues and the cares of his state in a fondly imagined Arcady—all of these are manifestations of the one primeval passion which reveals itself in church liturgy, in folk-mummings, and in masquerades, no less than in the tragedies of Æschylus and of Shakespeare. This universal nature of acting and of drama renders a study of the stage at once more fascinating and more difficult than the study of almost any other type of literature. It demands, in the first place, a careful investigation of religious ritual and of folk-customs, and, in the second, an equally careful investigation of the literatures of diverse races. No account of English drama can possibly be complete without reference to the services of the early Church, to the relics of pagan ceremonials preserved in half-fossilized forms among the peasantry, and to the development of dramatic activities in other lands.

At the very start of our inquiry into the origin and growth of the English stage, the need to look beyond the immediate to the general becomes apparent. Drama in England does not begin until the tenth century, and the impulse which brought it into being was completely independent, uninfluenced by any force from without. At the same time, we cannot dismiss the thought that, centuries before, the ancient Athenians had seen the stage evolving in their own culture and had brought that stage to a high level of achievement. From Greece, this drama was passed on to Rome and, although there it lost its early power, it pursued its activities to the time when the Empire eventually fell, in the fifth century, under the attacks of the barbarian hordes. Three aspects of the earlier dramatic movement demand at least some brief attention before we pass to the native English theatre. First, there is the interest of observing that, in essence, the ultimate source of the drama which rose in the tenth century is similar to that which brought the Athenian drama into existence. Secondly, there is corresponding interest in finding that, without any direct impress of the one upon the other, many of the same features are discernible in both. And thirdly, there is the fact that, while the earliest efforts of the English drama were wholly native and innocent of classical influence, we cannot escape references to the Greek and the Roman after the sixteenth-century period when English playwrights recognized their theatrical activities.

In Greece, both comedy and tragedy derived from religious ceremonial. We may think of the latter as starting from a chorus of worshippers standing or moving in a circle round the altar of a god, chanting in unison and indulging in unrehearsed dance. The first movement towards the dramatic came when one member of the chorus separated himself from the rest, uttering lines to which the chorus collectively replied. Once this single 'actor' had established his position, the rest was simple. Two actors, and then three, made their appearance, and with them formal dialogue took shape. On them the attention of spectators focused, and the chorus lost its original function as the protagonist.

Thus tragedy emerged out of a religious observance, and to the end it remained integrally related to the service of the gods. Audiences found that with their sense of delight in the performances went a feeling of awe and wonder. In consequence, only a formal august tone could be permitted in the elaboration of plot and dialogue. The stories told in these tragic dramas were restricted for the most part to a set series of legendary themes; the chorus, even when removed from its central position, helped to preserve a ritual element; the scenes took shape according to a set plan.

The formalism inherent in the Greek drama was further encouraged by the theatres in which the tragedies were produced. Because these tragedies were fundamentally religious exercises, they were presented on special days of festival when all the inhabitants of the city state, rich and poor, aristocratic and humble, flocked to witness them. At first, the theatre consisted of no more than a sloping hillside, which provided accommodation for the spectators, and a level tract, marked out in a circle, on which the players moved and spoke. Soon these primitive conditions were improved: a semicircle of stone seats became an auditorium; the space for the chorus became an 'orchestra', with the altar in its centre; facing the spectators, there rose a building the front of which came to serve as background for the performers. In its forepart a long, narrow raised stage offered a platform for the actors, while the chorus stood below them. These theatres were vast, and accordingly they encouraged statuesque methods of production. The actors wore high boots (the *cothurnus*) to give them added height; over their faces they had huge masks. Thus they could indulge in no violent movement, and for practical reasons their speech had to be stately and majestic.

Between the conditions in this Greek theatre and those in the bustling, secular playhouses of Shakespeare's time there is a vast measure of difference; in comparing the two our first thoughts must be of the distinctions which separate the one from the other. Yet the extraordinary thing is that, despite these distinctions, the Athenian and Elizabethan stages came to produce similar kinds of tragic expression. It may be assumed that for Shakespeare the Greek masters, Æschylus, Sophocles and Euripides, were no more than names, but his great tragedies may be critically discussed on similar terms. It is almost as though the spirit of the theatre itself, independent of time and place, had worked to realize identical ends.

In Athens, at other festivals, comedy also flourished—a comedy, lyrical and fantastic, which found its master in Aristophanes. These satirical, exuberant and often burlesque plays formed the fitting complement of the tragic dramas, but, unlike them, have few counterparts in later ages. Nevertheless, though in themselves they stand almost alone, some comic forms which are reflected in Elizabethan and other periods did rise from their inspiration. The plays of Aristophanes are generally described as the 'Old Comedy'; when the city state of Athens moved into its decline, and into different social conditions, a 'New Comedy' took shape. In this type of play, linked with Menander, the fantastic, lyric element vanished; the extravagant characters—the Birds and the Frogs and the rest of Aristophanes' imaginary figures—were abandoned; the wildly improbable plots laid aside. Instead, 'realistic' plots based on contemporary social life were chosen, and the audience was held by clever tricks and turns of action; the characters, no longer grotesques, were stage images of types that might have been found in any Hellenic city. Menander's play-world points forward to more than one kind of later social endeavour; it may be associated with the comedy of manners which flourished in the seventeenth century, and it may also have connections with the Elizabethan comedy of romance. His *Dyskolos*, after lying in obscurity for more than two thousand years, has come to light only recently, but many of its scenes summon thoughts of Shakespeare's sixteenth-century world.

This drama of Greece proved to be the chief model for the Roman theatre, and it was firstly through Rome that the classic achievements of Greece were handed down to later generations. Ancient tragedy meant, not the plays of Sophocles, but the closet dramas of Seneca. Menander remained unknown during periods when Terence was read and admired. When, however, we consider the forces which inspired a fresh dramatic development in the medieval period, we must put even these Latin playwrights out of our minds. With the fall of Rome in the fifth century the theatre virtually vanished; perhaps wandering entertainers carried on some of its traditions in a crude form amid their juggling and their jesting; but the production of drama, which in any event had been almost completely given over during the last years of the Empire, disappeared. While it is true that manuscripts of the Roman comedies and tragedies were still preserved in monastic libraries and read for the sake of their polished style, hardly anyone thought of them as plays. Indeed, the common idea was that the poet or one of his friends merely recited these pieces from a platform while entertainers mimed some of their actions on the ground below. There is no question of imitation here. Later on, Seneca and Terence and Sophocles came to influence the English drama, but that time lay several centuries ahead. In the tenth century, when the medieval plays first came into being, a completely fresh start had to be made.

The Growth of Native Drama: Tropes and Liturgical Plays

The prime interest of this fresh start is that it almost exactly paralleled the start of the Athenian drama. The drama of the Greeks had begun with the extension of religious observance, and similarly the medieval theatre developed, without conscious effort, out of the religious services of its time. Distinctively it was a creation of the Church.

For men and women of the Middle Ages, apart from the round of their daily affairs, the Church was virtually everything. There may have been grumblings about corruption among the clergy, and even anger at all the rabble of lecherous and greedy hypo-crites who sought, under its cloak, to fleece the poor; but here, after all, was rest for the weary, solace for the afflicted, bread for the hungry, succour for the oppressed; here was not only the church but the school, the meeting-place, the centre of art and, still more important, of amusement. The religion of the Middle Ages was a broad religion. It was serious and mystical, but it permitted laughter. Beside the real bishop stood the boy bishop with his crowd of hilarious attendants. The Church was ready and eager to provide for the people all the delight it could (as well as spiritual uplifting) by means of art and letters. Moreover, it was ready to show to an uneducated folk the Scriptural story in visible wise, thus counteracting the lack of vernacular versions of Holy Writ.

The very Mass itself is an effort in this direction. The whole of this service with its accompanying ritual is a symbolic representa-tion of the most arresting episodes in the life of Christ; it is only natural that the clergy should have attempted to make it even more outwardly symbolic as the knowledge of Latin among the ordinary people passed farther and farther into the background. More especially they must have seen the need, on the great feast-days of Christmas and of Easter, to bring before the con-gregation the salient facts of the New Testament story.

From a very early period various liturgical developments are traceable, all potentially conducive to a dramatic form. Most significant of these were the so-called 'tropes' which, particularly in the ninth century, permitted an extension, in music and even in language, of the service appropriate to the Easter ceremonials. It was out of such tropes that there rose, in the tenth century, the very first modern play, the *Quem Quæritis*. To call this a play may seem strange, since it consisted of only four lines; yet when we examine it carefully we must realize that it includes all the essen-tial ingredients of drama—the setting of a place of action, the presentation of fictional persons interpreted by performers, and the use of dialogue. One priest, standing near the altar, person-ates the Angel guarding the tomb of Christ, and towards him walk three other priests, personating the three Marys. The Angel chants:

Quem quæritis in sepulchro, O Christicolæ?
[Whom do ye seek in the sepulchre, O Christian women?]

The others reply:

Iesum Nazarenum crucifixum, O cælicola.
[Jesus of Nazareth who was crucified, O heavenly one.]

And the Angel tells them:

Non est hic, surrexit sicut prædixerat.
Ite, nuntiate quia surrexit de sepulchro.
[He is not here; He has risen even as He foretold.
Go; proclaim that He has risen from the sepulchre.]

Simple as this piece is, it gives the embryo of drama. Once born, it possessed all the elements needed for further growth; and that growth was fed in four chief ways. First, there was what we may style histrionic elaboration, by which the time taken in the chanting of the three brief speeches was lengthened. Already, by the close of the tenth century, a *Concordia Regularis*, prepared by Ethelwold, Bishop of Winchester, for the use of Benedictines, clearly indicates how this was accomplished even when the primitive drama remained part of the Church's service. While the third lesson was being intoned, four of the monks proceeded to dress themselves. One, clad in an alb, quietly moved to the altar and seated himself, palm-branch in hand. The other three, wearing copes and carrying thuribles of incense, then slowly approached the altar, 'stepping lightly in the similitude of persons seeking something'. After this came the question from the Angel, the reply of the Marys and the Angel's announcement; and at its end the trio of priests turned to the choir, crying, '*Alleluia: resurrexit Dominus* [Halleluia, the Lord has arisen!]', while the Angel called them back, intoning the anthem '*Venite et videte locum* [Come, see the place]', at the same time lifting a veil and showing them 'the place bare of the Cross, but only the cloths lying there in which the Cross had been enfolded'. Whereupon the Marys lifted up the cloth as though they would reveal to all that the Lord had arisen, and sang the anthem *Surrexit dominus de sepulchro*. Finally, the ceremony ended with the singing of the *Te Deum* and a joyful pealing of the bells.

A second force that led to further development was the expansion of the tiny playlet from within, in two directions. One of these was the splitting of the choral three Marys into individuals with speeches of their own that ran sometimes into many stanzas. The other was to attach to the central theme various subsidiary episodes. Thus, for example, the Marys were supposed to bear spices with which to anoint the body of Jesus, and we soon hear of the introduction of an additional character, an Unguent-seller, some of whose wares they pretend to buy before stepping up to the altar.

It will easily be imagined how in these ways the original little Easter ceremony was lengthened and diversified, but here we must take into account something still more important. Obviously what was being done for the Easter story could also be done for other cardinal episodes in the New Testament. Thus the question 'Whom seek ye in the sepulchre?' could without effort be changed into 'Whom seek ye in the manger, O shepherds?' and applied to the Christmas services. And the Christmas playlet offered as many opportunities for elaboration as the other: the shepherds could be shown chatting together, the star could be made to appear to them, they could be addressed by an Angel, they could seek for the rustic gifts they were to carry to the child Christ.

Lastly, a fourth force was one that we may style the 'theatrical' or the 'scenic'. At the very start, no attempt was made to suggest, even by the most primitive means, the supposed locality of the action: the words alone indicated that this was presumed to be near or at the tomb of Christ. But as the liturgical plays developed, and particularly as various episodes came to be included, a step was taken which would lead ultimately to the association of 'scenery' with the priests' performances. An architectural structure was erected close to the altar in the similitude of the tomb; a throne was provided for the Angel; and for the Unguent-seller a seat or stall was set up in another part of the church. By devices such as this, as we shall see, the principle of later medieval staging was established.

Though there existed all these several forces that led towards dramatic elaboration, quite obviously the play as play could not hope to reach far so long as it remained part of a larger religious service, nor could it develop freely while its dialogue was in Latin, not spoken but chanted. The very last force, therefore, and the most important of all, was that exerted by the separation of these playlets from the liturgy, and their consequent secularization.

Mysteries and Miracles

This secularization of the drama rose largely from the conditions of its staging. Medieval folk lacked means of entertainment; naturally, they flocked to watch the liturgical performances, and very soon the churches were unable to accommodate everyone. The obvious solution was to carry the performances outside into the spaces surrounding the church itself. This meant, however, that, even though the clergy still provided the actors, the plays were inevitably divorced from the services of which they had formed part. At the same time, some of the monks and priests, eager to make these dramatic pieces more appealing to an un-lettered public, began to introduce the vernacular into the dialogue—sometimes by reciting lines in Latin immediately followed by a translation, sometimes by uttering certain speeches in Latin with other speeches in tongues familiar to the spectators.

When this stage had been reached the ecclesiastical authorities recognized a danger ahead, and in diverse ways they sought to suppress what the Church itself had brought into being. Strict orders were promulgated, so that, as Robert Mannyng puts it in his *Handlyng Synne*, the cleric was forbidden by decree

> Miracles for to make and see:
> For miracles if thou begin,
> It is a gathering, a sight of sin.
> He may in the church through this reason
> Play the Resurrection . . .
> If thou do it in ways or greens,
> A sight of sin truly it seems.

However, the result of this prohibition was distinctly not that desired: when the clergy was instructed not to take part in these performances the laity eagerly seized upon the drama, abandoned the use of Latin dialogue, substituted vernacular speech throughout, and proceeded to expand the plays in both form and content. In many European countries this happened; the interest which the Biblical performances had roused in the medieval mind is amply shown by the foundation in France and Italy of societies specifically created to act and produce such pieces and by the willingness of English trade guilds to present them to the public.

The actors, then, were no longer restricted groups of priests and monks; large bodies of eager amateurs had taken their place; and it is not surprising that, in their hands, the scope of the drama was mightily extended. The medieval theatre had started with a brief four-line playlet introducing as characters only an Angel and the three Marys; very soon the whole story of the Bible, from the creation of Adam on to the Resurrection of Christ or the Last Judgment, was being given dramatic shape. For the performance of the plays impetus was offered by the establishment of a Corpus Christi festival, due each year on the Thursday after Trinity Sunday; first set by a papal decree of 1264, and later, in 1311, placed more formally in the calendar by an order of the Council of Vienne, that day was selected for the presentation of the amateur shows. Numerous records in England and abroad indicate that the months between performance and performance were busily spent in preparing for these holiday events so eagerly awaited at a time when recreations and amusements were relatively rare.

In this way, during the thirteenth, fourteenth and fifteenth centuries the mystery cycles, generally called 'miracle plays' in England, came into being. The term 'mystery' is somewhat difficult to explain and define, but in all probability it embraced the concept both of a religious ceremonial (as in the 'mysteries' of the Passion) and of a special art, skill or function (as in the trade 'mysteries' of the guilds). Abroad, scores of such compilations are extant; in England only four cycles have been preserved, but these, with other relevant records, are sufficient to show that English dramatic activities were fundamentally the same as those more fully traced in France and Italy. While it is true that we have nothing equivalent to the elaborate prompt-book which outlines the theatrical marvels aimed at in the Mons cycle, the general picture is the same—and it is this production method which we have to examine first.

Rarely were the mystery plays exhibited anywhere except out of doors, and no attempt was made to construct for them any 'theatre', in the modern sense. The fundamental principle was the application in an elaborated form of the staging device used for the liturgical and related plays in the churches. As we have seen, this involved the setting-up of special locations—often called *sedes*, or seats, *loci*, or places, *domūs*, or houses—assigned to the chief characters or events. Within the church all such locations were in view of the audience throughout; hence that method of stage representation described now as 'simultaneous setting' or 'multiple setting'. What happened, of course, was that when the Marys stopped to buy unguents at a stall, only this stall attracted the attention of the congregation-audience; and when the women moved towards the station of the tomb the existence of the stall was completely ignored. Two further things. The first is that the simultaneous setting constantly foreshortened distance; in a Christmas play, for example, the shepherds might first be shown tending their flocks and then coming to the manger; in fact the meadows where the sheep grazed would have been in the country, and the manger would have been in an inn at Nazareth, but spectators of the liturgical play saw these two places standing side by side. The second thing to note is that the area on which the individual stations were set up itself became part of the 'setting'; it could imaginatively be taken as the territory between location and location, so that the shepherds, in walking the few yards from their meadow to Christ's manger, might be supposed to have journeyed many miles, and on other occasions the actors could establish a specific location on any part of the open area by simply using words alone. The liturgical plays, therefore did not merely employ a series of stations visually presented to the spectators by means of seats or small platforms, but they also had available the *platea*, or place, on which these stations were set.

When the liturgical plays ceded their position to the mystery cycles, what happened was that the seats or small platforms were elaborated into 'mansions'—sometimes made into little rooms with curtains at the sides and back, sometimes decorated with pieces of carved and painted 'scenery'; at the same time the *platea* continued to serve its original function. In the placing of the mansions, two chief methods were employed. The first, generally styled the 'stationary' set, presented the mansions in a curving row facing the audience or else arranged them within a circle or a rectangular space. The second involved the placing of the mansions on wheels, so that they became 'pageants' which could be drawn from spot to spot; these, according to one contemporary, were fashioned 'like a house with two rooms, being open at the top'; in the lower room the actors 'apparelled and dressed themselves, and in the higher room they played'.

No doubt, in England at least, many of the effects aimed at were of a simple kind, yet we have ample evidence that as the years passed by numerous scenic tricks were introduced. The records, however, seem to show that greatest attention was paid to costuming. At Canterbury we hear of 'a pair of new gloves for St Thomas'; at Chelmsford a certain John Wright was paid for 'making a coat of leather for Christ'. In 1564 an inventory includes 'two Vices' coats and two scalps, five Prophets' caps, three flaps for Devils, four sheephooks, and four whips'. From Coventry we learn that in 1544 'a new coat and a pair of hose for Gabriel' cost three shillings and fourpence, while at Hull in 1494 'three skins for Noah's coat, making it, and a rope to hang the ship in the kirk' amounted to seven shillings; 'a pair of new mittens to Noah' cost fourpence. In 1504, at Leicester, 'linen cloth for the Angels' heads, and Jesus' hose' involved an expense of ninepence, and the painting of the Angels' wings cost eightpence. At Norwich, in 1565, an inventory of property belonging to the Grocers' Company listed, among many other items:

2 coats and a pair of hose for Eve.
A coat and hose for Adam.
A coat with hose and tail for the Serpent.
An Angel's coat and over-hose.
A face and hair [*i.e.*, a mask and wig] for the Father.
2 hairs [*i.e.*, wigs] for Adam and Eve.

No doubt the great guilds increasingly vied in the presentation of the separate plays. These inventories give us some idea of how they went about it.

The actors, as has been said, were all amateurs—members of the various companies who for a time put aside their labour to perform in the sacred mysteries. They were generally paid for their services, but never looked upon their work as a regular profession. At Coventry in 1573 a certain Fawson received from one of the companies fourpence 'for hanging Judas' and fourpence 'for cock-crowing'. An anonymous actor received as much as three shillings and fourpence 'for playing God', and five shillings went to 'three white [*i.e.*, saved] souls' and five shillings to 'three black [*i.e.*, damned] souls'. 'Two worms of conscience' earned sixteenpence between them. In 1483 at Hull Noah received one shilling; in 1494 in the same town Thomas Sawyr for personating God was given tenpence, while Noah's wife received eightpence. The plays and their performances were, therefore, distinctly the creation of the common people, with all the consequent defects and virtues. The *naïveté* of the few extracts from the records given above may prepare us for a similar *naïveté* in the handling of the plays—both, of course, ultimately dependent upon the people who wrote and who witnessed these dramas. The audience was profoundly devout and sincere, but at the same time it unconsciously sought for ways of escape from its piety in all manner of licence. One way is to be seen in the incredibly coarse *fabliaux* of the time, and even in certain ceremonies of misrule actually sanctioned by the Church, such as the notorious Feast of Fools and the Feast of the Boy Bishop. Here piety was thrown to the winds, and licence reigned. The gargoyles in the medieval cathedrals which grin down cynically upon the worshippers are another expression of this mood of abandon—a mood, however, which rarely becomes permanent. The gargoyles are but little outbursts of freakishness and gaiety in the midst of the mysterious grandeur of vaulted nave and solemn choir. For these people of the Middle Ages there was no such thing as form, as form is known in classic and in neo-classic art. With them drunkenness is found with the most mystic adoration, debauchery with the most lofty moral idealism, cynical ridicule with passionate worship, laughter with the solemnity of sacred thoughts.

It is natural that this grotesquerie should be reproduced in what is in some ways the most typical of medieval creations, the mystery or miracle play. The seriousness is there in the figures of God and of His angels, in the terrible Passion of Christ and in His resurrection from the dead, but there is also the laughter and the abandon, the escape from too high majesty. At one of the solemnest moments, as when the shepherds watch the star that is to herald the coming of a King over kings, this laughter breaks out, and we are treated to an engaging episode of the thievish Mak and his companions. The general satire of women could not be stilled even in face of the worship of the Virgin Mary, so Noah's wife becomes a shrew, jeering at her husband and flouting him uproariously. Even the flaming terror of Satan was not exempt; rapidly he developed into an almost comic figure, roaring and lashing his tail, and attended by groups of minor devils designed, in their grotesquely monstrous attire, to arouse both thrills of terror and shouts of laughter. Herod, too, suffered in dignity. This slayer of infants, murderer of murderers, developed into a comic type. His roaring and ranting became a recognized part of the performances of the time, and Shakespeare remembered him in later days. The plays in which these characters appeared were formless, lacking literary style often, and always wanting in 'correct' artistic proportions—the work, as eighteenth-century critics would have said, of the 'Gothick imagination'.

Still, in them lay the seeds that were later to blossom into the plays of Shakespeare and his contemporaries. There is freshness of fancy here, a free treatment of the material, a rich fund of humour, and at times a true sense of the profound and the tragic. If with the mysteries we are only on the borders of drama proper, we can see clearly the various traditions that flower gloriously in the time of Queen Elizabeth I.

These mystery plays were not confined to any one district of England. No doubt the record of many of them has perished, but acting can be traced during the thirteenth, fourteenth, and fifteenth centuries in over a hundred and twenty-five towns and villages of Britain, extending from the south of England to the north, from the Welsh mountains to Edinburgh and Aberdeen, even across the sea to Dublin and Kilkenny. Some of these towns, no doubt, had no regular series of mystery plays of their own, but numbers must have treasured for centuries their specially prepared individual cycles. Those which have come down to us must be only an infinitesimal portion of a literary activity once vast and far-reaching in its extent. Four such cycles have been preserved—those of Chester (twenty-five plays, with an extra drama probably abandoned at the time of the Reformation), York (forty-eight plays and a small fragment of another), 'Towneley' or Wakefield (thirty-two plays), and 'Coventry' (forty-two plays in the *Ludus Coventriæ* and two separate dramas from the Coventry Corpus Christi cycle). Besides these there are extant a Grocers' play of *The Fall* from Norwich; two dramas of *Abraham and Isaac*, one belonging probably to Northampton; a Shipwrights' play from Newcastle-upon-Tyne; the so-called *Croxton Sacrament*, dating from the second half of the fifteenth century; the 'Digby' plays of unknown origin; a stray drama of the *Burial and Resurrection*; the Shrewsbury fragments; and a set of five plays in the Cornish tongue, presenting interesting parallels with extant English examples.

It is impossible here to deal with all or even many of these plays in detail. First, to get an impression of their scope, we may turn to the best-preserved of the series, the York cycle, and allowing for individual variations, treat it as a type for all. This cycle contains forty-eight separate dramas, as well as a solitary fragment probably added towards the close of the fifteenth century. The various component parts are clearly apportioned to the various guilds:

(1) Barkers [*i.e.*, men who barked trees for the tanners]. *The Creation, Fall of Lucifer.*
(2) Plasterers. *The Creation to the Fifth Day.*
(3) Cardmakers [*i.e.*, makers of the implements used for carding wool]. *The Creation of Adam and Eve.* [Adam and Eve were then clothed in white leather].
(4) Fullers. *Adam and Eve in the Garden of Eden.*

(5) Coopers. *The Disobedience and Fall*.

(6) Armourers. *The Expulsion from Eden*.

(7) Glovers. *Cain and Abel*.

(8) Shipwrights. *The Building of the Ark*. [York was still an important port.]

(9) Fishers [*i.e.*, both fishermen and fishmongers] and Mariners. *Noah and the Flood*.

(10) Parchment Makers and Bookbinders. *Abraham's Sacrifice*.

(11) Hosiers. *Israelites in Egypt, Ten Plagues* and *The Passage of the Red Sea*.

(12) Spicers. *The Annunciation*.

(13) Pewterers and Founders [*i.e.*, makers and moulders of metal]. *Joseph and Mary*.

(14) Tile-thatchers [*i.e.*, tilers]. *The Journey to Bethlehem*.

(15) Chandlers. *The Shepherds*.

(16) Masons. *The Coming of the Three Kings to Herod*.

(17) Goldsmiths. *The Adoration*.

(18) Marchals [*i.e.*, men who shod and generally looked after horses]. *The Flight into Egypt*.

(19) Girdlers [*i.e.*, makers of small metal articles] and Nailers. *Massacre of the Innocents*.

(20) Spurriers and Lorimers [*i.e.*, makers of stirrups, bits, and bridle-fittings]. *The Disputation in the Temple*.

(21) Barbers [both in the modern sense and as teeth-extractors]. *The Baptism of Christ*.

(22) Smiths. *The Temptation of Christ*.

(23) Curriers. *The Transfiguration*.

(24) Capmakers [or Cappers; they made the elaborate medieval caps of maintenance]. *The Woman Taken in Adultery* and *The Raising of Lazarus*.

(25) Skinners [who were also furriers]. *The Entry into Jerusalem*.

(26) Cutlers. *The Conspiracy*.

(27) Bakers. *The Last Supper*.

(28) Cordwainers [*i.e.*, shoemakers]. *The Agony and Betrayal*.

(29) Bowyers [*i.e.*, makers of bows] and Fletchers [*i.e.*, makers of arrows]. *Peter's Denial* and *Christ before Caiaphas*.

(30) Coverlet-makers and Couchers. *The Dream of Pilate's Wife* and *Christ before Pilate*.

(31) Lytsterers [*i.e.*, dyers]. *The Trial before Herod*.

(32) Cooks and Waterleaders [*i.e.*, those who supplied water round the city]. *The Second Accusation before Pilate with the Remorse of Judas*.

(33) Tilemakers. *The Judgment on Christ*.

(34) Shearmen [*i.e.*, those who trimmed, or sheared, superfluous nap off cloth]. *Calvary*.

(35) Pinners [*i.e.*, makers of pins] and Painters. *The Crucifixion*.

(36) Butchers. *The Mortification of Christ*.

(37) Sadlers. *The Harrowing of Hell*.

(38) Carpenters. *The Resurrection*.

(39) Winedrawers [*i.e.*, carriers of wine]. *Christ appears to Mary Magdalen*.

(40) Sledmen [*i.e.*, carriers of heavy goods on sledges, or trolleys with wheels]. *Travellers to Emmaus*.

(41) Hatmakers, Masons and Labourers [probably not all at the same time responsible for the play]. *The Purification of Mary*.

(42) Scriveners. *The Incredulity of Thomas*.

(43) Tailors. *The Ascension*.

(45) Potters. *The Descent of the Holy Spirit*.

(46) Weavers. *The Appearance of Our Lady to Thomas*.

(47) Ostlers [*i.e.*, keepers of inns or hostelries, and those who took in horses for travellers]. *The Assumption and Coronation of the Virgin*.

(48) Mercers. *The Judgment Day*.

(49) [fragment]. Innholders. *The Coronation of Our Lady*.

The first point of interest is the close connexion of the plays with the guilds. We note how many plays were given to men specially qualified to deal with them; thus the mariners took the Flood, and the goldsmiths the Adoration. Secondly, it will be appreciated that the plays cannot be judged critically on standards applicable to other dramas. Each play stands alone, yet all are but parts in a vast cycle: we cannot indulge in the kind of critical study of either plays or cycles that would be appropriate to the work of Marlowe or Shakespeare, for the mystery plays have no authors—or countless authors, put it as we will. These cycles, typically medieval in their almost complete anonymity, were constantly changing; undoubtedly portions were periodically added to or taken away from particular plays. All we may do, then, is to indicate some of the chief points in one or two of the dramas or separate cycles, marking especially those elements which might have offered hints to the dramatists of later years.

From the literary point of view the York cycle may be the least notable. Its high-water mark of excellence is in the last few plays dealing with the Passion of Christ. Dramatically, however, its revivals in York, since E. Martin Browne recreated it in 1951 before the ruined north wall of the nave of St Mary's Abbey, have proved how exciting it can be.

The Chester cycle may have been influenced slightly by the plays of York, and certainly something seems taken from the great French *Mystère du Vieil Testament*, but there is about these dramas a genuine devoutness of tone which gives a special distinction. Not that the grotesque elements are wanting. They are displayed clearly in the Waterleaders' pageant of *The Deluge*, where Noah's wife appears in her traditional guise of a scolding shrew:

Noah Wife, come in! Why standest thou here?
 Thou art ever forward, that dare I swear.
 Come in, on God's half! Time it were,
 For fear lest that we drown.
Noah's Wife Yea, sir, set up your sail
 And row forth with evil hale!
 For, without any fail,
 I will not out of this town.
 Unless I have my gossips every one
 One foot further I will not gone.
 They shall not drown, by St John,
 If I may save their life.
 They loved me full well, by Christ.
 Unless thou wilt let them in thy chest.
 Else row forth, Noah, whither thou list,
 And get thee a new wife.
Noah Sem, son, lo! thy mother is wrath;
 Forsooth such another I do not know.
Sem Father, I shall fetch her in, I trow,
 Without any fail.
 Mother, my father after thee sends,
 And bids thee into yonder ship wend.
 Look up and see the wind,
 For we be ready to sail.
Noah's Wife Son, go again to him and say
 I will not come therein to-day.
Noah Come in, wife, in twenty devils' way,
 Or else stand there without. . . .
Noah's Wife That will I not for all your call,
 Unless I have my gossips all.
Sem In faith, mother, yet you shall,
 Whether you will or not. [*She is forced into the Ark.*
Noah Welcome, wife, into this boat.
Noah's Wife And have thou that for thy meed!
           [*She gives him a slap.*
Noah Ah! Ha! Marry, this is hot.

Whatever the jollity of such a scene as this, it is the emotion of the Chester plays that first matters: this is nowhere better expressed than in the play of *Abraham's Sacrifice*, performed by the Barbers and the Wax-chandlers. The portraits of Abraham and

Isaac are well drawn, and there is charm in the childlike presentation of a heart-touching story:

Abraham Make thee ready, my darling,
  For we must do a little thing.
  This wood upon thy back thou bring.
  We must not long abide. . . .
Isaac Father, I am all ready
  To do your bidding meekly.
  To bear this wood full ready am I,
  As you command me.
Abraham O Isaac, Isaac, my darling dear,
  My blessing now I give thee here.
  Take up this faggot with good cheer
  And on thy back it bring;
  And fire with me I will take.
Isaac Your bidding I will not forsake,
  Father, I will never slack to fulfil your bidding.
                    [*Here Isaac takes up the wood on his back,*
                        and they both go off to the hill.

Abraham Now, Isaac, son, go we our way
  To yonder mountain, if that we may.
Isaac My dear father, I will assay
  To follow you full fain.
Abraham Oh, my heart will break in three!
  To hear thy words I have pity.
  As Thou wilt, Lord, so must it be:
  To Thee I will be bound.
  Lay down thy faggot, my own dear son.
Isaac All ready, father, lo! it is here.
  But why make you so heavy cheer?
  Father, if it be your will,
  Where is the beast that we shall kill?
Abraham There is none, son, upon this hill
  That I see here in this place. . . .
Isaac Father, tell me of this case,
  Why you your sword drawn has
  And bear it naked in this place?
  Thereof I have great wonder.
Abraham Isaac, son, peace! I pray thee.
  Thou breakest my heart even in three.
Isaac I pray you, father, keep nothing from me.
  But tell me what you think.
Abraham O Isaac, Isaac, I must thee kill.
Isaac Alas! father, is that your will—
  Your own child here for to kill
  Upon this hill's brink? . . .

Abraham O my son, I am sorry
  To do to thee this great annoy.
  God's commandment do must I;
  His works are aye full mild.
Isaac Would God my mother were here with me!
  She would kneel upon her knee,
  Praying you, father, if it might be,
  For to save my life.
Abraham O comely creature! unless I thee kill
  I grieve my God, and that full ill.
  I may not work against His will,
  But ever obedient be.
  O Isaac, son, to thee I say,
  God has commanded me this day
  Sacrifice—this is no nay—
  To make of thy body.
Isaac Is it God's will I should be slain?
Abraham Yea, son, there is no denying:
  To his bidding I will be bound,
  Ever to His pleasing. . . .
Isaac Marry, father, God forbid
  But you do your offering.
  Father, at home your sons you shall find
  That you must love by course of kind.
  Be I once out of your mind,
  Your sorrow may soon cease.
  But you must do God's bidding.
  Father, tell my mother of nothing.

It is easy, in spite of the crude phraseology, to observe the emotional power which later dramatists would exploit.

Clear marks of composite authorship are given in the so-called 'Towneley' cycle, which probably belongs to the town of Wakefield. Some of the plays are evidently taken over from the York series or belong to some common source; others are independent, but of small literary value; and a few (plays iii, xii, xiii, xiv, and xxi) have a humour freer and bolder than anything visible in the other mystery cycles. Indeed, in those five plays we get the first sure signs of the hand of a writer with independent thought and individual expression. The five plays deal with Noah, the Shepherds, the Adoration, and the last days of Christ. Of these unquestionably the most interesting is the so-called *Second Shepherds' Play* (Nos. xii and xiii are both shepherds' plays), in which occurs the delightful pastoral farce of Mak and his companions. The shepherds are shown chatting 'in rustic row'; Mak enters to them, and, when they lie down to sleep, he succeeds in stealing a lamb. His companions awake, and find their loss. Together they troop down to Mak's cottage and knock at the door. Mak lets them in, and they see a cradle (in which the sheep is wrapped up). The third shepherd wishes to see the supposed child:

> Give me leave him to kiss and lift up the clout.
> What the devil is this? He has a long snout!
> **1st Shepherd** He is marked amiss. We wait ill about.
> **2nd Shepherd** Ill-spun woof, iwys, aye comes foul out.
> Aye, so.
> He is like to our sheep!
> **3rd Shepherd** How, Gyb? May I peep?
> **1st Shepherd** I trow kind will creep
> Where it may not go. . . .
> **Mak** Peace! bid I. What? Let be your fare.
> I am he that him got and yond woman him bare.
> **1st Shepherd** What the devil shall he be called? Mak? Lo, God.
> Mak's heir!
> **2nd Shepherd** Let be all that. Now God give him care, I say.
> **Wife** A pretty child is he
> As sits on a woman's knee.
> A-dillydown, perde,
> To make a man laugh.
> **3rd Shepherd** I know him by the ear mark. That is a good token.
> **Mak** I tell you, sirs, his nose was broken.
> Once told me a clerk that he was forspoken [*i.e.*, bewitched] . . .
> **Wife** He was taken with an elf;
> I saw it myself.
> When the clock struck twelve
> Was he forshapen.
> **2nd Shepherd** Ye two are both in the plot.
> **3rd Shepherd** Since they maintain their theft, let's do them to death.
> **Mak** If I trespass again, take off my head. . . .
> **1st Shepherd** Sirs, do as I say.
> For this trespass
> We will neither curse nor quarrel,
> Fight nor chide,
> But get it over quickly
> And toss him in a blanket.

This scene, because of its vivacity and realism, has become well known, but, although it cannot be matched elsewhere, it is typical of many others in which a crude kind of native comedy is struggling to birth. Thus in the most terrible scene of the *Cruci-*

fixion humour is introduced in the persons of four torturers. They work away at the cross, and start hauling it to its place:

3rd Torturer So, that is well, it will not burst.
  But let us see who does the best
    With any sleight of hand.
4th Torturer Go we now unto the other end.
  Fellows, fasten on fast your hands
    And pull well at this band.
1st Torturer I say, fellows, by this weather,
  That we draw all once together
    And look how it will fare.
2nd Torturer Let's now see, and leave your din!
  And draw we each sinew from sinew.
    For nothing let us spare.
3rd Torturer Nay, fellows, this is no game!
  We will no longer draw all together—
    So much have I espied.
4th Torturer No, for as I may have bliss
  Some can tweak, whosoever it is,
    And seek ease on one side or other.
1st Torturer It is better, as I hope,
  Each by himself to draw this rope
    And then may we see
    Who it is that ere while
    All his fellows can beguile
      Of this company.
2nd Torturer Since thou wilt so have, here for me!
  Now draw I, as might thou thrive!
3rd Torturer Thou drewest right well.
  Have here for me half a foot!
4th Torturer Alas, man! I trow thou dotest!
    Thou moved it never a bit!
  But have here for me that I may!
1st Torturer Well drawn, son, by this day!
    Thou goest well to thy work!
2nd Torturer Once more, whilst thy hand is in!
  Pull thereat with some good will!
3rd Torturer Yea, and bring it to the mark!
4th Torturer Pull! Pull!
1st Torturer   Have at it now!
2nd Torturer   Let us see!
3rd Torturer   Ah ha!
4th Torturer Yet one more draw!
1st Torturer   Thereto with all thy might!
2nd Torturer Ah ha! Hold still there!
3rd Torturer So, fellows!

Other mysteries need not detain us much further, although the *Ludus Coventriæ*, if only for its peculiar character as an unattached cycle and for its fanciful theology, deserves close attention. This series of forty-two plays has nothing to do with the regular Coventry Corpus Christi cycle, of which all but a fragment has perished, and was most probably performed at more than one town. Apart from these major series our most valuable relics are the actors' parts for three little plays of an exceedingly primitive type. These actors' parts, discovered at Shrewsbury in 1890, show clearly how the Latin anthems at Christmas and Easter were gradually adorned with fragments of dialogue in the vernacular. The *Officium Pastorum* gives us the basis of the later shepherds' plays, the *Officium Resurrectionis* the elaboration of the *Quem Quæritis* trope, and the *Officium Peregrinorum* the first stage of development in the ever-popular story of Christ's appearance before his disciples. The majority of the other extant mysteries and miracles have less intrinsic value. The Newcastle Shipwrights' play is in the ordinary tradition; the *Abraham and Isaac* probably belonging to Northampton is interesting for its association with the French *Mystère du Vieil Testament*; and the 'Digby' plays of *The Conversion of St Paul, St Mary Magdalene* and *The Massacre of the Innocents* show evidence of capable authorship.

What is to be our final judgment on this mystery tradition so far as it concerns the development of dramatic art? Obviously the plays have many defects; their construction is chaotic, for the cycle-method forbade a more ordered presentation of the material. Further, conservatism rules. The stories and the types were already before the authors when they sat down to write, so that a dramatist with possibly superabundant dramatic invention had hardly any scope. The stilted language affects us also; clearly the writers are fettered by the various rhymes and measures in which the dialogue is cast. On the other hand, we see many possibilities for future advance. The mysteries gave to the people of England a taste for theatrical shows; they prepared the ground for the Elizabethan drama of later date; they provided the basis for further development. Despite the restrictions, too, some of the authors displayed real liveliness: Cain becomes an English peasant, grasping and rapacious; the shepherds are not the shepherds of Palestine, but those of an English countryside; Noah's wife is a 'cursed shrew' of some provincial town. The serious scenes have a frequently realistic flavour. The murderers who surround Christ in the Wakefield play of *The Crucifixion* are native types and owe nothing to their historical surroundings. It is the freshness, then, of the mystery plays which deserves our attention, for it was this, added to a sense of form borrowed from a study of classical art, which gave to us the glories of the Shakespearian drama.

The Development of Professional Drama: Moralities and Interludes

In some of the mystery plays one or two personifications, such as Dolor or Misery, intrude now and then, and their appearance leads us towards the next development in drama—that of the morality play. Already in the fourteenth century there are records of Paternoster dramas, designed to reveal the triumph of the Virtues over the Vices, and the first years of the fifteenth century bring to us the interesting *Castle of Perseverance*, which shows the principle of the mystery plays applied to a new kind of subject-matter. For this production a series of mansions (or, as they are here called, 'scaffolds') were placed roughly in a circle, with one mansion at the centre. Midmost stood the Castle itself, and round about were the scaffolds of Caro, Mundus, Belial, Covetousness and Deus. The method of staging is the same as that for the Biblical plays through many years; but clearly the characters here are not taken from the Bible. Instead, the spectators had before them a drama the protagonist of which was Humanum Genus, mankind at large. To one side of him were grouped the persons of an evil angel, Malus Angelus, Mundus (the World), Belial, and Caro (the Flesh), whose minions were the Seven Deadly Sins; to the other side came a good angel, Bonus Angelus, associated with Confessio, Shrift, Penitencia and six Divine Graces. At the end a heavenly debate involved Misericordia (Mercy), Iustitia (Justice), Pax (Peace) and Veritas (Truth) before the person of God (Deus), seated on his imperial throne. Clearly we have moved to another dramatic world, one in which the plot, instead of being taken from a Biblical source, has been invented by the playwright, and in which the characters are all allegorically conceived.

Within the fifteenth century two other dramas of a similar kind show how the morality was developing. About 1450 came *Mankind*, in which the generic hero listens for a time to the beguilements of a rascally crew consisting of Mischief, New Guise, Nought and Now-a-days, and is eventually brought to repentance, receiving the blessing of Mercy. Towards the end of the period Henry Medwall produced a two-part play called *Nature* wherein the hero, at first brought up by Nature, Reason and Innocency, turns to Worldly Affection, Pride and Sensuality, rioting with them until finally Meekness, Charity, Patience, Occupation and Liberality become his guides.

When we think of the term 'morality', and consider that all the characters are abstractions, we may suppose that this kind of dramatic development involved retrogression rather than progress. The persons of the mystery plays were nearly all given individual names and, even although the primitive style of the authors was insufficient to make of them real characters in their own right, the basis was there for a drama rooted in reality; no such basis, we might continue, was to be found in the world of ideas and moral concepts presented in such plays as *Mankind* and *Nature*. But to dismiss these works so summarily would be false; the surprising thing is that playwrights, moving into this realm of abstractions, paradoxically came closer to the world around them, and in their technique introduced certain elements which were to exercise force on the later Elizabethan drama. The personifications were given contemporary features, and the audience was drawn into association with them. Even in these two early pieces the scenes can prove the latent vitality this dramatic form possessed. In *Mankind* Now-a-days, on his first entry, jostles his way on to the acting area through the very midst of the spectators:

Make room, sirs, for we have been long!
We will come give you a Christmas song.

Not satisfied with that, his companion Nought actually draws these spectators into their merriment:

Now I pray all the yeomandry that is here
To sing with us a merry cheer.

Later, we hear the roar of Titivillus, the devil, and his cry,

I come with my legs under me!

whereupon the rascally crew determine that this will serve as an excellent opportunity for proffering the collection-bag: 'We shall gather money unto,' says New-Guise. 'Else there shall no man him see'—

Now ghostly to our purpose, worshipful sovereigns,
We intend to gather money, if it please your negligence,
For a man with a head that is of great omnipotence.
Now-a-days Keep your tail, in goodness, I pray you, good brother!
He is a worshipful man, sirs, saving your reverence.
He loveth no groats, nor pence, or twopence;
Give us red royals if ye will see his abominable presence!
New Guise Not so! Ye that may not pay the one, pay the t'other!

The episode is racy, and the audience is caught up within the play. So, in *Nature*, Pride is not simply an abstract figure ideally conceived; he is an extravagant Osric of his day:

I love it well to have side hair
Half a wote beneath mine ear,
For evermore I stand in fear
   That mine neck should take cold.
I knit it up all the night,
And the daytime comb it down right;
And then it crispeth and shineth as bright
   As any purlèd gold.
My doublet is unlaced before—
A stomacher of satin and no more;
Rain it, snow it, never so sore,
   Methinketh I am too hot.
Then have I such a short gown,
With wide sleeves that hang a-down—
They would make some lad in this town
   A doublet and a coat.

And as we listen to these persons chatting among themselves, we realize that their words are the current speech of life. Sensuality is told by Man that he will rejoin the rioting crew. 'Oh then,' he says,

shall ye them comfort
And yourself also.
Wot ye who will be very glad?
Man Who?
Sensuality Margery!
Man Why, was she sad?
Sensuality Yea, by the mass! She was stark mad
  Even for very woe
When she heard talk of this chance;
And because she would live in penance
Her sorrow for to quench,

She hath entered into a religious place
At the Green Friars hereby.
Man Yea, has she?
Alack, good little wench!
Is it an house of strict religion?
Sensuality Yea, as any that ever was bygone
Sith the world stood.
Man Be they close nuns as other be?
Sensuality Close, quod a? nay, nay, perde!
That guise were not good—
Ye must beware of that gear!
Nay, all is open that they do there,
As open as a goose eye!
Man And cometh any man into their cells?
Sensuality Yea, yea, God forbid else!
It is free for everybody . . .
Man Be they not wedded, as other folk be?
Sensuality Wedded, quod a! No, so may I thrive!
They will not tarry therefor;
They can wed themselves alone.
'Come, kiss me, John'—'Gramercy, Joan,'
Thus wed they evermore.

These two or three early moralities, then, introduce us to something new—to plays which are independent entities and not simply parts of larger cycles; which call for the invention of plots and not only for the re-treatment of Biblical narrative; which move from a world of ancient history into a contemporary environment; which, especially in their scenes of riot, reflect the conditions of life known to the audiences. Moreover, and still more important, they bring us from the milieu of the trade guilds into a completely different theatrical environment.

The Castle of Perseverance, it is true, was performed with a setting similar to that used for the mystery plays, and a group of amateurs must have interpreted its large collection of dramatic characters. Amateurs, too, no doubt presented *Mankind* and *Nature*. But here there is a difference. Neither of these plays makes use of scenery; both must have been produced, without any attempt at the provision of a background, on the floor of a hall; in the latter the characters come in and out of doors, while the former was certainly a Christmas piece. When the collection-bag is passed round New Guise remarks that

At the good man of the house first we will assay.

We have not yet reached the world of true professionalism, but we are very close to it; probably the performers consisted of a group of local amateurs, not just members of some trade guild engaged in an annual festivity, but rather an association formed for the specific purpose of acting—a fifteenth-century amateur dramatic society.

Theatrical records of the period, though sparse, offer confirmation. During the latter years of the century, associations of 'players' called by the names of their towns or districts are recorded as receiving rewards for their services, and soon these tended to lose their amateur status. What probably happened was that the privileged group of minstrels attached to the houses of the gentry saw enviously what the amateurs could do and what the rewards were, and began to follow suit. So, in many districts, small companies were established, mostly with no more than four members: some, no doubt, already professionals, drawn from the minstrel class; others, carpenters and weavers caught by the glamour of the stage. In order to protect themselves, most of these put themselves under the patronage of prominent lords; at these lords' mansions they presented their Christmas shows, and for many months of the year they wandered round from place to place as strolling actors. An act of 1464 definitely associates 'players' of this kind with minstrels, and by the eighties of the century we hear not only of the King's players but also of such others as those under the patronage of the Earl of Essex and of Richard, Duke of Gloucester (later King Richard III).

The act of 1464 refers to 'players in their interludes', and in 1494 King Henry VII's actors were described as 'pleyars of the Kyngs enterluds'; here we first encounter a dramatic term of high importance. The word 'interlude', strangely, seems to be exclusively English. Whether in origin it meant only a play (or *ludus*) carried on between (or *inter*) several characters need not concern us; what is important is the fact that from the close of the fifteenth century until about 1575 it came to have a quite definite significance as the type of play, relatively short, suitable for performance by a small acting company at a lord's house. It was, then, a descriptive term for the typical pieces from which the professionals who came into being during those years composed their repertory.

It must not be assumed, of course, that with the appearance of the small professional troupes all other theatrical activities declined or vanished. Well into the sixteenth century, mystery plays continued to be performed as they had been for generations, and conditions which were fruitful for the rise of the strolling actors were also fruitful for the cultivation of performances of other kinds. In fact, the early years of the sixteenth century show a vast and variegated growth of all sorts of theatrical ventures. From the eighties of the preceding century the University of Oxford was displaying an interest in academic shows, and Cambridge soon followed; members of the Inns of Court early discovered the delights of dramatic activity; several of the larger schools brought play-acting into their curricula; the children of the royal chapels were similarly encouraged to present their stage offerings. The household of Sir Thomas More may not have been singular in the attention it paid to these early theatricals; and, at a slightly later date, at least a few worthy religious teachers, such as John Bale, saw that the drama could provide an excellent means of promulgating moral or theological opinions. Certainly the central element in this diverse activity was that of the small professional companies, yet it must be remembered that between 1475 and 1575 the drama was being fed from all these several sources.

In seeking to trace the growth of dramatic writing during this period it is impossible either to follow a strictly chronological progress or to keep distinct the various types of play cultivated by different kinds of performers. All we can do is to treat the early Tudor plays, roughly from the beginning of the sixteenth century up to near the accession of Elizabeth in 1558, as one general group; then to consider the contributions of the sixties and early seventies, when the professional companies were enlarging their scope, as the transition between the old world and the world of Shakespeare and his companions.

We can begin with the first three plays extant in printed form—*Everyman, Fulgens and Lucrece* and *Hick Scorner. Everyman*, still esteemed and acted, stands with one foot in the fifteenth century and one in the sixteenth. Related in some way with the Dutch *Elckerlijk*, it associates itself with the moralities; yet in its form, more consciously 'dramatic' than that of *The Castle of Perseverance, Mankind* or *Nature*, it points towards something new. With a kind of subdued and simple passion it shows Death, commanded by God, approaching Everyman; anxiously Everyman seeks solace and help from his companions, but Fellowship, Kindred, Goods and all worldly things forsake him; in the end only Good Deeds, frail and fainting, accompanies him over the passage of the grave. We cannot be quite sure what actors were in the anonymous writer's mind when he wrote this work, but almost certainly the second play, *Fulgens and Lucrece*, was intended for presentation by a group of amateurs in a private house. Here a humanistic theme is exploited, a maiden Lucrece being confronted by two lovers—Publius Cornelius, an aristocratic gallant, and the more lowly born but virtuous Flaminius. To a certain extent the piece might be regarded as a kind of dramatic debate, the lovers arguing their cases and the maiden finally deciding the question by offering her hand to Flaminius. This brief description does not suggest that the part has much vital interest, yet as soon as we turn to the text and listen to two boys, called simply *A* and *B*, chattering to each other, we recognize the work of a skilful dramatist. The pair, just come from a banquet provided by a cardinal, are full of excitement about a play which is to be performed for his guests. They are not supposed to be actors, but *B* knows the plot of the piece and tells it to his friend *A* (and incidentally and conveniently provides the audience with the 'argument'). Then, when the main performers come to speak their lines, *A* takes service with one of the wooers and *B* with the other, introducing an element of light comedy by their comments on the debate and by their own wooing of Lucrece's maid. To some extent the device is no more than a development of the technique used in *Mankind* to draw the spectators into the play-world, but obviously it is employed much more adroitly, and indicates how dramatic craftsmanship was being polished even in these early days.

The third play, *Hick Scorner*, differs from the other two, and almost certainly was intended for performance by professionals. Pity, Contemplation and Perseverance meet to bewail the evils of the time. Then suddenly Freewill pushes his way in:

> Away, fellows, and stand a-room!
> How say you? Am not I a goodly person?
> I trow you know not such a guest.
> What, sirs? I tell you my name is Freewill.

Soon he is joined by Imagination, and later by Hick Scorner himself—a merry character who regales the spectators with an account of his adventures:

> Sirs, I have been in many a country—
> As in France, Ireland and in Spain,
> Portugal, Seville, also in Almaine,
> Friesland, Flanders and in Burgoyne,
> Calabria, Pugle and Arragon.

This trio band together and put Pity in the stocks, where he sadly laments his fate in almost lyrical terms:

> Lo, lords, they may curse the time they were born,
> For the weeds that overgroweth the corn.
> They troubled me guiltless and wot not why.
> For God's love yet will I suffer patiently.
> We all may say 'Well-away' for sin that is now-a-day.
> Lo! virtue is vanished for ever and aye—
> > Worse was it never.

After all this grieving and this irreverent merriment, suddenly the plot turns to a happy conclusion. Perseverance and Contemplation return to rescue Pity from the stocks, while Freewill is converted from his evil ways.

Taking these three plays as pointers, it is possible to see in general outline the varied course of the drama during the first half of the sixteenth century. The tradition of what may be styled the 'amateur morality', established in *The Castle of Perseverance, Mankind* and *Nature*, and showing one form of development in *Everyman*, continued in several directions. With some writers it tended to shift towards political rather than religious themes, though we must also remember that in the Tudor age matters of Church and State were inextricably intertwined. Here comes John Skelton's *Magnificence* (probably about 1515), which introduces as central character a prince, Magnificence, led astray by Counterfeit Countenance, Cloaked Collusion, Courtly Abusion and Folly, brought to Poverty and Despair, and eventually embracing Good Hope and Redress. Skelton was a poet, and his scenes are vitally conceived, but his work must give place to the still more vital *Satire of the Three Estates* (1540–50), written by Sir David Lyndsay, produced several times in Scotland, and in our own day revived by Tyrone Guthrie at the first Edinburgh Festival of 1947. The core of this long and ambitious drama is a disputation, with Rex Humanitas in the centre, between Diligence and Wantonness, a disputation richly embroidered by episodes which attack corruptions ecclesiastical and political, and have as their central figure 'Pauper, the Poor Man'. Vigorous and forthright, Lyndsay's lines display imaginative power beyond anything of a similar kind in the contemporary English moralities, but unfortunately it stands alone in the Scotland of its time. Somewhat akin to it is an anonymous *Republica*, acted as a 'Christmas device' by a company of boys in 1553. In this play, too, the common folk find their representative in the People, an abstract character who, speaking in dialect, does not hesitate to complain of the evils of the age. 'Then let poor volk ha some part,' he says,

Vor we ignoram people, whom ich do perzent,
Wer ne'er zo i-polld, so wrong, and so i-torment,
Lord Jhese Christ, when he was i-pounst and i-pilate,
Was ner zo i-trounst as we have been of years late.

These political moralities may seem at first to exist in a sphere far removed from that of the Shakespearian drama, yet their significance in connection with what was to come is great. Out of them eventually developed the chronicle history play, and how that happened finds excellent illustration in a drama, *King John*, written by the worthy proselytizing vicar, John Bale, shortly before the middle of the century. In essence it does not differ overmuch from the other political moralities, even though its main emphasis is upon the evils of Catholicism rather than upon pride and magnificence, but the method Bale employed in its construction makes it the clear link between the old and the new, the abstract and the concrete. When we look at some of the scenes, and encounter dramatic persons such as 'Ynglond' (England), Sedicion, Civil Order, Commonalty, Private Wealth and Dissimulation, we might think that it is exactly the same as the other morality plays. The essential thing to note is that Bale, in order to make his arguments more potent, has deliberately avoided making his central figure a Prince Magnificence or a Rex Humanitas; instead, he has turned to English history and set King John on his stage throne, surrounding him not only by abstract virtues and vices, but also by individually named characters such as Stephen Langton, Cardinal Pandulphus and Symon of Swynsett. All that was required for the creation of the chronicle history was for a later dramatist to banish the personifications and stick more closely to actual historical events.

Alongside plays of this kind, others of the morality type sought to promulgate humanistic concepts and to plead for the pursuit of learning. To a certain extent that had been the object of Medwall's *Nature*, and the tradition was carried on in later works exemplified by John Redford's *Wit and Science* (c. 1540) and John Rastell's *Nature of the Four Elements* (c. 1517). In the former, Wit, the central character, enters with Study, Diligence and Instruction. Very soon Tediousness destroys his power, and he is trapped by the ensnaring wiles of Idleness until, at the close, Shame comes to him, and he returns to the arms of Science and Reason. In

Rastell's play, science also becomes the prime virtue, conceived mainly in terms of the discoveries currently being made by voyagers across the vast Atlantic Ocean.

John Rastell introduces us to an interesting company. He himself married Elizabeth, the daughter of Sir Thomas More, and his daughter Joan became the wife of John Heywood, author of several plays connected with the tradition to which *Fulgens and Lucrece* belonged. We are in the midst here of the More circle, and the More circle was interested humanistically in the theatre. Besides writing his own play, Rastell, a printer-publisher by trade, issued an anonymous adaptation of a Spanish work, *Celestina* (1499), under the title of *Calisto and Melebea*, thus bringing to English readers a narrative-drama not unimportant in the growth of the European theatre as a whole. The story tells how Calisto has become enamoured of Melebea, and how he confides in his servant Sempronio, who arranges to see the bawd Celestina. The heroine is almost persuaded to agree to an assignation with the hero when her father, Danio, tells her of an ominous dream he has had. In horror Melebea confesses her sinful thought, and the action ends with exhortations to virtue. The English version thus has a thoroughly moral ending, but quite obviously the author's attention is directed mainly towards the intrigue. The liveliest portions are those in which Celestina, a kind of prototype of Juliet's nurse, indulges in her lusty speeches. She can tell a tale at length and with evident gusto:

Now the blessing that Our Lady gave her son
That same blessing I give now to you all. . . .
Sempronio for me about doth enquire,
And it was told me I should have found him here.
I am sure he will come hither anon,
But the whilst I shall tell you a pretty game.
I have a wench of Sempronio's, a pretty one,
But the last day we were both nigh a stark shame . . .
She loveth one Crito better or as well.
This Crito and Elecea sat drinking
In my house, and I also making merry,
And, as the devil would, far from our thinking,
Sempronio almost came on us suddenly.
But then wrought I my craft of bawdery.
I had Crito go up and make himself room
To hide him in my chamber among the broom;
Then made I Elecea sit down a-sewing,
And I with my rock began for to spin
As who sayeth of Sempronio we had no knowing.

He knocked at the door and I let him in,
And for a countenance I did begin
To catch him in mine arms, and said 'See, see
Who kisseth me, Elecea, and will not kiss thee.'
Elecea for a countenance made her grieved,
And would not speak, but still did sew.
'Why speak ye not,' quod Sempronio. 'Be ye moved?'
'Have I not a cause,' quod she. 'No,' quod he. 'I trow.'
'Ah, traitor,' quod she, 'full well dost thou know.
Where hast thou been these days from me—
That the imposthume and evil death take thee!'
'Peace, mine Elecea,' quod he. 'Why say ye thus?
Alas, why put you yourself in this woe?
The hot fire of love so burneth between us
That my heart is with yours wherever I go.
And for three days' absence to say to me so,
In faith me thinketh ye be to blame.'
But now hark well, for here beginneth the game.
Crito in my chamber above that was hidden
I think lay not easily and began to rumble.
Sempronio heard that and asked who was within
Above in the chamber that so did jumble.
'Who?' quod she. 'A lover of mine.' 'Mayhap ye stumble,'
Quod he, 'on the truth as many one doth.'
'Go up,' quod she, 'and look whether it be sooth.'
'Well,' quod he, 'I go.' Nay, thought I, not so;
I said, 'Come, Sempronio, let this fool alone,
For of thy long absence she is in such woe,
And half beside herself, and her wit nigh gone.'
'Well,' quod he, 'above yet there is one.'
'Wilt thou know?' quod I. 'Yea,' quod he, 'I thee require.'
'It is a wench,' quod I, 'sent me by a friar. . . .'
Then he laughed. 'Yea,' quod I, 'no more words of this,
For this time too long we spend here amiss.'

The language is racy. We can appreciate how knowledge of such a piece might stimulate playwrights of the time towards fashioning and enriching their comic styles.

Heywood's dramatic essays breathe the same air. Their plots are simple, but their dialogue has liveliness, jauntiness and skill. *Witty and Witless* (*c*. 1533) takes shape as a simple debate between an intellectual and his opposite; *The Play of Love* (printed 1533) shows the debate in a slightly more elaborate form, involving four characters—the Lover-not-Loved, the Woman-Beloved-not-Loving, the Lover-Loved and Neither-Lover-nor-Loved. Although the persons are not given individual proper names, the world they live in is the same as that of *Calisto and Melebea*; indeed, as we listen to the tongue of Neither-Lover-nor-Loved wagging while he goes to the door—

> 'Knock soft,' quoth one who the same unlocked—
> An ancient wise woman who was never
> From this said sweeting, but about her ever.
> 'Mother,' quoth I, 'how doth my dear darling?'
> 'Dead, wretch,' cried she, 'even by thine absenting'—

we might well have the impression that Celestina is still rattling on. Yet further advance is made in *The Play of the Weather* (printed 1533; revived by Sir Barry Jackson at the Malvern Festival of 1932). Here the debate is extended and associated with groups of characters. Jupiter is more than a little worried to hear that many humans are grumbling about the weather he supplies to them, and he summons Merry Report to inquire into the matter. A Gentleman asks for days 'Dry and not misty, the wind calm and still,' a Merchant prays for the weather to be 'Stormy nor misty, the wind measurable', a Ranger wants 'good rage of blustering and blowing', a Water Miller seeks rain but is confronted by a Wind Miller who desires only breezes to move his sails; these are followed by a Gentlewoman, who demands 'weather close and temperate', a Launderer, who craves for sunshine, and finally by a little Boy whose sole interest is in 'plenty of snow to make my snow-balls'. In the face of all these suits what can poor Jupiter do save provide variety of weather at his own good will? Obviously we are moving away from the world of abstractions and of didacticism; genuine farce and comedy are in the making.

This farce and comedy emerge even more clearly in three other short plays which, though their authorship is not absolutely certain, may also have come from Heywood's witty pen. In *The Pardoner and the Friar* (*c.* 1519) a Friar steps on stage and to his disgust encounters a Pardoner; they quarrel about their respective virtues and functions, and each starts to deliver a sermon, the one seeking to outbellow the other—

Friar *Date et dabitur vobis.*
   Good devout people, this place of Scripture—
Pardoner Worshipful masters, ye shall understand—
Friar Is to you that have no literature—
Pardoner That Pope Leo the Tenth hath granted with his hand—
Friar Is to say in our English tongue—
Pardoner And by his Bulls confirmed under lead . . .

A Curate and Neighbour Pratt vainly attempt to still their clamour. There is no real plot here, nor is there in *The Four PP* (*c.* 1520), but the dialogue is vigorous and the fictional situation invites the introduction of just such tale-telling as gives raciness to *Calisto and Melebea* and *A Play of Love*. A Palmer, a 'Poticary and a Pedlar meet, and in the course of argument, agree to compete in the narrating of lies. Towards the end, the Pardoner explains that after a certain lady-friend of his had died, he went down to Hell to seek her. There he encountered a genial Satan:

> 'Ho, ho! quoth the devil, 'we are well pleased.
> What is his name thou wouldst have eased?'
> 'Nay,' quoth I, 'be it good or evil,
> My coming is for a she-devil.'
> 'What calls her,' quoth he, 'thou whoreson?'
> 'Forsooth,' quoth I, 'Margery Carson.'
> 'Now by our honour,' said Lucifer,
> 'No devil in Hell shall withhold her—
> And if thou wouldest have twenty more,
> Wert not for justice, they should go.'

Women, explains this devil, are such shrews that life in Hell is becoming most uncomfortable. As the Pardoner reaches this part of his story it seems that he must surely win the prize. Then very quietly the Palmer interrupts. The narrative, he says, is most peculiar, for in the whole of his varied experience he has never yet found any woman out of patience. For this lie the laurels are immediately awarded to him.

Finally, in *Johan Johan* (*c.* 1520; put on at the Birmingham Repertory in 1958) the debate is integrated into a simple plot. The piece opens excellently. Upon the stage wanders the henpecked husband whose name gives the title to the play, and at once he takes the audience into his confidence:

> God speed you, masters, every one.
> Wot ye not whither my wife is gone?

He tells them that she is continually gadding about. Working himself up into a passion, he promises that when she comes home he will beat her soundly,

> And at every stroke lay her on the ground
> And train her by the hair about the house round.
> I am even mad that I beat her not now.
> But I shall reward her, hardily, well enow.

There is never a wife between heaven and hell
Which was ever beaten half so well.

Then a doubt strikes him:

Beaten, quotha? Yea, but what if she thereof die?
Then I may chance to be hanged shortly.
And when I have beaten her till she smoke
And given her many a hundred stroke,
Think ye that she will amend yet?
Nay, by Our Lady, the devil a bit!
Therefore I will not beat her at all.

The reflection brings him back to his anger at her ways: he
resolves that, after all, he must punish her. Then the thought
occurs to him: What will his fellows say? He imagines one of his
neighbours asking:

'Whom chidest thou, Johan Johan?'
'Marry,' will I say, 'I chide my curst wife,
The veriest drab that ever bare life,
Which doth nothing but go and come,
And I cannot make her keep her at home.'
Then I think he will say by and by,
'Walk her cote, Johan Johan, and beat her hardily.'
But then unto him mine answer shall be,
'The more I beat her the worse is she,
And worse and worse make her I shall.'
He will say then, 'Beat her not at all.'
'And why?' shall I say, 'This would be wist,
Is she not mine to chastise as I list?'
   But this is another point worst of all,
The folks will mock me when they hear me brawl.
But for all that, shall I cease therefore
To chastise my wife ever the more
And to make her at home for to tarry?
Is not that well done? Yes, by Saint Mary,
That is the point of an honest man.
For to beat his wife well now and then.

Thus he works himself up into his passion again, and at this
opportune moment Tyb, his wife, enters on the stage behind
him:

Tyb Why, whom wilt thou beat, I say, thou knave?

Johan Who, I, Tyb? None, so God me save.
Tyb Yes, I heard thee say thou wouldst one beat.
Johan Marry, wife, it was stockfish in Thames Street,
  Which will be good meat against Lent.
  Why, Tyb, what haddest thou thought that I had meant?
Tyb Marry, I thought I heard thee bawling.
  Wilt thou never leave this wawling?
  How the devil dost thou thyself behave?
  Shall we ever have this work, thou knave?
Johan What, wife, how sayest thou? Was it well guessed
    of me
  That thou wouldest be come home in safety
  As soon as I had kindled a fire?
  Come, warm thee, sweet Tyb, I thee require.

The sense of what will be effective on the stage is obvious in this
introduction, and the play sustains its promise. The wretched
husband, much against his will, is sent off to invite the local priest
to share in the eating of a pie Tyb has baked. As they are about to
sit down, Johan is ordered to draw some water from the well;
when he returns he finds a hole in his pail and is forced to sit by
the fire, painfully softening wax, while the amorous priest and
Tyb gobble up the last morsels of the pie. Unable to bear his
indignities any longer, he goes berserk and drives the pair from
his house.

While work of this kind was being written for amateurs, professional actors were constantly adding to their own repertories,
specializing as a rule in interludes akin to *Hick Scorner*. Most of
the plays have vanished, so we have no sure basis for dogmatic
judgments about the material presented in lordly hall or on
village green. At least enough remains to suggest what it offered.
Surviving interludes indicate an effort to unite good healthy
instruction with much comic business. Two technical elements
especially demand our attention, the use of disguise and the
establishment of the dramatic character called the Vice. To an
extent disguise seems to have arisen chiefly out of the morality-
play pattern. The hero, or at least the central figure in a play, is
approached by some evil characters who wish to get him into
their clutches; if they come to him in their own shapes he may be
induced to dismiss them summarily, and so they pretend to be
other than they are. The notion is constantly used; we can believe
that sixteenth-century familiarity with it helps to explain the
popular disguise element in the later Elizabethan drama. Often
the idea is linked with the person of the Vice, a type ubiquitous in

early Tudor plays but not easy to analyse. Most modern dramatic historians are inclined to see his origin in the Seven Deadly Sins of the morality tradition; largely because of Shakespeare's allusion to the Vice with his dagger of wrath belabouring the Devil (*Twelfth Night*, IV.ii.124–31) there has been a tendency to suggest a diabolic association. For neither assumption is there any real evidence. True, the Vice is frequently connected with the morality-play Vices, but he remains distinct from them; and Vice and Devil are brought together in only two late plays. It is also to be observed that the term 'Vice' is often applied to characters, such as Neither-Lover-nor-Loved and Merry Report, who are in no wise connected with the Vices at all. In fact, the names Neither-Lover-nor-Loved and Merry Report offer us an excellent clue to his dramatic function. While at times he may come upon the stage as Politic Persuasion or even as Sin, fundamentally he is a completely amoral figure existing primarily, and sometimes only, to arouse laughter. He is the character who keeps the spectators bound up in the play, crying 'Make room, make room!' as he enters, and continually turning to them with comment and question. His share in the dialogue, generally more extensive than that of his companions, is enriched by an effervescent bubbling-over of words; he loves to rattle off lists of place-names, just as he loves to have long word-catalogues tumbling from his lips:

> The offals, the refuse, the rags, the parings;
> The baggage, the trash, the fragments, the sharings;
> The odd ends, the crumbs, the driblets, the chippings;
> The patches, the pieces, the broklets, the drippings;
> The flittance, the scrapings, the wild waifs and strays;
> The skimmings, the gubbings of booties and preys;
> The gleanings, the casualities, the blind escheats;
> The forging of forfeits, the scape of extreats;
> Th'excess, the waste, the spoils, the superfluities;
> The windfalls, the shreddings, the fleecings, the petty fees;
> With a thousand things more which she might well lack
> Would fill all these same purses that hang on my back.

Clad like the Fool in folk-dances and entertainments, he delights to sing and prance. Perhaps his name, as has been suggested, derives only from the wearing of a visor, or vise. Many a scene in these early plays he richly enlivens, and long after he disappeared in his own person from the stage his spirit would haunt the later drama.

Comedy, Tragedy and Tragicomedy

Our brief glance at early Tudor drama has carried us just a little past the mid-point of the century. During this period men slowly came to be aware of plays in other tongues both ancient and contemporary. A school-piece such as the farce of *Jack Juggler* (*c.* 1550) bases its farcical plot on Plautus' *Amphitruo*, and at the same time introduces Jack as a native Vice constantly taking the audience into his confidence:

> Our Lord of Heaven and sweet Saint John
> Rest you merry, my masters every one . . .
> And you too, sir, and you, and you also . . .
> How say you, masters, I pray you tell,
> Have I not requited my merchant well?

It is precisely this blend of native elements with elements classical and classically inspired that we observe in the development of the Shakespearean stage. During the years immediately before Queen Elizabeth's accession in 1558, we find our pace accelerating. In the decade after the Queen's enthronement the forms of drama so slow to evolve began to assume a new shape: it was due partly to further amateur efforts, partly to a fresh scope for the professionals.

About the year 1553 two plays were performed, both comedies, which mark a sharp break with the past. One is *Gammer Gurton's Needle*, written by a 'Mr S.' and presented at Christ's College, Cambridge; the other, intended for school production (probably at Westminster), is Nicholas Udall's *Ralph Roister Doister*.

In *Ralph Roister Doister* the impress of the two forces—of the interlude and of classical comedy—may readily be traced. In the form of the play, Terence is the master, and we realize how much playwrights of the time were to learn from him in two particular ways. Terence taught them how to shape, not merely a farcical episode, but a fully developed comic plot; *Ralph Roister Doister* is neither farce nor debate; it is a comedy full of incident and intrigue, well ordered and well planned. In addition, Terence showed the English playwrights how to vary and depict stage characters; the witty lovers, the testy old fathers, the intriguing servants, the blustering soldiers of late sixteenth-century drama were largely to take their inspiration from his example. Mere imitation, however, might well have led towards nothing save

insipidity and dullness. As *Ralph Roister Doister* shows, English
authors of this time had their own fully established native dramatic tradition to keep their scenes lively. Roister Doister himself
may be simply a version of the bombastic, boasting soldier of the
Roman plays, but his companion, Matthew Merygreeke, manifestly owes his being to the popular Vice.

The vitality in this new dramatic development is seen even
more clearly in *Gammer Gurton's Needle*. Again the influence of
Terence is patent, but instead of an urban environment, we are
carried off to a rustic setting, peopled by English village characters who owe little or nothing to ancient example. The plot is
simple—just the loss of a precious needle and the resultant suspi-
cions and jealousies, aggravated by the mischief of the Vice-like
Diccon. The author's skill is proved by his adroitness in keeping
attention alert both by the vigour of his dialogue and his inventive action.

This reference to dialogue reminds us that, while effective
dramatic expression requires careful and skilful planning,
architectural form alone cannot create good plays either comic or
tragic: the author must have an adequate and forceful medium for
his dialogue. In the days of the mystery plays many speeches
were cast in lines of varied, and often complicated, stanzaic
structure, and the tradition of these stanza forms was passed on
to the sixteenth century. Then, during the early Tudor period,
two things happened: more and more, playwrights tended to
seek for simpler rhythmic measures and gradually they began to
see what effective dramatic values could accrue from the use
of certain measures for particular situations or characters.
Thus, besides a toning down of the 'poetic' style, a vague principle was established whereby external rhythmic forms were used
to express outwardly the authors' purposes. Heywood's *The Play
of the Weather* illustrates this well. For Jupiter, as an omnipotent
god, the dignified rhyme royal is reserved:

> Right far too long, as now, were to recite
>   The ancient estate wherein ourself hath reigned,
> What honour, what laud, given us of very right,
>   What glory we have had, duly unfeigned
>   Of each creature which duty hath constrained;
> For above all gods since our father's fall
> We, Jupiter, were ever principal.

No other person is permitted to use this form. The more cultured
among the human characters, such as the Gentleman, are given

two methods of expression. When they address Jupiter they frame their lines in quatrains:

> Most mighty prince and god of every nation,
> > Pleaseth your highness to vouchsafe the hearing
> Of me, which, according to your proclamation,
> > Doth make appearance in way of beseeching,
> Not sole for myself, but generally
> > For all come of noble and ancient stock,
> Which sort above all doth most thankfully
> > Daily take pain for wealth of the common stock.

But when they are conversing with their fellows they descend for the most part to simple couplets. Thus, immediately after uttering the lines above, the Gentleman has some speech with Merry Report, concluding:

> Then give me thy hand. That promise I take.
> And if for my sake any suit thou do make,
> I promise thy pain to be requited.
> More largely than now shall be recited.

In contrast, the merry Vice, Merry Report, inclines to let his speeches fall into irregularly stressed couplets:

> Yea, farewell, good son, with all my heart.
> Now such another sort as here hath been,
> In all the days of my life I have not seen.
> No suitors now but women, knaves, and boys,
> And all their suits are in fancies and toys.
> If that there come no wiser after this cry,
> I will to the god and make an end quickly.
> O yes! if that any knave here
> Be willing to appear,
> For weather foul or clear,
> Come in before this flock;
> And be he whole or sickly,
> Come, show his mind quickly.

The principle, an excellent one, was to be of immense service to Shakespeare and his companions at the end of the century; but it had one fundamental weakness. It was set too high; on its top notes the dialogue rose to the artificial and undramatic rhyme royal, and its lowest notes did not reach beyond Merry Report's erratic couplets. Clearly, further advance was impossible without

Judi Dench as Mary: the York
Mystery Plays, 1957

Another scene, 1951: Lazarus
(Dudley Foster) emerging from
the tomb

The labels in the sketch read:

tectum

porticus

mimorum ædes

orchestra

ingressus

proscænium

planities siue arena

The Swan Theatre stage, *c*.1596: Johannes de Witt's
sketch copied by Arend van Buchell. The only contemporary
pictorial evidence of the interior of an Elizabethan playhouse

A Midsummer Night's Dream: a scene from Peter
Brook's Stratford-upon-Avon production, 1970

Dame Peggy Ashcroft as the Duchess of Malfi:
Aldwych, London, 1960

a recasting of the range in dialogue forms. Fortunately, such recasting was indicated during the fifties and sixties; the methods employed are shown clearly in two plays—a comedy called *The Supposes*, performed in 1566 by the members of Gray's Inn, and written by George Gascoigne; and a tragedy, *Gorboduc* or *Ferrex and Porrex*, presented by the Inner Temple in 1562, and written by Thomas Norton and Thomas Sackville. In the latter, the authors took the unprecedented step of using blank verse throughout; in the former the comic dialogue was expressed entirely in prose, a medium almost never employed previously for stage purposes. If we take these together, we realize that the dramatists, instead of depending upon a scale running from rhyme royal to irregular couplets, now had another scale extending from blank verse to prose; they could still make use, for occasional special effects, of such forms as couplets, quatrains and the like. In fact, this was the scale on which the Shakespearian drama was to rely.

In tragedy, *Gorboduc* occupies a position akin to that of *Ralph Roister Doister* and *Gammer Gurton's Needle* in comedy. Just as these plays were fashioned according to Terentian principles, so *Gorboduc* owed its shape to the study of Seneca, suddenly prominent in the early sixties. The translation of his works began with Jasper Heywood; no less a person than Queen Elizabeth tried her hand, in 1561, at versifying some passages from *Hercules Œtæus*; and within a few years all the tragedies were to appear in English costume. Sackville and Norton, therefore, were being thoroughly up to date in seeking to adapt his methods to the needs of the English stage. These needs were not for mere imitation; and the authors showed they knew what the public wanted by their deliberate departures from what Seneca had to offer. Rejecting a theme taken from classical myth, they used a plot based instead on ancient British history; instead of resting content with the exhibition of high passions and monstrous 'tragic' events, they made their play into a message for their own times. Their tale of a monarch whose arrangements for the succession to his throne were so unwise, obviously had direct pertinence at a time when all men, remembering the terrible days of the Wars of the Roses, were concerned and worried about the kingdom's future. To a certain extent, therefore, *Gorboduc*, though it has abandoned the use of personifications, may be regarded as a 'morality play'. This draws attention to the continuing force of the morality tradition, not only during this early period, but also when Shakespeare was turning from his comic realm to the realm of the tragedies.

All these plays were 'academic', and they were accompanied by numerous others designed for performance at universities, Inns of Court or schools. Gascoigne's *The Supposes*, adapted from *I Suppositi* by the Italian dramatist and poet Lodovico Ariosto, was partnered by an anonymous *Bugbears*, similarly adapted from other Italian comedy, A. F. Grazzini's *La spiritata*. A few years after *Gorboduc*, in 1566, the Inner Temple put on a second Senecan drama, the horrific *Gismond of Salerne*, which also deviated from the strict classic pattern by selecting a plot from one of Boccaccio's romantic tales. The significance of such comedies and tragedies were great; yet we must observe that the professionals too were playing their part in the enlargement of dramatic form and style; in particular, that they were extending their resources to permit them to make use of what the academics could offer. During the first part of the century, as we have seen, professional companies were very small, usually only four men or four men and a boy; it was obviously with such groups in view that publishers inserted on many title-pages the statement that 'four men may easily play this interlude'. Sometimes careful examination suggests that statements of this kind were over-optimistic, but clearly the publishers themselves felt that their little blurb had sales value. As we move into the early decades of Elizabeth's reign, signs of change become evident; references to the number of actors who, by doubling their parts, could perform the published dramas are extended to include six, seven, even eight players, and at the same time the popular plays tend to grow longer. Even though this is a period when comparatively little has come down to aid our judgments, enough remains to convince us that by 1575 the actors were finding a public much larger than any they had enjoyed in the past; that in consequence they were approaching the status of the great companies of Shakespeare's time; and that they could put on shows far in advance of the earlier short interludes. Alongside the growth of the adult companies, we must also take into account the children of Paul's and the Chapel. These continued to orient their productions towards the Court, but, as the years pass, we realize that more and more they too were becoming 'professional'. Some time would elapse before they offered serious rivalry to the adults, but already steps had been taken.

The public which attended shows given by both the adult actors and the children were clearly attracted by lyricism, wit, action and variety rather than by any stiffly 'classical' style; as we look at such plays of the period as have come down to us we see diverse essays in a 'tragi-comic' form rather than unrelieved tragedies from which lighter things have been banished, or comedies barren of serious thought. Dramatic works of this kind fall into more than one group. First come a series of moral interludes like *Nice Wanton* (*c.* 1550), *Wealth and Health* (*c.* 1555), *The Longer Thou Livest the More Fool Thou* (*c.* 1560), William Wager's *Enough is as Good as a Feast* (*c.* 1565), *The Contention between Liberality and Prodigality* (*c.* 1568), *The Trial of Treasure* (printed 1567), and George Wapull's *The Tide tarrieth No Man* (printed 1576). Not all of these are definitely linked with professional players; all are of a type that formed a large part of the offerings of the popular stage. All have common features: a moral theme is presented by abstractly named characters; farcical-comic business is plentiful; at the centre of the merriment is a gay fleering person usually named specifically as the Vice. Moreover, most of them make much use of song; a musical element developed in such a way as to show that at least some of the playwrights had observed the dramatic possibilities inherent in the use of lyrical material; in some plays the songs are introduced solely for variety, but in others they serve a definite function either in forwarding the course of the plot or in evoking atmosphere. Still further, several of the pieces in this group introduce stage directions of a sort rarely met with earlier—directions which suggest an increased awareness of theatrical effect. When, for example, in *The Longer Thou Livest*, Moros is bidden to enter 'counterfeiting a vain gesture and a foolish countenance', or when Worldly Man, in *Enough is as Good as a Feast*, is told to appear 'stout and frolic' and later to sport 'a strange attire', we realize that the authors, doubtless knowing more about the professional stage, have written in terms different from those of many earlier interludes.

In scope these plays are being brought to a level near to that of the later Elizabethan drama. An excellent example is provided by *Liberality and Prodigality*. Almost certainly that piece was originally acted, probably by boys, in 1567 or 1568, but when it was printed in 1602 the title page announced a Court revival before Elizabeth in 1601—the year when Shakespeare was engaged in the writing of *Hamlet*. We are therefore concerned here, not with something so primitive as to possess only historical value, but with a dramatic form which could still appeal to audiences thirty years later; which in fact exercised potent force on the formation of the stage in 'Shakespearian' times.

A second group of plays shows the mixture of the serious and the comic in another way. Here we meet *Horestes* (printed 1567) by John Pikeryng, Thomas Preston's 'lamentable tragedy mixed full of pleasant mirth', *Cambises* (probably 1561), Thomas Garter's *Susanna* (*c*. 1569), Richard Edwardes's *Damon and Pythias* (*c*. 1565), R. B.'s *Apius and Virginia* (*c*. 1565), and George Whetstone's *Promos and Cassandra* (printed 1578). In each of these the style is 'romantic', and in most the influence of the morality tradition is apparent. Haphazard in *Apius and Virginia* is the old rattling Vice; in *Cambises* the amoral Ambidexter carries on the ancient tradition of keeping in direct touch with the spectators, at one moment pretending he sees a pickpocket plying his trade—

> Is not my cousin Cutpurse with you in the meantime?
> To it! To it! cousin, and do your office fine . . .
> How like ye now, my masters? Doth not this gear cotton? . . .
> But how now, cousin Cutpurse, with whom play you?
> Take heed, for his hand is groping even now!—

at another moment turning to address an individual girl in the audience—

> I care not if I be married before to-morrow at noon,
> If marriage be a thing that so may be had.
> How say you, maid? To marry me will ye be glad?

At the same time, the plots are for the most part taken from classical sources, directly or indirectly: *Horestes* is simply Orestes with a cockney accent, and all the authors show that they are familiar with Terentian and Senecan styles.

Apius and Virginia is the most 'tragical' and also the most primitive in form. Here we are presented with a little *Measure for Measure* picture. Virginia, daughter of Virginius, fires the heart of the judge Apius. With the aid of Mansipulus and Haphazard he contrives to pass a decree that Virginia shall be given to him, but she prefers death at her father's hands to shame. The serious plot, written in a jogging rhythm, has little virtue except its moral; but when the author turns to comedy his lines suddenly acquire a spirited liveliness. 'Very well, sir,' says Haphazard, on his entry upon the stage,

> Very well, sir, it shall be done
> As fast as ever I can prepare.
> Who dips with the devil he had need of a long spoon,
> Or else full small will be his fare.

Yet a proper gentleman I am of truth—
Yea, that may ye see by my long side gown.
Yea, but what am I? A scholar, or a schoolmaster, or else some youth?
A lawyer, a student, or else a country clown?
A broom-man, a basket-maker, or a baker of pies,
A flesh- or a fish-monger, or a sower of lies?
A louse or a louser, a leek or a lark,
A dreamer, a drommel, a fire, or a spark?
A caitiff, a cut-throat, a creeper in corners,
A herbrain, a hangman, or a grafter of horners? . . .

The words gush forth in a long, amusing stream. Ridiculous though they may be, they give individuality to a rogue who might be regarded as the ancestor of Autolycus. Even to his death he goes gaily:

Must I needs hang? By the gods, it doth spite me
To think how crabbedly this silk lass will bite me.
Then come, cousin Cutpurse, come run, haste and follow me;
Haphazard must hang—come follow the livery.

A similar quality is apparent in *Horestes*. The mythical tale of Clytemnestra's murder moves heavily in long, crudely constructed, trailing couplets, but as soon as the Vice comes on stage pretending to be deep in thought and then addresses the spectators—

Ah, sirrah! Nay soft. What? Let me see.
Good morrow to you, sir. How do you fare?—

we find ourselves in a different realm, one of impertinent laughter and practical joking.

The juxtaposition of murder, assassination and cruel vengeance and of rollicking impudence reaches its most blatant expression in *Cambises*, a play in which the author exhibits his passion for theatrical effects, both in the dialogue and in the extraordinarily long stage directions. The main plot concerns the ambitious wars of Persia's monarch and the ugly intrigues of his Court. Cambises himself, the judge Sisamnes, prince Smirdis, and other 'historical' characters here justle with numerous personifications—Cruelty, Murder, Shame, Counsel, Diligence, Preparation, Commons Cry and Commons Complaint, 'Small Hability' and Execution—and with two classical deities, Venus and Cupid. Alongside these serious persons others carry on a vastly different business—Huf, Ruf and Snuf, three comic Soldiers with a Meretrix, the rustic Hob and Lob, accompanied by Hob's wife, Marian-May-Be-Good. And mingling with both the farcical and the heroic figures, the Vice Ambidexter laughs his way through the action. Never for a moment is the stage still: the Meretrix has a comic fight with Huf, Ruf and Snuf; one of the characters is smitten 'in the neck with a sword to signify his death'; 'a little bag of vinegar is pricked' to simulate bleeding; there is bombastic boasting, and wild fits of anger, and pleading, and lamentation. Obviously this was the kind of thing that excited and appealed to spectators.

Promos and Cassandra and *Damon and Pythias* introduce us to still another sort of tragi-comic drama. The former, based on a play by Giraldi Cinthio and on Claude Rouillet's *Philanira*, deals with the *Measure for Measure* theme. The choice of sources is significant; both the Italian playwright and the French were men who had critically deplored the over-dependence of their contemporaries upon classical material and had pleaded for a romantic drama more appropriate to the spirit of the world they lived in. Clearly Whetstone was similarly intent on familiarizing English audiences with the atmosphere of romance. Edwardes, in *Damon and Pythias*, pursued the same course and went so far as to style his work a 'tragical comedy'. The story here is one of friendship. Damon and Pythias arrive at Syracuse, and the former, having unwittingly allowed himself to give cause for suspicion to Carisophus, a parasite and informer, is condemned to death. On begging leave of the monarch Dionysius to return for a short time to Greece before his execution, he is permitted to go provided that Pythias remains in custody as his pledge of return. On the day appointed for the execution Damon has not appeared: Pythias is about to perish when his friend rushes in, embraces him, and demands to take his place. The king is so affected by this exhibition of loyalty that he pardons Damon and takes the pair into his Court. The story is expanded and lightened by several comic elements—by the pleasant humours of the kind-hearted but self-seeking philosopher Aristippus (a kind of transformed Vice), by the pranks of the merry serving-boys Jack and Will, and by the rustic adventures of Grim the Collier.

This development of romantic themes must be associated with the exploitation of another form of romance, the chivalric, apparently widely popular in the early seventies. The titles of numerous now lost plays from this period are known to us. We find among them many, such as *Cloridon and Radiamanta, Paris and*

Vienna, Mamillia, Predor and Lucia, Herpetulus the Blue Knight, Panecia, Phedrastus, Phignon and Lucia, Philemon and Felicia, Pretestus, and *The Red Knight,* which certainly or probably dealt with material of this sort. One extant piece gives us a good idea of what these were like—*The History of the Two Valiant Knights, Sir Clyomon Knight of the Golden Shield, Son to the King of Denmark, and Clamydes the White Knight, Son to the King of Suavia* (*c.* 1577). As produced by the Queen's company, this must have been an exciting show, with its varied scenes of love and rivalry, of farcical humour and of high adventure, and with a rich array of characters extending from comic servants, noble heroes, distressed maidens, cruel giants, to the imperial Alexander the Great. The gallimaufry of episodes and persons might at first seem unworthy of serious consideration, but when we read the text with the stage of the seventies in mind we have to acknowledge that it has been well constructed, and in a form apt to appeal to a growing theatrical audience.

This growing audience was responsible for many things, and for none more important than the building of London's first permanent playhouse in 1576. With its establishment, an old world gave place to a new. A prime sign was the disappearance of the term which had been used to describe professional plays; up to 1576 more than half the printed plays had been described on their title pages as 'interludes'; after 1576 not one was so styled. The 'interludes' belonged to a time when the professionals were strolling actors, few of them in a company and incapable as a rule of presenting anything more elaborate than short morals and farces. Now, in the new age, professional associations, established in permanent homes, could present works of extended scope—works for which 'interlude' was no longer appropriate. We are rapidly approaching the time of Shakespeare.

Two

The Elizabethan Drama

The Theatres

In 1576, when Elizabeth had been on the throne for eighteen years, the building of The Theatre in Shoreditch marked the start of the great dramatic development known by her name. What happened earlier was of prime significance; but it formed a basis, a foundation, rather than a firm structure.

Shoreditch was chosen for the first permanent playhouse because, though convenient to dwellers in the City, it lay beyond the jurisdiction of the civic authorities. During the time when professional actors were establishing themselves, the Queen and many of her lords had shown a real, if somewhat erratic, interest in theatrical affairs; as a result, the actors could work with a certain amount of freedom, and even of support. So long as the Queen and members of the nobility protected them, allowing them to form such companies as the Queen's Men, Lord Sussex's Men, Lord Essex's Men, they were not only at liberty to travel without risking arrest as vagabonds, they had also warrants likely to induce local officials to aid them. Not, even so, that these officials—many puritanically inclined—looked on the stage with favour; in particular, London's civic authorities had always shown themselves opposed to the stage. Their objections to it were religious, medical and economic. They regarded play-acting as ungodly, and the more severe among them were prepared to describe the theatre as the home of the Devil. With dismay they observed that greater crowds could be assembled for a performance than for a worthy sermon. Not unjustifiably they pointed out that such crowds added materially to the spread of infection during times of plague. Above all, they claimed that attendance at plays encouraged apprentices to slip away from their appointed tasks and gave to others an excuse for idleness. Consequently the fathers of the city sought to put all obstacles they could in the path of players who tried to act within London's boundaries.

Established in Shoreditch, the Theatre was in a position to carry on its work unmolested. As other playhouses were erected their chosen localities were all outside the walls. Some of them were built to the east, like the original Theatre itself; others were placed on the far side of the Thames, to the south, where they might be reached either by crossing the old bridge or by ferrying over the river. Soon, in the one district or the other, rival houses—the Rose, the Swan, the Globe and the Fortune—were called for by steadily increasing audiences.

Immediately before the erection of The Theatre, we have evidence that the players frequently made use of inn-yards, no doubt setting up some kind of trestle-stage at one end and accommodating spectators both in the yard itself and in the galleries which commonly ran round the walls. This may have formed a partial model in 1576 for the first building specifically set up to house an acting company, though it is possible that some of its features may have been influenced by what was known about theatrical experiment in Italy and elsewhere on the Continent. Basically, the open-air structure provided a benchless standing area for less affluent members of the audience, while galleries offered more comfort to those who could afford the additional cost; the limited few willing to pay still more were catered for in a 'lords' room', no doubt part of the lower gallery boxed off near the stage. These spectators saw before them a wide open platform, jutting out into the middle of the yard and some forty feet square, with a half-roof supported on pillars giving some protection to the actors during inclement weather. Above this was placed a tiny turret on which a flag was flown, and from which a trumpeter announced to all the beginning of a performance.

The main stage was bare, backed by a façade broken by two or more doors, through which the actors made their entrances and exits. In general, no attempt was made to localize the place of action by means of scenery, though the use of movable properties might imaginatively suggest indoor or outdoor settings as well as scenes supposed to take place in darkness. Thus a small tree could, if necessary, stand for a forest, a table and benches give the impression of a tavern, a wheeled-in bed indicate that the setting was a chamber, and the carrying-on of a flaring torch suggest in the warmth of a June sun the darkness of night. This conventional method of production had several results. Usually it meant that the players did not seek to localize their scenes with precision; the audience was content to know that a particular episode took place out of doors or indoors during the day or during the night. Secondly, the method imposed upon an author the need to do in words what later would be done by a scene-designer. Elizabethan tragedies and comedies include much descriptive material which would have been inappropriate in future dramatic writing. At the same time, the authors had very great freedom; untroubled by the problem of stage setting, they could introduce as many separate scenes as they cared—and, if need be, they could make an individual scene as brief as a dozen lines. Finally, the promoters would have no worrying thoughts about scenic expense.

The shape of the theatre also meant that the close proximity of actors to audience, a familiar feature of early Tudor performances, remained unaltered. The spectators almost surrounded the players and, as it were, they came *within* the play that was being presented. The Elizabethan actor stood on a conventional platform almost in the midst, and the uttering of his thoughts, addressed to those in close physical proximity to him, was completely in keeping with his surroundings. So too with the aside: in the Elizabethan playhouse it was merely an extension of generally prevailing audience-actor communion.

Besides the main stage, the actors had two other playing areas which they could use on occasion—some kind of rear stage and some kind of upper stage. How precisely the rear stage was formed is by no means certain. All that matters here is that, by drawing a curtain, by opening a large door, or by setting forth a tent-like structure, the players could provide the suggestion of an interior—a bedroom, a cave or a prison. The other area available consisted of a portion of the lower gallery immediately above the stage façade, an area which might be localized at will as Juliet's balcony, or as the walls of Calais, or a castle's battlements. While, however, the stage direction 'enter above' occurs frequently in play-texts of the period, it is notable that hardly ever do we find scenes proceeding on the gallery floor alone; almost invariably when characters are bidden to enter above, they are kept in contact with other characters standing on the main stage below. Perhaps even a third acting area was at their service; evidence is accumulating to show that quite frequently performers entered directly into the yard and from thence ascended to the stage—a practice clearly inherited from their predecessors, the interlude players.

The essential thing to remember while we are reading Elizabethan plays is that they were written for an audience trained to accept a conventional treatment of reality and to permit free scope for its own imaginative powers. One or two examples may clarify this. A situation not infrequent in both tragedies and comedies is that wherein some character is supposed to be in a room, pursued by his enemies. He dashes in and locks a door while his foes clamour without. On the Elizabethan stage this had to be done conventionally. All the doors in the façade could not be locked; in effect the spectators ignored the existence of all save the one immediately in use; fundamentally the same situation as in medieval productions, when 'mansions' not actually in dramatic service were dismissed from a spectator's mind. So too the old medieval convention of foreshortening space remained in familar use. A dramatist wishes to show two characters in Rome and then to carry them to Venice; he bids them go out by one door and in by another, and the voyage is done.

If those responsible for the productions spent relatively little on scenic effects they certainly laid out large sums on clothes. From the last years of the century we have some inventory lists of properties owned by the Lord Admiral's company, and these amply testify to the riches of the theatre's wardrobe. Here are doublets of orange-tawny satin and carnation satin and white satin and peach-colour satin, all 'laid thick with gold lace'; here are senators' gowns, hoods and caps; here are green jackets for Robin Hood's men, costumes for classical deities, suits for particular characters such as Herod, Henry V and Tamburlaine; there is even a 'ghost's suit and bodice'. The lists are long, and they show the sartorial wealth possessed by the greater companies. Properties, too, are in profusion—globes, sceptres, clubs, wooden heads and masks, Cupid's bow and quiver, snakes, pictures, armour, dragons, lions, popes' mitres, imperial crowns and crowns for ghosts—a miscellaneous collection revealing the resources now readily available for players who no longer had to trudge wearily with their bundles from stand to stand.

In trying to visualize an Elizabethan production, we must not permit ourselves to be misled by the absence of scenery. The main stage may have been bare, and the façade unchanging, but we can imagine that the audience saw a rich pictorial display of actors jetting round the platform in their silks and satins, and equipped with the appropriate property that they needed.

Shakespeare's Immediate Forerunners

When we pass beyond 1576 we have an impression of accelerated time. Through five decades, 1500 to 1550, the drama had moved with slow and unchanging pace, and between 1550 and 1575, in spite of many new theatrical experiments, the speed is not materially advanced. Then, after the establishment of The Theatre, we are rushed forward precipitately to the triumphs of the century's final years. The progress is steady and rapid; it may be convenient here to divide these last twenty-five years of the century into three; first the period from about 1576 to 1588; after this the sudden burst of energy that came during 1588–92; and, finally, the sure accomplishments of the last decade of Queen Elizabeth's reign.

It was during the first of these periods that John Lyly introduced a fresh kind of comedy to the English stage. *Alexander, Campaspe, and Diogenes* and *Sapho and Phao* appeared in 1584, *Galathea* about 1586, *Endimion* in 1588, and these were followed by others of similar quality—*Midas* (1589), *Mother Bombie* (*c*. 1590), *Love's Metamorphosis* (*c*. 1590) and *The Woman in the Moon* (*c*. 1592). In approaching these works, we must remember that Lyly's career, from first to last, was bound up with the child actors of Elizabeth's Court. It is important to bear this in mind for several reasons. Their methods of staging were not those employed by the adult players; in effect, they used a kind of simplified 'simultaneous setting' reminiscent of medieval practice, identifying various parts of the stage with such fictional localities as were required. Thus, in *Alexander, Campaspe, and Diogenes*, there are three locations—Alexander's house, Diogenes' tub and the shop of Apelles the painter—all exhibited to the audience at one time. If we try to read, say, Lyly's plays in terms of Shakespeare's stagecraft we shall form an entirely erroneous idea of their structure; awareness of Lyly's dramatic skill can come only when we consider his scenes in the light of the 'simultaneous setting' for which they were designed. We must realize also that the audience for whom he wrote was different from that which flocked to The Theatre and its successors. His plays were directed more towards courtly spectators, men and women less apt to make demand for bold effects, more likely to appreciate delicate turns and subtle nuances.

It was Lyly who was largely responsible for the first refined elaboration of romantic sentiment. As a university man, he was well acquainted with the classical dramatists, and his comedies show that his imagination was stirred continually by memories of ancient Greek myth. Yet he was no more inclined than the authors of the popular tragi-comedies to pursue a wholly imitative path. Where he differed from them was in his basic approach. They had mingled comic scenes with serious, paying little attention to congruity; their Hufs and Rufs and Snufs were crudely justled in alongside a Cambises and a Praxaspes. He sought for some atmosphere, or for some method of treatment, which might make a harmony of apparently antagonistic spheres of interest. There is, accordingly, in his comedies a mellowed spirit under which seriousness and laughter meet; a poetic fancy wherein the deities of classical mythology live and move by the side of human figures; wherein the clownish is made kin to the courtly. We might almost say that his characters are viewed through an idealistic coloured glass, bringing them together under one single illumination. Above all, he largely limits his dramatic themes to the exploitation of romantic love, and this romantic love he develops, not in its chivalric form, but in a form which led directly to Shakespeare's. Here are delicate colourings, a certain mellowed sadness, a spirit which the author himself described as 'delight'.

In pursuing this method, Lyly was able to make important advances in character-drawing. No doubt many of his stage persons remind us of types in the plays of Terence and elsewhere, but rarely do we find dully conceived replicas, and many have subtle individualistic touches. Mæstius and Serena in *Mother Bombie*, Eumenides and Semele in *Endimion*, Alexander and Campaspe and Apelles obviously anticipate romantic characters in the years to come.

Unfortunately, the feature which may have most delighted his contemporaries is precisely that which makes the plays difficult today. In his novel called *Euphues*, published in 1578, Lyly had exploited a new and highly artificial prose style—a style which rapidly became so popular in courtly speech and in the writings of other authors that it has won notoriety under the title 'euphuistic'. Basically, this prose form depends upon the constant use of antithetical clauses, often underlined by rather blatant alliteration, and upon an unending flow of similes, mostly derived from what has been called the 'unnatural natural history' beloved of the age. For us today, the euphuistic style seems dull, monotonous and uninteresting, but we must remember that it appeared fascinating and exciting in its own time. Men found in it a prose utterance clearly based on artistry, possessing an element of grace, and cultivating refinement of thought and of phrase instead of blundering blindly forward. All men and women of culture began to converse in euphuistic style, and the commoners tried at least to ape the aristocrats.

This style Lyly has used for the dialogue of his plays. True, he has greatly modified the artificiality of his original *Euphues*, and in many scenes the speeches he gives to his characters are reasonably effective. Still, enough remains to make most of his dramatic work somewhat boring to modern ears. In reading his comedies, we need to exercise our historical imagination. We must take these plays as they were taken by their first audiences. We read, for example, such a passage as this:

Dromio Now, if I could meet with Risio, it were a world of waggery.
Risio O that it were my chance, *obviam dare Dromio*, to stumble upon Dromio, on whom I do nothing but dream.
Dromio His knavery and my wit should make our masters that are wise, fools; their children that are fools, beggars; and us two that are bond, free.
Risio He to cozen and I to conjure would make such alterations that our masters should serve themselves—the idiots, their children serve us—and we to wake our wits between them all.

Its artificially balanced cadences, repeating themselves from scene to scene, may have a soporific effect upon us, yet we have to recreate in our imagination the delight they gave to those for whom they were novel and fresh. Some years later Shakespeare might satirize the euphuistic style good-humouredly. Still, his own precise prose owed as much to Lyly as did his maidens in men's habits, his romantic lovers, and his grotesques, such as Don Adriano de Armado with his page.

What precisely the adult players were offering to the public during these years we do not know, since this is a period from which few texts have been preserved; but several plays which are extant give at least a glimpse of their repertory. *Common Conditions*, published during the year when The Theatre was built, shows the old methods employed for the treatment of romantic adventure. We are introduced to three tinkers, Thrift, Drift and Shift, planning to hold up and rob some traveller. Sedmond comes in, accompanied by Clarisia and his servant Common Conditions; they indulge in conversation cast in the dreary kind of serious verse which had been usual in plays of the *Clyomon and Clamydes* school:

The silly traveller that is attach'd through wearied toil
And forc'd through mere necessity to trace from native soil,
Though wearied at his journey's end with painful travail past,
Is glad in heart he hath attain'd his journey's end at last.

Then the fun begins. The tinkers surround the small party of travellers and decide that Common Conditions must be hanged. Begging leave to do this office for himself, he succeeds in persuading his captors to let him climb a tree with a halter in his hand. Once he has reached a bough far above their heads he raises such vociferous halloos for help that the robbers hastily decamp in terror. This adventure leads to others in which romantic love, strange dangers and hilarious mirth are freely exploited. As with the Queen in the much later *Cymbeline*, a Duchess finds herself consumed with jealousy because the fair, innocent, gentle heroine is beloved by the people more than her own children; as in *The Two Gentlemen of Verona*, one of the characters (Common Conditions) is seized by bandits who, immediately recognizing his cleverness, ask him to be their captain; as in *Pericles*, the heroine is lost at sea and sold into servitude. Despite the dullness of much of the serious talk and the crudity of the comic, no one can avoid seeing here some of the foundations of Shakespeare's world of romance.

With *Common Conditions* we can place two interesting pieces, *The Three Ladies of London* and *The Three Lords and Ladies of London*, important because they were written by one man, Robert Wilson; because that man was a popular actor; and because they can be dated with assurance, the first appearing about 1581 and the second in 1588. Even when all allowance is made for the maturing power of the author, there is the possibility of catching a glimpse here of the way in which dramatic progress was effected during the passage from the beginning to the end of the eighties. Both plays derive from the moral-interlude tradition, but there is a marked distinction between them. *The Three Ladies*, using the ancient abstractions, such as Fame, Love, Conscience, Dissimulation, Fraud and Simplicity, attacks the prevalent vices of the age, and introduces several striking episodes. The most significant is the story of a merchant, Mercadore, who goes off to Turkey in the service of Lucre; there he meets and cheats a Jew called Gerontus; brought to court, he discovers that in law a Turk cannot be forced to pay his debts to a foreigner; at once he declares his willingness to abandon the Christian faith and become a Mahommedan; whereupon Gerontus, shocked by this proposed apostacy, offers tε absolve Mercadore from the debt so that he may not be tempted to commit such a crime. Incidents like these show Wilson's quality of mind, but it must be confessed that for the most part his dialogue is awkward, cramped and old-fashioned. While we cannot acclaim *The Three Lords* as a play of outstanding worth, it does exhibit an ease and assurance lacking in the earlier work. The abstractions are handled with greater skill, the scenes are more elaborate, the story is more complex, and the style of dialogue moves forward from patterns set in the older interludes to those being established when Shakespeare first applied himself to the stage. Perhaps these two plays may be taken as symbolic of what was happening generally to the drama during this decade.

Still further variations on the theme of romance appear in *The Rare Triumphs of Love and Fortune* (1582), a tragi-comical drama which anticipates several later Elizabethan plays in presenting its main action within a fully developed 'framework', so that, as in *The Taming of the Shrew*, for example, the play itself takes shape in the form of a theatrical representation given before or by another group of characters. In *The Rare Triumphs* we are first introduced to a meeting of mythological deities during which Venus and Fortune quarrel about their respective powers over humanity. The main play thus becomes, as it were, a test of these powers —the first episode revealing Fortune's strength, the second that of Venus, with a finale wherein the influences of both are displayed. Romantic love and magic are predominant. The hero, unexpectedly named Hermione, and apparently of low birth, is devoted to Fidelia, daughter of Duke Phizantius. The girl's brother, Armenio, in a jealous rage, challenges him to fight, and because of their combat the lover is exiled. Wandering abroad in despair, he comes to a cave where his high-born father Bomelio, also banished, lives in seclusion poring over his magical books, and by Bomelio's aid a happy end is reached. We are looking forward here to *The Tempest*, and though the anonymous author was no great poet, the varied style of the dialogue can foreshadow the poetic subtleties on which Shakespeare's achievements were to be based.

Finally, *Fedele and Fortunio*, or *The Two Italian Gentlemen* (1584). If, as seems probable, this was Anthony Munday's work, then it introduces us to a man whom at least one contemporary acclaimed as 'the best for comedy' in his time and 'our best plotter'. Most of his dramatic writings have perished, but one other at least, *John a Kent and John a Cumber*, was written some time before 1590 and may also be dealt with here. *The Two Italian Gentlemen* is only a modified version of an Italian *Il Fedele* (1576) by Luigi Pasquaglio, but the other play has unquestioned importance. Again the main plot revels in romantic love and rare adventure, and these Munday has enveloped in a richly variegated atmosphere. Continually complicating the narrative come two magicians—the Welsh John a Kent and his morose Scots rival, John a Cumber. One of them says:

> Here's love and love, good Lord, was never the like.
> But must these joys so quickly be concluded?
> Must the first scene make absolute the play?
> No cross? No change? What? No variety?

and these words might almost be taken as a motto, expressing what appealed most to the audiences of the time and what Munday sought to give them. Besides these two active wizards, other characters add to the diversity of the play. Particularly significant are the quaint 'Antiques', fairies or spirits, in the service of one of the magicians, and the group of clownish humans, Turnop and his rustic crew, busily engaged in rehearsing a rude entertainment for the pleasure of their lord. If *The Rare Triumphs* calls *The Tempest* to mind, here *A Midsummer Night's Dream* is manifestly anticipated.

The Arrival of Shakespeare

Precisely when Shakespeare started to work for the London stage cannot be accurately determined; all we know for certain is that by 1592 he had won such success as to cause his rival, Robert Greene, to utter a jealous attack. Some believe that Shakespeare had presented his first plays as early as 1585; others would place it some five years later. The exact date may not particularly matter: what is important is his standing as a central figure in the swift dramatic movement between about 1587 and 1592, precursor of the great dramatic development which enriched Elizabeth's last years.

In 1592 the dying Greene had called Shakespeare a 'Johannes fac totum', a Jack-of-all-Trades; an epithet not without justification. During the immediately preceding seasons Shakespeare had gained popularity in tragedy (*Titus Andronicus*), chronicle history (the three parts of *Henry VI*) and comedy (*The Comedy of*

Errors, *The Two Gentlemen of Verona*, perhaps a first version of *Love's Labour's Lost* and other pieces). These early plays reflected accurately the three kinds of drama which marked the period as a whole. No other playwright exhibited such a range, even though his own dramatic power was aided by the efforts of others, contemporaries or immediate predecessors.

In tragedy two such companions set the pace, Christopher Marlowe and Thomas Kyd. When Marlowe, about 1587, sent his prologue-speaker to introduce *Tamburlaine* to the public, providing him with an aggressive and self-confident challenge,

> From jigging veins of riming mother-wits
> And such conceits as clownage keeps in pay,
> We'll lead you to the stately tent of war
> Where you shall hear the Scythian Tamburlaine
> Threatening the world with high-astounding terms,

at one stroke he established a new theatrical realm. Until that time no author had been poetically (and invigoratingly) fervent. Prevailing styles in dialogue were rhythmical and metrical: some writers made them mildly effective, but until *Tamburlaine* audiences had had no chance to listen to this kind of majestic and lyrical speech. From 1587 onward, blank verse became the established norm for serious dramatic dialogue; other playwrights—most notably Shakespeare—were to modify and make more varied its basic rhythms; but Marlowe stood forward as the precursor and prophet.

Tamburlaine was followed quickly by *Dr Faustus* (*c*. 1588) and *The Jew of Malta* (*c*. 1589). The three works have qualities in common. In the first two particularly, we recognize at once Marlowe's power of identification with his heroes. Tamburlaine seizes us because the poet has had a vision of military grandeur, and the fusing of the author's own personality with that of his creation becomes patent in the lines. Suddenly, amid scenes of conquest and carnage, Tamburlaine has the speech that begins:

> If all the pens that ever poet held
> Had fed the feeling of their masters' thoughts,

and ends with the concept of a poetic vision beyond the power of words; this is not the victorious monarch speaking, but Marlowe himself. Similarly, Tamburlaine's passionate seizing of the Persian lord Meander's line

> And ride in triumph through Persepolis

in his

> 'And ride in triumph through Persepolis?'
> Is it not brave to be a king, Techelles,
> Usumcasane and Theridamas?
> Is it not passing brave to be a king,
> And ride in triumph through Persepolis?

reflects the poet's and not the prince's delight in rich, sonorous phrases. This fusion of the author and the hero becomes even threefold in *Dr Faustus*. Faust is a scholar, not an ambitious conqueror; but he and Tamburlaine and Marlowe all meet at times in one:

> Nature, that fram'd us of four elements
> Warring within our breasts for regiment,
> Doth teach us all to have aspiring minds.
> Our souls, whose faculties can comprehend
> The wondrous architecture of the world
> And measure every wandering planet's course,
> Still climbing after knowledge infinite
> And always moving as the restless spheres,
> Will us to wear ourselves and never rest
> Until we reach the ripest fruit of all,
> That perfect bliss and sole felicity,
> The sweet fruition of an earthly crown.

The Marlovian approach, therefore, brings intensity, admiration and wonder into tragedy. At the same time, it must be realized that these qualities exist for their own sake. Our impression after reading *Tamburlaine* is that Marlowe was intoxicated by his contemplation of the aspiring man who, starting as a simple Scythian shepherd, ends as a king over kings. Nevertheless, the admiration thus aroused could not banish the thought that Tamburlaine was a monster of cruelty. Wonder at Faustus's aspiring courage in making his pact with Mephistophilis could not deny the fact that this action damned his soul. The admiration and the wonder were stimulated, not by appreciation of moral virtues, but solely by the exhibition of individualistic striving, in spite of humanity's weakness, towards superhuman power. This means that the intensity, admiration and wonder could come as easily from watching extreme villainy as from looking at virtuous aspiration. Thus, after presenting Tamburlaine and Faustus, Marlowe appropriately completed the trio by creating his thoroughly evil Barabas in *The Jew of Malta*.

This concentration upon intensity and this self-identification of the poet with his central characters offered much to Shakespeare and his fellow-tragedians, but it seriously restricted Marlowe's own dramatic achievement. Not only was he so involved in the creatures of his imagination that they tended to become lyrical rather than theatrically poetic characters, he was also inhibited from creating a larger and comprehensive dramatic universe. *Tamburlaine*, it might be said, exists solely for Tamburlaine, *Dr Faustus* exclusively for Faust. Other characters are mere dummies, inanimate figures, their only excuse to offer opportunities for the hero's eloquence; the play's structure has no significance apart from that hero's being. Marlowe was incapable of giving life to a Horatio, a Cassio, a Banquo or a Kent; he could not have imagined the architectural complexities of a *Hamlet*.

That is precisely what his companion Kyd was fitted to do. In the year when *Tamburlaine* appeared on the stage, *The Spanish Tragedy* captured an excited public, and its dramatic (as opposed to poetic) power is amply demonstrated by both its immediate success and its long-continuing popularity. There are no heroics here: the element of wonder and admiration is absent. Though Kyd's blank verse has a variety and at times an appealing quality of a kind not to be found in Marlowe, it lacks entirely the fierce passion and lyrical fervour which Marlowe possessed; instead of concentrating upon one single hero, Kyd writes something in the nature of a psychological thriller. The play, opening with the soliloquy of a ghost, tells a story of love, murder and vengeance. Bellimperia, daughter of the Duke of Castile, exchanges vows with Horatio, son of Hieronimo, but her brother Lorenzo, having planned his sister for his friend Balthazar, breaks in upon their amorous conversation and hangs the lover in an arbour. Awakened by the noise, old Hieronimo finds his son dead and the shock deranges his brain. He seeks revenge, but at first he cannot be sure of the identity of those responsible; when he determines the truth revenge is delayed both by fits of madness and by the fact that his enemies are lords of high estate. Only after numerous hesitating steps does he succeed in enticing them to take part in the performance of a play and in killing them during the course of its action. Partly, this is a Senecan drama; the ghost, the revenge element, many stylistic features testify to its origin. But Kyd knew the tastes of his audience, and he adapted what he took from Seneca to popular demands. The play has a strong, well-developed and at times intricate plot: its stage effects are excellently managed; the scenes are varied and built so as to hold the spectators' attention; and, in the play-within-the-play, the whole tragedy rises to an exciting climax.

Clearly, the plot and the development of *The Spanish Tragedy* are similar to those of *Hamlet*; in the one a father, seeking to avenge his son's murder, is afflicted with madness; in the other a son endeavours to avenge a father's murder, and exhibits both real and feigned disturbance of mind. Shakespeare's indebtedness to Kyd is apparent. But, even though a Hamlet play was in existence by 1590, the *Hamlet* we know did not arrive until the beginning of the seventeenth century, and it is only with Shakespeare's youthful work that we are now concerned. During this period he wrote his gruesome *Titus Andronicus*, a tragedy in which he combined the essential qualities of Marlowe and of Kyd. Its story, replete with death, horror, vengeance, links it with *The Spanish Tragedy* in well-constructed planning and the exploitation of intrigue; the dramatist does not concentrate on one person alone but examines a group of characters skilfully contrasted. Shakespeare has added something of Marlowe's intensity; the figure of Aaron the Moor grips the imagination by its vigorous and self-centred evil. While no one would be prepared to say that *Titus* is one of Shakespeare's masterpieces, it manifestly shows the hand of a dramatist greater than either Kyd or Marlowe: the style can have a directness, a subtlety and a diversity of its own. The public, fascinated by these tragedies, was also much attracted by historical dramas of every kind, some of them certainly concerned with 'tragic' material, others giving more weight to romantic adventure. Once more, the loss of so many plays does not permit us to say with confidence when and by whom the chronicle history was inaugurated; possibly several authors concurrently contributed to its establishment, but if so Shakespeare was assuredly one of the first. His three parts of *Henry VI*, in spite of immaturity of style and in grasp of character, have an ordered dramatic presentation of historical events that is indiscernible in any similar extant plays which might have been produced earlier. If we find ourselves inclined to dismiss this trilogy as unworthy of theatrical notice, we need only compare it with the contemporary *Edward I* of George Peele in order to appreciate its virtues. *Edward I* makes every attempt to win popularity; it is spectacular and patriotic, and the strands of its plot are woven into a complicated pattern. But the pattern itself has no design; historical matter has here been mixed up with folk-lore elements and with romantically conceived inventions; there exists no sense of purpose beyond an effort to make an immediately popular appeal. More of a historical sense of purpose appears in *Jack Straw*, but the handling of its simple story of Wat Tyler's rebellion and of Richard II's endeavour to avoid bloodshed shows the history play hardly advanced to a structure richer than that of the interludes. *Henry VI*, despite the lack of assurance in many of its scenes, displays a masterly grasp of complex chronicle material and an innate sense of dramatic requirements. Even if we assume that other writers before Shakespeare had managed to deal with English history without the introduction of Bale's abstractions, there can be little doubt that *Henry VI* was the force which inspired the chronicle play's later popular development.

Henry VI was completed by Shakespeare's own *Richard III*, a drama planned more in Marlowe's tragic form. Eminently 'threatrical' in conception, it focuses all its attention upon the central figure, presented as a monster of villainy. The difference between the true dramatist and the lyrical poet becomes apparent as soon as we compare this character with Tamburlaine, Faustus or Barabas. Their portraits are humourless, drawn in hard unshaded lines, beings to be wondered at but lacking human features. On the surface, Richard seems to be delineated in a similar way, but when we examine his speeches we realize that it is not mere intensity that gives him his peculiar theatrical vigour. A grim sense of humour animates his words and actions from the first maliciously mocking soliloquy; though the wooing of Anne is undertaken to further his political ends, it is enlivened by the delight he takes in his consummate skill. We cannot discuss Richard's personality as we discuss Hamlet's, but the man has an individuality that Marlowe's protagonists lack: basically, it is because he has been conceived by a dramatist able to stand apart from his creations.

Marlowe attempted one work of this kind. In *Edward II* he dealt with a young king whose impolitic and unhealthy devotion to a favourite brings him to ruin. There are no heroics: Marlowe, it might seem, is showing a genuine dramatic power distinct from the lyrical intensity of his other major plays. Still, with the aspiring hero's disappearance, this poet-dramatist's virtue fades. Though *Edward II* has some affecting scenes and one or two poetic arias, its dialogue as a whole is undistinguished. Moreover, Marlowe has ignored for a private story of homosexual infatuation the breadth and range that mark Shakespeare's chronicle histories. No doubt *Edward II* was a strong influence on *Richard II*. Recognition of this merely serves to emphasize the essential dramatic difference between the plays.

Much as tragedy and chronicle history excited spectators then, the theatre depended mainly on essays in the treatment of romance. There Marlowe's companion, Robert Greene, stands out as leader. Lyly had contributed much to romantic comedy during the early 1580s; but his work was more suitable for child actors than for adults, and it was left to Greene to fashion romance material into a more popular mould. His method in *Friar Bacon and Friar Bungay* (*c*. 1588) and *James IV* (*c*. 1590) was to select a vaguely historical setting and within its frame to weave a variegated design of love, adventure and magic. Clearly he was following experiments in the romantic style, yet his plays, in their charm, their effective dialogue, strongly drawn characters and enveloping atmosphere, remain distinct from anything earlier. *Friar Bacon* concerns two rival magicians, each trying to outdo the other in wizardry; a low comedy element is provided by Bacon's stupid scholar Miles and a Devil who finally runs off with the magician on his back. Beside these characters are Edward, Prince of Wales, and Lacy, Earl of Lincoln, both in love with the low-born Margaret. We have, accordingly, a mingling of three different worlds—the world of wizardry, the world of aristocratic life and the rustic world. Instead of remaining separate, as so often in preceding plays, these have been merged in a harmonizing mood, rather resembling that which Lyly spread over his comedies, but less delicate and visionary. The same method is seen in *James IV*. Here the Kings of England and of Scotland, surrounded by a group of courtiers, meet Bohan, a melancholy Scot, and Oboram, or Oberon, King of the Fairies; here too is a narrative of romantic love, with Dorothea, the best-drawn heroine of sixteenth-century drama outside Shakespeare's plays, as the main figure. The whole is fused into a unity by Greene's humour; realism and idealism are interfused.

Shakespeare's indebtedness to Greene is by no means confined to his romantic patterns. Greene did much to expand the resources of poetic dialogue. Although deeply influenced by Marlowe, he modified the example he found in *Tamburlaine* and made it more supple. Sometimes his rhythms remind us of Shakespeare's, as in

> Why? Thinks King Henry's son that Margaret's love
> Hangs in the uncertain balance of proud time?

Sometimes lines such as

> Poring upon dark Hecate's principles

strike out interesting variants upon the blank-verse norm. And throughout there is an adaptation of this measure to dramatic requirements, less rhetorical, less lyrical and more varied than Marlowe's.

Other dramatists in diverse ways exploited the romantic forms, frequently following Greene's method in choosing some 'historical' framework for their adventures, occasionally falling back upon dramatic devices inherited from the interludes, and once or twice suggesting lines of further advance. Three plays illustrate this. In *John of Bordeaux* we have a piece obviously in the Greene style, introducing a 'historical' plot. The central character, John, takes service with the German Emperor; with his adventures goes the magic wrought by two wizard rivals, Bacon and Vandermast; low comedy is provided by Perce, Bacon's man. Audiences, apparently, did not tire of the same dramatic elements served up again and again. Nor were they averse to methods inherited from former years. *A Knack to Know a Knave* has its historical setting in the reign of King Edgar, and its magician (here a thoroughly worthy character) in Bishop Dunstan; but its romantic atmosphere is coloured by the mood which produced the old moralities. We hear much of the sins of the age, the evil courtiers, the cozening knaves, the grasping farmers; and among the ordinarily named persons we actually encounter an abstract figure, Honesty, as well as a Devil who bears off a wicked bailiff to Hell. How easily at this period the old and the new could co-exist is apparent in the humorous whimsy of George Peele's *The Old Wives' Tale*, with its fresh treatment of romantic material. The central notion is clever. Antic, Frolic and Fantastic enter lost at night in the depths of a forest. Old Clunch, lantern in hand, encounters them and takes them to his cottage. There, after a rustic repast, his wife Madge begins to tell them a fairy-tale, and its persons suddenly assume bodily form to enact their story. With the crafty development of its play-within-the-play, its sly satirical touches, the fusing of the actual world with that of the romantic imagination, Peele's work does remain durable. In spirit it seems removed by decades from the contemporary *Knack to Know a Knave*.

This was the realm which the young Shakespeare entered with his *Two Gentlemen of Verona* and his *Love's Labour's Lost*, and in entering it he became its master. It is obvious that he took over much from his predecessors and fellows; there is no difficulty in tracing the episodes and devices he borrowed from Munday and Greene and the rest. Nevertheless, he wrought the romantic comedy into a new shape. Not for a moment was he tempted to follow the pattern set by others, and to place his romantic stories in a vaguely historical setting. Instead of using a misty background of the English past, he deliberately elected to 'distance' his plots by taking them abroad to Italy and elsewhere. Instead of heaping adventure upon adventure, he tended to keep his plots limited to a fairly simple story. Instead of submerging himself completely in the realm of the impossible, he sought to make the impossible seem real, he used his low-comedy persons to comment upon the extravagances of romantic passion. Stepping into this world of the imagination, he was careful to see that his feet came down on firm ground. *The Two Gentlemen of Verona* is by no means a great comedy, and no doubt the first version of *Love's Labour's Lost* lacked the witty effervescence of the play which has descended to us; but already Shakespeare was indicating the course his particular treatment of the romantic material was to take.

The Final Achievements of Elizabethan Drama

During the seasons of 1592 and 1593 the plague cruelly ravaged London, and for much of that time the theatres had to be closed. When regular performances started again it was evident that mature mastery had replaced apprentice work. There must have been crude stuff in plenty, hastily written to satisfy the continual demands of the several stages now active in London, but in most of the plays which have been preserved we find a new assurance and a firm confidence.

In general, we gather that spectators were less responsive to tragedy than to other dramatic forms. Apart from *Julius Caesar*, at the very end of the period, Shakespeare wrote only a single tragic play, *Romeo and Juliet* (1595), one that might well be regarded rather as a romantic comedy which has taken a wrong turning than as a 'tragedy' in the stricter sense. Perhaps contemporaries saw it as such; when printed in 1597 it appeared as 'An excellent conceited tragedie', and the use of the epithet 'conceited'

—otherwise used exclusively to describe comic dramas—is revealing. *Romeo and Juliet* is a triumph, but it stands apart, not only from the rest of Shakespeare's tragic works, but also from all other tragedies preserved from these years. It derives neither from *Tamburlaine* nor from *The Spanish Tragedy*; it does not lead to *Hamlet* or *Macbeth*; in spite of its tale of woe, it is kin rather to *Much Ado About Nothing*.

Judging from such plays as are extant, we may hazard that the tragedies produced—comparatively few of them—were not of prime importance, and that they belonged to two categories. If *Alphonsus, Emperor of Germany*, comes, as seems likely, from this period it may serve as one illustration. Here Marlowe and Kyd meet in a plot which shows Alphonsus, a monster of vice, proceeding by poison, dagger-thrust and intrigue to destroy those who stand in his way. An image of sheer wickedness, the revenge motif and a display of horror-incidents are calculated to freeze the spectator. The second (and more interesting) category produced something entirely new. Just before 1592 an anonymous author presented in *Arden of Feversham* a 'tragedy' based on an almost-contemporary middle-class murder—that of a man named Arden sordidly done to death by his wife Alice. Already, in his three first plays, Marlowe had shattered the ancient principle which had insisted that tragedy could deal only with princely characters. Tamburlaine certainly became a monarch, but he started as a Scythian shepherd; Faustus was an ordinary German scholar; Barabas was a Jewish merchant. These persons, however, he had invested with his own enthusiastic dream of grandeur; in spite of their humble origins they did not depart overmuch from the splendour attached to a formal tragedy's kings. The author of *Arden of Feversham* takes the final and perhaps in a sense the logical step of making the hero of his play humble in every respect. There is no ecstatic, wondering lyricism; the dialogue, even when not expressed in prose, aims at making the action seem as 'realistic' as possible.

From the titles of a number of lost plays produced within the decade, we know that other authors experimented in the style of domestic tragedy, and these experiments, since they point the way towards dramatic forms typical of the modern stage, are obviously of much significance. It may be doubted whether they made really great appeal in their own time. Elizabethan audiences found more joy in plays less drearily realistic; particularly in the chronicle histories and in various forms of romantic drama. Shakespeare himself, having completed one tetralogy covering the reigns of Henry VI and Richard III, now turned to write another dealing with Richard II, Henry IV and Henry V. *Richard II* (*c.* 1595), was moulded as a tragedy, with no comic relief, its action depending almost entirely upon two contrasting figures, the pettish but imaginative king and the unimaginative but practical Bolingbroke. Then came the two parts of *Henry IV* (1597), built upon an entirely different plan. Instead of dwelling exclusively in palaces and conversing with courtiers and quarrelling lords, we are asked to spend much of our time in an Eastcheap tavern and to enjoy the company of a John Falstaff, one of Shakespeare's most vital creations even though in his relations with the young Prince he takes the place of the Vice in the old moralities. Finally the set of four plays was completed by the patriotic *Henry V* (1599), its far-flung tale of military conquest lightened by the presence of two groups of humorous characters, Nym, Bardolph and Pistol and the representatives of Wales, England, Scotland and Ireland. Even if we neglect *King John* (*c.* 1595), in which for some reason Shakespeare deviated from the theme animating his two tetralogies and reverted to a much earlier reign, we must acknowledge that this vast historical canvas, executed with such skill and variety, revealing both abstract principles and living persons, testifies as much to Shakespeare's greatness as do his tragedies and comedies.

Other dramatists during these years eagerly ransacked the chronicles, seeking for material in diverse reigns, and still others experimented with what might be called the biographical chronicle play. Munday wrote a *Sir Thomas More* (*c.* 1595)—a play of special significance, not only for its own sake, but also because the extant manuscript contains additions which many scholars believe to be in Shakespeare's own hand. Munday, with three collaborators, also shared in another drama, *Sir John Oldcastle* (1599–1600), which likewise has Shakespearian affiliations, although of a different kind. In *Henry IV* the character of Falstaff had originally been called Oldcastle; it seems that complaints by some descendants of that historical person induced Shakespeare and his company to rename the comic knight and to present a half-hearted apology in the epilogue to *Part Two*: 'Oldcastle', said Shakespeare, 'died a martyr, and this is not the man.' Probably these irate descendants sought even further vindication of their ancestor by encouraging the preparation of the *Oldcastle* play. Confessedly written to rebut Shakespeare's work, announced as a 'true and honourable history', it aimed to show that Sir John was 'no pampered glutton' but 'a valiant martyr and a virtuous peer'.

These were all serious essays in the interpretation of historical events from the chronicles; commoner, maybe, were other plays in which the events were imaginatively embroidered and treated in a manner more cavalier. Typical are the two parts of *Robert Earl of Huntingdon* (1598), written by Munday in collaboration with Henry Chettle. This two-part drama exploits the popular interest in the legendary Robin Hood and moulds the 'historical' material to its special needs. Skilfully, the playwrights wrought their scenes into a kind of play-within-the-play, a device, eminently in keeping with the folk-lore stories, that doubtless was partly responsible for the success of the work when acted by the Lord Admiral's men. Its success may well have been so great as to have encouraged Shakespeare to write a rival attraction for his company, the Lord Chamberlain's; there is some reason for believing that his excursion into the greenwood of *As You Like It* (1599) and even, perhaps, the very title of that play were inspired by the popularity of Munday's and Chettle's effort.

As You Like It leads us into Shakespeare's romantic comedy, a world enriched by *A Midsummer Night's Dream* (*c.* 1595), *The Merchant of Venice* (*c.* 1596) and *Much Ado About Nothing* (*c.* 1598). Shakespeare has passed far beyond the achievements of Lyly and Greene. His architectural planning is now masterly, his language vibrant and assured, his sense of character deepened, his romantic idealism and practical good sense wrought into a single harmony. Above all, there appears an appreciation of the contrast between appearance and reality, between being and seeming, made still more profound by an imaginative likening of the stage to the world of men. 'These things', says Demetrius in *A Midsummer Night's Dream*,

> seem small and undistinguishable,
> Like far-off mountains turned into clouds,

and Hermia answers him,

> Methinks I see these things with parted eye
> When everything seems double.

At times the dream becomes the only reality; at times reality is changed into the dream; and, as for the plays in which this vision is expressed,

> The best in this kind are but shadows, and the worst
> are no worse if imagination amend them.

It is important that in the period's entire range of drama we can find nothing similar to this. Shakespeare had many mighty contemporaries; in his youth, and even later, he was often content to base his efforts upon theirs; sometimes we catch glimpses of him writing in rivalry; yet his achievement remains distinct. The individual vision inspiring his scenes, the adroit weaving of the variegated strands in *A Midsummer Night's Dream*, the fusing of the almost incompatible elements in *The Merchant of Venice*, the subtle admixture of the ludicrous and the serious, the artificial and the real, in *Much Ado*—all prove that his eminence depends upon his ability not just to do better what others were doing but essentially to grasp something far beyond their reach.

The contrast is clear when we move from his comedies to other works familiar to the contemporary public. William Haughton's *Englishmen for My Money; or, A Woman will have her Will* (1598), certainly drew crowds in the year when *Much Ado* was probably performed. We may admit that it exhibits dramatic skill; in the end we are obliged to agree that basically it consists of no more than a pleasant, shallow display of love, intrigue and disguise informed by a strong patriotic sentiment. The piece no doubt proved effective in stage action, with its story of three girls designed by their miserly father for a Frenchman, a Dutchman and an Italian, and managing by a series of tricks to gain the hands of their English lovers; but beyond its story it has nothing valuable to offer. Occasionally we encounter something a little richer, such as *Old Fortunatus* (1599) in which Thomas Dekker could toss off such lines as these:

Behold yon town, there stands mine armoury,
In which are corselets forged of beaten gold,
To arm ten hundred thousand fighting men,
Whose glittering squadrons when the sun beholds,
They seem like to ten hundred thousand Joves,
When Jove on the proud back of thunder rides,
Trapped all in lightning flames: there can I show thee
The ball of gold that set all Troy on fire. . .

Dekker also wrote *The Shoemaker's Holiday* (1599). Even these do not touch the fringe of Shakespeare's gown. The former cleverly mingles its mortals with creatures of the imagination, its dialogue is poetically delicate—and still it never approaches the quality of Shakespeare's comedies. *The Shoemaker's Holiday*, with its merry Simon Eyre, Lord Mayor of London ('Prince am I none, yet am I nobly born!'), its love affairs, and its cheerful Firk and Rodger from the 'gentle craft', may be accepted as one of the period's most romantic diversions; yet we have to acknowledge that the charm rests upon the surface. It does not penetrate within.

Three

The Jacobean and Caroline Drama

Audiences and Theatres

Politically, one age ended and a new age began in the year 1603, when Elizabeth, after her long reign of over four decades, finally passed away, and when James VI of Scotland made his slow progress southward to assume the crown of England as James I. In the theatre, however, the break between the old and the new came several years earlier, at the very end of the sixteenth century. If the Elizabethan drama began in earnest with the building of The Theatre in 1576, it may be said to have ended with the opening of the Globe in 1599 and of the Fortune in 1600. At the very time that these two great houses were being built to accommodate the Lord Chamberlain's Men and the Admiral's Men, the children's companies, quiescent since Lyly's day, suddenly entered the professional field. In 1596 James Burbage bought part of the buildings which before had been Blackfriars monastery, converted them into a playhouse, and let this to two impresarios who presented the Children of the Chapel. The venture was an immediate success from its beginning in 1599 or 1600, and within a few months Shakespeare was speaking in *Hamlet* of the 'aery of children, little eyases [unfledged hawks], that cry out on the top of question, and are most tyrannically clapped for't'; these little players, he observed, 'are now the fashion'; they have carried away Hercules and his load (the emblem of the Globe theatre), and the adult players are forced to take to the road. Thus the 'private' playhouse, roofed in, comfortably appointed and more expensive than the public ones, was firmly established in London. One or two later structures were modelled on The Theatre, the Globe and the Fortune, but the Blackfriars inspired those stages more typical of the early seventeenth century. About 1608 the Lord Chamberlain's Men themselves took over that theatre from the children and made it their principal home; other companies followed this lead by performing their repertories at the Cockpit or Phoenix in Drury Lane (1616), Salisbury Court (1629) and similar private playhouses. So far as we can tell, the transference of plays from the public theatre platform to the smaller private theatre stage involved no fundamental alteration in the methods of performance; nevertheless, because the private playhouse was indoors, artificial lighting was introduced for the first time, and there were chances later to experiment in the use of scenery.

The success of the private theatres was due largely to changing social movements and moods. During the last five years of Elizabeth's reign many men were anxious, disturbed and worried. No one was quite sure what would happen on her death; the Wars of the Roses remained as a persistent memory. In addition, the Essex affair had spread gloom over England. Those opposed to Essex feared possible dangers ahead; among thousands on whom he had cast his strange spell his execution aroused bitterness and dismay. Thus, between about 1598 and 1603, a darker spirit prevailed than in the exultant years immediately following the Armada's defeat in 1588. When James I came to the throne he brought a new atmosphere to the Court; numerous hangers-on travelled down with him from Scotland, he was inclined to lavish honours upon favourites, he loved banquets and revelry; and the Court party slowly became estranged from the mass of serious-thinking folk. In these circumstances, those who belonged to the 'high' English Church, and who acknowledged the idea of the divine right of kings, formed a body of opinion completely opposed to the continually growing and hardening school of Puritan thought which stood for the power of Parliament. James, dying in 1625, bequeathed all troubles to his son; and Charles I, though personally dignified and worthy, helped to widen the cleavage in the nation. He angered the Parliamentarians; he married a princess who was a devoted Catholic, and in his court Catholic gallants were freely welcomed. The end came in 1642 when civil war broke out; seven years later the King was executed.

Puritan doctrine was bitterly against the theatre, and with its gradual spreading the number of playgoers dwindled. Other things contributed. During Elizabeth's last years the prevailing mood had encouraged the rise of a group of angry young men who sought to express themselves through satire, and who aimed at a 'realistic' drama of social errors and vices. Though they began in the public playhouses, they were soon more at ease in the private ones; their public was not general, they appealed mainly to intellectuals; and the 'little theatre', with its expensive seats and matching audience, was more congenial than the popular Globe or Fortune. This was a beginning. The vogue of the private theatres grew with the years, and before the Civil War the drama had become the almost exclusive delight of the king's courtiers. One of the first acts of the victorious Parliamentarians—the suppression of all theatrical performances—showed how the stage had become identified in the public mind with the despised and detested Cavaliers.

From one point of view we can regard as a single unity the drama produced from the beginning of the century until the closing of the theatres. Still, here it is convenient to divide it into three sections: the early Jacobean, covering the last years of Elizabeth and extending to about 1610; the late Jacobean, to 1625; and the Caroline, 1625 to 1640. True, one fades into the other, yet each has its special qualities.

Satirical and Citizen Comedy

Though from 1587 to about 1598 the theatre's general atmosphere was romantic, there were signs already of a movement towards realism. *Arden of Feversham* took tragedy into a middle-class milieu. Its counterpart in comedy was Henry Porter's *Two Angry Women of Abington* (1598), in which a couple of bourgeois families, involved in strife, blunder their way through the confusions of a night's darkness. Still, the realistic method was purposeful in neither of these. The years immediately ensuing brought the resolute young anti-romantics and their social criticism, usually satiric in spirit.

In the new form of comedy one man, Ben Jonson, is pre-eminent. Shakespeare's company, the Lord Chamberlain's, put on the first version of *Every Man in his Humour* in 1598, but Jonson would soon find more fitting audiences and actors in the private playhouse. *Every Man in his Humour* was followed by *Every Man out of his Humour* (1599), *Cynthia's Revels* (c. 1600), *The Poetaster* (1601), *Volpone* (1606), *Epicœne; or, The Silent Woman* (1609); *The Alchemist* (1610), and the slightly later *Bartholomew Fair* (1614). Through these, Jonson became one of the most discussed dramatists of the time; and though some contemporaries raised their eyebrows, the publication of his plays as *Works* in 1616 testified to his eminence. No previous playwright had had the distinction of a collected edition of his writings for the stage, and not one had dared to suggest that these writings deserved such a high-sounding title.

By no means all of Jonson's plays are realistic in form; the first version of *Every Man in his Humour* had an Italian setting. But they are all animated by one spirit, and in general they make use of similar methods. The main object is clearly expressed in the prologue to his first play. There he protests that, though he seeks for an audience's approval, he is not prepared to sacrifice his integrity by serving 'the ill customs of the age'. He will not follow his romantic predecessors and contemporaries by making

> a child, now swaddled to proceed
> Man, and then shoot up, in one beard and weed,
> Past threescore years; or, with three rusty swords
> And help of some few foot-and-half-foot words,
> Fight over York and Lancaster's long jars.

The contemptuous allusion to Shakespeare's chronicle histories is patent. Instead, Jonson

> rather prays you will be pleased to see
> One such to-day as other plays should be—
> Where neither chorus wafts you o'er the seas,
> Nor creaking throne comes down the boys to please,
> Nor nimble squib is seen, to make afeard
> The gentlewomen, nor rolled bullet heard
> To say, it thunders, nor tempestuous drum
> Rumbles to tell you when the storm doth come.

He wants

> deeds and language such as men do use,
> And persons such as comedy would choose
> When she would show an image of the times.

Obviously, Jonson is thoroughly opposed to romantic comedy and historical chronicles, objecting to these on two grounds —first, because they are what we would call 'escapist', and secondly because they lack classically precise form and use cheap theatrical effects. He seeks to correct both faults by reverting to the tightly wrought pattern of Latin drama, and by making his comedies comment upon the errors of his age. To carry out his purpose, moreover, he adopts a special approach to his characters. The word 'humour' appears in the title of his first play, and familiarly his form of comedy is now called 'the comedy of humours'. Here we must appreciate the then widely prevailing medical belief that in man there were four basic 'humours' or 'moistures' (the word 'humour' being akin to our modern 'humid'). In the well-balanced individual these humours existed in due proportions, so that an even harmony ensued; but in many men the growing force of one humour, or two humours in conjunction, could destroy the operation of the others, and create disease. This medical concept Jonson applies to character, and once more he has succinctly explained his objectives:

> in every human body
> The choler, melancholy, phlegm, and blood,
> By reason that they flow continually
> In some one part and are not continent,
> Receive the name of humours. Now thus far
> It may, by metaphor, apply itself
> Unto the general disposition—
> As when some one peculiar quality
> Doth so possess a man that it doth draw
> All his effects, his spirits and his powers,
> In their confluctions, all to run one way—
> This may be truly said to be a humour.

In effect, to present his satirical picture of society, Jonson seeks to put upon the stage not individuals but types—the testy old father, the curmudgeonly miser, the flamboyantly bombastic soldier, the jealous husband. Undeniably, he is a powerful and vigorous technician; his dialogue is stinging, witty and at times deadly accurate, and many contemporaries were inclined to rate him more highly than Shakespeare. Yet, magnificent satirist though he is, his satire is not accompanied by any positive vision, and it tends to become personal in a double sense. He could see the errors and vices in the society of his age; what he could not show was any picture of a better world. He lashed at boastfulness and arrogance, and these were precisely his own demerits. Professing to take a wide, impartial view of the social world, he marred many of his plays by petty personalities. In *Every Man out of his Humour* the central plot has been excellently planned, but because so many of the characters, such as Clove, Carlo Buffone and Puntarvolo, are obviously caricatures of Jonson's opponents, the scenes are reduced to a level of self-centred petulance. Further, there is little sympathy in his work. *Volpone* impresses us as a terrible indictment of human greed, duplicity and lust; its Corbaccios and Voltores are like creatures born of a nightmare; its selfish intrigues grip our attention; but in the end, for want of any contrasting elements among the monsters, fools and knaves, we may find ourselves unhappy. For all that, *Volpone*, with certain speeches of sensuous beauty such as the cry,

> A diamond, would have bought Lollia Paulina
> When she came in like star-light, hid with jewels,
> That were the spoils of provinces

has had some famous twentieth-century revivals, those in particular of Sir Donald Wolfit on various occasions, and one at the National Theatre in 1977, with Paul Scoffield as the fox of Venice.

Epicœne is a singularly bright comedy in the midst of the more bitter plays; to Jacobeans *The Alchemist*, with its quacks and gulls, would have been as topical as a revue, for in 1610 alchemy and its gibberish were part of the town's small-talk; and *Bartholomew Fair* is a packed panorama of Smithfield, a sustained gust of character-comedy. With these plays Jonson's truly creative work in the theatre ended. He did write other comedies, notably *The Devil is an Ass* and *The Staple of News*, but these are less cunningly constructed and are marred by exaggeration and personal pettiness. Other dramatists, who eagerly followed Jonson's style, adapted it to their own purposes (as writers have been doing in the 1970s). George Chapman, Jonson's classically minded friend, had written as early as 1597 a comedy, significantly named *A Humorous Day's Mirth*, in which he showed a similar approach to character; for years after this he was contributing to the stage. His method usually differed from Jonson in its mingling of satiric purpose with romantic appeal. *The Gentleman Usher* (*c*. 1602) thus introduces the elderly, sack-loving widow Cortezza, the foolish Poggio and the pedantic Sarpego within an almost tragi-comic framework of love and adventure; in *Monsieur D'Olive* (1604) the episodes which exhibit a Jonson-like gulling of the titular hero are set against a tale of emotional grief in which Marcellina has vowed herself to eternal seclusion and Count St Anne lives as a hermit mourning the loss of a dead wife. Even *The Widow's Tears* (*c*. 1609), satirically revealing the shallowness of a woman's devotion, has been placed in a romantic environment. Chapman's settings, and an effervescent pleasure in practical joking, separate his comedies from Jonson's; the only one in which he chooses a 'realistic' approach is *Eastward Ho!* (1605), with John

Marston and Jonson himself as collaborators. This piece, localized in London (and appropriately revived at the Royal Exchange
in the City during 1953) offers a moralizing satirical picture of the
good apprentice marrying his master's daughter and of the bad
apprentice rioting his goods away and ending in the hands of the
watch.

Chapman was Jonson's friend; Thomas Dekker, one of the
freshest and liveliest theatrical writers of the time, was his
enemy. Among Dekker's earliest works, indeed, was *Satiromas-
tix; or, The Untrussing of the Humorous Poet* (1601), in which one of
the main persons, Horace, is palpably a contemptuous carica-
ture. This Horace, or Jonson, is a dogmatic, conceited little ver-
sifier who tries to write by the aid of a kind of rhyming-
dictionary, and the happiest scene in the comedy presents him in
his study trying to compose an ode:

> O me thy priest inspire,
> For I to thee and thine immortal name
> In—in—golden tunes—
> For I to thee and thine immortal name—
> In—sacred raptures flowing—flowing—swimming—swimming—
> In sacred raptures swimming—
> Immortal name—game—dame—tame—lame—lame—lame—
> Pox! hath—shame—proclaim—Oh!
> In sacred raptures flowing will proclaim—
> O me thy priest inspire!
> For I to thee and thine immortal name,
> In flowing numbers fill'd with spright and flame—
> Good! Good! In flowing numbers fill'd with spright and flame. . . .

Dekker's true gifts lay not in satire but in the exploitation of
realistic comedy with a kind of warmth and affection. Jonson
hates; Dekker has a good-humoured sympathy. *The Shoemaker's
Holiday* showed this at the start of his career, and it is equally
evident in the sentimentally conceived portrait of *The Roaring
Girl; or, Moll Cutpurse* (c. 1610) more than a decade later.

Dekker's devotion to London streets finds a reflection in
Thomas Middleton, but here, without Jonson's bitterness,
Middleton reports a darker side of existence. Like Chapman, he
began with plays in romantic settings—*The Old Law* (1599), *Blurt
Master-Constable* (c. 1601) and *The Phœnix* (c. 1603)—but his real
virtues were exhibited only when he adopted the realistic style in
A Trick to Catch the Old One (c. 1605) and *A Mad World, My Masters*
(c. 1606). We are in a world of abstract types, Lucres and Hoards,
and Lampreys and Moneyloves, but the dialogue is consistently

fresh and the intrigues are managed with skill; crime and vice form the main ingredients; the scenes bustle with vitality and life. The first play illustrates another feature of the drama cultivated by realistic writers, the opposition of youth and age, and the tendency to take youth's side. In *A Trick to Catch the Old One*, the hero is Witgood, a profligate but a merry wit, who has been cheated of his estates by his uncle, Lucre. He devises a plan: he introduces his uncle to one of his mistresses, a courtesan, pretending that she is a rich widow and that he is her favoured suitor. Thus misled, Lucre is persuaded to restore to him the titles to his lands. Plots of a similar sort were to become frequent, and Witgood's descendants would flourish mightily. The gallants, the tavern-haunters, the needy younger brothers, were given here a flattering glass in which their wit could constantly triumph over age's severity and greed.

The Flourishing of Tragedy

The most stimulating thing about this period is the fact that the new mood which encouraged satire and realistic-sentimental scenes also had the power to encourage the greatest development of tragedy since the ancient Athenians. As we have seen, the tragic stage did not flourish luxuriantly after the days of Marlowe and Kyd; the decade between 1589 and 1599 found its desires expressed more aptly in romantic comedy and the chronicle-history play. By 1599, however, the well of the English chronicles had been drawn nearly dry. Every reign from that of Edward I to the end of the sixteenth century had had its dramatic treatment after the production of Shakespeare's *Henry V*. It is true that Elizabeth's death made it possible for playwrights to go to the early Tudor period which, during her lifetime, they dared not touch, and several of them eagerly seized the chance. Thomas Dekker and others thus collaborated in *Sir Thomas Wyatt* (*c*. 1604), the pathetic fate of Lady Jane Grey. Samuel Rowley, in *When you see me, you know me* (1604) wrote a play about Henry VIII. Thomas Heywood capped this with the two parts of *If you know not me, you know nobody*; or *The troubles of Queen Elizabeth* (1604); a chronicle of Elizabeth before her accession, with some later events of her reign; and Shakespeare, at the very close of his career, joined John Fletcher in *Henry VIII* (1613): we can only speculate on the precise division of labour. Not much more could be done in this kind of play, and gradually it disappeared. When John Ford worked on his belated and moving *Perkin Warbeck* in 1633 (the Royal Shakespeare Company staged it at Stratford-upon-Avon in 1976) he was forced to acknowledge that the history play had long since gone 'out of fashion': probably because few dramatists were able then to write in the high vein expressed by Ford's James IV of Scotland when he meets Warbeck and says:

> He must be more than subject who can utter
> The language of a king, and such is thine.

Despite the rise of the realistic school, the romantic comedy managed to retain its popularity. Shakespeare was not alone in seeking to bring to it a spirit which might meet the desires of a new age. *Twelfth Night* (*c.* 1600), though invested with a melancholy absent from his early comedies, remained pure romance; but already in *The Merchant of Venice* (1596), with many of its scenes set on the Rialto, and in *Much Ado About Nothing* (*c.* 1598), with its theme of desertion and threatened death, he had begun to deepen his work; in *All's Well That Ends Well* (*c.* 1602) and *Measure for Measure* (1604) he was definitely reflecting in his own way the mood that was animating Jonson. The reflection becomes even clearer when we turn to the strange *Troilus and Cressida* (1602), which contemporaries found impossible to classify, and which obviously expresses a sense of perplexity and unease. The change in material and mood has induced us to speak of the 'dark comedies' or the 'problem plays', and treating them so we realize they are among the most absorbing of Shakespeare's works. At the same time, we have to admit that they are dramatically unsatisfying precisely because an attempt has been made to force more into the romantic form than it can assimilate. *All's Well That Ends Well* seldom appealed in the theatre until various British mid-and-late-twentieth-century productions by such men as Tyrone Guthrie, John Barton and Jonathan Miller; even in the best productions of *Measure for Measure* (and there have been many good ones since William Poel's day) audiences find it difficult to harmonize the almost tragic intensity of the Angelo story with the twists, tricks and turns of the romantic plot; and though the verse of *Troilus and Cressida* (also frequently revived now) can shape the ice-flowers of Ulysses or miraculously 'heel the high lavolt',[1] its contrasts can still be puzzling.

---

[1] *Troilus and Cressida*, iv.4.85. The lavolta was a lively dance. See also *Henry V*, III, 5.32–3: 'They bid us to the English dancing-schools/And teach lavoltas high and swift corantos.'

Others beside Shakespeare sought to use the romantic style for new purposes, and their plays produce the same impression. One example may serve for many. In 1602 or 1603 Middleton wrote *The Phœnix*, selecting an imaginative setting appropriate for a comedy of romance, the court of an only vaguely identified Duke of Ferrara. Within this frame he places a series of episodes in which artificial intrigue is mingled with social satire. Phoenix, the young prince who has been ordered to travel abroad, remains at home in disguise to reveal the ill practices of various evil lords; a worthy matron is sold to one of these by her husband; a young girl is assigned to the care of her uncle, Falso, who steals her money and incestuously seeks to seduce her; Falso's three servants are aided by their master to rob the poor; his daughter, a jeweller's wife, maintains a dissolute lover; and a rascally lawyer delights in ruining his clients by encouraging them to indulge in law-suits. Two things are manifest: the incompatibility of the romantic framework with the exploitation of social satire and a tendency to revert to methods used in the old moralities. *The Phœnix* has many points of interest; but as a play it fails.

Fortunately, Shakespeare and several of his companions realized that what they might wish to achieve in this new social and theatrical atmosphere demanded a dramatic form other than that of romantic comedy. In 1599 Shakespeare presented his *Julius Caesar*, and John Marston the two parts of his peculiar *Antonio and Mellida*. The former play is an undoubted triumph, and the latter, by no means a masterpiece, most valuably aids our understanding of the period's changing temper. In the first part of *Antonio and Mellida* Marston offers a 'satirical' romantic comedy akin in style to *The Phœnix*. Antonio and his father, Andrugio, Duke of Genoa, have been defeated by Piero, Duke of Venice, and a price is on their heads. Disguised as an Amazon, or martial woman, Antonio penetrates into Piero's court and steals away his beloved mistress Mellida. Adventure follows adventure until at the end Piero suddenly abandons his jealous rage and welcomes the banished son and father. We are here on familiar ground. The second part of the play, however, starts abruptly with a completely changed atmosphere. Piero enters 'unbrac't, his arms bare, smear'd in blood, a poniard in one hand bloody, and a torch in the other'; revenge and murder become the theme; Andrugio is slain and appears in ghostly form to his son; Piero finally perishes at Antonio's hand in the midst of a court masque. The atmosphere of romantic comedy has gone and a new kind of tragic spirit has taken its place. Marston's work is in many respects ridiculous, yet it may serve as an image of the time. In the first part of *Antonio and Mellida* he has adopted the romantic comedy style, and tried to fit it to ends other than those for which it was originally calculated; in the second part he has gone right back to the style of *The Spanish Tragedy* and frankly embraced a tragic form. Still further, in the form he has selected, he points steadily in the direction of *Hamlet*.

Hamlet must have appeared on the stage two years later, in 1601; *Othello, Macbeth* and *King Lear* followed between 1603 and 1606; *Antony and Cleopatra, Coriolanus* and *Timon of Athens* must have been written almost immediately thereafter. In these, Shakespeare, who had been trying uncertainly to expand the scope of the romantic comedy, manifestly found what he required; and the success of the four plays from *Hamlet* to *King Lear* shows that he was giving his public what at that time they wanted. After many years the spirits of Marlowe and Kyd were revived, fused with one another, and endowed with fresh strength. Marlowe's intensity and sense of grandeur received new dramatic force; not only was the theme of *The Spanish Tragedy* reflected in the theme of *Hamlet* but, throughout, the qualities which had given distinction to Kyd's work were taken over and refashioned. The bitterness, uncertainty and melancholic sentiment of the period were here expressed so fittingly as to give these tragedies enduring existence. The expanded romantic comedy could provide little beyond an unsatisfactory amalgam of discordant elements; realistic comedy, even in the hands of a master like Jonson, could hardly rise beyond the topical and the temporary; in Shakespeare's tragedies the immediate present was enlarged into the eternal.

In saying this, we must be careful to observe that the last three tragedies, the so-called 'Roman' plays, are of a kind different from their predecessors. Not only are they distinct from the others in dealing with classical themes, they are also cast in another form. From *Hamlet* to *King Lear* we recognize that Shakespeare's supreme aim is to produce work calculated for the stage; the dramatist is completely in control. From *Antony* to *Timon* we are inclined to feel that the poet is overmastering the playwright. Even if allowances are made for the fact that *Timon* was apparently left unfinished, its basic concept is poetic rather than dramatic; *Coriolanus* is a masterly achievement without being a thoroughly satisfactory play; and *Antony and Cleopatra*, in spite of many brave revivals, impresses us more in its text than in the theatre.

It is unnecessary in any general survey to write more about plays so well known, but it is important to fit them into the wider pattern of the contemporary theatre. Many of Shakespeare's fellow-playwrights, from Jonson downward, essayed the tragic form during this decade. Not one produced a play worthy to be set by his; none was able to match his complex command of living characters, of inevitable movement from proposition to final conclusion, of integrated individual, political and metaphysical action, of complete mastery in the handling of diverse material. At the same time, the tragic form, closely bound up with the demands of the period, did yield a series of dramas which, even without a thoroughly harmonious poetic vision, contributed notably to the theatre. There were, of course, numerous failures of contrasting kinds. Jonson's own *Sejanus* (1603) and *Catiline* (1611), ambitious and carefully wrought, have practically no dramatic value, and they may stand as representative of several other works inspired rather by a scholarly dream than by theatrical fervour. At the opposite extreme are plays such as Henry Chettle's *The Tragedy of Hoffman; or, A Revenge for a Father* (c. 1602) and the anonymous and undatable *Alphonsus, Emperor of Germany*, wherein theatricality runs riot. In the first, lurid incident follows lurid incident as the gloomy hero, seeking to avenge his father's murder, proceeds to assassinate his enemies and himself perishes because he has allowed 'fickle beauty and a woman's fraud' to deflect him from his main purpose. In the second, Alphonsus, a monster of vice, moves from crime to crime until he is caught by one of his intended victims, forced to deny God, and then stabbed to the heart.

Obviously, contemporary audiences derived some delight from crude pieces of this sort, enjoying the contemplation of intense evil and the pleasure of watching involved intrigue. They were also prepared to welcome tragedies of deeper intent. George Chapman wrote a series of dramas which, though replete with sensational scenes, were inspired by a philosophic concept. In 1604 his *Bussy D'Ambois*, based on contemporary events in the French Court, presented a strong-willed, aggressive hero cast in an almost Marlovian mould. The story of his adventures, told boldly, with scenes of fighting, devil-conjuring, ghostly visitations, letters signed in blood, might all have seemed ridiculous had Chapman not been able to convince us that basically his object was to set upon the stage the image of one kind of greatness, the individual who determines to be a law unto himself and will bow to neither God nor man. The ghost of the dead

Bussy dominates a second companion piece, *The Revenge of Bussy D'Ambois* (*c*. 1610), in which the dead Bussy's brother Clermont, a calmer, deeper and more balanced character, is driven to seek a revenge against which his instincts are opposed. Another two-part play, *The Conspiracy and Tragedy of Byron* (*c*. 1605), traces the career and final defeat of a second ambitious and trampling hero, the dramatic picture of a man with the virtues and weaknesses of the recently executed Earl of Essex—to whom, indeed, Chapman specifically likens him. Finally, in *The Tragedy of Chabot Admiral of France* (*c*. 1613) these essays in political tragedy end with the treatment of a noble-minded, though low-born, servant of a king who moves forward faithfully amid others' corruption until his master's ill-founded suspicion breaks his heart.

A vastly different purpose animates the plays of John Webster. *The White Devil* (*c*. 1610) and *The Duchess of Malfi* (*c*. 1614) are among the relatively few non-Shakespearian tragedies of the time to preserve their fame. Both inhabit a world of intense evil. The first concentrates upon a woman, Vittoria Corombona, who might be almost the female counterpart of the Marlovian hero—prepared to indulge in any crime to achieve her ambitious ends. The second shows a noble Duchess caught in the toils of cruel and ambitious men, tormented in spirit and in body, and done wretchedly to death. Webster's was a peculiar half-genius. In some respects he exhibits the true dramatist's skill in the ordering of his scenes; hardly any could match him in the conjuring up of dark, macabre situations illuminated by a poetic imagination ever dwelling on the thought of death. Yet neither of these plays gives full satisfaction; the vision flags at times, vanishes for a space or loses itself in perplexed confusion. Perhaps he is the man who comes nearest to Shakespeare in his power of character delineation but his tragedies rather serve to illuminate Shakespeare's magnificent balance than to vie with him.

Webster's world of evil appears in a variant form in *The Revenger's Tragedy* (1607) and *The Atheist's Tragedy; or, The Honest Man's Revenge* (*c*. 1608), the second certainly and the first probably written by Cyril Tourneur. *The Revenger's Tragedy* offers a cynically melodramatic plot, introduced by the hero, Vindice, who, with the skull of his murdered mistress in his hand, soliloquizes on the wickedness of his enemies and on his resolve to achieve their ruin. The action moves with lugubrious inevitability towards a scene in which an amorous Duke is confronted, in a darkened room, with the dummy figure of a woman. On the top is placed the skull, smeared with corrosive poison. The Duke, induced to salute the 'lady', falls writhing to the ground, and is stamped to death. It might be thought that such a play could have no value; yet the nervous tension of its dialogue and the poetic virulence of its longer speeches give it a quality of strength matched in no other tragedy of the time. Vindice's apostrophe to 'the skull of his love dressed up in tires' in itself reveals the strange, extraordinary passion:

> Does every proud and self-affecting dame
> Camphire her face for this? And grieve her Maker
> In sinful baths of milk, when many an infant starves
> For her superfluous outside, all for this?
> Who now bids twenty pounds a night, prepares
> Music, perfumes and sweetmeats? All are hush'd.
> Thou mayest lie chaste now. It were fine, methinks,
> To have thee seen at revels, forgetful feasts,
> And unclean brothels—sure, 'twould fright the sinner
> And make him a good coward, put a reveller
> Out of his antic amble,
> And cloy an epicure with empty dishes.
> Here might a scornful and ambitious woman
> Look through and through herself. See, ladies, with false forms
> You deceive men, but cannot deceive worms—

In contrast with *The Revenger's Tragedy* (revived by the Royal Shakespeare Company in 1967, with Ian Richardson as Vendice), *The Atheist's Tragedy* brings forward a hero who, confronted by an enemy as confirmed in wickedness as any Jacobean villain, deliberately rejects the idea of executing his own vengeance and leaves God to punish the evil-doer. The fact that this hero's name is Charlemont suggests a close connexion between Tourneur's play and Chapman's *Revenge of Bussy D'Ambois*, with its not dissimilar portrait of Clermont. The revenge theme, we must remember, appealed to this age not only because of its theatrical potency, but also because it raised fundamental philosophical and religious questions.

Amid all these experiments in tragedy one other must be noted. *Arden of Feversham* in 1591 had essayed an absolutely novel form, that of the domestic drama, and during the late Elizabethan and early Jacobean periods several attempts were made to follow it. In 1599 Shakespeare's company produced *A Warning for Fair Women* (an anonymous play about a murder in 1573), which carried the naturalistic style a stage further. Though some of its scenes are almost melodramatically absurd, others, such as that where the children sit down to play by the door, and that where the husband, Sanders, angers his wife by refusing to give her money for the settlement of a milliner's bills and thus in effect seals his own doom, prove that the author was seeking for what we now should call a 'documentary' effect, and that he had some skill in recording common speech and characters. Maybe the greatest interest of this piece is its illuminating introduction—a debate by Tragedy, History and Comedy, which casts much light on contemporary interpretations. Tragedy's way with the murder is in effect a reply to Comedy's satirical description of prevailingly romantic tragic styles; these, she declares, show

> How some dann'd tyrant, to obtain a crown,
> Stabs, hangs, impoisons, smothers, cutteth throats;
> And then a Chorus, too, comes howling in
> And tells us of the worrying of a cat,
> Then of a filthy whining ghost,
> Lapped in some foul sheet or a leather pilch,
> Comes screaming like a pig half-stick'd
> And cries 'Vindicta! Revenge! Revenge!'
> With that a little rosin flasheth forth,
> Like smoke out of a tobacco-pipe or a boy's squib.
> Then comes in two or three like to drovers,
> With tailors' bodkins stabbing one another.
> Is this not trim? Is not here goodly things?

We might almost say that this domestic drama aimed at creating for contemporaries a 'progressive theatre'; the kitchen sink (of which we heard so much in the 1950s) had hardly been created then, but the 'kitchen-sink' kind of play was being adumbrated.

Others followed this lead. *A Yorkshire Tragedy* (c. 1606) is a potted play evidently intended as part of a composite *All's One; or Four Plays in One*. Though crude, it is remarkable for the fierce intensity of its central figure, the husband who destroys his family in a wild fit of passion. At the opposite extreme in length come the two parts of Dekker's *The Honest Whore* (1604–5), a work which might almost be taken as anticipating the modern 'domestic drama' not tragically conceived but intent on dealing with a 'problem'. True, the setting, instead of being a bourgeois English home, is romantic, but the entire atmosphere belongs to contemporary London. The sub-plot is comic, concentrating upon the patient, pacific citizen Candido, whose wife seeks many means to make him angry. This serves as contrast and comment on the main story which, among a fair amount of intrigue, focuses upon a courtesan, Bellafronte; meeting the pure-minded Hippolito, she is deeply moved by his words of reproof, and completely converted. Dekker's method in the second half of his play is particularly enlightening. Here (virtually a reversal of the first) we see Hippolito, in sudden lust, pursuing Bellafronte, now married to an honest man, and being rejected by her. We are far removed from the world of *Arden of Feversham*; some of the dialogue, with its scalding fury, is close in spirit to Tourneur's, while the humorous scenes remind us of citizen comedies of the period. Nevertheless, in spite of these qualities and its romantic framework, *The Honest Whore* obviously derives from a concept that animated the writers of realistic tragedy.

One particular play from this group is still remembered, and indeed occasionally produced: Thomas Heywood's *A Woman Killed With Kindness* (1603); praise for it is merited. Heywood has done several things in it. The play, revived by Barry Jackson at Malvern in 1931 and by the National Theatre at the Old Vic forty years later, is a 'tragedy' with a theme related to those of *Arden of Feversham* and *A Warning for Fair Women*, but instead of simply exhibiting a domestic murder, it mingles a story of death with the presentation of a problem, and the treatment of this problem is enriched by a deliberate avoidance of sensational incident. Secondly, it binds together two entirely different plots in such a manner as to make them complementary. Finally, it succeeds in putting upon the stage real-life scenes in which, when occasion demands, the language can soar beyond the common pitch. The first plot introduces a couple of friends, Sir Francis Acton and Sir Charles Mountford, who go hunting and fall into a violent quarrel over a triviality; flying into a passion, Mountford kills two of Acton's men, thus ruining himself; Acton plans a personal vengeance but is deflected from his purpose when he falls in love with Mountford's sister. This serves as background for the other, and main, plot, which opens on the picture of a happy domestic interior; John Frankford and his wife are devoted to each other; the former befriends a man named Wendoll and brings him to his house; there, in spite of all attempts to quench their infatuation, the wife and Wendoll become lovers. Frankford's old servant divines the truth and tells his master; at first the husband, blind with rage, plans to murder the pair, but calmer thoughts prevail; he sends his Anne to live in seclusion at a lonely manor, and when, dying of shame and a broken heart, she begs him to come to her, he acquiesces, and she passes away pardoned. The treatment of the two stories is imaginatively individual, and the language adds strength and colour. Thus, as Frankford looks upon the guilty lovers in their bed, Heywood is able to find (for a thought that Shakespeare had used before him, and later dramatists would repeat), a form of expression at once 'realistic' and 'poetic':

O God, O God! that it were possible
To undo things done, to call back yesterday,
That time could turn up his swift sandy glass
To untell the days and to redeem these hours!
Or that the sun
Could, rising from the west, draw his coach backward,
Take from the account of time so many minutes,
Till he had all these seasons call'd again,
Those minutes and those actions done in them,
Even from her first offence, that I might take her
As spotless as an angel in my arms!
But O! I talk of things impossible,
And cast beyond the moon. God give me patience,
For I will in to wake them.

Years later, in the sixteen-twenties, Heywood wrote another play which, although removed from it in time, deserves to be taken along with *A Woman Killed with Kindness*. In *The English Traveller* the story once more is of an erring wife, but the emphasis is upon the man who falls in love with her. Geraldine, a fine, sensitive young gentleman back from foreign travel, goes to the home of an older friend, Wincott. There he meets and becomes devoted to Wincott's wife, who returns his love. The pair vow that they will not betray the husband, and pledge eternal, chaste affection, at least until the wife is free; Geraldine, in order not to risk temptation and to avoid possible scandal, absents himself from the house; but the wife, against her better nature, finds herself drawn into a sordid affair with the evil-minded Dalavill. Like Anne Frankford, she dies repentant after her unfaithfulness has been discovered. In this, as in his earlier play, Heywood shows that he is not interested in sin as such; rather in the reflection of that sin in the minds of others. Frankford is more carefully studied than Mrs Frankford; Geraldine more than the erring wife. This approach to his material gives Heywood a special position of his own in a period when most of his companions were inclined, Tourneur-like, to concentrate on the exhibition of evil for its own sake.

In spirit, if not in plot, one other later play, *A Fair Quarrel* (*c*. 1616) by Middleton and Rowley, might be seen as a kind of companion-piece to Heywood's dramas. Here also two contrasting plots have been interrelated. The first tells of a girl Jane, secretly married to Fitzallen, whom her money-seeking father plans for a rich and foolish Cornishman, Chough. The father has Fitzallen falsely arrested. Jane discloses her pregnancy to a doctor who makes advances to her. Rejected, he reveals her condition to Chough, who promptly rejects the thought of marrying her; and the father is obliged to get Fitzallen released. In the second curious plot a Captain Ager quarrels violently with his superior, a colonel, whereupon his mother (who has been traduced) tries vainly to stop a duel by falsehood. But the duel is fought and the captain profits remarkably from the wounded colonel's repentance. The play is swiftly written, and its people live; at the same time, its realistic approach veers at moments towards the sentimental. Though *A Fair Quarrel* cannot justly be styled sentimental as a whole, it does—excellent as it is—betray signs of the almost inevitable trend of the domestic drama towards the mawkish and the artificial.

The impulse which inspired, directed and partly created Shakespeare's tragedies continued to rule the theatre during the latter part of James's reign. Although it is easy to trace signs of debility, the appearance of many plays worthy of remembrance and the evolution of new dramatic forms proved that its formative strength had not yet been lost.

Three or four playwrights may illustrate the course of the tragic drama. First, Francis Beaumont and John Fletcher, who gave their names to a dramatic style almost as influential as those of Shakespeare and Jonson. In 1616 the *Works* of Ben Jonson, completed by a second volume in 1640, had ushered in a novelty—the collected edition of an author's writings for the stage. In 1623 this was followed by the *Comedies, Histories, and Tragedies* of Shakespeare. The only other corresponding publication during this period, if we omit a not quite complete one-volume edition of Marston's plays in 1633, was the folio issued in 1647 as *Comedies and Tragedies written by Francis Beaumont and John Fletcher Gentlemen*. In fact, the title of this last work was a misnomer; Beaumont shared in only a few of the plays; Fletcher wrote some unaided and some in collaboration with other authors; and in several neither Fletcher nor Beaumont took part. Though such a portmanteau term should be used with discretion, the term 'Beaumont and Fletcher' can be used, not to suggest that the men were responsible for such and such a play, but simply to label a general dramatic style illustrated in the 1647 volume. W. Bridges-Adams, in *The Irresistible Theatre* (1957), notes, in the 'commendatory reference to "Fletcher's keen treble and deep Beaumont's bass" ', a possible clue to authorship. When, he says, we compare plays produced by the partnership with those afterwards, the voice perceptibly missing is Beaumont's, who used 'the firm decasyllabic as an instrument of deep emotion'; Fletcher's was a looser measure.[2]

The Maid's Tragedy (c. 1611) exhibits their tragic form at its best. The plot is simple. Amintor, married by royal command to Evadne, discovers on his wedding night that she is the King's unashamed mistress. His thoughts of revenge are barred only by contemplation of the divinity which hedges a king. When Evadne, stirred to repentance, murders her royal lover, Amintor's anguish sweeps her into fresh despair. There is a powerful imagination at work, but the play fails to hold us as it should—mainly, perhaps, because attention is focused less on the characters than upon the central problem. We may feel at times that, despite the intensity of its passions, *The Maid's Tragedy* comes closer to the spirit of later romantic tragi-comedy than it does, say, to *Othello*.

Constantly, in other 'Beaumont and Fletcher' tragic dramas, the typical romance material and attitudes appear, with emphasis more on a patterned theme than the persons involved. In *Cupid's Revenge* (c. 1612) we are interested less in the persons than a story in which the god Cupid, angered at the lack of devotion to his shrine, descends to earth and causes havoc. *Thierry and Theodoret* (c. 1617) exists rather for its sensational presentation of a terrible mother and her two tragic sons than for any real attempt to make these people live. Indeed, in the 'Beaumont and Fletcher' plays we can see clearly how the individualization of character which had given force and distinction to earlier dramas was being submerged by a reliance upon stock types. A king becomes merely a monarch, good or bad according to the needs of the plot; a heroine is made all innocent, a hero all noble; a faithful friend takes shape almost as the personification of Loyalty in a morality. Some of these 'Beaumont and Fletcher' tragedies have interest, but at core they are theatrical rather than dramatic; invested with no driving sense of purpose, but aiming only at immediate response from their audience.

[2] 'Each style,' says Bridges-Adams, 'is the complement of the other. But in attempting these distinctions we must of course not forget that the two friends may often have been subject to each other's influence.' Beaumont's dates were 1584–1616; Fletcher's, 1579–1625.

Philip Massinger's work is far different, but in many of his plays, and in spite of their sensational incident, we feel a lack of excitement, of subtlety, of inner penetration—with the result that they leave us relatively unmoved. There may be a terrible villain in *The Duke of Milan* (*c*. 1622), but he is made to protest too much; Sforza may be a great lover, but the rhetoric given to him tends to make his love seem more like lust. Further indications of weakness are apparent in *The Unnatural Combat* (*c*. 1623), where a number of genuinely effective scenes are nullified by melodramatic effects (including the death of a character struck by lightning) and especially the hiding of certain basic information until the last act for the sake of a sudden surprise. If these plays show some of Massinger's weaknesses, the *Virgin Martyr* (1610) and *The Roman Actor* (1626) illustrate his strength. The former, creating tragic passion out of Christian faith, succeeds in giving life to its central character, Dorothea; the latter, in the person of the actor Paris, achieves a kind of dignified grandeur.

A view of these plays as a whole suggests that Massinger was unfitted to write genuinely impressive tragedy because he lacked intensity of vision and deep sensitivity. Both of these qualities find expression in two of Middleton's plays, *The Changeling* (1622) and *Women beware Women* (1621), although the vigour of the first is vitiated by the combination of the main plot with another plot wholly inappropriate, and that of the second by a plethora of romantic intrigue. *The Changeling*, like *Macbeth*, shows crime being born of crime. W. Bridges-Adams, calling it a 'half-masterpiece', has said of it: 'Nobody today remembers the intricate sub-action from which the play takes its name. All we remember is the affair of Beatrice-Joanna and the wolfish De Flores.' Beatrice, daughter to the Governor of Alicante, to escape marrying a man she does not love, engages a Court hanger-on, De Flores, to get rid of the unwanted suitor. The murder is effected; De Flores is offered money but contemptuously demands a greater and more intimate reward. When Beatrice proudly draws his attention to the distance between her noble blood and his, the reply inexorably brings her down to reality:

> Look but into your conscience; read me there;
> 'Tis a true book; you'll find me there your equal.

Beatrice gives herself with loathing to De Flores, but gradually the evil she has let loose penetrates her soul. The atmosphere of *Women beware Women* resembles this, yet as we struggle through its complicated plot we realize the quality that is wanting in Middleton's tragic world: his figures are all voluptuaries, knaves, lechers, and the unrelieved blackness, instead of making a deep impression, can pall upon us. Even so, both plays have been revived with success in the modern theatre, *The Changeling* at the Royal Court in 1961, and *Women Beware Women* by the Royal Shakespeare Company at the New Arts in 1962.

The Cult of Tragi-Comedy and Social Comedy

Most of the tragedies written at this time, whatever their poetic virtues, merely developed forms that had been established earlier. Still, in other fields, the late Jacobean theatres did manage to evolve types of drama previously unexploited or only vaguely suggested. Two are especially important.

In 1608 the play of *Pericles* immediately drew a public. Though its provenance is impossible to determine exactly from the mutilated text published in the following year, Shakespeare was probably responsible for much of it. Its form is a dramatized story, the poet Gower acting as Prologue and Chorus, narrating some of the events and introducing those performed by the players. In keeping with this device, the plot is spread across the years and in many places: it shows Pericles, the Prince of Tyre, sorely plagued by man and fortune in his Levantine wanderings, and arriving eventually at a haven of rest. Though there are clear connections between this work and Elizabethan romantic comedies, the differences are equally obvious. A spirit of wonder is evoked; at times an element of mystery moves the action towards the symbolic; romance is being exhibited in a new way.

This mood colours Shakespeare's next three plays—with the exception of his share in *Henry VIII*, his last—*Cymbeline* (*c*. 1609), *The Winter's Tale* (*c*. 1610) and *The Tempest* (1611). The protracted plots of the first two; the visions and the scenes of wonder; the stress on the word 'tale', linked with the narrative method used at the beginning of *The Tempest*; the hints of symbolism, accentuated by such names for the heroines as Marina, Perdita and Miranda; the quality of the poetic style; the theme of the lost one fortunately found again—all these features bind the four plays in a single group. Some critics find in them the aftermath of Shakespeare's tragic passions, 'reconciliation' following torment; others believe that they originated in the new kind of playhouse, the 'private' Blackfriars, that Shakespeare's fellow-actors took over in 1608 or 1609; still others seek to argue that he was here exploiting a new sort of tragi-comedy initiated by Beaumont and Fletcher. Though we may never be able to answer the question directly, there is no evidence to suppose that these were other than Globe Theatre dramas; indeed, such evidence as we do possess connects them rather with the public than with the private stage. Further, the facts available to us suggest that, instead of Beaumont and Fletcher influencing Shakespeare, he most likely influenced them. No doubt he borrowed freely from others, but there is no need to assume that throughout his career he was incapable of thinking and inventing for himself.

Anyway, a vast chasm separates Beaumont and Fletcher's tragi-comedies from Shakespeare's. His are deep and theirs shallow; his manifest a profound imaginative vision, whereas even the best of theirs aim simply at theatrical effect; rarely do they present more than stock characters, and assuredly none worthy to stand beside the living persons Shakespeare created. *Philaster* (c. 1610) provides us with little more than a skilfully told story of a hero who has some dangerous political and pathetic amorous adventures; its incidents are controlled, not by thought of the persons involved, but by a desire to keep the audience constantly alert. This theatricality in the Beaumont and Fletcher tragi-comedies originated a relatively new dramatic pattern—an apparently inevitable tragic ending suddenly twisted to a happy and surprising conclusion. In *A King and No King* (1611), for example, we see a young monarch gripped by an incestuous passion for his sister and apparently heading for inexorable ruin; then, unexpectedly, the last act reveals that the girl is not his sister, that he is not the king, and that she is really the queen. Occasionally, as in the tragic *Bonduca* (c. 1612), these authors could escape for a moment from their desire to pander to a weakening public taste, but in general theatricalism rules—a refined theatricalism, no doubt, compared with the cruder efforts of some minor Elizabethans, yet as artificial as theirs. Scene after scene is devised for contrast and surprise; never for a moment are we allowed repose. *The Custom of the Country* (c. 1620) introduces a hero Arnoldo newly married to Zenocia; the lord of the country demands that she should be sent to him on her wedding night; the couple flee by boat, accompanied by Arnoldo's brother; Arnoldo arouses lustful passion in Hippolyta, who tries to poison Zenocia and ruin the hero, but incredibly repents in time to avoid disaster; the brother apparently kills a stranger in a street brawl and is protected by this stranger's mother; later he is obliged to take service in a male brothel; the supposedly slain man is found to be alive; and all ends happily. As another stage figure, Wilde's massive Lady Bracknell, would say 270 years later: 'A life crowded with incident.'

Dozens of such plays, some feeble, some competent, poured from Fletcher and his collaborators. *The Sea Voyage* (1622), like *The Tempest*, bears us to a distant island, but its inhabitants, a group of Amazons, are used merely as an excuse for amorous affairs romantically strange. Sometimes, as in *The Maid in the Mill* (1623), comic intrigue modifies the romantic; sometimes pathetic sentiment predominates, as in *The Two Noble Kinsmen* (1613), a dramatization of Chaucer's *Knight's Tale* in which some believe Shakespeare (especially in the first act) to have been Fletcher's collaborator. Most of the plays are adroitly constructed, and Fletcher's easy poetic style gives quality to their dialogue; but fundamentally these were ephemera that appealed to the audiences of courtiers who flocked to Blackfriars and occasionally to the Globe. The tastes of these spectators were becoming jaded. They could, from time to time, accept the sensationalism of some revenge play, especially if it brought in unexpected incidents; they could also applaud a cleverly wrought tragicomedy which offered pleasing surprises; but they were rapidly losing the power of appreciating the serious drama in any of its forms.

The result is that, even when we look beyond the 'Beaumont and Fletcher' plays, we are confronted by patent artificiality. Massinger was a worthy playwright; he knew how to construct a drama effectively, and he possessed a strong, if rhetorical, poetic style. Though these qualities are present in *The Bondman* (1623), they cannot hide from us that not one of the characters has other than a theatrical existence; although the theme of *The Renegado* (1624), dealing with a Christian induced to abandon his faith, promises an interesting and forceful play, the author is prepared to vitiate his work by one of the usual happy-ending twists; in *The Maid of Honour* (1621), which also promises well, we are confronted only by a pathetic lover, Adorni, a comic Signor Sylli, a noble innocent heroine, Camiola, a commonplace headstrong king, Roberto, and a lustful woman, Aurelia—stock persons all. The significance of this becomes obvious when we reflect that Massinger was unquestionably one of the most serious-minded, accomplished and ambitious playwrights of his time; if he failed we may have a measure for estimating the extent of the general decline, not only in tragedy, but also in tragi-comedy.

During the second part of James's reign, even while artificial tragi-comedy won applause, audiences of young gallants also favoured the development and expansion of a kind of comedy which foreshadowed the comedies of manners so typical of the later years of the century.

Jonson, as we know, first consciously opposed the romantically inspired works so popular before 1600; and his influence was probably most potent in encouraging various other dramatists, between the beginning of the century and 1610, to exploit London's citizen world. This provided the foundation. In Middleton's *A Trick to Catch the Old One* something further was suggested. There the hero was a young spark, impoverished but able by the exercise of his wit to win money for himself: the type of hero taken over and elaborated by Fletcher and his associates. In focusing attention on these witty young men, Fletcher once more showed his keen awareness of what would please the public. He recognized that the private theatres were largely supported by youthful courtiers, inns-of-court men and their companions, who in any clever, audacious hero discovered an idealized picture of themselves, and heard the polished, witty conversation towards which they aspired in their own society. Many a gallant took his place in the theatre, notebook in hand, ready 'to write down what again' he might 'repeat at some great table, to deserve' his 'meat'. Wit had indeed now become 'the word in fashion'—so much so that audiences sought for it not only in the dialogue but also in the prologues to plays. The use of the prologue had been common for a long time; we may even trace it back to the time of the medieval mysteries; but in the past it had generally been employed merely to explain the content or objectives of the drama to which it was attached. Thus in *Romeo and Juliet* the opening verses simply outline the main course of the action, while those which preface *Henry V* apologize for setting such great events as the battle of Agincourt upon a bare platform. Now, in James's later years, the prologue was 'advanced above the fabric of the whole work', and not infrequently any dislike of it caused what followed to be condemned.

This emphasis upon wit led too to the growth of a critical spirit in the auditorium such as had not been usual before;

> He that can
> Talk loud and high is held the witty man;

such a man

> censures freely, rules the box, and strikes
> With his court nod consent to what he likes.

In the theatres there were many

> deep-grounded, understanding men
> That sit to censure plays, yet know not when
> Or why to like;

the authors recognized that

> Some in a humorous squeamishness will say
> They come only to hear, not see, the play;
> Others to see it only; there have been,
> And are good store, that come but to be seen,
> Not see nor hear the play.

It was in this milieu that the youthful, well-born Fletcher won his success by transferring witty conversation to the stage. Many plays with which he was associated were romantically set, but whether supposed to take place in a vague France or Italy or amid London surroundings they brought to the spectators the sprightly immodest libertine whom they could admire, or the eccentric character at whom they could laugh, or the cleverly conceived plot from which they could derive intellectual delight. In *The Woman's Prize; or, The Tamer Tam'd* (c. 1611) they derived merriment from watching a Petruchio subjugated by his second wife, an English girl; they were pleased to see the careless, roguish Valentine win a lively widow in *Wit without Money* (c. 1614); they laughed at the foolish dapper La Writt, in *The Little French Lawyer* (c. 1619), who fondly imagines he has become a valiant duellist; and above all they enjoyed watching a Witty-pate Oldcraft (*Wit at Several Weapons*, 1609) gaily cheating those less intellectually alert but richer than himself. One particular comedy, *The Wild-Goose Chase* (1621), suggests what later was to be fashioned out of Fletcher's example. Though this is different in many respects from the Restoration comedies of manners, it anticipates them in others; the merry heroine Oriana, who indulges in a series of tricks to win her elusive Mirabel; her sisters, Rosalura and Lillia-Bianca, and their lovers, the blunt Belleur and the witty Pinac, clearly suggest the social circle inspected by Etherege and his companions. It was not by chance that Farquhar selected this comedy as the basis for his own comedy of manners, *The Inconstant*.

Cavalier Spectators and their Tastes

In moving from the Jacobean to the Caroline drama, it is again essential to consider the typical audiences and their theatres. Fundamentally, the gentlemen and their ladies who supported the actors were the same as those who dominated the theatre in James's time; yet there were several important differences. In 1625 the Civil War was not far off; the Puritans were growing in power and severity; the Cavaliers more and more were becoming self-consciously aware of themselves as a social unit dependent upon the Court; and, when the Puritans attacked the stage in such vituperative terms as appear in William Prynne's *Histrio-mastix* (1633), these Cavaliers replied by making the playhouse a kind of appendage of Whitehall.

Their interests, therefore, were predominant and they induced the actors to move from the hitherto prevailing Elizabethan methods of production towards a new style. The courtly spectators had been familiar for many years with the elaborate royal masques developed from the collaboration of Ben Jonson and the architect-designer Inigo Jones. The first of these had come in 1605, *The Masque of Blackness*; and James, who delighted in such shows, encouraged Jonson and other poets to devise similar spectacular pieces. Organizations such as the Inns of Court followed suit, and various wealthy nobles sought, in their own mansions, to emulate the practice of the palace. Throughout the reigns of James and Charles these spectacular aristocratic entertainments followed one another in magnificent procession.

Though the masque itself remains outside the range of the drama proper, its influence on comedy and tragedy alike during the Jacobean period is easily traceable. Undoubtedly, Shakespeare's last plays were partly inspired at least by the idea of the masque, and much other work, comic and serious, would contain short masque-like interludes. Until about 1625 the influence was indirect rather than direct; the professional stage still remained for the most part a bare platform backed by a façade, and scenery (in the modern sense) was virtually unknown. During Charles's reign there are numerous signs of change. No doubt most plays were given in the older manner, but with the still closer association of Court and theatre there were several attempts to reproduce on the professional stage effects akin to those with which many of the spectators were familiar at Court. When we hear that in the performance of Thomas Nabbes's *Hannibal and Scipio* (1635)

The places sometimes chang'd too for the scene,
Which is translated as the music plays
Betwixt the acts,

and when we find that Heywood's *Love's Mistress* (1635), after being given three times before royalty, was presented publicly at the Phœnix, we realize that we stand upon the threshold of a new theatre. In his preface to the last work, Heywood specifically praises Inigo Jones,

> who to every act, nay almost to every scene, by his excellent inventions gave such an extraordinary lustre, upon every occasion changing the stage to the admiration of all the spectators that, as I must ingeniously confess, it was above my apprehension to conceive, so to their Sacred Majesties and the rest of the auditory it gave so general a content that I presume they never parted from any object, presented in that kind, better pleased or more plenally satisfied.

The days when poet and player alone were of account had begun to vanish.

At Charles I's Court, especially under the tutelage of Queen Henrietta Maria, there was an active cult of the Platonic romance then so fashionable in Paris; young courtiers of literary pretensions were encouraged to practise writing in this style for the stage. Until then nearly all plays had been written by authors who remained well outside aristocratic circles—the Shakespeares, the Chapmans, the Dekkers, the Heywoods. Fletcher, it is true, was an exception, but he did not himself walk the Court's corridors or lounge in its anterooms, and most of his collaborators came from humble environments. Now, during the reign of Charles, the Cavalier poet makes his appearance: in the main to flatter royal taste by cultivating a kind of drama, much influenced by the Platonic romances, which was bound to remain caviare to the general.

All of this does not mean the older styles disappeared, to be supplanted suddenly by new forms. What it means is that, during these fifteen years, the stage looked more and more towards the Cavalier audience. It slowly changed its shape and, without completely severing itself from the Elizabethan tradition, suggested an entirely different kind of theatre to come.

While the strictly 'Cavalier' playwrights—such as Lodowick Carlell, with the two parts of his *The Passionate Lovers* (1638) and the corresponding parts of his *Arviragus and Philicia* (1636) —hardly need examination here, three writers of tragic and tragi-comic plays are notable for the manner in which they illustrate the changing styles and for the merit of some of their own achievements. The first, James Shirley, might be taken as representative of dramatists seeking to preserve the earlier tradition. *The Traitor* (1631) and *The Cardinal* (1641), the first set in Italy and the other in France, so inflate the tragedy of revenge and villainy as to make their scenes, despite poetic passion, become absurd. Extravagance has been sustituted for intensity, and the result is often ludicrous: when one of the characters, stabbed and dying by the side of his enemy, cries out:

> Now must I follow:
> I'll fight with him in t'other world,

we recognize how 'literary' and artificial are Shirley's conceptions. Almost the final words of the play are from one of the few survivors: 'Here is a heap of tragedies'; but the very excess of blood prevents us from being as impressed as Shirley desired. 'By these you see', he made one of his persons say,

> There is no stay in proud mortality;

but the crop of murders leaves us strangely cold. When, similarly, a Duchess observes in *The Cardinal*:

> He says he loves me dearly and has promised
> To make me well again, but I'm afraid
> One time or other he will give me poison,

the audience might well respond with a laugh rather than a shudder. The older kind of tragic expression had lost its potency.

John Ford sought another path. Subtly and imaginatively sensitive, and at the same time an avid student of such writings as Burton's *Anatomy of Melancholy*, he sought to create what might be called 'psychological' tragedy. *The Lover's Melancholy* (1628) in its very title reflects the general trend of his work. This, a tragicomedy, does not possess much value, but *The Broken Heart* (1629) and *'Tis Pity She's a Whore* (c. 1627) have had much romantic praise. The former (which Sir Laurence Olivier directed at the Chichester Festival of 1962, playing both the Prologue and Bassanes), lingers fondly upon thwarted love, strained emotions and bizarre situations. While willing to admit that Ford is a true poet and that certain scenes, such as that in which Calantha learns of the death of lover, friend and father, are striking on both page and stage, one cannot accept the play as masterly. The very nature of his persons' names show Ford's 'literary' approach: Ithocles, he explains, is 'The Honour of Loveliness', Orgilus is 'The Angry One', Calantha is 'The Flower of Beauty', Penthea is 'Complaint'. Symbolic titling may be proper in such a play as *The Tempest*: Ford's employment of it betrays the falsity of his tragic attitude. Perhaps *'Tis Pity* (familiar in performance nowadays) exhibits greater power, yet its action must leave us unsatisfied. Ford had every right, if he so wished, to take as his theme a tale of incestuous passion between a brother and sister; but one can be uneasily oppressed by his treatment, sometimes (it seems) chosen deliberately not because it fired his imagination, but because the choice of relationship would excite jaded listeners. Intensity, instead of being generated by a poetic vision, is sought through the nature of the plot itself.

Finally, we can glance at an author far less gifted as a poet but much more important in the mid-century theatrical world. Before 1640 a favoured courtier and the privileged master of a playhouse company, Sir William D'Avenant, was among the first to stimulate dramatic activity when the Puritan interregnum had ended; to a certain extent he would be a moving force in the development of the 'love and honour' drama of the Restoration period. In his first independent efforts, *Albovine* (1628) and *The Cruel Brother* (1627), he was a crude exponent of the gloomy and murderous tragedy where lust, ambition, rapine and violence are pervasive. But when, in 1634, he gave the significant title of *Love and Honour* to a rumbustious tragi-comedy, when in the following year he called another play *The Platonic Lovers*, and when (1638) he made Eumena of *The Fair Favourite* a king's platonic 'mistress', it was as if he were setting up a great signpost pointing directly and accurately towards John Dryden some thirty years ahead. His Theander and Eurithea are not far removed from Almanzor and Almahide.

All through this period tragi-comedy flourished, and its styles were various. *The Spanish Gipsy* (c. 1623) by Middleton and Rowley mingles, rather charmingly, the story of a licentious Roderigo who deflowers Clara, but later, repentance-struck, marries her, and a second story which shows the banished Alvarez and his delightful daughter living disguised in a gipsy camp. Sudden flights of lyrical utterance, passages of rhetorical sentiment, complex intrigue and scenes coarsely designed to catch the attention of the public mark most of the romantic tragi-comedies with which James Shirley supplied the stage from *The Brothers* (1626) onward, through *The Grateful Servant* (1629) and *Changes; or, Love in a Maze* (1632), to *The Young Admiral*, *The Gamester*, and *The Bird in a Cage* in 1633. Robert Davenport comes forward with his fairly successful *City Night-Cap* (1624) in which one part of a double plot concerns a pathologically jealous husband who actually suborns a friend to tempt his wife, and the other deals with an overtrusting Lodovico, who allows to his priggish and riggish wife all liberty. During the final years of Charles's reign, such plays as William Habington's *The Queen of Arragon* (1640), Thomas Rawlins's *The Rebellion* (*c*. 1636), Sir William Berkeley's *The Lost Lady* (1637) and Thomas Randolph's *The Royal Slave* (1636) illustrate the pathos, sentimentalism and extravagant incident so dear to the tastes of the Court, and so influential when the theatres reopened on the restoration of the monarchy. With these go the related experiments in pastoral style. About the year 1608 Fletcher had tried his youthful hand at a *Faithful Shepherdess*, but apart from this the earlier decades had largely avoided a pastoral mood. Now numerous poets turned to it during these years just before the outbreak of the Civil War: the veteran Jonson with *The Sad Shepherd* (*c*. 1637) and its lovely opening in Sherwood:

> Here she was wont to go! and here! and here!
> Just where those daisies, pinks, and violets grow:
> The world may find the spring by following her;

Shirley with *The Arcadia* (printed 1640), Randolph with *Amyntas* (*c*. 1630), Rutter with *The Shepherds' Holiday* (*c*. 1634)—none of them, it is true, producing any memorable dramatic achievement.

We find much more of positive value in the extension and elaboration of the realistic comedy established when the century was young, and now in harmony with the taste of a Cavalier audience. Some authors, such as Philip Massinger, pursued the Jonsonian course with some distinction. Indeed, Massinger's *A New Way to Pay Old Debts* stands out in early seventeenth-century drama as one of the durable successes: it stayed in the repertory until the nineteenth century (and Edmund Kean at Drury Lane), and it has also had a few twentieth-century revivals with such actors as Robert Atkins and Donald Wolfit. In his terrible portrait of a 'cruel extortioner', the powerfully vital figure of Sir Giles Overreach, Massinger showed that he could take a 'humour' cast in Jonson's mould and give it living quality. Here he fused the dramatic methods of both Jonson and Shakespeare. His comedy *The City Madam* (1632)—acutely recreated at Birmingham Repertory Theatre in 1964—has a certain similar (and bitter) force. Though none of its persons shares Overreach's vitality, the picture of a merchant's household, with its selfishly ambitious Lady Frugal and its hypocritical Luke, does have genuine theatrical virtue.

William Rowley's work is rather comparable in purpose. *A New Wonder, A Woman never vexed* probably appeared at about the same time as *A New Way to Pay Old Debts*; like Massinger's play, it deals seriously and morally with social problems. Set vaguely in a historical milieu, its characters and situations are contemporary: the tale of a self-righteous merchant who casts off his good-hearted spendthrift brother and disinherits his own son. At length he is in difficulty himself. Succoured by son and brother, he comes to a deeper understanding of human values. Once more the double influence of Jonson and Shakespeare is apparent.

Though various Stuart comedies share kindred merits, most of those that still speak to us were individual efforts, single successes by minor men. Massinger apart, the only prolific dramatists with styles of their own were Richard Brome and James Shirley. Brome began as a follower of Jonson; he had been, in fact, Jonson's servant, and his early efforts were blessed and aided by his master. Even if we decide that he was not a great poet or writer, he had a real talent for the stage; several of his plays succeeded in their own time, and a few remained popular well into the eighteenth century. He was able to modify the Jonsonian 'humours' comedy so that it approached the later comedy of manners; and he exploited the musical element in his plays so that they pointed vaguely towards the ballad-opera of later years: *The Northern Lass* (c. 1629) and *A Jovial Crew; or, The Merry Beggars* (1641) are examples. The first has a novelty in its dialect-speaking heroine who comes to London, falls in love with Sir Philip Luckless, and, before gaining his hand, is involved in a world of marriage-hunters, fools and would-be wits: the whole of the action is diversified by a free use of songs and masques. The atmosphere of *The Northern Lass* is carried a stage farther in *A Jovial Crew*, which has the double interest of being the last play performed before Parliament closed the theatres, and of reappearing in triumph during the next century as a ballad-opera. Charmingly, Brome tells his story of a worthy old squire who, after his steward Springlove has left him for a company of beggars, discovers to his joy that the young man is really his son by a beggar-woman. Still, the story itself matters little: for the author (and for ourselves) the piece rests upon its imaginatively conceived scenes within the beggars' camp.

Brome's work shows one way in which Jonsonian comedy was being extended; another is in the plays of Shirley. Already, in *The School of Compliment*, staged in 1625, the year when Charles I came to the throne, Shirley had marked the path he would take. Though this comedy has not much value, with neither an effective plot nor living characters, its fantastic 'school' where young gallants are taught how to deliver highly flowered compliments does prove that the dramatist was concerned with the manners of his time and not with social problems and evils. It is this that distinguishes *The Witty Fair One* (1628), *Hyde Park* (1632) and *The Lady of Pleasure* (1635). All depend upon wit and social polish; all display a new, anti-romantic attitude towards the relationship between men and women. 'Come,' says the hero of *The Witty Fair One* to the heroine, 'remember you are imperfect creatures without a man; be not you a goddess; I know you are mortal, and had rather make you my companion than my idol; this is no flattery now.' The Petrarchan sonneteer has gone; so has the deity he worshipped; we have stepped into another world. In 1642, as the theatres shut their doors, they have come close to what would be the spirit of the Restoration stage after 1660. Shirley's comedy of manners, Brome's modification of the Jonsonian style, D'Avenant's themes of love and honour, all laid the foundations of a new house.

Four
Restoration Drama

Drama under the Puritans

The theatres were officially closed by Commonwealth ordinance in 1642; theoretically there was no further acting in England until the restoration of Charles II. But appearances are often deceptive, and we have evidence that in various ways the theatrical tradition established during the early seventeenth century was carried on to the years after 1660.

Undoubtedly the Puritan authorities were anxious to put a stop to all sorts of amusement, innocent and otherwise; but equally we know that actors and spectators frequently evaded the vigilance of the soldiery and defiantly presented their shows. Acting in the Commonwealth period was of two kinds: at the old theatres with performances by some of the players of Caroline days, and at theatres, booths, inns, halls, by bands of actors who chose 'drolls' or farces, usually derived from already existing plays. Thus, the more broadly comic portions of *A Midsummer Night's Dream* were extracted and performed under the title of *Bottom the Weaver*. Of these 'drolls' two collections are extant, one entitled *The Wits*, published in 1662, and the other *The Stroler's Pacquet Open'd*, issued in 1742. This 'droll' tradition is important, for it ran its course by the side of the regular theatre tradition right on to the end of the eighteenth century. Nor does the acting of 'drolls' exhaust the theatrical activities of the Commonwealth period. Regular plays were frequently seen. Whenever the actors could gather an audience together in one of several half-dismantled playhouses they would, no doubt in most unseemly haste, hurry through some Beaumont and Fletcher or Shakespeare drama. Sometimes their performances were interrupted by the rude entrance of Puritan soldiers, and then the affair was reported in the primitive newspapers of the time; more often than not the players must have got off unscathed, all record of the performance being lost irretrievably. There are many extant accounts of acting during these years, and those accounts, we must presume, are but roughly indicative of a fairly constant series of irregular performances both in London and in the provinces. Thus, in two distinct ways, the continuity of tradition was being preserved.

These were not the only means by which the earlier Caroline theatre was connected with the later. After Cromwell came to power, some actors formed themselves into a company and set off for Germany under the leadership of one George Jolly, who was later in partnership with William Beeston, formerly master or governor of the King's company of child players at Salisbury Court. With what must have been a repertory of well-known Elizabethan, Jacobean and Caroline plays, he would have carried on an earlier acting tradition during an interregnum of eighteen years. William Beeston himself forms another link. This man, whom Dryden called the 'Chronicle of the Stage', was the son of Christopher Beeston, who had known Shakespeare in the opening years of the seventeenth century. It is likely that William Beeston, owner in 1660 of the Salisbury Court and associated in D'Avenant's theatrical undertakings, played the part of a maestro to the younger players. These acting links are completed in Sir William D'Avenant, intimately connected with the theatre in the days of Charles I and leader of a patent company under Charles II. His own operatic endeavours, in *The Siege of Rhodes* and other similar pieces performed towards the close of the Commonwealth, provide a pleasant little oasis of licensed acting in the midst of an otherwise arid desert.

Many who were not of the severest Puritanical convictions looked back to the theatrical glories of the past and kept alive in their hearts the love of acting. The tradition of the written play was also preserved in several distinct ways. Many of the actors, finding their regular sources of income removed, were forced to dispose of what in earlier days they had jealously guarded. In the early seventeenth century some players seem to have believed that a drama unprinted was more likely to be popular in the theatre than a drama published. Accordingly they held in their tiring-rooms stacks of manuscripts which they refused to sell to the 'stationers'. Only in times of distress—as when the playhouses were shut because of the Plague—did they reluctantly dispose of their treasures. There are obvious exceptions. Heminge and Condell issued in 1623 many then unpublished works of Shakespeare, apparently as a kind of last service to their

A composite drawing showing the kind of improvised stage that might have been in illicit use during the Puritan interregnum

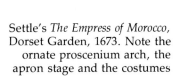

Settle's *The Empress of Morocco*, Dorset Garden, 1673. Note the ornate proscenium arch, the apron stage and the costumes

Addison's *Cato*, 1713. Observe the blend of
contemporary and Roman dress

Mrs Siddons as the Tragic Muse: painted by Sir
Joshua Reynolds

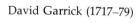
David Garrick (1717–79)

William Charles Macready
(1793–1873) in 1821

deceased friend; Jonson evidently looked upon his plays as his own property and had his *Works* printed in 1616; but various dramas were regarded as the possessions of the companies which produced them first. During the Commonwealth many of these plays were released by the actors. Apart from numerous separate comedies and tragedies, the period offered the rich array of the Beaumont and Fletcher dramas, published in 1647, as a large folio volume. We must assume that it could not have been published without a corresponding reading public: many, remembering pleasant days in the theatre, turned from the stage to the study and to the texts of their favourite tragedies and comedies of Shakespeare, of 'Beaumont and Fletcher', or of Shirley.

The Restoration Theatre

In 1660 Charles II returned to his throne amid the rejoicings of a nation wearied of the excessive restrictions of the Commonwealth; the band of devoted Cavaliers, who had shared his exile, joined with the many people in England eager for a return of earlier Caroline traditions. No sooner was Charles on his throne than bodies of actors were formed into companies. George Jolly hurried back from Germany; William Beeston hastily reopened the Salisbury Court theatre; Killigrew gathered together the remnants of the old King's Men; D'Avenant collected a body of young actors, untrained, but eager for histrionic glory. The King, however, was anxious to keep the affairs of the theatre in his own hands; within a few months of his accession he had issued orders and patents by which the number of companies was limited to two, one under Killigrew and another under D'Avenant. These settled down to a comfortable monopoly, the first at the various Theatres Royal, the second at the Duke's houses in Lincoln's Inn Fields and in Dorset Garden. In 1682 the companies were amalgamated, and remained so until a number of the best actors seceded in 1695. The first point, then, is this, that, while for thirteen years one theatre supplied all the needs of London, for the other twenty-seven years to the end of the century only two theatres were open. When we remember that a smaller London, thirty or forty years before, had been able to support as many as six theatres concurrently, it becomes obvious that some great change had affected the playgoing public. That change is really the culmination of a gradual movement from the early years of the century: the theatre has degenerated completely into a thing of the Court; the middle classes for the most part keep away. A few bourgeois people, such as Pepys, may have attended the playhouses during these years, but such people were those who sought for Court preferment or who aped in one way or another the manners and tastes of the Cavaliers. All we know proves conclusively that a typical audience was composed of the courtiers, their ladies, the gallants and the 'wits', with a sprinkling of town riff-raff. The Theatre had become the often riotous haunt of the upper classes, and in consequence plays written for it were calculated to appeal to a courtly and Cavalier house. It is this that explains both the rise of the heroic tragedy and the elaboration of the comedy of manners. One appealed to artificial aristocratic sentiments on the subject of honour; the other reflected the morally careless but intellectually brilliant atmospheres of boudoir and tavern.

Further, the playhouses changed their shape. In three particular ways the Restoration theatre differed from the Elizabethan. Except for a few years after 1660, when actors used some of the still existing buildings, the old open-air 'public' theatre vanished. The new theatres, with one early exception, were roofed in and artificially lit. Moreover, the first new premises were not of the square inn-yard type, but converted tennis-courts, oblong in shape. It is obvious that in theatres of this sort the Elizabethan platform stage would have been out of the question; on the other hand, tradition pointed to a stage surrounded by the audience. Hence a compromise whereby a proscenium arch, known to the early seventeenth century only in Court masques, cut off part of the theatre, and an 'apron' in the form of a semicircle jutted into the midst of the pit. There is here the union of two mutually opposing systems. Players could still be intimate with the audience when they moved forward (or 'downstage'), and yet there remained the possibility of scenic display in the background. We shall expect to find, then—and do find—that, technically, the plays written for this theatre show many anomalies. They are transition plays, simultaneously looking back to the earlier platform with its free conventions, and forward to the development of a new theatre. For the first few years it was natural that the dramatists should not have learned to write for the altered stage; their plays were cast in Elizabethan form. Gradually, the changed conditions had their effect; dramatists realized what the actors needed, and their plays, because of scenic influence, became more co-ordinated and less episodic than those from Shakespeare's time. It is only in the period's spectacular productions that we discover such rapid shifting of locality as there had been in an *Antony and Cleopatra* or a *King Lear*.

The presence of this scenery, added to the primitive sort of lighting that now accompanied all plays, meant the loss of one important Elizabethan convention. We remember how Shakespeare and his fellows were forced, because of the absence of scenery and performances in daylight, to explain where the actors were supposed to be and at what time the action was supposed to take place. In the Restoration theatre the information would have been superfluous, and we can see how gradually more and more was left to designer and machinist: more, that is, to the eye, less to the ear. While this aided concentration in the plays themselves and prevented minor dramatists from wandering into disquisitions on Nature's loveliness, it detracted to a certain extent from the poetic quality inherent in earlier dramas; verbal splendour was subdued.

Another most important change was the coming of the actress. Formerly the players were men or boys; but the pleasure-loving Charles II, who had seen many performances by women during his exile abroad, decided that the introduction of actresses here would be a good thing. Cynically, he pretended that this was in the interests of morality. Probably no one believed him. Yet no one objected, and a woman may have first appeared on the English stage on 8 December 1660 in Vere Street, Clare Market. The company was Thomas Killigrew's in a free version of *Othello*. The prologue that night announced:

I come, unknown to any of the rest,
To tell you news; I saw the lady drest:
The woman plays today; mistake me not,
No man in gown, nor page in petticoat:
A woman to my knowledge.

The Desdemona could have been Margaret Hughes or Anne Marshall. Though at first the number of woman capable of fulfilling their tasks in the London theatre must have been small, and boys continued occasionally to take the feminine roles, by 1670 the new conditions had been fully established. Not only were Betterton, Mohun and the rest praised, but also Mary (Moll) Davis, Nell Gwyn (famous for other reasons), Mary Betterton (Saunderson), Mary Knepp, and other precursors of the great Barry, Bracegirdle and Oldfield. It became more and more necessary to provide suitable parts for the newcomers. When D'Avenant (if he indeed were guilty) altered *Macbeth* he saw the need for enlarging the roles of both Lady Macbeth and Lady Macduff; and when the same author in collaboration with Dryden sought to improve *The Tempest* they provided Miranda with a sister and Ariel with a spirit mate. Shakespeare suffered from his Restoration adapters, particularly from Nahum Tate (then a young man) in a version of *King Lear* (1681) which survived for a long time. There Lear, Cordelia and Gloucester are spared at the end, and Lear hands his daughter to Edgar with suitable expressions. Tate wrote in his dedication to an 'esteem'd friend': "Twas my good Fortune to light on one Expedient to rectifie what was wanting in the Regularity and Probability of the Tale, which was to run through the Whole, as Love betwixt Edgar and Cordelia, that never chang'd Word with each other in the Original. . .' Lear says in Tate's last scene:

> But, Edgar, I defer thy Joys too long:
> Thou serv'dst distrest Cordelia; take her Crown'd;
> Th'imperial Grace fresh blooming on her Brow;
> Nay, Gloster, thou hast here a Father's Right,
> Thy helping Hand t'heap Blessings on their Heads.
> **Kent** Old Kent throws in his hearty Wishes too. . .
> **Gloster** Now, gentle Gods, give Gloster his Discharge.
> **Lear** No, Gloster, thou hast Business yet for Life;
>   Thou, Kent, and I, retir'd to some cool Cell
>   Will gently pass our short Reserves of Time
>   In calm Reflections on our Fortunes past. . .

In all respects the Restoration stage was pursuing a new path, even if it could not quite shake off old memories, the 'fortunes past'.

Love and Honour Drama

The Restoration is remarkable for the development of several species of drama destined either to become typical theatrical forms or to breed equally typical cognate forms in the next century. These types, of which the heroic tragedy, the comedy of manners, the opera and the farce, are chief, all display a union of diverse forces. Each, from one point of view, is the lineal descendant of some species of pre-Restoration drama, yet each is coloured and modified by the influence of contemporary Continental work. The heroic tragedy may thus be considered as merely a further elaboration of the romantic plays first made popular by Beaumont and Fletcher. D'Avenant knew of the contest between Love and Honour, and the exaggerated, flamboyant language in the writings of Dryden and Settle was anticipated by more than one dramatist of the early seventeenth century. On the other side, we have the testimony of Roger Boyle, Earl of Orrery, the first to attempt the introduction of the heroic style into England, that the employment of rhyme in place of blank verse in these heroic plays was due to the influence of France, exerted through the enthusiasm of the King. Nor was it only in outer form that the Restoration dramatists modified their styles to accord with prevailing tastes in Paris. The heroic drama, with its grandiloquent sentiments, is to be regarded as the representative in the theatre of the mood and atmosphere of the heroic poem, a form of literature which, popularized by such men as Chamberlayne and D'Avenant, had come from France in the middle of the century. The comedy of manners, likewise, is an admixture of similar ingredients. Its source lies in Jonson's comedy of 'humours' and Fletcher's comedy of intrigue. Everywhere we can trace in its form the older strains altered a trifle to suit a later age. Congreve's witty, debonair, callous, philandering air is thus born of the sterner and more satiric Jonson. Yet much of what we know now as the comedy of manners would have remained unwritten, or would have been written in a different style, if the English theatre had not possessed Molière for a guide and a model. The same analysis of forces is true for farce and opera. Farcical elements enough are apparent in sixteenth- and seventeenth-century comedies, and the later farce of the Restoration and Georgian eras owes a great deal of its vitality to older examples. But the first afterpiece, and first true English farce—Otway's *The Cheats of Scapin* (1676)—was but an adaptation from the French, and many similar pieces produced in the last decades of the seventeenth century, and in the years that followed, were either alterations of French farcical works or farcical renderings of true comedies originally written by Molière and his companions. In the same way, the Restoration opera, made glorious by the music of Purcell, was a purely native development, though it might not have come into being without the operatic efforts of Renaissance Italy and contemporary France. We cannot assert too often that, despite the immense change in the English theatre on Charles II's advent, the substratum of all dramatic activities during the latter part of the century was mainly English. The great wave which had risen to a surge with Shakespeare was still eddying along the shore, slightly disturbed but not clearly altered in its course by neighbouring cross-currents.

In serious drama the first two decades of Charles's reign are marked by the cult of the heroic play, sometimes with a tragic ending, sometimes with one reasonably happy. Instead of continuing the use of blank verse, dramatists deliberately turned to rhymed couplets, realizing, no doubt, that the blank verse proper in Shakespeare's day was no longer in harmony with changing speech-patterns; moreover, with Fletcher and his fellows, the medium had lost much of its original precision and vigour. Plots and situations, too, were different. Emotions were boldly but artificially expressed; violent ranting and inflammatory speeches ruled; and virtually the only conflict admitted was that between love and honour. The period's heroic plays could be just as absurd as the satirical scenes in the Duke of Buckingham's burlesque, *The Rehearsal* (1671); even the delightful soliloquy of Prince Prettiman over his boots, one symbolizing honour, the other love. This ends with him hobbling from the stage, one boot on, the other off.

John Dryden is the best (perhaps the first) dramatist of the heroic play. If he did not invent it, at least he gave it impetus, and when in 1677 he recanted and bade adieu to his long-loved mistress, rhyme, most of his companions followed the lead. Beginning with *The Indian Queen* (1664), written with Sir Robert Howard, he led the van of the love-and-honour playwrights, producing before 1675 *The Indian Emperor; or, The Conquest of Mexico by the Spaniards* (1665), *Tyrannick Love; or, The Royal Martyr* (1669), *The Conquest of Granada by the Spaniards* (1670), and *Aureng-Zebe* (1675), besides the rhymed 'opera' wrought out of Milton's *Paradise Lost* and entitled *The Age of Innocence* (printed 1677). All the five heroic plays are built upon a set plan: in each a hero of superhuman prowess and boundless pride; a heroine of unsurpassed constancy and beauty; a stirring story of fighting and martial enthusiasm; and, in several of the characters, an inner conflict between love and honour. All of this is expressed in couplet form, the artificiality of the medium corresponding to the artificiality of the situations and the persons. Shakespearian echoes can be found, but the language as a whole bears the same relation to Shakespeare's as a bad gramophone record to the voice of a skilled singer. The tones are exaggerated and harsh; there is the continual drone of metallic rhymes; instead of imaginative vitality, only mechanical accomplishment.

In saying this, we must remember Dryden's basic objective. In his plays, as in his non-dramatic poetry, he was determined to establish something fresh. During the Caroline period the impulse that had produced Shakespeare was weakening dangerously. Against this the Restoration period sought for a new clarity and precision. In prose and verse alike the need was for logical and direct utterance, so the substitution of heroic couplets for the older blank verse was a particular manifestation of a general movement of change. Though—inspired as it was by an intellectual concept—it failed completely to delineate the passions, it was admirably adapted to any rhetorical utterance. We can judge this from a single passage in *The Conquest of Granada*. Almanzor, intent upon seeing his mistress, enters to be confronted by the ghost of his mother; obviously, his words are totally inadequate to summon the desired atmosphere of awe and wonder:

Almanzor A hollow wind comes whistling through that door,
    And a cold shiv'ring seizes me all o'er:
    My teeth, too, chatter with a sudden fright.
    These are the raptures of too fierce delight,
    The combat of the tyrants, Hope and Fear,
    Which hearts, for want of field-room, cannot bear.
    I grow impatient: this or that's the room.
    I'll meet her: now, methinks I hear her come.
[*He goes to the door. The Ghost of his Mother meets him. He starts back. The Ghost stands in the door.*
    Well may'st thou make thy boast, whate'er thou art;
    Thou art the first e'er made Almanzor start.
    My legs—
    Shall bear me to thee in their own despite:
    I'll rush into the covert of thy night,
    And pull thee backward by the shroud to light.
    Or else I'll squeeze thee like a bladder there,
    And make thee groan thyself away to air.
[*The Ghost retires.*
    So! Art thou gone? Thou canst no conquest boast.
    I thought what was the courage of a ghost.

This is sheerly ridiculous; but there follows another speech, uttered by the ghost, which aims, not at arousing emotion, but at making a logical statement:

Ghost I am the ghost of her who gave thee birth,
    The airy shadow of her mould'ring earth.

Love of thy father me through seas did guide;
On seas I bore thee, and on seas I died.
I died; and for my winding sheet a wave
I had, and all the ocean for my grave.
But when my soul to bliss did upward move,
I wander'd round the crystal walls above,
But found the'eternal fence so steeply high
I flagg'd and flutter'd down, and could not fly.
Then, from the battlements of the heav'nly tower,
A watchman angel bid me wait this hour,
And told me I had yet a task assign'd,
To warn that little pledge I left behind,
And to divert him, ere it were too late,
From crimes unknown and errors of his fate.

The first passage is foolish; the second rises to assured dignity and effectiveness.

Beside Dryden there roared and ranted a goodly company of heroic dramatists, most of them of little account. Elkanah Settle, with his wretched *Cambyses, King of Persia* (1671) and, not much better, *The Empress of Morocco* (1673), hardly deserves more sympathetic treatment than he received in Dryden's satiric verses. John Crowne's work is almost equally negligible. *The Destruction of Jerusalem by Titus Vespasian* (1677) is his most accomplished effort, but even this is a long way after *The Conquest of Granada*. Among the rout of heroic rhymesters only three stand forward with occasionally noteworthy scenes.

Roger Boyle, Earl of Orrery, one of the first to experiment in the heroic form, took a path somewhat different from Dryden's. The latter, in the line of native dramatic development, wrote plays which were the descendants, if far removed, of Shakespearian tragedy. Orrery is more deeply influenced by the rhymed tragedy of France. His atmosphere has a chilly attempt at classical restraint, which marks him as a follower of Corneille and Racine rather than of the Elizabethans. Yet, somewhat surprisingly, he reverted in some of his plays to the long-forgotten chronicle-history tradition. If in *Mustapha, Son of Solyman the Magnificent* (1665) and *Tryphon* (1668) he adopted those Eastern themes so popular with the heroic writers, in *The History of Henry the Fifth* (1664) and *The Black Prince* (1667) he took up the chronicle-history tradition abandoned by almost all Caroline dramatists. True, his treatment of these native historical themes is totally unhistorical and owes nothing to sixteenth-century example, yet the very fact that Orrery thought of English history at a time when grotesque visions of Peru and Persia and Egypt prevailed, shows that he had a mind of his own. Probably his practice had some influence upon later dramatists who turned for inspiration to the history of their native land.

Of different importance is Nathaniel Lee, the Bedlamite. This man, who first appeared in the full flush of 'heroicism' with *Nero, Emperor of Rome* (1674), and who continued to write his rhymed and blank-verse plays until 1689, was one of the unhappy creatures who, born with an undue share of enthusiasm and passion into a world of intellect and reason, find relief only in madness. Akin to Cowper and Smart and Blake, the light flashing from his brain in lucid intervals gleams all the more brightly because of the surrounding gloom. The follies of Lee's rhapsodies are patent, yet beneath the absurdities of *Sophonisba; or, Hannibal's Overthrow* (1675), of *Gloriana; or, The Court of Augustus Caesar* (1676), and of *Theodosius; or, The Force of Love* (1680), we can discern elements to praise. Formless and hysterical though his plays may be as a whole, his ability to create individually impressive scenes does demand recognition.

The only other heroic writer who needs attention is Thomas Otway. Before he wrote his two minor masterpieces, he gave to the theatre a rhymed *Alcibiades* (1675) and *Don Carlos, Prince of Spain* (1676), both with surer touches than we find anywhere in the period save in the work of Dryden. *Alcibiades*, for all its foolish scenes, has a strength of utterance; and *Don Carlos* is one of the best heroic dramas, with a theme less exaggerated than usual and passions not artificialized out of all likeness to human emotions. At the very opening of his career, and working in a dramatic sphere peculiarly difficult and circumscribed, Otway shows a quality which later he would refine and deepen in *The Orphan; or, The Unhappy Marriage* (1680) and in *Venice Preserv'd; or, A Plot Discover'd* (1692), both plays that would be often revived. (In London during 1953 Sir John Gielgud and Paul Scofield acted in a celebrated *Venice Preserv'd*, directed by Peter Brook.)

The Return to Shakespeare

These two dramas introduce a dramatic development certainly influenced by the heroic play, and that development was due unquestionably to a new appreciation of Shakespeare. In 1677 Dryden had written his *All for Love* confessedly in imitation of Shakespeare's style, and two years later Otway turned from his heroic plays to *The History and Fall of Caius Marius*, in which, surprisingly, he mixed a story from Plutarch with an adaptation of Romeo and Juliet. Thus, even though *The Orphan* may seem to look forward towards Shakespeare, the force which inspired it was evidently an admiration of what the Elizabethans had achieved, and a wish to recapture some of their power. The story of a fatal error by which a brother deflowers his brother's wife has been dealt with in a manner deeply influenced by Shakespearian tragedy, though the stress upon pathetic situations is imposed by the author's sense of what the audiences of 1680 demanded. Even more 'Elizabethan' in form is *Venice Preserv'd*, with its contrasts between the stern yet generous Pierre, the vacillating Jaffier and the troubled Belvidera, in perhaps the most effective tragedy of its period.

Dryden's *All for Love* was not simply an adaptation: rather it set out to fashion the theme of *Antony and Cleopatra* into a shape harmonious with the dramatic philosophy of the late seventeenth century. Abandoning the wide passionate sweep of Shakespeare's tragedy, even while constantly inspired by its spirit, the play presents a clearly wrought and economically patterned version of the historical events, reducing the lovers' complex emotions to a simpler form such as the spectators of the time might appreciate. It marks the upward reach of Dryden's power, and its long popularity during years when the original *Antony and Cleopatra* could not be successfully staged is a testimony to its excellence within its own kind.

Dryden's other tragedies have hardly the same strength and fervour. *Amboyna* (1673) is a crude drama written purely as a piece of propaganda against the Dutch; *Troilus and Cressida; or, Truth found too late* (1679) is merely a retreatment of Shakespeare's tragi-comedy; while *Don Sebastian, King of Portugal* (1689) and *Cleomenes, the Spartan Hero* (1692) return to heroic sentiments, even though couched in blank verse instead of rhyme. Altogether Dryden's efforts in this realm are disappointing. Except for *All for Love*, his best work was in the heroic drama, a type which, however absurd at times, best suited his talents.

As tragedy developed after 1679 two tendencies (inherent in *All for Love* and *The Orphan*) became apparent. The first is pseudo-classicism, leading to strictness of form, including the retention of the three unities, and to chill of dialogue and simplification of plot. The other, which takes diverse forms, is the movement towards pathos and pity. These tendencies dominated almost the whole of tragedy from the last decades of the seventeenth century to the latter part of the eighteenth. The pseudo-classical school, at least that part of it which held most strictly to the 'rules' of propriety and good conduct, hardly obtained a secure footing in the seventeenth century itself; and even in the Augustan age proper (from the reign of Anne to the last quarter of the eighteenth century) it failed to produce anything of intrinsic value. These dull dramas were mounted and revived, but none proved genuinely popular, unless we assume that Addison's *Cato* (1714) succeeded entirely on its own merits, unaided by political prejudice. Still, if the more extreme pseudo-classicists had little hold during the Restoration period, the rules they cherished penetrated all the realms of drama and came to influence greatly both comedy and tragedy.

In reaction to this, although frequently it took a course parallel to the pseudo-classical movement, and even joined paths with it, we find the development of pathetic and pitiful sentiments and scenes. This tendency, already apparent in *The Orphan*, has been noted several decades earlier in some dramas of the period 1610–40. Now it flourished more abundantly. Love and honour themes had led men to stress more deeply than in Elizabethan days the subject of amorous passion, so that by the end of the seventeenth century hardly any tragedy failed to introduce as a main theme a tale of love. Instead of the deep and diverse emotions which marked the tragedies of Shakespeare, we find now constant plaints and passages of amorous bombast in the sincerity of which we cannot believe. With the change of atmosphere went an alteration of tragic plan. In the Elizabethan world tragedy had been predominantly masculine, the hero at the centre of the play and all attention focused on him. When love became so popular a theme, the heroine rapidly grew more prominent; but at a time of pure heroics her progress was hindered by an emphasis on martial prowess; from this—for few heroines were Amazons—she was banished. Still, the fashion for pathos favoured the heroine; towards the end of the century we reach the 'she-tragedy' where the hero has almost completely vanished and a woman dominates the entire action. Though the climax was not reached until the eighteenth century, when Rowe fully established the type, the tendency is clearly traceable in preceding decades. Rowe's most important predecessor in this sphere was John Banks. Beginning with a couple of heroic dramas, *The Rival Kings*; or, *The Loves of Oroondates and Statira* (1677) and *The Destruction of Troy* (1678), he passed from these to write a series of pathetic plays on historical themes, *The Unhappy*

Favourite; or, The Earl of Essex (1681), *Virtue Betray'd; or, Anna Bullen* (1682), *The Island Queens; or, The Death of Mary, Queen of Scotland* (printed 1684) and *The Innocent Usurper; or, The Death of the Lady Jane Gray* (printed 1694). The titles of these tragedies clearly show their general scope. None is remarkable in itself, though Banks was a more capable writer than usually allowed, but their historical value is great. Several of them remained long on the stage. Rowe certainly was acquainted with them, so that Banks became one of the most potent forces in the development of eighteenth-century tragedy. Indeed, in several dramatic schools his influence, direct and indirect, for forty or fifty years after his death was second only to Shakespeare's.

Opera and Spectacle

The heroic, pathetic and other movements all combined with a general operatic tendency. Scenery had come into general use; we have noted the growing exaggeration and artificiality of plot and character; and the age still kept that enthusiasm for music so marked in the Elizabethan period. All was ready for the elaboration of the opera. To trace this accurately we must return to the dramatic work of Sir William D'Avenant, both an inaugurator of the heroic drama and a popularizer of the operatic form in England. When he was the only person authorized during the Commonwealth to arrange theatrical performances, he had probably convinced authority that these were not plays but musical entertainments. Certainly *The Siege of Rhodes* (1656)—like *The Cruelty of the Spaniards in Peru* (1658) and *The History of Sir Francis Drake* (1658)—was entertainment of this sort, written in rhyme, and designed, on the lines of Italian opera, to be sung in recitative and aria; it left its impression both on the opera and upon heroic drama. The new scenes, the orchestral accompaniment, the pleasant airs, all attracted playgoers, and within a few decades other writers were working similarly.

The first approach to opera after 1660 was towards adapted Shakespeare. *The Tempest*, after much sophisticated alteration and addition, was made operatic by Dryden and Shadwell. An unknown author, conjecturally identified with D'Avenant himself, dealt with *Macbeth*; and numerous references, scathing as well as flattering, showed that the new fashion was popular. Inevitably, it flowered into the composition of original operas, even more ornate. Dryden, always ready for a promising current novelty, wrote his *Albion and Albanius* (1685) and his *King Arthur; or, The British Worthy* (1691). D'Urfey, Settle and others competed in works each more gorgeous and crowded than the last. All of these operas were on the English plan and commonly described as 'dramatic' to distinguish them from the 'Italian': the presence or absence of recitative was the cardinal difference. All the dialogue of the dramatic opera is spoken; these were in fact spectacular plays with many incidental songs and a full accompaniment of instrumental music. Italian operas, designed wholly to be sung, permitted spoken dialogue only in occasional comic scenes. With Purcell's aid the dramatic type held the stage throughout the Restoration; but by the beginning of the eighteenth century there were efforts—finally successful—to supplant the English-style opera by the foreign.

The approach was made at first through translation. Two theatrical workers, MacSwiny and Motteux, seem to have been chiefly responsible for preparing the first two operas of this kind, *Arsinoe* (1705) and *Camilla* (1706). The singers were all English, and the original music was adapted to the conditions under which the works were produced. But soon the stock of English vocalists was limited; every one praised the voices of Italy; and, accordingly, managers offered high sums to tempt away from the Continent a few of the more noted singers. Even yet the production of operas in the Italian tongue was delayed, the managers making the English singers perform in English and the Italians in Italian: a convention rich in absurdities that Addison chronicled satirically in several well-known *Spectator* essays. Such a compromise could not endure for long, so we are not surprised to find within a few years the appearance of Italian operas in all their original glory. Once established upon the stage, these held their position. Handel came to England and aroused still more enthusiasm for the type; hardly a year passed without several new productions; the Italian opera became the fashionable haunt of society, and in its own way it helped to weaken native dramatic work.

Undeniably it had several well-marked influences upon the English stage. The dramatic operas were rapidly cast into the background. Though *The Tempest* and *The Prophetess* remained as stock pieces, few new works of the same class were written. While the older successes kept something of their charm, the form was clearly felt to be old-fashioned, and authors who tried to produce something to rival the Italian works wrote their verses in recitative and aria. Beyond this, the new fashion placed its mark upon the age. The success of the opera-house frequently caused a corresponding failure of the other theatres. Upper-class society in the eighteenth century was often short of money, and the high prices for opera subscriptions left many people unable to patronize regular plays.

Comedies of Humours and of Intrigue

It is not hard to see why tragedy and opera gave no real master-piece to the theatre in this age. The men of the Restoration period were searching for truth, not in the realm of passion and 'enthusiasm', but in that of common sense and reason. The rich music of the Elizabethan playwrights and the bizarre stanzas of the metaphysical poets were alike displaced in favour of the heroic couplet, a verse-form which demanded for successful execution little beyond a good ear, a sense of proportion and a lively intellect. Moreover, a new prose was discovered, one fitted for the enunciation of logical thoughts and witty fancies. More and more men turned to this prose as a medium to express their desires, so that comedy, which alone depended on prose dialogue, became the dramatic form most capable of expressing the temper and spirit of the age. The Restoration period could produce no tragic dramatist greater than Otway and Dryden; but it did produce some of the finest comic writers in the history of the English theatre.

The typical style developed during these years was the comedy of manners, but in thinking of the contributions made by Etherege, Congreve, Vanbrugh and Farquhar, we must remember that the 'manners' form was rivalled by many others. These proved as popular, if not more popular, with contemporary audiences; and the old comedy of humours took a prominent place. Jonson was still the acclaimed chief of comic dramatists, and his intellectualism appealed to an age weary of degenerate imagination. Even Dryden, much as he revered Shakespeare's name, did not dare to place him above Jonson. His influence on the period is twofold. We find, in the first place, a number of comedies obviously modelled directly upon his style; and, besides these, many dramas not prevailingly Jonsonian in essence betray the influence of his work in dialogue, scene or character. Even the masters of the comedies of manners frequently showed that they had learned at least part of their art from the early seventeenth-century playwright.

Among his stricter disciples Thomas Shadwell is without doubt the leader. No man more insisted on Jonson's greatness; no man attempted more to carry on his dramatic method, and it must be admitted that Shadwell was no mean disciple. His style, certainly, is rough, lacking refinement and careful polish, but he had a true flair for the theatre and much skill in the depiction of humorous types. In a sense, he is the truest mirror of the age that we possess. Congreve may show more brilliantly the fine wit of the time, but his very brilliance takes away from the reality of the portrait; Shadwell, rising to less exalted heights, displays more accurately the ordinary life of his time. Of his eighteen dramas three or four stand out—the early *Sullen Lovers* (1668), *The Humorists* (1670), *Epsom Wells* (1672), *The Virtuoso* (1676), *The Squire of Alsatia* (1688) and *Bury Fair* (1689). In each of these we meet a lively story of contemporary life, an array of eccentric and extravagant humours, and a somewhat loose love-plot. In each the scenes are presented with gusto and the life of the age is keenly observed. *The Sullen Lovers* contains some recognizable caricatures of individuals; *Epsom Wells* gives a racy picture of the world of sport and dalliance; *The Virtuoso* ridicules amateur antiquarians and scientists; in *The Squire of Alsatia* the author penetrates the underworld. Spread out before us here is a kind of Restoration documentary.

Others followed the Jonsonian line. Sir Robert Howard, brother-in-law of Dryden, won success with *The Committee* (1662), a moderately good-humoured attack upon Puritan hypocrisy, well-written and vivacious, with characters not too heavily exaggerated and one particularly popular figure in Teg, or Teague, a loyal Irish servant, ancestor of many similar types in later years. With Howard goes the rougher and more plebeian John Lacy, who in *The Old Troop; or, Monsieur Raggou* (1663), contributed another anti-Puritan satire to the theatre. Beside this Lacy has left an adaptation of Shakespeare in *Sauny the Scot; or, The Taming of the Shrew* (1667), one of Molière in *The Dumb Lady; or, the Farrier made Physician* (1669), and a more original work in *Sir Hercules Buffoon; or, The Poetical Squire* (1884). All of these are marked by the same features, a tendency to follow Jonson in the depiction of grotesque humours, a certain roughness and vulgarity of texture, and a decided propensity towards farce. This may be due to the fact that Lacy himself was an actor, fully alive to every possibility of laughter. A companion of Lacy in farcical 'humours' is John Wilson; *The Cheats* (1663) has an amusing plot and some fairly ludicrous dialogue, though it is marred, like most of these Jonsonian works, by coarseness and lack of delicacy in style and treatement.

These comedies of 'humours', even from the first, were a trifle out of date. Dryden was more in accordance with the changing tendencies of the age when he strove in his comedies to unite the strength of Jonson, the courtly spirit of Beaumont and Fletcher and the new air of intellectual wit. Had Dryden possessed more of the debonair, outwardly brilliant, but not necessarily profound, temperament of Etherege and his successors he might have succeeded in founding the comedy of manners. As it is, his undercurrent of emotion, his lack of fine wit, his inability to throw himself completely into the thoughtless follies and amusements of his time, prevented him from capturing the precise note of the 'manners' school. He stands as a link between the earlier and the later, incapable of casting off his enthusiasm for the Elizabethan drama, yet not content merely to reproduce, as Wilson and Lacy strove to do, the exact style of the earlier period. His first comedy, *The Wild Gallant* (1663), comes closest to previous models, the inspiration obviously derived from Jonson; but even here Dryden showed that he felt the needs of his own age. In the portraits of Lady Constant and Loveby he showed clearly enough his consciousness that Stuart society demanded something more than the rough Jonsonian satire. *The Wild Gallant* is not a good comedy, but it certainly shows the main features of Dryden's style, developed with much greater skill in his later plays. In the comic intrigues of *Secret Love; or, The Maiden Queen* (1667), he introduced something finer. The air of careless abandon, the hilarious wit, the setting free of all conventional restraint—all features of his earliest play—are here crystallized in two figures, Celadon and Florimel, who will always remain monuments of his power and genius. This pair reappear, in variant form, as Wildblood and Jacintha in *An Evening's Love; or, The Mock Astrologer* (1668), Palamede and Doralice in *Marriage A-la-mode* (1672), Ascanio and Hippolita in *The Assignation; or, Love in a Nunnery* (1672), Mercury and Phaedra in *Amphitryon; or, The Two Socia's* (1690), but without surpassing the gaiety and witty abandon of the original couple. In these plays Dryden shows his position in the development of the comic theatre. He owes a debt to Jonson, chiefly in his minor characters; he owes another to Beaumont and Fletcher and the comedy of intrigue; but above all, he takes a path of his own in striving to express something of the new spirit of the age. In thus fusing many diverse elements Dryden did great service to the English theatre, but the very fact that he did so has taken something from his posthumous fame. His comedies, fine as they are and excellently fitted for stage representation, have not the individual flavour which distinguishes the work of Etherege and Congreve. One other thing makes them less acceptable to modern readers. Congreve dwells almost wholly in the world of the intellect; his amours are not of passion, not of the heart but of the head. Dryden still retained something of the Elizabethan age, and in consequence his scenes of licence are often less palatable than similar scenes in the comedies of 'manners'.

Few of the many other comedy dramatists can be dealt with here. One is Mrs Aphra Behn. As Shadwell is the chief representative of the comedy of 'humours' in this period, so she is the chief representative of the comedy of intrigue. Her dramatic career began in 1670 with a tragi-comedy, *The Forc'd Marriage; or, The Jealous Bridegroom*, but her main work in later years was in the realm of comedy proper. Her most popular success was *The Rover; or, The Banish't Cavaliers* (1677; second part, 1681); besides this she has several plays well worth reading, especially *The Dutch Lover* (1673), *The Town-Fop; or, Sir Timothy Tawdrey* (1676), *Sir Patient Fancy* (1678), and *The City-Heiress; or, Sir Timothy Treat-all* (1682). There is little wit, but a good deal of intrigue cleverly worked out, and a decided skill in comic portraiture. Vivacity is her chief merit; bustling movement governs all her work. This species of comedy of intrigue, made popular by the Spanish tastes of the Court, was adopted by a few other writers, such as John Crowne in *Sir Courtly Nice; or, It Cannot Be* (1685), but it was not taken up again with the same enthusiasm until the appearance of Mrs Centlivre in the eighteenth century.

Among this varied comic writing, one form deserves attention, not because of its intrinsic value, but because of its influence on the later history of the theatre. Though farcical elements may be found in many earlier plays, this was the period when farce evolved as an independent dramatic type. Thomas Otway, in 1676, produced a tragedy called *Titus and Berenice*; when published, it appeared along 'with a Farce call'd *The Cheats of Scapin*'. Within a few seasons Nahum Tate (who had had his own form of pleasure with *King Lear*), was delighting audiences with *A Duke and No Duke* (1684), winning such success that in 1693 he added a preface to the printed text, giving 'an account of the *personae* and *larvae* of the ancient theatre' and providing a critical defence of the newly established dramatic type. Thus, within little more than a decade, farce had fully set itself on the stage beside the time-honoured genres of tragedy and comedy.

Most of the earliest experiments in farce were derivative, taking shape either as crude adaptations of already existing comedies or as versions of Italian–French *commedia dell' arte* performances at that time being introduced to the public. *The Cheats of Scapin* has its source indicated by its title; *A Duke and No Duke* is a version of a comedy written by Cockain in imitation of the Italian style; Edward Ravenscroft's *Scaramouch a Philosopher, Harlequin a Schoolboy, Bravo, Merchant and Magician* (1677) was specifically described as 'after the Italian manner'; the same author's *The Anatomist; or, The Sham Doctor* (1696) was a reworking of a French comedy, and Tate's *Cuckold's Haven; or, An Alderman No Conjuror* (1685) was derived from a selection of scenes from *Eastward Ho!* and Jonson's *The Devil is an Ass*. The original source of farce, therefore, was twofold—one impulse coming from the Italian–French comedians and the other from an elaboration of that 'droll' tradition once popular at the fairs. Very soon farce would expand beyond this limited sphere, and during the eighteenth century it became one of the most popular and staple elements in the theatre's repertory. As such, these early experiments, even if they have nothing of value to offer, do need to be remembered.

The Comedy of Manners

They need to be remembered particularly because their popularity grew during the very years when the comedy of manners reached its finest form. These types of play stand at opposite poles, one aiming to rouse rude laughter by absurd incident, crude humour and physical gesture, the other laying all stress upon polish, wit and sprightliness. We cannot gain a complete picture of the theatre during this period unless we realize that spectators who encouraged farce also relished a form of comedy far more intellectually brilliant than anything the English stage had so far known.

The comedy of manners, as its name implies, concentrates upon the depiction of men and women in a social world ruled by convention. Its 'manners' are not simply the behaviour of humanity in general but the affectations and cultured veneer of a highly developed and self-conscious group. In the Whitehall ruled over by Charles II, Restoration gallants and their mistresses had sought first for intellectual refinement, epigrammatic wit and easy dalliance; and these are the qualities reflected in 'manners' comedy. Already, soon after the playhouses were reopened in 1660, Dryden had given a foretaste of what was to come, but he was unfitted by nature to enter completely into this new world. Though the typical comedy of manners gives delight by showing the contrast between natural man and man conditioned by the social code, it tends to tone down and to intellectualize ordinary emotions. Love may cause the young, reckless, careless, cynical hero to follow his mistress into the horrors of a lonely country house far removed from the dear delights of Town; a confirmed bachelor, anxious to retain his freedom, may be led to the marriage noose, and his freedom-loving sweetheart may be persuaded to dwindle into a wife; but basically the natural emotions are kept in the background for contrast; the foreground is reserved for the exercise of intellect. Dryden, in presenting his Celadons and Florimels, was anticipating the fashionable pairs who would follow them, but he was sufficiently 'Elizabethan' to refuse a strictly intellectual approach. In his early comedies the emotional element refuses to be subdued.

Others besides Dryden contributed towards the new comic form, and even before 1640 dramatists such as Shirley were beginning to give it shape. For its first clear outline we have to wait until the debonair Sir George Etherege turned to the theatre. He began with *The Comical Revenge; or, Love in a Tub* in 1664 and followed with *She wou'd if she cou'd* (1668) and *The Man of Mode; or, Sir Fopling Flutter* (1676). In the first of these he almost completely failed to develop a personal style. Somewhat similar to Dryden's *Secret Love*, *The Comical Revenge* is an unintegrated piece in which scenes in rhymed couplets alternate with others in dallying prose. Had this been his only contribution to the theatre, Etherege's name would not now be remembered. The four years between the appearance of this work and *She wou'd if she cou'd*, wrought a mighty change. In his second play the fine gentlemen and witty ladies are presented in a new light; the shape and form of Restoration society is evoked in all its scenes; the dialogue succeeds in recording the very tones of contemporary civil conversation. And the eight further years between this comedy and *The Man of Mode* show an advance almost equally great. Although *She wou'd if she cou'd* established the Restoration comic style, it still lacked final distinction; that distinction came with the arrival of Dorimant, the fashionable hero, of Harriet, the clear-eyed lady on whom his own wandering eyes fix their gaze, and of Sir

Fopling Flutter, the beau who carries fine manners to excess and becomes a figure of ridicule.

By the early seventies, the influence of *She wou'd if she cou'd* had inspired several playwrights to imitate its style, and before *The Man of Mode* appeared, William Wycherley produced three plays—*Love in a Wood; or, St James's Park* (1671), *The Gentleman Dancing-Master* (1672) and especially *The Country-Wife* (1675) —which contributed notably to this comic form. All three revel in a world of fops and fools and gallants; all are concerned with the eternal love-chase; in all there is a sure handling of character and of situation.

In these works Wycherley gave himself wholeheartedly to the spirit which had animated Etherege, but deep within himself he concealed a sense of moral purpose of which Etherege was impenitently innocent. Wycherley has been called a Puritan with the veneer of a Restoration gentleman, and the description seems admirably to fit. He adopted the current modes of contemporary society, but in the end he was unable to prevent the assertion of his native self and to avoid a bitterly satirical attack upon the very vices with which he had amused himself in his first plays. Thus in 1676 came *The Plain-Dealer*, in which the hero is no longer an easy careless libertine, but a gentleman whose very name, Manly, puts him in opposition to the elegant Dorimants of the time. One might have thought that this sort of play would have been a failure on the Restoration stage; in fact, it was Wycherley's greatest triumph, a witness not only to his dramatic power but also to the public's widely varying interests.

If Wycherley, in *The Plain-Dealer*, seems to be shattering the fabric of the comic style Etherege had established, William Congreve carries the style to still further achievements. Untroubled by any puritanical reflection, this author at once differs from, and bases his dramatic work upon, the creator of *The Man of Mode*. He has not the same firm command of plotting, but he possesses an airiness of fancy and a pointed delicacy of style which goes beyond Etherege's. In Congreve's dialogue the words and phrases pirouette and bow; they pierce; they laugh and flirt and dally. All is subordinated to brilliance of wit and modulations of style. His four comedies—*The Old Bachelor* (1693), *The Double Dealer* (1693), *Love for Love* (1695) and *The Way of the World* (1700)—illustrate in their variety the delicate balance for the full expression of the new comic spirit and the ease with which that balance could be disturbed. The first play, though confused in plot and including characters somewhat out of place, was a decided success, finer, more scintillating, than anything which had gone before: no previous writer had achieved a comedy so rich in racy, cultured, easy, debonair conversation. *The Double Dealer* was, by comparison, a failure—due, it seems, to the fact that Congreve permitted an emotional quality to disturb the play of his wit. In *Love for Love* there is a return to the mood of *The Old Bachelor*, but again a disturbing element intrudes—here because Congreve has brought in some characters and situations of what might be called a 'realistic' kind. Fundamentally, his genius depended upon the creation of a world which, though it might appear to mirror life, was a refinement and not a copy of reality; thus the episodes involving Miss Prue and Tattle, so far from extending the comedy's range, almost destroy its essential spirit. (We must agree that the play continues to hold the stage.)

Only perhaps in *The Way of the World* was Congreve able to reach perfection. There is no false note. Millamant sails gloriously through its scenes, affected and fascinating; the servants, the fools, the lovers, the wits all seem to take from her something of the air of modish triviality which makes her so delightful. We may say that the plot is no plot, only a series of often impossible and confusing incidents, streams of metaphorical conceits and bewildering flights of fancy; but in fact we do not want more than Congreve has given us; his power lay, not in the fashioning of dramatic incident, but in his mastery of wit and command of dancing words. The melodies charm our ears:

Mirabell Do you lock yourself up from me to make my search more curious? Or is this pretty artifice contrived to signify that here the chase must end and my pursuit be crowned, for you can fly no further?

Millamant Vanity! No, I'll fly and be followed to the last moment: though I am upon the very verge of matrimony, I expect you should solicit me as much as if I were wavering at the grate of a monastery [a composite term, then!], with one foot over the threshold. I'll be solicited to the very last—nay and afterwards.

Mirabell What? After the last?

Millamant O, I should think I was poor and had nothing to bestow if I were reduced to an inglorious ease, and freed from the agreeable fatigues of the solicitation.

Mirabell But do you not know that when favours are conferred upon instant and tedious solicitation that they diminish in their value, and that both the giver loses the grace and the receiver lessens his pleasure?

Millamant It may be in things of common application, but never, sure, in love. O, I hate a lover that can dare to think he draws a moment's air independent on the bounty of his mistress. There is not so impudent a thing in nature as the saucy look of an assured man, confident of success. The pedantic arrogance of a very husband has not so pragmatical an air. Ah! I'll never marry unless I am first made sure of my will and pleasure.

Two years before Millamant and Mirabell reached the theatre, a chill blast had blown over the stage. In 1698 a stern Nonconformist clergyman, Jeremy Collier, had startled actors, authors and spectators with a work entitled *A Short View of the Immorality and Prophaneness of the English Stage*. Within the next few months the presses were busy printing pamphlets by those who sought to rebut its arguments and by those who for moral or religious reasons were anxious to reform or to overthrow the theatre. In many respects the attack was justified, even though many of Collier's own arguments verge upon the absurd; and the truth which underlay his attack is amply apparent in the replies of the poets arraigned at the bar of Nonconformist justice. Dryden had been singled out especially. In his magnanimous way he confessed his errors, regretting that he had written in a fashion he deplored. Others were unwilling to admit their faults; instead they tried to distract attention to the sect of which Collier was a member, and to concentrate on his more trivial strictures. His main contentions were for the most part unanswered, and these made their impact. The mood that dominated the Whitehall of Charles II had vanished; James II had been driven from the throne because of his Catholic affiliations; and William of Orange had brought to England a different spirit. There was a veneer of moral sentiment. The upper middle classes, which had stood apart from aristocratic society, were now entering its previously closed circle and leavening its codes of behaviour with their influence.

Everything conspired together, and the comedy of manners, licentious, vain, worldly, found itself under attack. The days of Congreve, the days of thoughtless, brilliant, careless wit, were virtually over, and the old free grace was never completely to be recaptured. For a time comedy strove to preserve something of its old abandon, but its light soon flickered out, quenched by a rising tide of sentimentalism.

Among those who helped to keep alive something of the spirit of Congrevian comedy were George Farquhar and Sir John Vanbrugh, whose careers stretched from a period contemporaneous with the Collier attack to the middle of Queen Anne's reign.

Farquhar's first play, *Love and a Bottle*, was produced in 1698, his last, *The Beaux' Stratagem*, in 1707; Vanbrugh's *The Relapse; or, Virtue in Danger* appeared in 1696, his last farces in the early years of the eighteenth century. The careers of both men are alike; taken together, they indicate the general trend of theatrical tastes. Both began in the seventeenth century with largely 'immoral' comedies, full of wit and striving to capture the fine grace that had distinguished the Stuart Court; both, as they progressed, showed with frequent touches of satire and cynicism a descent to sentimentalism and farce. Not that the two had precisely similar natures. Farquhar is at one and the same time nearer to the spirit of Congreve and more foppish than Vanbrugh. In *The Constant Couple* (1699), in *The Inconstant* (1702), and in one of his most durable plays, *The Beaux' Stratagem*, he has caught something of the true 'manners' style. His plots are more carefully elaborated than those of Congreve, but he retains at least a reflection of the Congreve wit. In *The Twin Rivals* (1702) and in *The Recruiting Officer* (1706), he displays clearly the impress of the newer age. The first play is deeply tinged with hypocritical sentimentalism; the second has a realistic touch quite alien to the comedy of manners. Vanbrugh is much more robust than Farquhar, and that robustness removes him from Congreve, leading him to draw comedy down to the lower depths of farce. More than any other writer of this kind of play, he relies upon action for comic effect. His plots are designed, not, as Congreve's were, for the expression of fancies of the mind, but for the elaboration of comic situations. This is not so noticeable in his early works, *The Relapse*, *The Provok'd Wife* (1697) and *Æsop* (1696–7), nor is it especially apparent in *The Confederacy* (1705) or in *The Mistake* (1705), but it is abundantly evident in *Squire Trelooby* (1704), a collaborative farce made out of Molière's *Monsieur de Pourceaugnac*, and in *The Country House* (1698), another farce taken from Dancourt. Like Farquhar, too, Vanbrugh turned to a type of sentimentalism, evidently insincere, in *The False Friend* (1702). The truth is that men of Farquhar's and Vanbrugh's calibre did not know where to stand. They had lost freedom of action in the conflicting moods of the time. Spectators, perhaps, were just as pleasure-loving as they had been in the days of Charles II, but there were now societies for the reformation of manners, and statutes against oaths, and other dreadful things to be feared. Efforts in the older style were bound, therefore, to be only half-hearted, or, if indulged in boldly, to be followed by a moment of painful reflection.

Five

Drama in the Eighteenth Century

The Changing Playhouse World

While no strict frontier can be drawn between the seventeenth and eighteenth centuries, the year 1700 may be held to mark the division between old and new. True, signs of change were apparent during the years 1690–9 and perhaps they are traceable even earlier, but the season of *The Way of the World* saw the last of the Restoration comedies, and later plays were clearly written in a different mood and in a different style.

In considering the eighteenth century as a whole, we observe several theatrical developments: first, three movements related to each other—the growth of a new audience, the enlarging of the 'patent' theatres and the springing up of the 'minor' ones. From 1682 to 1695 a single theatre met London's needs; even so, actors often complained of meagre audiences. Then, in 1695, Betterton headed a group of dissentient players and once more set up a second house, operating under the authority of the 'patent' which had temporarily lapsed thirteen years before. In itself this action was a sign that conditions were altering: slowly the play-going public was beginning to expand. That expansion in turn depended largely upon the altering structure of society. In Charles II's days, as we have seen, the theatre belonged essentially to the Court; hardly any middle-class spectators entered its doors. But, as the century waned, it became clear that the old, tightly knit aristocratic society was beginning to disintegrate; many of the older families were in financial difficulties, and numerous merchant families, having made themselves affluent, were anxious to enter society. In consequence, marriages of convenience began to break down the former barriers. Naturally, in these circumstances the newcomers turned to diversions which had delighted the aristocratic world, and so the potential play-going public was enlarged.

This enlargement continued throughout the century. The theatre, instead of being reserved for a privileged few, took on an upper middle-class atmosphere; and its new body of spectators had to be accommodated. The opening of a second theatre in 1695 met the needs for a time, but very soon even two were found inadequate to cope with growing demands. Thereupon the 'patent' theatres were periodically reconstructed so as to provide more seating space, and numerous 'minor' playhouses were built and operated outside the 'patent' authority. In 1737 the notorious Licensing Act sought to curb their activities, but in devious ways they managed to carry on their work—work which, on occasion, proved even more popular and valuable than that of Drury Lane and Covent Garden: it was at one 'minor' theatre that *The Beggar's Opera* was presented, and on the boards of another 'minor' the great David Garrick made his first appearance in London.

The entry of the middle classes is important, and not only because they added to the potential number of playgoers. Undoubtedly families which had become related through marriage to people of quality tended to accept the conventions of society, yet inevitably they brought with them some of their inherited bourgeois, and occasionally Puritan, tenets and tastes. Thus the union of the two led to the creation of an audience at once less homogeneous than that in the Restoration theatre and lacking the harmonized generality of the audiences in Elizabethan times. Society still enjoyed the licence of the comedy of manners; Shadwell, Dryden, Etherege, Wycherley and Congreve still held the stage: but the new groups of spectators, with more serious predilections, also delighted in moralizing, in sentimentally conceived situations, in scenes of pathos. As we watch the development of eighteenth-century drama we see a constant and silent struggle between the force of intellectual dalliance and the more solemn objectives of the mercantile world, until during the sixties and seventies the sentimentalists finally triumphed.

While London remained the theatrical focus from the beginning of the century to its end, increasing audiences there were paralleled by a growth of playgoing in the provinces. Touring players had been numerous in the sixteenth and early seventeenth centuries, and, though they had little success in Restoration times, they still pursued their traditional circuits during Charles's reign. After 1700 their position was more secure and their influence spread more widely. Hitherto the 'pomping folk', as they have long been known in south Cornwall, had no permanent homes, producing their plays wherever they could find some empty hall or barn. Now, during the eighteenth century, they began to build their own theatres, some even graced with the title of Theatre Royal, and a few companies had enough local support to abandon their laborious tours and settle down in permanent 'stock'. Though, for the most part, their repertories consisted of London successes, and they offered little to the drama of the age, they soon came to be the schools where stage aspirants were trained. David Garrick first practised on their stages, and it was from one of these provincial theatres that Mrs Siddons and her brother, John Philip Kemble, came to startle London.

In all these ways, the eighteenth-century playhouse established its own traditions, traditions which would be passed on to the nineteenth century and even to the present day.

Pseudo-classic and Pathetic Tragedy

In tragedy the eighteenth century inherited three or four traditions—the heroic; that which led towards renewed appreciation of Shakespeare; the pathetic style (often in the form of English historical plays) as expressed by Banks and Otway; and the gradual development of pseudo-classical theory and practice. Of these, in the seventeenth century, the last was infinitely the weakest. All the more chill pseudo-classical dramas written and produced before 1700 were unsuccessful; audiences still admired the bombast of Dryden, the pathos of Otway, the natural warmth of the Shakespearian style. In the eighteenth century pseudo-classical theory became more and more predominant. Addison, Pope, Steele and a host of lesser men, including Dennis and Gildon, helped to establish firmly the strict set of laws which bound poetry for well over half a century, and still exercised its influence in the days of Byron. According to these rules imitation of the 'Ancients' was the best that a modern author could do. His plays must preserve the three unities of time, place and action. He must not permit more than a certain number of characters to appear in his work. He must, above all, endeavour to secure decency, propriety, order and common sense; and he must aim at intellectual rhetoric rather than passionate rhapsody. These rules dominated almost all the poetic and dramatic activity of the reigns of Anne and the early Georges, but dominated it as a force from without. Some writers may have found the pseudo-classic theory well to their tastes, but spectators looked for something more inspiring, something more bombastic, than they could find in the chill of classical tragedy. So, in this period, a constant struggle went on between the pseudo-classicists and those who preferred other styles. Heroic tragedy continued to exert its charm on the audience; imitations of Shakespeare constantly appeared; Otway ruled over a large body of dramatists and spectators. But the lack of a central purpose told heavily on the fortunes of the tragic stage. Few playwrights seemed to know their own aims, and the majority compromised by observing the unities, filling their plays with pathos, and seasoning them with heroic ardour and hints from Shakespeare. The result is simply an uninspired mass.

It was for want of neither courage nor patience that the pseudo-classicists failed to reform entirely the tastes of their age. Again and again they tried, but few succeeded. In the early years of the century Dennis and Gildon made serious attempts, and failed; so did Dr Samuel Johnson in the pomp of his *Irene* (1749), a tragedy that got some small applause only through the services of his former pupil, David Garrick. Barely three or four of these dramas were popular, and all lack true energy and tragic fervour. The first to establish itself was *The Distrest Mother* (1712), written by Ambrose Philips ('Namby-Pamby'), Pope's rival in pastoral poetry. This play was an adaptation from Racine, distinguished by a few passages of speakable dialogue, introducing two fairly persuasive characters, and yet remaining an alien growth.

In the year after *The Distrest Mother* Joseph Addison saw the production of his *Cato* at Drury Lane. If this, at once accepted by his friends and associates as a masterpiece, has been long forgotten in the theatre, we may admit that the original praise was by no means unjustified; what could be done within the pseudo-classic form Addison has done, and our only legitimate criticism is of the style of drama to which *Cato* belongs. Instead of absurdly making a love-theme the centre of an intellectual tragedy, Addison took as his hero a philosopher whose nature and problems could be revealed appropriately in rhetorical dialogue, certainly more so than the natures and problems of violently passionate lovers and their mistresses. Addison had shown his acumen in boldly choosing a theme suited to the restricted sphere in which he worked. One or two phrases still linger:

'Tis not in mortals to command success,
But we'll do more, Sempronius, we'll deserve it.

and

> From hence let fierce contending nations know
> What dire effects from civil discord flow.

Few other writers of the period realized the reason for Addison's success. His companions continued to devote their scenes to love affairs, introducing weeping Andromaches and dismal Hecubas. Just for a moment, towards the middle of the century, it looked as though this style of play might receive a fresh impetus from James Thomson, author of the widely popular *Seasons*, but the promise was greater than the actual achievement. In *Sophonisba* (1730) Thomson appeared, like Addison, to divine what was demanded in classically influenced rhetorical drama; instead of a heroine inspired wholly by amorous emotions, he strove to show one dominated by patriotic sentiment, intent to benefit her native land. Something of the same approach distinguished his treatment of *Agamemnon* (1738). Later Thomson turned to plays of a different kind in *Edward and Eleonora* (printed 1739) and *Tancred and Sigismunda* (1745); the titles indicate that, while groping towards themes outside Greek legend, Thomson was reverting to the methods of his predecessors.

During the second half of the century this kind of tragic writing offered nothing of worth; soon the type was overwhelmed by the onrush of spectacular melodrama, better suited, with its flagrant rant, to a public already animated by the rise of romantic, and at times revolutionary, sentiment.

Relics of the heroic drama were numerous during these years. Even Gildon, despite his strict critical views, sought to emulate Dryden's bombastic flights. No single play of this sort exhibited any real quality. Joseph Trapp's *Abra-Mule; or, Love and Empire* (1704) contains one or two striking passages, but its characters are hopelessly stereotyped and the language is rarely above mediocre competence. Benjamin Martyn's *Timoleon* (1730), as well as David Mallet's *Eurydice* (1731) and *Mustapha* (1739), may similarly be lifted from the rout, but they have no great virtue. At most, a few occasional scenes give them a merit denied to their companions.

The school of pathos has a little more of worth to offer. No dramatists in this style have left any plays with enduring qualities, but precisely because they limited their aims they could produce something worthy of at least some praise. Prominent during the early part of the century was Nicholas Rowe, a disciple of Otway and Banks, and to an extent an ancestor of George Lillo. In his work there are echoes of the heroic style, touches which remind us of Shakespearian tragedy and a general structure deeply influenced by pseudo-classical theory: yet, despite these elements, they were clearly designed to evoke pity rather than awe. His first drama, *The Ambitious Stepmother* (1700), confessedly inspired by Otway's style, was hardly more than an apprentice piece, and not much may be said for the 'heroically' designed *Tamerlane* (1701), but *The Fair Penitent* (1703), *The Tragedy of Jane Shore* (1714) and *The Tragedy of the Lady Jane Gray* (1715) possess an individual note which rightly put Rowe at the head of Augustan tragic writers. Each is a 'she-tragedy', with a heroine instead of a hero; each throws its main stress upon pathetic situations and scenes. Rowe is skilful in the exploitation of pitifully distressing emotions; his persons come fitfully alive; and he has the gift of pleasant if not very powerful blank-verse dialogue. As a whole, his dramas, whatever their weaknesses and defects, are among the best serious plays of their time.

During later years English and related historical themes provided material for a cognate species of drama, often with echoes of Shakespeare and Otway. Mrs Haywood attempted a tragedy on *Frederick, Duke of Brunswick-Lunenburgh* (1729); Ambrose Philips one in *Humfrey, Duke of Gloucester* (1723), and such dramatists as Henry Brooke in *Gustavus Vasa* (1739), William Havard in *King Charles the First* (1737), William Shirley in *Edward the Black Prince; or, The Battle of Poictiers* (1749), and John St John in *Mary Queen of Scots* (1789). These plays for various reasons appealed more to contemporary audiences than the stricter 'classical' essays. Often they introduced patriotic sentiments; mostly their plots and characters were nearer to the spectators than those which dealt with ancient legendary persons; frequently they allowed the introduction of at least some bustle and action. Yet not one now is anything more than a title; not one held the stage for more than a few performances.

Their failure must be attributed to the style in which the authors worked. We may illustrate it from the solitary play of this kind which had power to arouse a certain amount of excitement and was remembered beyond the period of its original production. In 1756 John Home's *Douglas* was presented to an Edinburgh audience, and stimulated it to a frenzy of excitement. Here, some men said, was the triumph of a Scots Shakespeare. In the following year the drama came to Covent Garden and, though the reception was not so fervent, its qualities were esteemed, and it became accepted as a stock-piece, frequently revived. It seemed to be providing exactly what the time needed; a spirit of romanticism was beginning to stir, and at a period when the way was being prepared for Percy's *Reliques* and Chatterton's 'medieval' experiments, the material of *Douglas* might have been thought likely to encourage a revival of serious poetic drama. As soon as we turn to the text, we realize that this could not be. We need go no further than that speech of 'The Stranger' which endured for so long as a recitation piece:

My name is Norval. On the Grampian hills
My father feeds his flocks; a frugal swain,
Whose constant cares were to increase his store
And keep his only son, myself, at home.
For I had heard of battles, and I long'd
To follow in the field some warlike lord,
And heaven soon granted what my sire denied.
This moon which rose last night, round as my shield,
Had not yet fill'd her horns, when, by her light,
A band of fierce barbarians, from the hills,
Rush'd like a torrent down upon the vale,
Sweeping our flocks and herds. The shepherds fled
For safety and for succour. I alone,
With bended bow and quiver full of arrows,
Hover'd about the enemy and mark'd
The road he took, then hasted to my friends,
Whom with a troop of fifty chosen men
I met advancing. The pursuit I led
Till we o'ertook the spoil-encumber'd foe.
We fought and conquered.

As a passage for parlour declamation, all very well, but clearly the language is stilted and rhetorical. There could be no hope for the creation of successful serious drama within this style. In our time *Douglas* had a remarkable revival at the Edinburgh Festival of 1950 when, thanks to Dame Sybil Thorndike as Lady Randolph, genuine tragedy ennobled Home's melodramatic anecdote, and for two hours or so tinsel shone to gold.

The Ballad-Opera and Pantomime

We have glanced at the spectacular and operatic tendencies of the Restoration, and at the development of Italian opera in the eighteenth century itself. These are to be interpreted as an expression of popular taste moving against the restrictions of severer poets and critics. Men and women of the time liked show; music appealed to them, and dancing. After listening in bored silence to the ceaseless drone of the heavier tragedy they flocked for recreation to the opera, or applauded vigorously the singers, instrumentalists and dancers who gave *intermezzi* before and after, and occasionally in the midst of, regular performances in the theatres.

Four popular species of entertainment must be noted—the operatic, the spectacular, the terpsichorean and the mimic. From the Restoration (and even in Elizabethan times) dancing formed a popular part of dramatic performances. Many plays ended with a dance, and we know how such an actress as Moll Davis charmed her public. To satisfy the craving for these dances theatrical managers in the late seventeenth century called in the services of dancing-masters from Paris; we learn many of their names from the prominence given to them in early eighteenth-century newspaper advertisements. Their performances were limited in scope at first, but presently a taste developed for mimic dancing where a story was told silently in expressive movement: here we reach the beginnings of pantomime, a form which owed much to the various French and Italian troupes that appeared in London from season to season. From its beginning the *commedia dell'arte* had encouraged the display of gesture and action on the stage, and because only a few English spectators could understand French and Italian, the physical skill of the foreign comedians appealed more than any of their dialogue. Not surprisingly, when the time came for native experiment in a related style, English managers encouraged wordless performances compact of music, dance, mime, comic business, lavish scenery and machinists' tricks. Thus the typical English pantomime came into being, delighting the public, and gradually extending its fantastic empire.

Though these pantomimes cannot be said to have driven ordinary drama from the stage—for they were mostly played with, and not instead of, regular comedies and tragedies—their establishment and expansion much changed the typical theatre repertories. They helped the disintegration of true dramatic taste; they lowered the general power of appreciation; and they established fully the reign of the after-piece. The after-piece, as we have noted, was inaugurated in England with the appearance of Otway's *The Cheats of Scapin*, and in the first years of the eighteenth century it was fairly common for a tragedy or comedy to be given with a one-act farce. Still, these were merely sporadic, not essential, appendages to the ordinary plays. Then, with the success of pantomime, the public came to demand some light refreshment when a tragedy or sentimental comedy had ended: if not a pantomime, a short farce or ballad-opera. An audience saw nothing extraordinary in listening to Lear's last agony at half-past seven and laughing hilariously at pantomime or a farcical afterpiece at eight o'clock. There was a further result. Pantomime led dramatists who might otherwise have written serious work to indulge in the minor forms, knowing that a one-act farce paid better than a full-length tragedy, and that even trivial words for an operatic pantomime were well rewarded. So farce came to occupy a playwright's mind; many men, such as Lewis Theobald, editor of Shakespeare and a capable scholar, turned to the foolish ditties of pantomime.

Pantomime would move with the reign of the ballad-opera. In origin, this 'ballad-farce', as it was often called, was at once a burlesque and a rival of Italian opera, and it included many satirical attacks upon the follies inherent in that form. Not that it would have succeeded if musical enthusiasts had not already prepared the way. Men were used now to hearing a story sung; they were delighted when their favourite airs, native, popular or Italian, were provided with new and witty lyrics and set in a plot (told in English) that they could understand, and (being comic) they could enjoy.

The ballad-opera was invented, almost by chance, by the erratic John Gay. Already, in some earlier dramatic efforts, he had shown tastes that favoured the extravagant and the satirical. *The Mohocks*, described as a 'tragi-comical farce' when it was printed in 1712, was designed to make fun of contemporary vices and stupidities, and the peculiar play entitled *The What D'Ye Call It* (1715) indicates in its very title the mixed style in which Gay delighted. Though he found success only when he came to write *The Beggar's Opera*, that success was immediate and lasting. When his musical piece was given at the little Lincoln's Inn Fields Theatre in 1728 the whole of fashionable London flocked to see it; its month-long run set up a long-remembered record, a triumph due both to the novelty of the form and to Gay's own skill. In effect he gave to audiences of the time something which might be called the fantasy of rationalism. Shakespeare, in *A Midsummer Night's Dream*, with its dim-wood setting, its antique background, its mingling of fairies, lovers and artisans, offers emotional fantasy; in *The Beggar's Opera* the time of action is contemporary, and the characters are rogues and vagabonds; by jesting and exag-

gerating, Gay has created a fantastic new world of his own:
'Where is my dear husband?' cries Polly:

> Was a rope ever intended for his neck? O, let me throw my arms about
> it, and throttle thee with love! Why dost thou turn away from me? 'Tis
> thy Polly. 'Tis thy wife.

Macheath Was there ever such an unfortunate rascal as I am!

Lucy Was there ever such a villain?

Polly O, Macheath, was it for this we parted? Taken! Imprisoned! Tried!
Hanged! Cruel reflection! I'll stay with thee till death; no force shall
tear thy dear wife from thee now. What means my love? Not one kind
word! Not one kind look! Think what thy Polly suffers to see thee in
this condition.

> Thus when the swallow, seeking prey,
> Within the sash is closely pent,
> His consort, with bemoaning lay,
> Without sits pining for th' event.
> Her chatt'ring lovers all around her skim;
> She heeds them not, poor bird, her soul's with him.

Lucy and Polly quarrel over the wretched man:

Lucy Art thou then married to another? Hast thou two wives, monster?

Macheath If women's tongues can cease for an answer, hear me.

Lucy I won't. Flesh and blood can't bear my usage.

Polly Shall I not claim my own? Justice bids me speak.

Macheath How happy could I be with either,
> Were t'other dear charmer away!
> But while you thus tease me together
> To neither a word will I say.

Having seen *The Beggar's Opera* delight its audiences two
hundred years after the original performance, we can well
imagine the excitement it caused in 1728.

Unfortunately, Gay was unable to repeat his triumph. The
sequel, which he called *Polly*, was printed in 1729, but because
the authorities discerned, or pretended to discern, revolutionary
sentiments, it did not appear on the stage until 1777. Less skilfully wrought than its predecessor, it fails to capture the old
spirit; the realistic elements are not so consistently fanciful and
wayward, and the style lacks the easy abandon of *The Beggar's
Opera*. Nor does Gay's later attempt in the same form, the burlesque *Archilles*, particularly matter.

Others applied themselves with enthusiasm to the kind of
drama he had invented. In diverse shapes the ballad-opera pur-

sued its course, dozens of authors eagerly striving to rival Gay in his newly won popularity and affluence. Only a few of the pieces have any distinctive feature: sometimes, as in Henry Carey's *The Dragon of Wantley* (1737) and its sequel, *Margery; or, A Worse Plague than the Dragon* (1738), burlesque predominated; sometimes, as in Colley Cibber's *Damon and Phillida* (1739) and John Hippisley's *Flora* (1729), the scenes were pastoral. A few plays succeeded, but most of them died after their first runs. Among them all, the only one worthy of praise is Sheridan's much later *The Duenna*, produced in 1775. Here the characters are cleverly drawn; the lyrics are pretty and melodious; the dialogue is rarely dull and often witty. Still, *The Duenna* brings us to a form of dramatic entertainment which should be considered separately from ballad-opera. This play, and others, such as Isaac Bickerstaffe's *The Maid of the Mill* (1765) and *Lionel and Clarissa* (1768) really belong to the category of comic opera, and though *The Duenna* of 1775 cannot be dissociated from *The Beggar's Opera* of 1728, the two remain in several ways distinct.

Gay's *Achilles* reminds us of the connection between ballad-opera and burlesque: their original impulse is similar, even if many of the eighteenth-century burlesques are not musical. In 1728 Henry Fielding wrote his first play, *Love in Several Masques*; and probably the same year's example of *The Beggar's Opera* encouraged his tragic burlesque, *Tom Thumb* (1730), afterwards reworked and renamed *The Tragedy of Tragedies*. In the mood of Buckingham's *The Rehearsal*, this aims at the absurd situations, the flatness of language, the stereotyped characters in the tragedy of its time. Witty and piercing, it was long popular both in its original form (revived more than once in the twentieth century) and in a later ballad-opera version. Many of Fielding's plays are inspired by the same literary-satirical purpose, *The Covent Garden Tragedy* (1732), *Pasquin* (1736), *Tumble-down Dick; or Phæton in the Suds* (1736) and *The Historical Register for the Year 1736* (1737). All have a keen sense of what the audience wanted; to read them gives a vivid picture of what was happening to the stage in their period. Thus, in *Pasquin*, a rather stupid tragic poet, Fustian, is watching a rehearsal of his new play with the critic Sneerwell (a name that one day Sheridan would annex). A battle scene has been acted; the curtain falls; and the dramatist says, preening himself:

There, there, pretty well; I think, Mr Sneerwell, we have made a shift to make out a good sort of a battle at last.

Sneer Indeed I cannot say I ever saw a better—

Fust You don't seem, Mr Sneerwell, to relish this battle greatly.

Sneer I cannot profess myself the greatest admirer of this part of tragedy; and I own my imagination can better conceive the idea of a battle from a skilful relation of it than from such a representation; for my mind is not able to enlarge the stage into a vast plain, nor multiply half a score into several thousands.

Fust Oh! your humble servant; but if we write to please you and half a dozen others, who will pay the charges of the house? Sir, if the audience will be contented with a battle or two, instead of all the raree-fine shows exhibited to them in what they call entertainments——

Sneer Pray, Mr Fustian, how came they to give the name of entertainments to their pantomimical farces?

Fust Faith, Sir, out of their peculiar modesty; intimating that after the audience have been tired with the dull Works of Shakespeare, Jonson, Vanbrugh, and others, they are to be entertain'd with one of these pantomimes, of which the master of the playhouse, two or three painters, and half a score dancing-masters are the compilers. What these entertainments are, I need not inform you who have seen 'em; but I have often wond'red how it was possible for any creature of human understanding, after having been diverted for three hours with the productions of a great genius, to sit for three more, and see a set of people running about the stage after one another, without speaking one syllable, and playing several juggling tricks . . . and for this, Sir, the town does not only pay additional prices, but lose several parts of their best authors, which are cut out to make room for the said farces.

Sneer It's very true, and I have heard a hundred say the same thing, who never fail'd being present at them.

Fust And while that happens they will force any entertainment upon the town they please, in spite of its teeth [GHOST OF COMMON-SENSE *rises*]. Oons, and the devil, madam! What's the meaning of this? You have left out a scene; was ever such an absurdity, as for your ghost to appear before you are kill'd?

Ghost I ask pardon, Sir, in the hurry of the battle I forgot to come and kill myself.

Fust Well, let me wipe the flour off your face then; and now if you please rehearse the scene. Take care you don't make this mistake any more tho'; for it would inevitably damn the play, if you should. Go to the corner of the scene, and come in as if you had lost the battle.

Ghost Behold the ghost of Common-Sense appears.

Fust 'Sdeath, madam, I tell you you are no ghost,
You are not kill'd.

Ghost Deserted and forlorn, where shall I fly?
The Battle's lost, and so are all my friends.
[*Enter a* POET.

Poet Madam, not so, still have you one friend left.
Ghost Why, what art thou?
Poet Madam, I am a poet.
Ghost Whoe'er thou art, if thou'rt a friend to misery,
  Know Common-Sense disclaims thee.
Poet I have been damn'd
  Because I was your foe, and yet I still
  Courted your friendship with my utmost art.
Ghost Fool, thou wert damn'd because thou didst pretend
  Thyself my friend; for hadst thou boldly dar'd,
  Like *Hurlothrombo*, to deny me quite;
  Or, like an opera or pantomime,
  Profest the cause of ignorance in public,
  Thou might'st have met with thy desir'd success.
  But men can't bear even a pretence to me.
Poet Then take a ticket for my benefit night.
Ghost I will do more, for Common-Sense will stay
  Quite from your house, so may you not be damn'd.
Poet Ha! Say'st thou? By my soul a better play
  Ne'er came upon a stage; but since you dare
  Contemn me thus, I'll dedicate my play
  To Ignorance, and call her Common-Sense.
  Yes, I will dress her in your pomp, and swear
  That Ignorance knows more than all the World.

There could be no better commentary on the day's theatrical affairs. However satirically exaggerated, it bears the weight of truth.

Though burlesque, partly because of Fielding's own endeavours, proved highly popular in the mid-eighteenth century, few of the pieces rise above mediocrity. One of the best early examples is Henry Carey's *The Tragedy of Chrononhotonthologos: Being the most Tragical Tragedy, that ever was Tragediz'd by any Company of Tragedians* (1734) with its famous first lines:

SCENE, *An Antechamber in the Palace.*
[*Enter* RIGDUM-FUNNIDOS, *and* ALDIBORONTIPHOSCOPHORNIO.
Rigdum-Funnidos Aldiborontiphoscophornio!
Where left you Chrononhotonthologos?

This is a short piece, extravagant rather than wittily satirical. Much more subtle is Richard Brinsley Sheridan's *The Critic; or, A Tragedy Rehearsed* (1779), with its character of Puff, who has reduced the gentle art of advertisement to regular rule and scientific method. To Sneer, who questions him on the point, he cries:

O lud, Sir! you are very ignorant, I am afraid. Yes, Sir—PUFFING is of various sorts—the principal are, The PUFF DIRECT—the PUFF PRELIMINARY—the PUFF COLLATERAL—the PUFF COLLUSIVE, and the PUFF OBLIQUE, or PUFF by IMPLICATION.—These all assume, as circumstances require, the various forms of LETTERS TO THE EDITOR—OCCASIONAL ANECDOTE—IMPARTIAL CRITIQUE—OBSERVATION FROM CORRESPONDENT—or ADVERTISEMENT FROM THE PARTY.

Sneer The puff direct, I can conceive——

Puff O yes, that's simple enough. For instance—A new comedy or farce is to be produced at one of the theatres (though, by the by, they don't bring out half what they ought to do). The author, suppose Mr Smatter, or Mr Dapper—or any particular friend of mine—very well; the day before it is to be performed, I write an account of the manner in which it was received—I have the plot from the author,—and only add—Characters strongly drawn—highly coloured—hand of a master—fund of genuine humour—mine of invention—neat dialogue—Attic salt! Then for the performance—Mr Dodd was astonishingly great in the character of Sir Harry! That universal and judicious actor, Mr Palmer, perhaps never appeared to more advantage than in the Colonel;—but it is not in the power of language to do justice to Mr King! Indeed he more than merited those repeated bursts of applause which he drew from a most brilliant and judicious audience! As to the scenery—The miraculous powers of Mr De Loutherbourg's pencil are universally acknowledged!—In short, we are at a loss which to admire most,—the unrivalled genius of the author, the great attention and liberality of the managers—the wonderful abilities of the painter, or the incredible exertions of all the performers!——

Sneer That's pretty well indeed, Sir.

Puff O cool—quite cool—to what I sometimes do.

These quotations both point out the evils and show the virtues of their time.

The Growth of Sentimentalism

In both tragedy and comedy, the age's chief weakness was the lack of a clear orientation. The comedy of manners, which had produced Etherege, Wycherley and Congreve, was rapidly degenerating when Farquhar and Vanbrugh took it over. A few other dramatists, such as Charles Burnaby and Mrs Centlivre, tried to keep its spirit alive; but it had lost its original force, and could never again assume quite the same delicately careless and polished tone of the earlier years.

Dramatists were turning chiefly to the expression of moral sentiment. Sometimes they were not prepared to go beyond the enunciation of well-intentioned platitudes; sometimes they went further towards the expounding of social concepts and the delivering of 'messages'; sometimes, during later years, to the presentation of humanitarian views and to encouraging pity for the 'distressed'.

We are bound to deplore the effect this development had upon the spirit of comedy, and the weight of ridiculously lachrymose scenes which it imposed upon the theatre. On the other hand, we are compelled to acknowledge that, for good or evil, it gave birth to an entirely new sort of play. We may regret that there could never appear another Etherege or another Congreve blissfully ignorant of any moral obligations, but we must admit that the new humanitarianism, the recognition of social problems, the endeavour to make the theatre express in its own way the many social issues before its audience, were an inevitable reaction to what had gone before. With Congreve the moving power of the old comedy had vanished; the serious dramas, heroic and other, offered little that might be related to their spectators' lives. The new middle class wished to see its interests reflected on the stage; it found itself instead in an alien and artificial realm which lacked even the merit of excitement; in the comedies it had to watch uneasily the scenes of gallantry that inwardly it condemned. What it sought, and what the sentimental dramatists gave, was an intermediate kind of play where occasional comic scenes alternated with others that made serious, if facile, comments on the contemporary world.

This sentimental trend may be observed as far back as the early eighties of the seventeenth century, and it seems probable that the political interest aroused during the last days of Charles II, the reign of James II and the Rebellion, had something to do with the shifting of focus from brisk intrigue to scenes more serious. Political disturbance caused men to think of problems of government and of religion, and from these they were led naturally to consider the problems of social life in general. This coincided with the development of a reaction to the excesses of the Stuart Court, and together the two forces moved on rapidly. Men such as Thomas D'Urfey, women such as Mrs Behn, proved that they were aware of difficulties that rose from social conventions of the time. Even Shadwell felt the spirit of the age, and showed it in his later work. It must be understood, of course, that before 1700 all these trends were merely tentative and experimental; even towards the very end of the century nothing more had been achieved than the occasional introduction of a 'moral' note into plays concerned mainly with flagrant exhibitions of the love-chase. Typical is *Love's Last Shift* (1696) by Colley Cibber, always eager to satisfy popular tastes. Here the best is being made of two entirely different worlds. The licentious comic characters and themes of the old comedy are freely exploited, and the author goes so far as to warn the spectators that his hero is 'lewd' throughout the first four acts; then, in the fifth we have an artificially conceived conclusion in which the erring gallant is made to promise a mending of his ways. Thus were all the spectators made happy: the reformers rejoiced because virtue triumphed; the pleasure-loving were willing to accept a wholly incredible conversion for the sake of the careless intrigue and loose dialogue of the preceding scenes.

Cibber and others went on to dozens of similar transitional plays; the only marked development was a tendency to tone down the licentiousness and to concentrate attention in the comic situations rather upon fashionable foibles than upon intrigue. Cibber's *She wou'd and she wou'd not* (1702), *The Double Gallant; or, The Sick Lady's Cure* (1707), *The Lady's Last Stake; or, The Wife's Resentment* (1707), and *The Refusal; or, The Ladies' Philosophy* (1721) all agree in emphasizing affected, vain women and their foppish courtiers. In a sense, these plays may be taken as a kind of 'she-comedy' paralleling the contemporary 'she-tragedy'. The heroines become of more consequence than the heroes, and the general atmosphere is more 'genteel'. Wit of Congreve's quality has disappeared, nor is there any rich play of fancy. Instead we are presented with all the fashionable follies, all the darling delights, of the town. The men and women are here seen changing their interests and relationships. Men tend to become mere beaux intent, not on a satire, a lampoon or a witty jest, but on ribbons and wigs; women, less intellectual than their Restoration sisters, spend their lives in trivialities.

Among such plays as these, others appear in which the later growth of sentimentalism is more clearly foreshadowed. Especially important are the works of Sir Richard Steele, joint-author of *The Spectator* and the writer of a seriously reflective essay called *The Christian Hero*. Steele's inclinations, in spite of his own somewhat careless life, were all on the side of morality. He believed in domestic happiness, he believed in faithful love, he believed in the goodness of the human heart. It is not surprising, therefore, to find that in his four comedies—*The Funeral; or, Grief A-la-Mode* (1701) *The Lying Lover; or, The Ladies' Friendship* (1703), *The Tender Husband; or, The Accomplish'd Fools* (1705) and *The*

Conscious Lovers (1722)—he should have tried to utter his own genuinely sincere reflections upon life. The first of these plays expresses his hatred of hypocrisy through the characters of Lady Harriot and of the honest old servant Trusty. In *The Lying Lover* his hatred of duelling is exemplified. Domestic virtue occupies him in *The Tender Husband*, and in *The Conscious Lovers*, his best play, he develops an emotional theme which at times takes us far from the comic. The hero, Bevil junior, about to be married to Sealand's daughter Lucinda, has met and befriended an unknown girl named Indiana, with whom he ultimately falls in love. Unlike earlier rakes, he will neither betray this girl nor marry her without his father's consent. For a time it seems that the play must end unhappily: then Sealand discovers in Indiana his own daughter. An artificial conclusion; but the dialogue is capable, the characters are persuasive and the situations cleverly contrived.

It must be obvious that such a play as *The Conscious Lovers* is moving towards a dramatic form distinct from what the term 'comedy' had implied, and it was this new form that typified developments during the later years of the century. Doubtless, comedies of a mixed kind—such as Mrs Centlivre's *The Gamester* (1705), with its attack upon gambling, and William Taverner's *The Artful Wife* (1717), with its morally reflective observations—can stand for the majority of plays in this period, but the style indicated in *The Conscious Lovers* was now destined to be the mode, aided by an influence from abroad. In Paris, numerous writers, encouraging a trend similar to London's, made certain definite and significant contributions of their own. In particular, instead of simply cloaking earlier kinds of comedy with moralizations and virtuous statements, they had begun to dream of an entirely new dramatic genre worthy of taking its place beside the others hallowed by classical precept and practice. True, the formal expression of this new critical approach did not come until Diderot and Beaumarchais propounded it in the fifties and sixties of the century, but several decades before that the concept of a new kind of drama was already in the air. Hence the interest of John Kelly's *The Married Philosopher* (1732), the first adaptation of a French sentimental drama in English—and one certainly aiming at what later was to be styled the 'serious comedy'.

The fuller development of the sentimental play in England had to wait for some years, and for two dramatists, Hugh Kelly and Richard Cumberland. Of this pair, Kelly is more closely allied than Cumberland to the older native traditions: such a play as *The*

School for Wives (1773) has obviously been based on the older type of 'genteel' comedy, though his emphasis on the virtues of natural affection and on the evils of social conventions carries these older forms into an entirely different atmosphere. Foibles which before had been an occasion for laughter are now condemned; seriousness rules. In *False Delicacy* (1768), one of the triumphs of its age, vociferously applauded by spectators and avidly read at home, two heroines nearly ruin their lives because they are inclined to sacrifice the dictates of their hearts to society's demands, and there is a happy ending simply because an unconventional gallant, inspired by sentimental motives, dares to plead the cause of nature. Similarly, in *A Word to the Wise* (1770), a girl's happiness is nearly destroyed because of her father's insistence that she should marry the man of his choice; smiles follow tears only because the proposed bridegroom, kindly, good-natured and sentimental beneath his foppish exterior, is prepared, magnanimously, to release his bride-to-be.

In devising these situations, Kelly and his companions sought to be 'realistic', but in fact they imposed upon the stage a kind of dialogue insipid and ridiculously artificial. 'O, Sir George,' exclaims the heroine, when she has decided to reveal her true affections to the man she does not love,

> O, Sir George, to the greatness of your humanity let me appeal against the prepossession of your heart. You see before you a distressed young creature whose affection is already engaged and who, though she thinks herself highly honoured by your sentiments, is wholly unable to return them.
> **Sir George** I am extremely sorry, madam—to have been—I say, madam—that—really I am so exceedingly disconcerted that I don't know what to say—
> **Miss Dormer** O, Sir George, you have no occasion for apologies, though I have unhappily too much. But I know the nicety of your honour, and I depend upon it with security. Let me then entreat an additional act of goodness at your hands, which is absolutely necessary as well for my peace as for my father's—this is to contrive such a method of withdrawing your addresses as will not expose me to his displeasure.

There is, then, in these plays a strange dichotomy, an attempt to cultivate the 'natural' and at the same time a hopelessly artificial approach.

Precisely the same dichotomy is apparent in Cumberland's work. This relies mostly on two dramatic devices. The first is the presentation of the reckless libertine whose faults and vices are external to his true nature. In *The West Indian* (1771), a popular piece, the hero, an inherently benevolent but rakish youth, having tried to seduce the heroine, eventually marries her, though given to believe that she is poor. Improbably reforming himself from all his former vices, he is rewarded materially by finding that his bride is a wealthy heiress. The other note in Cumberland's plays is his deliberate choice of characters he can pity. In one play he seeks to give a feeling heart to the Irishman, hitherto a familiar stage booby; in another he tries to do the same for the stock comic Scotsman; and in his best-known work, *The Jew* (1794), for a moneylender who becomes a generous friend of the distressed; it is he who rescues Sir Bertram's son from ruin, and who acts as a kindly *deus ex machina*. We can acclaim Cumberland's purpose in writing the play, but we cannot avoid seeing it as a tissue of artificialities: his propagandist aim makes his situation mawkish, and his characters as unreal as their dialogue.

Kelly and Cumberland did not stand alone in elaborating the sentimental *genre*, neither were their works the best in this kind. As early as 1748, Edward Moore wrote a well-planned play, *The Foundling*, which, though a comedy, was designed to 'steal the pitying tear from beauty's eye' in its treatment of a theme (unknown parentage) prized by sentimentalists from the time of Steele's *The Conscious Lovers* to that of Cumberland's *The West Indian*. A son sentimentally seeking his father, or a maiden cast parentless upon the world, was sure in the eighteenth century to call for a free use of handkerchiefs. So also, at a later date, Thomas Holcroft took the sentimental play yet farther. *The Road to Ruin* (1792; last seen in London, 1937, in an unfortunate revival) long remained as a popular stock piece: thanks largely, we imagine, to the character of Goldfinch, the 'ridiculous horse-jockey oaf' (with his catch-phrase, 'That's your sort!') who appears in 'a high-collared coat, several under-waistcoats, buckskin breeches covering his calves, short boots, long spurs, high-crowned hat, hair in the extreme, etc., etc.' He goes on like this in a breathless compression that Dickens may have remembered when he created Alfred Jingle:

Harry Dornton A fine woman!
Goldfinch Prodigious! Sister to the Irish Giant! Six feet in her stockings!—That's your sort!—Sleek coat, flowing mane, broad chest, all bone!—Dashing figure in a phaeton!—Sky-blue habit, scarlet sash,

green hat, yellow ribbands, white feathers, gold band and tassel!—That's your sort!

Harry Ha, ha, ha! Heigho!—Why, you are a high fellow, Charles.

Goldfinch To be sure!—Know the odds!—Hold four in hand—Turn a corner in style!—Reins in form—Elbows square—Wrist pliant —Hayait!—Drive the Coventry stage twice a week all summer: —Pay for an inside place—Mount the box—Tip the coachy a crown—Beat the mail—Come in full speed;—Rattle down the gateway!—Take care of your heads!—Never killed but one woman and a child in all my life—That's your sort!

However, the hero of *The Road to Ruin* is a young man (Harry Dornton) who is destroying himself by his passion for gambling. Riotous though he is, he is thrown into despair when he hears that his follies are about to bring his father to disaster. Nobly, he decides to sacrifice himself by proposing marriage to an ugly but rich old widow. In the nick of time all comes right; the good in heart are duly rewarded. Superficially, this play seems to be no more than another example of the brand of drama thoroughly exploited by others, yet Holcroft was essentially different from Kelly and Cumberland. When the prologue-speaker advances to address the audience, he pretends that the author's original script has been lost and that he is obliged to improvise. 'The author', he says,

> had mounted on the stilts of oratory and elocution—
> Not but he had a smart touch or two about Poland, France, and
> the—the Revolution,
> Telling us that Frenchmen and Polishmen and every man is our
> brother,
> And that all men, ay, even poor Negro men, have a right to be free, one
> as well as another.
> Freedom at length, said he, like a torrent is spreading and swell-
> ing,
> To sweep away pride and reach the most miserable dwelling,
> To ease, happiness, art, science, wit, and genius to give birth—
> Ay, to fertilize a world and renovate old earth!

In fact, these supposedly extemporized lines reveal Holcroft's real objective. He was typical of those sentimentalists who towards the end of the century were moving from virtuous platitudes to the inculcation of revolutionary ideas. We have made a long journey within the hundred years since the comedy of manners was first being modified by its early reformers.

Comedy's Temporary Revival

In essence the sentimentalists looked not towards comedy but towards 'drama'. Instead of laughter, they sought tears; instead of intrigue, melodramatic and distressing situations; instead of gallants and witty damsels, pathetic heroines and serious lovers. Most of their plays may have been labelled 'comedies', but the development of the comic theme did not interest them.

We must not assume that this sentimentalism completely dominated the stage. Farce was still popular, and many saw the follies of the sentimentalists' endeavour. Whitehead expressed a fairly common thought when, in *A Trip to Scotland* (1770) he satirically makes one of his characters declare: 'The good company will perceive, that, whatever effect the late run of sentimental comedies may have had upon their audiences, they have at least made the players men of honour'. Cobb has a characteristic passage in *The First Floor* (1787):

Young Whimsey Hey-day! What's become of the exquisite luxury of a feeling mind in relieving distress?
Furnish It may do very well for people of fortune, but a tradesman should never indulge in luxury.
Young Whimsey Consider, generosity is part of the business of man.
Furnish And a d—d losing trade it is; therefore it shan't be a part of *my* business.

In diverse ways, through satire and burlesque and through practical experiment, numerous authors tried to keep the comic spirit alive. Samuel Foote, a prolific actor-dramatist of the third quarter of the century, thus devoted himself to more or less farcical pieces enlivened by satirical stings: *The Knights* (1749), *The Minor* (1760), *The Orators* (1762) and similar pieces. Such plays as *The Maid of Bath* (1771), with its portrait of Miss Linley (later Sheridan's wife) and with its attacks on the Methodists, were written amusingly with topicalities in mind. Foote's work was rough, if vigorous, but even in its roughness it preserved something of the old spirit.

More important is George Colman, generally known as 'The Elder' to distinguish him from his son, George Colman the Younger. Though his plays contain episodes and characters obviously influenced by the sentimental style, he consistently supported the cause of laughter and ridiculed the cult of pity.

Polly Honeycombe (1760), a clever satire of contemporary absurdities, anticipates both in general outline and in definite phrases Sheridan's more polished satire in *The Rivals*. Colman's opposition to sentimentalism is seen clearly enough in his selection of Fielding's novel *Tom Jones* for the plot of his more ambitious *The Jealous Wife* (1761), a comedy which, while it lacks Congreve's wit, is effectively written in the style of the comedy of manners. The same style predominates in his excellent *The Clandestine Marriage* (1766), which he wrote a few years later in collaboration with David Garrick. For its aged but indomitable Lord Ogleby, a portrait of a crumbling fop intimately conceived and genuinely comic in its execution, *The Clandestine Marriage* would deserve remembrance. We have been grateful in twentieth-century revivals not only for Ogleby (who has been acted by Sir Donald Wolfit and Alastair Sim), but also for a great deal of alert dialogue, with action to match.

More sentimental touches appear in the plays of Arthur Murphy, yet he too has three comedies, *The Way to Keep Him* (1760), *All in the Wrong* (1761) and *Know Your Own Mind* (1777), which make an evident effort to preserve the integrity of the comic tradition. While the Cumberlands and Kellys and Holcrofts allowed their distressed heroines to talk in terms far removed from those of ordinary conversation, Murphy can introduce his lively Lady Bell reciting part of a love-lyric:

> Yes, I'm in love, I own it now,
> And Cœlia has undone me;
> And yet, I swear, I can't tell how
> The pleasing plague stole on me.

What would I give to have some miserable swain talk in that style to me? 'Belinda has undone me!' Charming!

Miss Neville A lively imagination is a blessing, and you are happy, Lady Bell.

Lady Bell I am so. But then I am not talked of. I am losing my time.

Lady Jane Why, you bold creature! I hate to hear you talk with so much intrepidity.

Lady Bell Prudery, my dear sister, downright prudery! I am not for making mysteries of what all the world knows.

Lady Jane And how do I make mysteries, pray?

Lady Bell Why, you confident thing, I'll prove it against you.

Lady Jane But what? What? What will you prove?

Lady Bell That you are ready to jump out of your little wits for a husband, my demure, sober sister. Miss Neville, a poet is not more eager for the success of a new comedy, nor one of his brother poets more desirous to see it fail, than that girl is to throw herself into the arms of a man.

In a kindred manner Mrs Hannah Cowley, author of nearly a score of comedies, farces and tragedies, strove to work in the older tradition. *A Bold Stroke for a Husband* (1783), *The Belle's Stratagem* (1780) and *A School for Greybeards* (1786) are all equally vivacious, adding to intrigues intricately contrived, and reminiscent of the plays of Mrs Behn and Mrs Centlivre, characters which take life in performance. In *The Belle's Stratagem*, frequently revived, Doricourt, handsome, witty and gallant, succeeds in recalling the vanished Dorimants and Mirabells. These comedies, merely a few, prove that even prevailing sentimentalism could not banish laughter. We ought not to forget the prolific blind Irishman, John O'Keeffe, for the sake of *Wild Oats* (1791) which the Royal Shakespeare Company so happily rediscovered in 1976, with Alan Howard in the once celebrated part of Rover, nonpareil of the pomping folk and a kind of quotation-dictionary. We may not say of O'Keeffe, as Hazlitt would, that 'in light, careless laughter and pleasant exaggerations of the humorous, we have had no one to equal him'; but the return of *Wild Oats* does mean now that it is likely to linger in the repertory.

All the comedies of the late eighteenth century have been overshadowed by the work of Goldsmith and Sheridan. Oliver Goldsmith first attacked the sentimental drama in 1759 when he published his essay on *The Present State of Polite Learning*, and a decade later (1768) *The Good-Natur'd Man* was directed shrewdly at the style of Kelly, Cumberland and their kind. Spectators realized how clever it was, even if they were too squeamish to accept without protest the 'low' scenes that Goldsmith had introduced. In reading this comedy we may not discern where exactly Goldsmith left the sentimentalists. Certainly its last lines are exactly in Cumberland's spirit:

Honeywood Heavens! How can I have deserved all this? How express my happiness, my gratitude! A moment like this overpays an age of apprehension.
Croaker Well, now I see content in every face; but Heaven send we be all better this day three months.
Sir William Henceforth, nephew, learn to respect yourself. He who seeks only for applause from without has all his happiness in another's keeping.
Honeywood Yes, Sir, I now too plainly perceive my errors—my vanity, in attempting to please all, by fearing to offend any; my meanness in

approving folly, lest fools should disapprove. Henceforth, therefore, it shall be my study to reserve my pity for real distress, my friendship for true merit, and my love for her, who first taught me what it is to be happy.

This shows that Goldsmith had not completely thrown over the style he condemned, and similar passages are scattered throughout the play. But when we reach the bailiff scenes in the third act Goldsmith's sly satire is obvious. The bailiff says:

Looky, Sir, I have arrested as good men as you in my time—no disparagement of you neither—men that would go forty guineas on a game of cribbage. I challenge the town to show a man in more gen-teeler practice than myself. . . . I love to see a gentleman with a tender heart. I don't know, but I think I have a tender heart myself. If all that I have lost by my heart was put together, it would make a—but no matter for that. . . . Humanity, Sir, is a jewel. It's better than gold. I love humanity. People may say, that we, in our way, have no human-ity; but I'll shew you my humanity this moment. There's my follower here, little Flanigan, with a wife and four children; a guinea or two would be more to him, than twice as much to another. Now, as I can't shew him any humanity myself, I must beg leave you'll do it for me. . . . Sir, you're a gentleman. I see you know what to do with your money.

The Good-Natur'd Man (revived by the National Theatre at the Old Vic in 1971) cannot be regarded as truly successful; com-plaints no one can make of *She Stoops to Conquer; or, The Mistakes of a Night* (1773). This comedy, of deserved fame, presents a pecu-liar and interesting fusion of different forces. If it owes part of its inspiration to the school of which Farquhar was the last true representative, in essence its spirit is closer to Shakespeare's romantic comedies, then more popular than at any time since the early seventeenth century. In effect, the conception of Hard-castle, Tony Lumpkin, Diggory and the lovers exhibits, not a witty intellectual approach, but the exercise of humour: the sly smiles, the subtle sallies, the humane sensitiveness. Basically, Tony Lumpkin is born of Falstaff's company: he is a fool and yet a wit; while laughing at his follies we recognize that often the laugh is turned back upon ourselves. Though setting and personages seem far from Shakespeare's Rosalinds and Orlandos, Bottoms and Dogberrys, it seems certain that Goldsmith was looking back fondly over a period of nearly two hundred years.

Having nothing in common with Goldsmith except his objection to sentimentalism, Richard Brinsley Sheridan sought also to keep laughter on the stage. His work for the theatre is strangely various. We have noted the comic opera *The Duenna* (1775). *The Rivals*, performed in the same year, has no Shakespearian reminiscence (unless we hold that Dogberry might have admired the verbal adventures of Mrs Malaprop), but it speaks clearly enough of Jonson and Congreve. Many of the names, such as Sir Lucius O'Trigger, Sir Anthony Absolute and Lydia Languish, take us back to the comedy of 'humours', and much of the dialogue recalls the late seventeenth-century style. The Julia-Faulkland scenes, particularly amusing in the modern theatre, are concessions to a sentimentality of which we know Sheridan's real opinion very well: consider his treatment of Lydia. Further, though patently wishing to keep to the level of comedy, he freely introduces farcical episodes; indeed, all suggests that as yet Sheridan has no very determined intentions: *The Rivals*, in spite of its vigorous writing and of such an inimitable portrait as Mrs Malaprop, is not an integrated whole.

The School for Scandal (1777), on the other hand, is a completely harmonious masterpiece. Nothing disturbs the constant glitter of its wit, and the complicated plot is kept moving with consummate skill. Satire of the sentimental strain, expressed in the person of Joseph Surface, falls into its proper place. All is amply clear, and never for a moment does the author deviate from his effort to follow Etherege and Congreve in the exploitation, for comic ends, of the manners of society. The famous fourth-act Screen scene in which old Sir Peter unwittingly destroys the 'man of sentiment' he has prized is one of the show-pieces of English comedy:

Sir Peter Teazle Well, there is nothing in the world so noble as a man of sentiment.
Charles Surface Pshaw! he is too moral by half;—and so apprehensive of his good name, as he calls it, that I suppose he would as soon let a priest into his house as a girl.
Sir Peter No, no,—come, come,—you wrong him. No, no, Joseph is no rake, but he is no such saint in that respect either.—I have a great mind to tell him—we should have a laugh. (*Aside*).
Charles Oh, hang him! he's a very anchorite, a young hermit!
Sir Peter Hark'ee—you must not abuse him: he may chance to hear of it again, I promise you.
Charles Why, you won't tell him?
Sir Peter No—but—this way.—Egad, I'll tell him.—(*Aside*). Hark 'ee, have you a mind to have a good laugh at Joseph?

Charles I should like it, of all things,
Sir Peter Then, i'faith, we will!—I'll be quit with him for discovering me. He had a girl with him when I called (*Whispers*).
Charles What! Joseph? you jest.
Sir Peter Hush!—a little French milliner—and the best of the jest is—she's in the room now.
Charles The devil she is. (*Looking at the closet*).
Sir Peter! Hush! I tell you. (*Points to the screen*).
Charles Behind the screen! Odds life, let's unveil her!
Sir Peter No, no—he's coming—you shan't, indeed!
Charles Oh, egad, we'll have a peep at the little milliner!
Sir Peter Not for the world!—Joseph will never forgive me.
Charles I'll stand by you—
Sir Peter Odds, here he is!
(*Joseph Surface enters just as Charles Surface throwns down the screen*).
Charles Lady Teazle, by all that's wonderful!
Sir Peter Lady Teazle, by all that's damnable!

Sheridan never matched this again, though *The Critic; or, A Tragedy Rehearsed* is a masterly burlesque. Sheridan, who had then directed the Theatre Royal, Drury Lane, for three years, brings on the flamboyant Mr Puff, the stage-struck Mr Dangle and a Mr Sneer (all the name implies) to witness a rehearsal of Puff's tragedy, *The Spanish Armada*. Puff knows the tricks. Thus we have the readily communicative and expository Sir Walter Raleigh, the responsive Sir Christopher Hatton ('It is . . . We do'), the Earl of Leicester in heroic blaze with 'trope, figure, and metaphor' as plentiful as noun-substantives, the unanimous resolution—with Puff's comment, 'When they *do* agree on the stage, their unanimity is wonderful', the prayer (nothing like it in great emergencies), and the morning cannon in triplicate, though credit for this goes to the stage management. Then there are the flower-catalogue of Tilburina—a long way after Perdita's—the debate with her father in 'a sort of small-sword logic which we have borrowed from the French', the Beefeater's soliloquy that would have been a great deal longer if he had not been observed, Burleigh's Nod (the Lord High Treasurer speechless but in spate), the Beefeater again, 'discovering' himself by throwing off his upper dress and appearing in a very fine waistcoat, and Tilburina, stark mad in white satin, with her Confidant stark mad in white linen. Grand nonsense: modern audiences have had the felicity of seeing Laurence Olivier's Puff soaring to heaven on a wave and descending upon a cloud. Sheridan did little more: *A Trip to Scarborough* (1777), for all its individual quality, is only an adaptation of a play by Vanbrugh; and when we reach the melodramatic version of Kotzebue's *Pizarro* in 1799 we see that the dramatist of *The School for Scandal* has utterly forgotten the comic stage. One day Leigh Hunt would call *Pizarro* (in its time a familiar country hack piece) 'downright booth at a fair—a tall, spouting gentleman in tinsel'. In many respects, the writing of these two works by the same man is symbolic. In his great comedy Sheridan said almost the last word for the kind of play Congreve brought to perfection; in *Pizarro* he was saying almost the first word for nineteenth-century melodrama.

The Domestic Drama

The melodrama was born out of many things, and not least out of the domestic 'tragedies' which were part of the sentimentalists' contributions to the theatre.

Domestic tragedy in Elizabethan times had produced an *Arden of Feversham* and *A Woman Killed with Kindness*, but this type of drama soon vanished amid heroic ardours and pseudo-classic rhetoric. About the period when we can discern the first glimmerings of sentimentalism, some signs appear to indicate a revival: Otway's *The Orphan* concentrates upon characters who, if aristocratic, are at least not royal; Banks, in his historical plays, emphasizes the pathetic 'domestic' situation; in *Oroonoko* (1695) Southerne makes his hero an ill-used, dark-skinned native chieftain. In these works and others which followed we observe both a deliberate attempt to tone down the heroic, rhetorical style and to make it more 'ordinary', and the development of the concept of 'fate'—maybe because, in turning from regal splendours, some compensating 'tragic' element was essential, and also because these 'fatal' situations offered a chance for pathetic sentiment.

During the first years of the eighteenth century we can watch the slow elaboration of this type of play. In 1704 comes the anonymous *Rival Brothers*, obviously based on *The Orphan*; barely two decades later, in 1721, Aaron Hill casts his eyes back to the early *Yorkshire Tragedy*, and in *The Fatal Extravagance* gives us the first play of its time which deals with middle-class English characters in a 'tragic' manner. These, and other, plays foreshadowed George Lillo's *The London Merchant; or, The History of George Barnwell*, a play which fluttered all London society when it was first produced in 1731, and which remained a stock piece for many years. Here at last was a writer daring enough to make the hero of his tragedy a mere apprentice; here was one bold enough to write his serious dialogue in prose. It is true, of course, that this prose was not only artificial in its pattern but also strongly influenced by the blank-verse measure. The Uncle enters and soliloquizes in a manner almost identical with that of any of the scores of contemporary dramas about more heroic persons:

> If I was superstitious, I shou'd fear some danger lurk'd unseen, or Death were nigh. A heavy melancholy clouds my spirits; my imagination is fill'd with gashly forms of dreary graves and bodies chang'd by death—when the pale lengthen'd visage attracts each weeping eye and fills the musing soul at once with grief and horror, pity and aversion. I will indulge the thought. The wise man prepares himself for death by making it familiar to his mind. When strong reflections hold the mirror near, and the living in the dead behold their future selves, how does each inordinate passion or desire cease or sicken at the view! The mind scarce moves; the blood, curdling and chill'd, creeps slowly through the veins, fix'd, still and motionless, like the solemn object of our thoughts. We are almost at present what we must be hereafter, 'till curiosity awakes the soul and sets it on inquiry

Throughout the entire play, not only in soliloquies, this style rules, so that the dialogue assumes almost the quality of a burlesque. But, in 1731, this prose of Lillo's was a novelty that seemed to its public to be bringing 'reality' upon the stage. Audiences wept; men of letters praised the work; royalty read it in the palace boudoir; foreign playwrights hastened to adapt it and to write imitations. Ridiculous though it may seem to us, *The London Merchant* marked the downfall of the classical tragedy.

Lillo followed this lachrymose play with *Fatal Curiosity*, a not ineffectively written drama about an ordinary peasant couple led by poverty to commit a terrible crime. Like *The London Merchant*, it was translated into several languages, and its echoes were long heard on many stages.

Other dramatists attempted similar plays. Thus John Hewitt came forward with *Fatal Falsehood; or, Distress'd Innocence* (1734) and Thomas Cooke with his peculiarly named play *The Mournful Nuptials; or, Love the Cure of all Woes* (printed 1739; acted as *Love the Cause and Cure of Grief; or, The Innocent Murderer*, 1743), but these were dull works, wanting vitality. Much more forceful was Edward Moore, who in *The Gamester* (1753) produced an affecting domestic drama of unrelieved misery. Beverley, the hero, is ruined through his passion for gambling. Reduced to his last few coppers, he takes his wife's jewels, and, playing recklessly, loses them. Meantime, Lewson, the lover of Beverley's sister, discovers the evil machinations of the hero's pretended friend Stukely. Realizing that his exposure is imminent, Stukely instructs his agent to murder Lewson, and the blame is cast on Beverley, who in his misery takes poison and dies—just as he hears that a large sum of money has been left to him. Moore's success rests on two things. First, his drama has a grimly concentrated atmosphere, akin to, but stronger than, that of *The London Merchant*. Secondly, although influenced by Lillo's style, he is able to bring his language nearer to reality. As a contrast with the Uncle's soliloquy already quoted, Beverley's soliloquy in prison shows both the indebtedness to and the improvement on the speech-forms of the earlier drama:

> Why, there's an end then. I have judg'd deliberately, and the result is death. How the self-murderer's account may stand I know not. But this I know—the horrors of my soul are more than I can bear. [*Offers to kneel.*] Father of mercy! I cannot pray. Despair has laid his iron hand upon me and seal'd me for perdition. Conscience! Conscience! thy clamours are too loud! Here's that shall silence thee. [*Takes a vial out of his pocket and looks at it.*] Thou art most friendly to the miserable. Come, then, thou cordial for sick minds, come to my heart. [*Drinks.*] O, that the grave wou'd bury memory as well as body! For if the soul sees and feels the sufferings of those dear ones it leaves behind, the Everlasting has no vengeance to torment it deeper. I'll think no more on't. Reflection comes too late. Once there was a time for't, but now 'tis past.

It is obvious that the language in these soliloquies by Lillo and Moore savours of what we now call the 'melodramatic'; the quality becomes even more apparent when we move from reflections uttered by men about to die to the speeches which accompany sensational actions. In *The London Merchant* the apprentice-hero, goaded by a prostitute, determines to murder and rob his uncle. Barnwell, according to a stage direction, 'sometimes presents the pistol, and draws it back again; at last he drops it—at which his uncle starts and draws his sword':

Barnwell O, 'tis impossible.
Uncle A man so near me, arm'd and mask'd!
Barnwell Nay, then there's no retreat.
　　[*Plucks a poniard from his bosom and stabs him.*
Uncle O, I am slain! All-gracious Heaven, regard the prayer of Thy dying servant. Bless, with Thy choicest blessings, my dearest nephew; forgive my murderer; and take my fleeting soul to endless mercy.

[*Barnwell throws off his mask, runs to him, and, kneeling by him, raises and chafes him.*

Barnwell Expiring saint! O, murder'd, martyr'd uncle! Lift up your dying eyes and view your nephew in your murderer.

We need not be surprised, then, that when romanticism came with its predilection for 'Gothick' ruins and Oriental strangeness, the style set by Lillo and Moore should have governed the melo-dramatic plays which flooded the stage during the first half of the nineteenth century. Though from 1750 the theatre had sentimen-tal dramas by the score, and though *The London Merchant* and *The Gamester* were warmly applauded, audiences of the time were not really interested in 'tragedy'. They found greater delight in plays which presented sinners reclaimed, distressed maidens saved, sympathy rewarded, and evil exposed—plays, too, with oppor-tunities for colour and music, for a mingling of excitement and laughter. All of this the melodrama gave them. Serious attempts at the writing of domestic 'tragedy' had again to wait until many decades had gone by.

Six

Drama in the Nineteenth Century

Decay and Change

After Sheridan and Goldsmith's period the drama rapidly decayed—first of all because of the size of the theatres. The Theatre Royal, Covent Garden, was enlarged in 1787 and rebuilt five years later; about the same time there was a new Drury Lane. Results could have been predicted. Though profits increased, often largely, the gulf that separated stage from pit and galleries rendered any form of subtle acting impossible: in the vast, many-tiered cavern of Covent Garden, which held 2,800 people, it could seem a day's march from the stage to the back of the pit, and players had to boom out into the candle-lit immensities (always lighted before the coming of gas made it possible to dim the auditorium). Naturally, companies moved to rant and bombast. Mrs Siddons herself had to make her inflections coarser and rougher; any flash of repartee was impossible, a tender whisper or an excited aside rendered absurd by the actor's need to shout if he were to be audible in the topmost galleries. Obviously, in these conditions anything that approached the comedy of manners would have been intolerable, the finer tragedy would have been dissipated, and only the roughest and crudest effects were safe. Hence the rise and popularity of spectacle. Never had scenic artists and machinists so much to do; dialogue was subordinated to the gorgeous effect and the resounding chorus. Melodrama, with its songs, its boldly adventurous plotting, and its stereotyped characters, began to rule the stage.

Probably the very size of these theatres intensified the evils of the audience. Sane, sober people who might have helped the growth of a finer drama were obliged to keep themselves aloof. Society, libertine and vulgar, set an example aped by the more dissolute of the bourgeoisie. Prostitutes thronged the foyers; coarse language, rioting, drunkenness, abounded. James Boaden has a typical story in his *Life of Kemble* (1825). On a November evening in 1806 Sarah Siddons was appearing as Volumnia with her brother, John Philip Kemble, as Coriolanus. During the supplication, when Mrs Siddons urged the conqueror to spare Rome, 'when every ear should have been burning with the pure flame of patriot vehemence', as Boaden said sternly—at such a moment an apple was thrown upon the Covent Garden stage and fell between Mrs Siddons and Kemble. When the actor protested vigorously, someone shouted back that the apple had been thrown at 'disorderly females in the boxes'.

The many 'minor' theatres which grew during these years also encouraged melodrama. At first authority allowed the 'minors' to continue if they avoided spoken dialogue, so in various productions at the end of the eighteenth century and early in the nineteenth plots were explained partly in mime, partly by a few songs, and partly by the use of title-boards with a few snatches of written dialogue (like captions in the era of the silent film). Later concessions permitted three-act plays against a constant musical background and with a stipulated minimum of songs. Obviously, as in the big theatres, spectacular musical melodrama flourished: it was easy for meagrely paid hacks to keep up the supply, and many writers who might have done something in the theatre forsook it for other literary forms. Meanwhile managements would employ 'house authors' who guaranteed to turn out, season by season, so many melodramas apiece. Though several poets took to playwriting, very few succeeded, and for various reasons: they still thought in terms of pseudo-Elizabethan blank verse, or current stage conditions did not encourage them to learn their trade within the theatre itself. Most of these poetic plays seem condescending: the authors, we feel, were conscious of their higher station and blamed the managements, not themselves, when they were rejected. Some wrote poems in dialogue form which (they said) were not intended for performance: never before were so many unacted, and frequently unactable, dramas published.

Towards the middle of the century there were signs of change. In 1873 a reviewer in the *Westminster* claimed that English drama was irrevocably dead: yet by then (and even in the sixties) there had been hopeful signs of a wider life ahead. Already an epoch-making Act for 'regulating' the theatres had been passed in 1843—and not too soon. The 'minors', precariously at work without legal support, were then almost in charge of the drama; Drury Lane was struggling for solvency, and Covent Garden would soon be an opera house. Such a state of affairs was ridiculous, and, logically, the Act of 1843 destroyed the power of the 'patents' while putting the 'minors' at liberty. Planché noted the new freedom in a Haymarket entertainment, *The Drama at Home* (1844). Here the Drama, about to emigrate, was stopped by Portia in her 'Doctor of Laws' gown:

I say you're free to act where'er you please,
No longer pinioned by the patentees.
Need our immortal Shakespeare mute remain
Fixed on the portico of Drury Lane;
Or the nine Muses mourn the Drama's fall
Without relief on Covent Garden's wall?
Sheridan now at Islington may shine,
Marylebone echo Marlowe's mighty line;
Otway may raise the waters Lambeth yields,
And Farquhar sparkle in St George's Fields;
Wycherley flutter a Whitechapel pit,
And Congreve wake all 'Westminster to *wit*.'

Not many signs of change were observable at first; managers kept to the same type of play. But as the years passed and new theatres were built, more intimate, better fitted for tragedy and comedy, the theatrical world as a whole began to assume a new shape. Actors had no longer to mouth grandiloquently; a subtler, more delicate, method had its chance; and playgoers who had once given up in despair began at last to return.

Largely because of the influence of Queen Victoria and her Court, life generally was becoming more sober and respectable. When the Queen began to 'command' leading actors to perform with their companies at Windsor she gave, as it were, a direction to her people. In these days the quiet middle class could go to the play without being affronted by flamboyant rowdyism. Moreover, certain managements were making the theatres more comfortable, cushioning stalls, laying carpets and inventing the 'dress circle' and (for less wealthy patrons) the 'family circle'. At the beginning of the century doors were opened early, and a show could go on to near midnight: in one evening a farce, a tragedy, a pantomime, with entr'acte divertissements. By the end of the century doors opened later and closed earlier; a single play, with a 'curtain-raiser', was the rule; and most theatres had their specialities. A playgoer, knowing more or less what to expect, could go comfortably at an hour to suit his convenience.

Still, improvements are rarely without disadvantages, and the new system had two in particular: the first, and most important, the coming of the long run. Until the mid-eighteenth century, even well into the nineteenth, runs of any length were unknown except for pantomimes. Before 1640 the nine performances for Middleton's *The Game at Chess* was a much-bruited record, and the month's run of *The Beggar's Opera* (1728) quite extraordinary. Normally theatres worked on a repertory system with constantly changing bills: only pantomimes, elaborate and costly to stage, were done more often. In the new theatres tradition had to be put aside. A manager who had given much time and money to settings, costumes and rehearsals, and who found the potential public much larger than it had been, was obviously inclined to let his piece run so long as it could attract an audience. This led to something else. In the old days a theatre had a stock company, engaged at the start of a season, which would present every chosen play. Now, with the coming of the long run, managers found it more profitable—as well as artistically better—to engage players for particular parts; if a piece succeeded these might remain for months or years; if not, then they had to look for other engagements. The drastic alteration in theatre economics caused a cleavage between managers and players—less acute during the nineteenth century, when many actors were also managers and concerned closely with the production of their plays. The cleft widened early in the twentieth century, when hundreds of actors would be victimized by men concerned only with profits. Obviously, one day players and managers would form their own official bodies: trade unionism (Equity is the present label) had reached the theatre.

As in London, so in the provinces. Dozens of Theatres Royal, all of which had had their resident companies, came under managers who were often simply businessmen. The railway had long made travelling easier and more rapid; London productions could be sent with profit on long tours, or, more usually, special companies could be engaged to tour in a new metropolitan success. Frequently provincial managers seemed to be only booking agents occupied in filling their seasons; and, the country over, theatres were no longer—as they had been—training-grounds for the young actors. Hence in time the creation of a dramatic school, something animatedly discussed since 1750; in London what began as the Edwardian 'Tree's Academy' would turn to the Royal Academy of Dramatic Art.

Wherever we look in the theatrical landscape we can see changes that began quietly in the late eighteenth century. Theatre illumination, for example. David Garrick, while managing Drury Lane, brought in an improved method of stage lighting capable of effects hitherto unknown; in essence, substituting something 'realistic' for the older conventions. His interest in this caused him to engage a scenic designer named De Loutherbourg, who spent most of his time in experiments with light, and whose name is linked with a device (the 'Eidophusikon') which could show a stage set that continually changed its atmospheric quality. Obviously, such an attempt as this, at a time when candles and lamps were the only means of illumination, could not go very far; but, just as the idea of the late eighteenth century 'flying coaches' anticipated the railway, so De Loutherbourg and Garrick anticipated in idea the theatrical wonders that gas-lighting and later electricity would make possible. For the theatre-worker these were entirely new instruments, able with comparative ease to simulate the effects of nature. More important, the house lighting could be so controlled as to separate the stage world from that of the auditorium.

Becoming more and more complex, the theatre needed one dominating figure in command. In the waning century, when a play was being rehearsed, its actors were no longer members of a stock company trained to work together, but a group of individuals engaged for a single occasion. Most of those who undertook to co-ordinate stage action were either player-managers (such as Henry Irving at the Lyceum) or authors (such as W. S. Gilbert and Arthur Wing Pinero); but already, before 1900, a new figure was rising, the 'producer'—one day he would be 'director'—a new and governing functionary, a man who neither wrote nor acted, but who gave all his effort to the general ordering of the stage.

There were various other changes. As audiences grew, so did the amount of published drama criticism. Its first great utterances came early in the nineteenth century, from William Hazlitt (who has been said to have 'invented' Edmund Kean) and Leigh Hunt: there were such Victorians as G. H. Lewes, John Oxenford, Henry Morley, Joseph Knight; and in the later years, when William Archer, A. B. Walkley and (for a brief, glittering period, Bernard Shaw) reached the stalls, an impressionist writer, Clement Scott, of *The Daily Telegraph*, had more power than any critic before him. The profession had its own newspapers in *The Era*, and afterwards *The Stage*; and *The Theatre*, born in 1880, was for some time a monthly journal that surpassed anything before it.

Until the last Victorian decades only a few men had closely studied stage history. Then, in a fresh historical-critical approach to the past, scholars began (for example) to speculate on the shape of the Globe Theatre on Bankside and to realize how the stage had altered across the centuries. In a limited way, William Poel's productions for the Elizabethan Stage Society proved the value of these researches. But dramatists too found that a study of the theatre's history enabled them to clarify their ideas; to appreciate the original cause of such and such a convention and why now it might be abandoned or modified. It was the basis for a fresh dramatic theory: studying Shakespeare in his own working conditions, they could see more surely what elements in his work belonged exclusively to his own age, and what might give suggestions to themselves. Antiquarian research delighted such actor-managers as the painstaking (and humourless) Charles Kean, the more exciting and flexible Henry Irving, and Kean's legitimate successor (with an added sense of humour), Herbert Beerbohm Tree. Still, already some were wondering whether ornate stage decoration was worth so much trouble; whether after all the drama had not been more impressive when the stage was a bare platform, something that an audience's responsive imagination must transform to the castle of Macbeth, to Arden, Agincourt or the tall towers of Troy. Lavish spectacle might dominate, but at least the right questions were being asked.

Poetic Plays

Many between 1790 and the realistic 'cup-and-saucer' experiments of T. W. Robertson in the eighteen-sixties pondered upon the 'decline of the drama'. Many authors tried to provide something worthier than facile melodrama or nondescript farce; but almost all these attempts were doomed because they originated not from within the theatre but from without. Instead of coming to the level of the stage and seeking gradually to raise the standards of performance, literary men persisted in standing aloof, self-consciously lowering their precious tragedies and dismally monotonous comedies as though these were divinities, machine-borne, by which alone the evil course of events might be altered. This sense of superiority, allied to a sad ignorance of theatrical conditions, marred practically every effort.

Generally, serious drama in the eighteenth century had been classical, though a certain liberalizing element had intruded because of a genuine enthusiasm for the plays of Shakespeare, Otway and Rowe, and though, in hesitating imitation of these, the stricter forms of the pseudo-classic stage were sometimes abandoned—a sparkle of life gleaming fitfully in scenes otherwise mechanically conceived and hopelessly chilled by convention—the classic mood did predominate. There were two other notable forms: the first, domestic tragedy, inaugurated by Lillo; the second, a type of serious play which might be called pseudo-romantic. Home's *Douglas* belongs to this category, and the work of several other writers, among them the not unimportant Robert Jephson, with his *The Law of Lombardy* (1779), a tragic rendering of the tale told in *Much Ado about Nothing*, and *The Count of Narbonne* (1781), based on the 'romantic' novel of Horace Walpole, *The Castle of Otranto*. Walpole himself provided an even more startling unacted play of the type in *The Mysterious Mother* (1768).

Of these three styles of tragic drama—classic, domestic and pseudo-romantic—the first, quite naturally, received little formal recognition in an age when poets were revolutionaries, battling against the forces of critical restraint imposed on literature by Pope and his companions. There were certainly some belated supporters, such as John Delap, who had started his career with *Hecuba* in 1761, and who carried on his activities until the printing of *Abdalla* in 1803; and there were others who, like Byron, professed an admiration for the old literary laws, and made fitful attempts to follow them in practice. Yet, for the essential purposes, we may say that the rule of the Augustans was dead.

Domestic tragedy, it might have been thought, would have provided legitimate and inspiring activity for the romantics. There was something novel here; the possibility of searching criticism of life; a field comparatively untilled which dramatists might cultivate and sow as they desired. But the poets preferred to soar to realms more fantastically conceived: they preferred the way of Home and of Jephson. These had both been deeply influenced by Shakespeare, an influence that is the most marked feature of the literary drama during the early nineteenth century. Sometimes it becomes confused with the strain of German medievalism—the spectacular excitement of Kotzebue or the sensationalism of Schiller—but everywhere it is apparent. It influences the choice of theme; it induces repetition of imitated characters; it fetters the dramatist to a blank-verse style which, because no longer in its vigorous youth and harmonized to the speech of the age, strikes us as false, shallow and artificial. This Shakespearian influence is deeply marked, at the very beginning of the century, in the plays of John Tobin. The plot of *The Honey Moon (1805)* is a patchwork of ideas taken from *The Taming of the Shrew, Twelfth Night, Romeo and Juliet* and *Henry IV*, with some suggestions from Fletcher's *Rule a Wife and have a Wife*. Rolando is a poor imitation of Benedick who, for purposes of variety, is made to love, not a Beatrice but a Viola, here called Zamora. In *The Curfew* (1807) Shakespearian and 'Gothick' suggestions are allied. Gloomy and dismal caves, marauding robbers, a stock 'Baron', appeals to superstitious sentiment, recognitions of long-lost wives and long-lost sons—all are introduced into a hotchpotch of romantic imaginings, and expressed in language which seems an equal mixture of debased Shakespeare and adulterated Fletcher.

Typical too are the *Plays on the Passions*, issued in three volumes by Joanna Baillie, dated 1798, 1802 and 1812. These are well-meaning enough, but the path of true drama cannot be paved with good intentions alone. Though Joanna Baillie's talent is genuine, and though her language rarely sinks to mediocrity, and rises at times to genuinely impassioned utterance, her work fails because she had no real knowledge of the stage; she was merely a woman of letters condescending to show the theatre what it ought to be; she was not honestly anxious to make herself acquainted with its many requirements. Beyond that, too, her tragedies have their weaknesses. She has gone the wrong way to work. Shakespeare, we may believe, did not say to himself, 'I shall write a play on Jealousy', and turn out *Othello*, or 'I shall write a play on Pride, and turn out *Lear*. The cardinal passion of Shakespeare's dramas depends upon the characters and the theme; Joanna Baillie's plays have character and theme dependent on a preconceived passion, an error shared by other more distinguished poets: Coleridge's *Remorse* is a cardinal instance. Moreover, the greater dramatists do not limit themselves to one emotion. Joanna Baillie never seems to trust herself to speak of pride when her theme is jealousy, or to speak of hate when her theme is ambition. She has successfully documented men's emotions and boxed them up in nice little romantic caskets, to be opened one at a time with excessive care. Still further, her plays can be markedly crude. Her love of murder as a dramatic device stereotypes many of her situations, and her way of revealing the whole pattern of the plot in her first act renders the development of her tragedies uninteresting. The only one of her plays at all successful on the stage was *De Monfort* (acted 1800), and that she owed apparently less to her own genius than to a wonderful piece of stage-carpentry by which the theatre was turned into a fourteenth-century church magnificently decorated.

Of the several members of the early, or 'Wordsworth' group of romantic poets, all tried their hands at play-writing. Take Robert Southey first, because of his influence on the others. His dramas all belong to the early 'pantisocracy' period when he was excited by visions of a millennium heralded by the French Revolution. *The Fall of Robespierre*, written with Coleridge, appeared in 1794, and his enemies issued *Wat Tyler* surreptitiously in 1817 when Southey had long left his youthful republican sentiments and turned to Toryism instead. Both of these plays are pitiful enough, and *Wat Tyler* reads almost like a parody of sentimental, humanitarian melodrama. Samuel Taylor Coleridge was a trifle more successful in his *Remorse* (1813), a revised version of the early *Osorio* which had been sent to Sheridan as early as 1797 and impolitely refused. The far from vital *Remorse* can remind us of Joanna Baillie. Here the evil Ordonio plots against his brother, the upright hero, Don Alvar; after much dramatic complication, during which Ordonio and an honest Moor are slaughtered, Alvar throws off his disguise and the piece ends on a note moderately happy. In general atmosphere it shows clearly the impact of German romantic drama, and its theme of two contrasting brothers closely resembles the popular *Robbers* of Schiller.

For both Coleridge and William Wordsworth abstract philosophic emotions mattered more than any concrete presentation of character. Wordsworth's *The Borderers* (written 1795–6 and published in 1842) may also be traced to Schiller. The crime committed with the best-intentioned motives is clearly a legacy from German drama, but Wordsworth has nothing of Schiller's power over dramatic form. For all its attempts at decoration, this chaotically constructed debate on the fascination of evil makes an exceedingly glum play set during the reign of Henry III in a wild region on the borders of England and Scotland. We are in the company of Marmaduke, who leads an independent band of borderers. A cold voluptuary named Oswald incites the poor man to crime; Wordsworth, who seems throughout to be arguing with himself, oblivious of any possible spectator, pours out unrestrained pages of blank verse in his least inspired mood.

Sir Walter Scott too wrote several plays. His studies in German literature led him early to a rather pedestrian version of Goethe's *Götz von Berlichingen*. Among his later works was a drama called *The Doom of Devorgoil*, a weird blend of melodrama and extravaganza remembered only for its ballad of Bonny Dundee

('To the Lords of Convention 'twas Clav'erse who spoke:/ 'Ere the King's crown shall fall, there are crowns to be broke'). In 1952 the play had an unexpected Pitlochry Festival production which Jean Forbes-Robertson did as much as anyone to animate. Scott's other plays included *The House of Aspen* (1829), thoroughly in the German style and ranking only with such spectacular melo-dramas as *The Castle Spectre;* it has none of the power which had made Scott one of the greatest literary figures in Europe.

Others hoped fondly for success in the theatre. Charles Lamb, who furnished Coleridge with a prologue for *Remorse,* wrote a tragedy, *John Woodvil,* which he called originally *Pride's Cure* (written 1799; printed 1802). This, which Lamb submitted unasked to John Philip Kemble, has the usual defects of the current poetic drama; its poetry (as one would expect) frequently echoes the Elizabethans, but it has no coherent central power, and at best its characterization is a sketchy patchwork. We need not worry about Lamb's fated one-act and one-night farce (no poetry here), *Mr H.,* done at Drury Lane in 1806. Lamb had the delusion about names that Bernard Shaw—not, perhaps, a natural companion—also had in later years. Each of them held that the sound of a funny name could shatter the audience, and Lamb believed in the potency of his Mr Hogsflesh.

Of the Byronic group of romantic authors, Keats, Shelley and Byron all tried to write for the theatre. Keats's lumbering *Otho the Great* was written during about six weeks in 1819 at a period of great emotional strain and passion. Armitage Brown, after agree-ing to give Keats the title, characters and dramatic conduct of a tragedy which Keats would then 'wrap in poetry', described in detail the progress of each scene. The poet, without knowing what might happen later, would obediently put the material into verse—until the fifth act, when he rebelled and wrote as he wished. The plot, set within a single day in tenth-century Ger-many, has a resolute villain and villainess, an injured hero and a distraught heroine; Otho is no more the leading character than, say, Cymbeline. The man who (at various times) the collaborators had hoped that Kean or Macready would play is Ludolph, 'a hot-blooded character' or hysterically abandoned lover. The writ-ing is pictorial and hollow; nothing seems to matter, though the speakers talk at the pitch of their voices and two of them die at the end in and round 'a banqueting hall brilliantly illuminated and set forth with all costly magnificence'. Throughout we have echo upon echo; thus in one speech by Auranthe we can catch the voices of the Attendant Spirit from *Comus* and of Shakespeare's

Richard II (not that the dreary woman is like either). *Otho*, which the impatient authors withdrew from Drury Lane (where it had been accepted), and which came back unopened from Covent Garden, was not acted until a Sunday performance in London during 1950. Appropriately, it was a foggy evening.

Shelley's *The Cenci* (1819) does live in its own right, though we have to guard against overrating it. The plot, one of incest, parricide and retribution, is founded upon the horrors which ended in the extinction of one of the noblest families in Rome—in the year 1599, during the pontificate of Clement VIII. At the centre of the tragedy, as Shelley turned it to his use, are the dreadful Count, violent, cruel, incestuously passionate, and the daughter who—with her stepmother—is driven to murder. Defects are obvious. Many passages are needless dramatically, and Beatrice herself is an oddly contradictory figure. Even so, in our century such actresses as Sybil Thorndike (in 1923, when the play was at length licensed for public performances) and Barbara Jefford (Old Vic, 1959) have been uncommonly moving; and the last speech lingers in the mind. The Cardinal bows before Beatrice when (with her stepmother) she goes out to execution, and she speaks to him very quietly:

> Give yourself no unnecessary pain,
> My dear Lord Cardinal. Here, Mother, tie
> My girdle for me; and bind up this hair
> In any simple knot; ay, that does well.
> And yours, I see, is coming down. How often
> Have we done this for one another; now
> We shall not do it any more. My Lord,
> We are quite ready. Well, 'tis very well.

Lord Byron, among the poets, comes nearest to success. His plays are surer in theatrical technique than those of his companions; and their range, from *Manfred* (1817), through *Marino Faliero, Sardanapalus, The Two Foscari* and *Cain* (all 1821) to *Werner* (1830) is very wide. All reveal the presence of a creative spirit at once more intense than any of the other poets and more in touch with ordinary life. The Romantic writers habitually put themselves forward in their dramas, but though Coleridge, Shelley or Keats could not have been tragic heroes, Byron is in the mould from which Marlowe's heroes were formed. Like Faustus and Tamburlaine, Byron had his aspirations; he was a lonely figure setting himself up against the world. The creator of *Childe Harold*

Edmund Kean as Richard, Duke of Gloucester, in
Richard III

THEATRE ROYAL, COVENT-GARDEN

This prefent FRIDAY. April 30, 1819,

Will be acted the new Tragedy of

EVADNE;

Or, THE STATUE.

With new Scenery, Dreffes, &c.
The Principal Characters by

Mr. ABBOTT,

Mr. MACREADY,

Mr. YOUNG,

Mr. C. KEMBLE,

Mr. CONNOR, Mr. Norris, Mr. George, Mr. White,

Mr. Louis, Mr. Grant,

Mr. Healy, Mr I King, Mr. Guichard,

Mifs O'NEILL,

Mrs. FAUCIT.

After which, will be performed (for the 2d time) a FARCE, (with fome Mufick) called

A Roland for an Oliver

The MUSICK arranged by Mr BISHOP.
The SCENERY painted by Mef. Phillips and Grieve.
The principal Characters by

Mr. FAWCETT,

Mr. JONES,

Mr. ABBOTT,

Mr. EMERY,

Mr. J. ISAACS, Mr. KING,

Mef. Norris, Crumpton, Montague, G Pyne, George, Healy, Parfloe

Mifs FOOTE,

Mifs BEAUMONT, Mifs GREEN.

☞ *NOT AN ORDER can be admitted.*

A Private Box may be had for the Seafon, or nightly, of Mr. Brandon at the Box-office

VIVAT REX.

The new mufical Drama of

THE HEART OF MID-LOTHIAN,

creates the moft heartfelt intereft—and is received throughout with every expreffion of applaufe & fatisfaction—It will be repeated Tomorrow, Monday,
and Tuefday

On account of the great demand for Places,

The Tragedy of EVADNE will be repeated this evening.

The New Farce of

A ROLAND FOR AN OLIVER.

having been received throughout with a continued roar of laughter, and
fhouts of univerfal applaufe,
will be repeated every evening till further notice.

On Wednefday will be produced, for the firft time, a NEW TRAGEDY, which has been long
in preparation, (with new Scenes, Dreffes and Decorations) called

FREDOLFO.

The principal characters by

Mr. YOUNG, Mr. C. KEMBLE, Mr. YATES, Mr. CONNOR,
Mr. MACREADY, Mr. EGERTON, Mr. JEFFERIES, Mr. COMER,
Mifs O'NEILL.

A Covent Garden playbill, 1819

A water melodrama at Sadler's Wells: a print
illustrating the atmosphere in the minor theatres of
the early nineteenth century

Mrs Patrick Campbell as Paula in Pinero's *The Second Mrs Tanqueray*, 1893, painted by Solomon J. Solomon

Henry Irving as King Lear, 1892, drawn by Bernard Partridge

and of *Don Juan* might well have had the stuff of which great drama is made, and in fact his plays are not without their own value. *Manfred*, theatrically the weakest, fully exhibits his appreciation of grandiose ambition, his misanthropic hatred and his feeling for nature's solitary spaces. In *Werner; or, The Inheritance*, with decayed palace, raging night, secret passage, remarkable disclosure, we can see more clearly the German influence; dedicated to Goethe, it bears the stamp both of *Götz von Berlichingen* and of Schiller's *Die Räuber*. Siegendorf, disguised as Werner, is set against his arch-enemy Stralenheim, who is murdered by young Ulric, Werner's son. An innocent soldier is accused of the crime, and, in searching for the truth, Werner (acted by William Charles Macready in his own version) is led to recognize that the guilt lies immediately with his own son, and, ultimately, with the pride and passion he had inspired in that son's heart. The story, although improbably melodramatic, contains some not ineffective scenes. *Sardanapalus*, too, with its complex hero, effeminate, yet capable of heroic action, and its skilfully drawn heroine, is impressive in the spectacular-sentimental vein, but even here, as in the other plays, we feel something lacking. The total effect is vitiated by an unrelieved and constant stress upon a few 'passions' which become in the end drearily monotonous.

Still, though Byron knew so much more about the theatre than did his contemporary poets—he was for a long time on the Board of Drury Lane—he does seem now to speak to us at several removes. Maybe there is an unfortunate confession, expressed unconsciously in a line and a half from *Childe Harold* on the city of Venice:

And Otway, Radcliffe, Schiller, Shakespeare's art,
Had stamped her image in me.

'Radcliffe' is a reference to *The Mysteries of Udolpho*; Byron had some of Otway, some of Schiller, too much perhaps of Anne Radcliffe. Possibly stage production could animate much that is cold upon the page. *The Two Foscari* and *Marino Faliero* are tragedies of Venice. Francis Foscari is the eighty-year-old Doge who dies when the bell of St Mark's is already sounding for his successor; Macready is remembered, among other things, for the rhetoric of the Doge condemned to die. Each play has a certain dramatic drive.

Apart from the major poets, several other writers endeavoured to persuade audiences of their worth and were successively hailed as prophets of a new age. Charles Robert Maturin won transitory fame with his *Bertram* (1816), produced by Kean at the solicitation of Lord Byron. This, as well as the showy *Manuel* (1817) and *Fredolpho* (1819), is marked by its sense of verbal beauty, but excessive sentimentality and pathos reduce all these plays to minor dramatic importance. Richard Lalor Sheil failed because he tried to capture the stage by storm, heaping excess upon excess in wild confusion. *Adelaide* (1814) is a typically German-type play on the French Revolution, and *The Apostate* (1817) is full of grandiloquent passages which often sink to bathos. Sometimes Sheil comes as near as any of his contemporaries to a truly dramatic note, yet none of his plays, with their admixture of Elizabethan, romantic and 'Germanic' elements, can stir our hearts today.

Henry Hart Milman was another of these men. *Fazio* (1816) was designed as an 'attempt at reviving our old national drama with greater simplicity of plot', but it fails because of its rambling blank verse and its want of intensity. The plot, a peculiar one, is concerned mainly with the alchemist Fazio, in whose home Bartolo, an old miser, dies. Fazio seizes the man's bag of gold and then pretends he has found the philosopher's stone. In a fit of jealousy his wife accuses him of Bartolo's murder; and he is arrested and hanged, while she dies of remorse. It is hardly a theme for tragic treatment. William Sotheby turned to Russia for the material of his *Ivan* (1816), a poorly contrived drama of palace intrigue and would-be philosophical sentiment, typical, in its lack of coherence, of so many tragedies of the time. The few tragedies of Mary Russell Mitford, *Julian* (1823), *The Foscari* (1826) and *Rienzi* (1828), do possess individuality and a few telling scenes, but again they exist in a literary-imaginative world far removed from the contemporary stage.

It seemed for a while that one writer might draw the literary drama from the rut of mediocrity or incompetence, but we realize now that James Sheridan Knowles had nothing fresh to give to the drama of his period. More than most of his companions, he was prepared to use devices to fix the attention of an audience; he had sufficiently lofty ideals and critical acumen enough to keep his aim steady; and he understood something of the middle-class demands of the contemporary theatre. More than once, too, he had Macready to interpret him. Yet with all this he had, at core, nothing new to present. *Virginius* (1820) is merely a bourgeois rendering of a classic story ('The scene is the Forum', said R. H. Horne, 'but the sentiments are those of the Bedford Arms');

William Tell (1825) is only a superior melodrama; and *The Wife; A Tale of Mantua* (1833) is hopelessly artificial in its romantic mode, with long-lost loves miraculously revealed.

Later writers followed energetically. Walter Savage Landor, without much dramatic craft, early essayed tragedy in *Count Julian* (1812), and again, after a quarter of a century, in *Andrea of Hungary* and *Giovanna of Naples* (1839) and in *The Siege of Ancona* (1846). Various plays by his brother, Robert Eyres Landor, were no more significant. Thomas Noon Talfourd came closer to the theatre with his classically based *Ion* (1836), hailed by many as the long-awaited drama destined to lead men towards a new world. The tragedy cannot hold us now as it held the imagination of Macready, reflecting on it in his country garden under the high, bright moon of a May night. Today it must strike us as rather prim and frigid, apt to run into such a soliloquy as this:

Adrastus Yet stay—he's gone—his spell is on me yet;
  What have I promised him? To meet the men
  Who from my living head would strip the crown,
  And sit in judgment on me?—I must do it—
  Yet shall my band be ready to o'erawe
  The course of liberal speech, and if it rise
  So as too loudly to offend my ear,
  Strike the rash brawler dead!—What idle dream
  Of long-past days had melted me? It fades—
  It vanishes—I am again a King!

Talfourd was just as unrewarding with the romantic theme of his later *Glencoe; or, The Fate of the Macdonalds* (1840). It was a play (with a subject from the previous century) that again refused to rise from the careful patterns of its text.

Everywhere the story was the same. Blank verse meandered through classic or Shakespearian meadows, but it was never allied to true dramatic authority. Great poets fared no better than the minor ones. Robert Browning should have had genuine dramatic qualities: he was not merely a man for the melodious cadence that would soon pall, or for sub-Shakespearian repetitions. He had a dominant will, a knowledge of men and a love of reality; in mid-career he would create his famous gallery of 'Men and Women'. Undoubtedly he was qualified beyond most to write the strong and durable drama. Yet, with the rest, he failed. Several things prevented him from achieving anything truly vital. His love of the soliloquy, admirably suited for 'dramatic lyrics', does not meet theatrical demands. His love for the odd, the peculiar, the extraordinary, grows tiresome when exploited throughout the length of a play.

True, his introduction could have been auspicious. Macready (ever the name) asked him especially for a play ('Will you write me a tragedy and save me from going to America?'). The dutiful result was the over-rhetorical *Strafford*, written in ten days, produced in 1837 and soon discarded. The chaotic splendour of the poem *Sordello* intervened between *Strafford* and Browning's next plays *King Victor and King Charles* (1842) and *The Return of the Druses* (1843). The first was one of his nearest approaches to dramatic success. Confining himself to four characters, he has been able to concentrate and animate his scenes. Victor, resolute and occasionally treacherous; his son Charles, perplexed and at odds with himself; Charles's noble wife; and the politician D'Ormea are impressively manœuvred. *The Return of the Druses* evokes a Syrian race, living under the domination of the Templars. Goaded to rebellion by an old Prefect's tyranny, these men accept Djabal, a born leader, as a god reincarnated to free them from oppression; and in consequence they reject the efforts of an honest member of his order to release them from their bondage. The age found in neither play what it sought. Bold and imaginative plot and treatment do not compensate for a lack of theatrical vigour and for dialogue marred by obscurities, and these defects are even more apparent in the later *Blot in the 'Scutcheon* (1843) and *Colombe's Birthday* (1844; acted 1853).

If Browning, of all people, failed, we cannot wonder that others gave even less than he to the stage. Thomas Lovell Beddoes, certainly, had a true eye for the needs of the time. 'The man', he said, 'who is to awake the drama must be a bold, trampling fellow. . . . With the greatest reverence for all the antiquities of the drama I still think that we had better beget than revive—attempt to give the literature of this age an idiosyncrasy and spirit of its own.' What he produced himself was *Death's Jest Book* (completed in its first form 1826; printed 1850) with its macabre visions, its violently passionate blank verse, and its lyrics, all reminiscent of the Jacobean Webster and Tourneur. There are certainly fine passages:

> To trust in story
> In the old times Death was a feverish sleep,
> In which men walked. The other world was cold
> And thinly-peopled, so life's emigrants
> Came back to mingle with the crowds of earth;
> But now great cities are transported thither,

> Memphis, and Babylon, and either Thebes,
> And Priam's towery town with its one beech,
> And dead are most and merriest; so be sure
> There will be no more haunting till their towns
> Are full to the garret; then they'll shut their gates,
> To keep the living out, and perhaps leave
> A dead or two between both kingdoms.

Jeremiah Wells's much-praised *Joseph and His Brethren*, originally published in 1824 and frequently revised up to 1879, owes its being to a literary and not to a dramatic impulse. Even the more theatrical plays of Richard Henry Horne—*Cosmo de Medici* (1837), *The Death of Marlowe* (1837), *Gregory VII* (1840) and *Judas Iscariot* (1848)—although imaginative in conception and written in a style more apt for the stage betray the general weakness. They are imitations of earlier dramatic activity; they are out of touch with their age.

During the last quarter of the century many men imagined that Lord Tennyson might be the man likely to re-establish a vital poetic drama. With the support of the Kendals and of Henry Irving, he managed to get a hearing from the public, but the reception of those tragedies that were staged was polite, formal and dictated rather by regard for his non-dramatic verse than by any theatrical enthusiasm. *Queen Mary* (1876) cannot fully sustain its theme; but *Harold* ('Here rose the dragon-banner of our realm;/Here fought, here fell our Norman-slander'd King') does have some declamatory vigour: it was printed in 1877, and just over half a century later Barry Jackson staged it at the Court, with Laurence Olivier, the Harold, in one of his first major parts. *Becket* (printed 1879, revised by Irving, 1893) may be remembered only for Irving's performance and the fact that his last words before death at Bradford were Becket's 'Into Thy hands, O Lord—into Thy hands!' It does lack, in the words of Beddoes, 'an idiosyncrasy and spirit of its own'.

Undeniably, we must respect the general aim of these poets in devoting themselves to the stage—a wish to invest the drama with poetic fire and to revive Shakespearian glories. Yet we have to admit that, for various reasons, none had the quality to fulfil so laudable a purpose.

Melodrama, Farces and Extravaganzas

For the energy, the theatrical sense and the air of excitement so lacking in the serious poetic dramas of this period we have to turn to an entirely different world. One of the potent forces which led to the establishment of melodrama at the turn of the century was the impact of the contemporary German theatre, and we must note the peculiar fact that the same plays which had so impressed the poets also stimulated the hack-writers they despised. During the decade from 1790 to 1800 publishers were busily printing translations of German dramas; most of these were never staged, but the extraordinary number of editions many of them reached shows how avidly they were read. Nothing quite like this had been known in earlier years. There can be no doubt that several of the dramas, written by men of high distinction, Lessing, Goethe and Schiller, were genuinely important; *Die Räuber* (disappointingly revived in London in 1976) was a notable achievement, and even Goethe's youthful *Götz von Berlichingen* was framed in a richly imaginative form. We need not wonder that they excited the romantic poets who took them as models. On the other side, the structure of these plays has a decidedly 'melodramatic' quality; here are ruined castles, the trappings of 'Gothicism', the outlaws, the noble heroes, the distressed heroines—all capable of captivating the less literary and less exalted. Moreover, many German plays brought to the notice of the English public were by men who certainly had none of the masters' power. Among these August von Kotzebue won most esteem; in several respects he was accomplished; he knew the stage well, and in some of his plays, such as *Menschenhaus und Reue* and *Falsche Scham*, he showed that his purposes were serious, if sentimental. Yet his work, far more than the others', descends towards the melodramatic. For many English readers at that period the newly discovered German drama meant Kotzebue (Sheridan's version of *Pizarro*, for example) rather than Schiller and Goethe. From 1786, when James Johnstone prepared the first rendering of a German drama—*The Disbanded Officer*, adapted from Lessing's *Minna von Barnhelm*—the chief theatrical influence of these plays was towards increased sentimentalism, to stock characters, to the insertion of sensational scenes, and, in fine, the exploitation of 'Gothick' material, or material of an exotic type which, in its strangeness, could create a kindred mood among the public.

Meanwhile, in the midst of this, there was fresh news from Paris. There Guilbert de Pixérécourt was setting himself up as Kotzebue's French counterpart, and Holcroft's version (1802) of *Cœlina, ou l'enfant du mystère*, under the title of *A Tale of Mystery*, introduced a play commonly regarded as the first true melodrama on the English stage. We must always bear in mind that the French and German influences were not against native English tradition, and that their force was due, not so much to their novelty as to their expression, in a more emphatic form, of a trend amply visible in the London theatre's eighteenth-century repertories. The sentimental hero of Steele's *The Conscious Lovers* is the direct ancestor of the hero, eager to rescue innocence in distress, who appears in such a play as Thomas Morton's *Speed the Plough* (1800)—with its famous Mrs Grundy ('what will Mrs Grundy say?')—hovering on the border between serious comedy and frank melodrama; the line of development from Home's *The Fatal Discovery* to James Boaden's *Fontainville Forest* (1794) is easy to trace. In this piece (set in the fifteenth century against a ruined Gothic abbey) the villain, a Marquis, finds that the heroine he covets as his mistress is actually the daughter of his own brother whom long since he had murdered. Whereupon he commits suicide. All the accessories of the romantic melodramatists are here: an ancient abbey, a highway robbery dictated by abject hunger, a ghost in a darkened room, a long-concealed murder startlingly exposed—and this as early as 1794, before ever Pixérécourt and Kotzebue had become familiar to English audiences.

Similar melodramatic plots captured the English theatre at the beginning of the century, and, coming by the hundred, they would exert their hold for many years. A few examples will serve. *The Iron Chest* (1796), based by George Colman the younger on William Godwin's novel *Caleb Williams*, can stand for plays transitional between the ebb of the sentimental style and melodrama proper. Here Sir Edward Mortimer, head-keeper of the New Forest, has been tried for murder and acquitted; when the noble Wilford discovers this, Mortimer—to get rid of him—accuses him of robbery. But Wilford is the hero, and because heroes must always win, a document that has been strangely concealed in an iron chest finally reveals the crime. Closely related in plan and execution is William Dimond's *The Foundling of the Forest*, produced more than a decade later, in 1809. Here the villain is a Baron Longueville. Loving Geraldine, daughter of De Valmont, he seeks to murder Florian, a foundling. His plot fails; meantime, it is discovered that De Valmont's long-lost wife still lives; and the Baron's conscience-stricken agent discloses that Florian is really De Valmont's son. Again a story of criminal purpose and of distressed virtue triumphant.

Nearly all the settings for these early melodramas were medieval or Oriental, and many used supernatural effects. Such writers as 'Monk' Lewis, in *The Castle Spectre* of 1797 and *Adelmorn the Outlaw* (1801), tried every kind of eerie and sensational incident. In a passage from the second, Ulric is the villain, intent upon slaying the innocent Adelmorn; Lodowick is the comic honest man, companioned by Hugo, a ministrel, and Innogen is the distressed heroine. Ulric, confronted by the forces of the good, is ordered to swear his innocence. He begins to obey:

Ulric As I have hopes of happiness hereafter, by all that is holy in Heaven, by all that is fearful in Hell, I swear that—
> [*As he proceeds, the* Ghost *rises slowly with a flaming dagger in his hand, and stands opposite to* Ulric, *who stops and remains gazing upon him for some time without motion.*

Sigismond Why stop you?
Ulric [*motionless*]. My Lord!
Sigismond What gaze you at?
Ulric My Lord!
Sigismond Proceed.
Ulric He cannot be a witness in his own cause.
Sigismond Who?
Ulric He! He! My uncle! See you not my dagger? Flames curl round it! Lo he points to his bleeding bosom! But 'tis false—'tis false! The wound I gave him was not half so deep!
> [*All utter a cry of mingled joy and horror.*

Innogen [*wild with joy*]. Heard ye that? Heard ye that? O, father, heard ye that?   [*Embracing* Sigismond.
Adelmorn They are Ulric's lips, but the voice is Heaven's!
Ulric Look off me! I cannot bear thy glance! Flames shoot from thine eyeballs, and fire my brain! O, look off me!
Sigismond Mark how passion shakes him.
Ulric [*frantic*]. Thy grave was deep: why hast thou left it? To save thy darling? To drag me to the block prepared for him? This prevents it! [*Drawing his dagger, and rushing towards the* Ghost, *who till now has remained fixed like a statue, but on his approach raises his arm with a terrible look and motions to stab him.* Ulric *utters a cry of horror.*] Mercy! I am guilty, but not fit to die!
> [*He falls on the ground, while the* Ghost *sinks.*

Lewis explained, rather charmingly, of one of his characters in *Adelmorn*: 'I must again request the reader to observe that, wherever Lodowick's speeches appear *ludicrous*, he is supposed to intend them to produce that effect.'

The same atmosphere breathes in Edward Fitzball's *The Flying Dutchman; or, The Phantom Ship*, produced fifteen years later, in 1827. Here we find ourselves in the 'Devil's Cave':

An overhanging rock, leading into the cave—a grotesque rock in the centre resembling an antique table, and massy book, closed. Music. LESTELLE *discovered, supporting herself against the rock in an attitude of distress.* VANDERDECKEN *comes down, with a torch and points to the magic book.*

Lestelle Thine, earthly or unearthly, never! Terrible being, thou mayst indeed trample on my mortal frame, but the soul of Lestelle is far above thy malice.

> [*Music. He is angry. He takes her hand, and, approaching the book, it flies open and displays hieroglyphics.* LESTELLE *screams and sinks at the base of the rock. Footsteps heard without.* VANDERDECKEN *listens.*

Mowdrey [*calling*]. Lestelle! I am here! You are safe! [*He descends and sees* VANDERDECKEN.] Ah, wretch, is it thou! Tremble!

> [*Music.* VANDERDECKEN *laughs, then draws a sword. A terrific fight.* MOWDREY, *after repeatedly stabbing his opponent in vain, is taken up by* VANDERDECKEN *and furiously thrown down.*

Vanderdecken Mortal, die! [*Thunder.*] Ah, what have I done? [*He displays bodily agony.*] I have spoken. [*Music.*] The spell which admits my stay on earth is destroyed with my silence. I must begone to my phantom ship again, to the deep and howling waters. But ye, the victims of my love and fury, yours is a dreadful fate—a hundred years here, in torpid life, to lie entombed till my return. Behold!

> [*Points to the book. A chord.*

Melodrama was written in exclamation marks; it plunged into blazing gulfs; it was lit by Germanic marsh-lights; it thundered and volleyed. English poetry was in its high midsummer; but the stage could merely shake a thunder-sheet over 'a castle decayed and partly ruinous' or 'A half-ruined castle—on one side the entrance to a dungeon'. Even while we note the basic clichés, we should remember that melodrama was always vital enough to satisfy changing tastes. Authors in search of fresh plots went very soon to the flourishing world of contemporary fiction. Sir Walter Scott had many stories which, when stripped down to the bone, could be easily adapted to melodramatic requirements: thus *Rob Roy* contained the stock bandit of sympathetic heart, a hero in young Osbaldistone, a graceful heroine (with the usual secret) in Diana Vernon and a thorough villain in Rashleigh Osbaldistone. Since there was no dramatic copyright, the melodramatists were free to use this heaven-sent material as much as they desired. Hearts of Midlothian throbbed on every stage.

Partly through this research in the world of fiction, partly because of altering tastes, melodramatic themes began to change during the thirties and forties of the century. Having ransacked Scott, 'minor' playwrights quite naturally looked back to the fiction-writers of earlier years. They tried their hand at Fielding and Smollett, and discovered in Defoe an author who, because of his love of action, well suited their purposes. But when one of them had turned, say, *Moll Flanders* into a play, and when others followed with kindred picaresque themes (such as B. N. Webster, in 1832, with his *Paul Clifford, the Highwayman of 1770*), it was found possible to approach contemporary life more nearly than the customary bizarre or romantic stories would allow. The way now was clear for the 'naturalistic' melodrama, a form given fresh impetus by the dramatization of Dickens's novels. These, full of character and exciting incident, were avidly seized; proof-sheets were snatched as they came wet from the press; as many as half a dozen separate dramatic versions of a novel were produced within a week of its publication. Through such plays the public became accustomed to see familiar scenes presented in the now accepted melodramatic style: in sobbing over Little Nell and hissing Scrooge, they discovered a fresh and added excitement because Little Nell was nearer to them than a shadowy Adeline and Scrooge a more potent villain than a nebulous Marquis.

From this it was only a step to the sentimental depiction of all kinds of life—mostly lower-class life—known to the spectators. Usually, for action and sensation were obligatory, the themes had some background of crime, war or rebellion, and, as the century advanced, dramatists became progressively ingenious with plots likely to appeal to popular audiences. Actual contemporary murders were put upon the stage; Maria Marten would die again and again in the Red Barn. The introduction of domestic melodrama, allied to the effects of the epoch-making Theatre Act of 1843, soon brought something new. Minor dramatists, who turned from the Middle Ages, the East and the supernatural to the common themes of daily existence, quite naturally lost some of their artificiality of style and sought to fortify the new naturalism. Sometimes they were unable to imagine anything better than the introduction of familiar objects—street-lamps, or hansom-cabs, or later, actual weapons used by the criminals who were their protagonists. Then, gradually adopting subtler methods, their technique was improved. Though fuller 'realism' could not be developed from the melodramatic style, these plays took at least a step towards the dramatists of 1890–1920. Whatever we may think of the theatre's too enduring realism, we can welcome this nineteenth-century change from the chill rhetoric of classic and romantic literary drama.

The work of such men as Tom Taylor and Charles Reade is

much stronger than the earlier melodramas. Sometimes, it is true—as in *Two Loves and a Life* (1854), written by Reade and Taylor in collaboration—they might choose a romantic theme: here one from the rising of 1745. But their domestic melodramas are most typical: Taylor's *Still Waters Run Deep* and *The Ticket-of-Leave Man* (1863) treat the contemporary criminal world with a shrewdness unknown before. Even the young Henry Arthur Jones could attempt this form. In *The Silver King* (1882) he produced a vigorous melodrama, ascribed to him and the negligible Henry Herman, that pleased even Matthew Arnold. It contains a famous line with a long pedigree: 'O God, put back Thy universe and give me yesterday.'

From about 1840 the literary drama was correspondingly popularized. The author known best as Bulwer Lytton (he was then Edward Lytton Bulwer) had written *The Lady of Lyons* for Macready in 1838; and Dion Boucicault's *London Assurance*, put on by Vestris at Covent Garden, arrived in 1841. Each in its own way is important. *The Lady of Lyons* (and other plays such as *Richelieu*, with its 'curse of Rome' speech, would succeed it) showed 'literary' authors how to make their work more immediately acceptable. In *Lyons* (the period is 1795, post-Revolution) Claude Melnotte, a peasant who has vainly loved a proud beauty, Pauline—'as pretty as Venus and as proud as Juno'—woos her in his disguise as the Prince of Como. Two of Pauline's rejected suitors had planned the trick to discredit her; but, given his chance, Claude speaks to Pauline (who had never known him as the gardener's son) with a passionate eloquence. They are married; there is a fatal revelation; then, after more than two years, Claude (as a Colonel and a hero) and his wife are happily reunited. The passage for the lovers in the second act became a theatrical show-piece:

Claude Nay, dearest, nay, if thou would'st have me paint
 The home to which, could Love fulfil its prayers,
 This hand would lead thee, listen! A deep vale
 Shut out by Alpine hills from the rude world;
 Near a clear lake, margin'd by fruits of gold
 And whispering myrtles! glassing softest skies
 As cloudless, save with rare and roseate shadows,
 As I would have thy fate!
Pauline My own dear love!
Claude A palace lifting to eternal summer
 Its marble walls, from out a glossy bower
 Of coolest foliage musical with birds

Whose songs should syllable thy name! At noon
We'd sit beneath the arching vines and wonder
Why Earth could be unhappy, while the Heavens
Still left us youth and love!

Lytton's comedy *Money* (1840) has a more positive significance. Playgoers in the mid-nineteenth-century theatre were largely middle-class. This tale of a will and its legatee, a poor relation who tests the affections of two girls and of his entourage, proved that Lytton, unlike other literary dramatists, knew how spectators were asking for comedy and tragedy expressive of their own conditions.

Much of Dion Boucicault's work also deals with the social life of the day. *London Assurance*, 'made to order, on the shortest possible notice', when the young Irishman was twenty, was a stock piece for many years: it came back, received almost as new, in a Royal Shakespeare Company revision during the summer of 1970: in 1932 Barry Jackson had put on the original text at a Malvern Festival. It is a mercurial comedy with a complex of wooings and a plot that shifts from Belgravia to Gloucestershire; there is no need to linger with the obvious derivations, for the result is Boucicault's own and might be called, after one of its most actable parts, a gay spanker. The principal figure, Sir Harcourt Courtly, is the vainest of elderly bucks, who fancies himself as an animated Greek marble; curled and petulant, he insists for his own comfort that he has never looked stupid in his life. Donald Sinden, who acted the massive, pouting Narcissus for the RSC, resembled the Prince Regent crossed with Max Beerbohm's Lord George Hell. In *The School for Scheming* (1847) Boucicault discusses aristocratic fashions, the ambitions of the merchant class, the virtues of the poor. Though a sentimentalist, he had a swift instinct for the theatre. His Irish melodramas, in which he joined theatrical sensation to a genuinely humorous spirit, were justifiably applauded: *The Colleen Bawn* (1860), *Arrah-na-Pogue; or, The Wicklow Wedding* (1864) and *The Shaughraun* (1874) still possess virtues of their own.

Away from melodrama and sentimental comedy, the purely comic theatre, with one exception, continued to languish in vapid opera and stupid farce: primitive, often coarse, physical action had replaced epigram and glittering metaphor. But the exception is important. Early-nineteenth-century audiences were not always unaware that the work they enjoyed was essentially foolish: beside sentimental melodrama there flourished the burlesque, and though it produced no masterpiece—for the many travesties of *Hamlet* or of current serious drama were mostly faint and repetitive—the burlesque style did contribute to a form entirely of its age, and usually called 'extravaganza'. For its English vogue we have chiefly to thank James Robinson Planché, a prolific writer who began with *Amoroso, King of Little Britain* (1818) and continued until the second half of the century. His extravaganzas abound in puns; his style can be rough; his ideas are often weak and trivial—but he did achieve one thing: the translation of a romantic love of the wonderful from an impossible Orientalism, and from a medieval atmosphere absurdly broadened, to something honestly fresh and creative. To lightly touched satire and burlesque he joined the imagination of fairytale: consider, say, *Olympic Revels; or, Prometheus and Pandora* (1831), mingling spectacle, topical allusion and a parody of classical legend. Planché himself also altered the costume of burlesque; before him its characters were dressed as vulgarly as might be, whereas he insisted on dresses as rich and historically accurate as he could devise. This speaks for his work: the bringing of delicacy and refinement to a form that had been insensitively crude. Other authors followed him. Robert Brough had an early success with *Camaralzaman and Badoura; or, The Peri who loved a Prince* (1848); Brough, in his turn, bequeathed the style to H. J. Byron, so copious during the 1860s and 1870s. Byron was a determined word-twister, but probably the most redoubtable pun of its time turned up in *The Field of the Cloth of Gold* (1868) by William Brough, Robert's brother. Here a character, disembarking in France, observed:

Yesterday all was fair, a glorious Sunday,
But this sick transit spoils the glory o'Monday.

It was then that W. S. Gilbert arrived. His dramatic career began during the seventies in a variety of moods. He was a cynical, satirical wit; he enjoyed parody and burlesque, and he added a personal and strangely poetic fancy and a whimsical humour. Seeing the other side of the picture as the romantic poets could not, he managed to retain something of their fervour. Always too he kept the paradoxical, topsy-turvy manner which added 'Gilbertian' to our language. His qualities were at once apparent in *The Palace of Truth* (1870): all who enter the enchanted place must speak the truth, so a cold princess becomes hysterically passionate; a gushing prince, blasé and chill; a man sardonically bitter, a genial philosopher. *Pygmalion and Galatea* (1871) is more serious, with an element of sadness—often concealed elsewhere—that is emphatically expressed in *Broken Hearts* (1875); at more or less the same time Gilbert was writing the farce of *Tom Cobb* (1875), and his sharpest work away from the Savoy operas, the mischievously witty *Engaged* (1877) which the National Theatre company would revive at the Old Vic (1975) without the acclamation it needed.

Gilbert's most shining and durable triumphs are the libretti of the so-called Savoy operas, preserved for us down the years by the dedicated D'Oyly Carte company. He had an invaluable composer in Arthur Sullivan; their partnership, broken in life, remains unbreakable in history. The libretti can be satirical, as in *Patience; or, Bunthorne's Bride* (1881) and its demolition of the aesthetic 'sunflower' cult; but few who go now to the operas, to *Iolanthe; or, The Peer and the Peri* (1882), *The Mikado; or, The Town of Titipu* (1885), the more serious *The Yeomen of the Guard* (1888), with one of Gilbert's finest lyrics, 'Is life a boon?'), and *The Gondoliers; or, The King of Barataria* (1889), think first of the sting behind the laughter, serious purpose behind apparently irrepressible paradox. Gilbert, by no means an easy man, was one of the uncommon dramatists of his century. However original his genius, he rose not from the poets who aspired to the stage, but from those despised writers of melodrama, burlesque and the farcical sketch. There could be no better example of the vitality of one group and the theatrical sterility of the other.

The Dramatic Revival

Between the years 1845 and 1865 a young man, then quite obscure, was busy with a sequence of melodramas, farces and comediettas. They were no different from scores of others by contemporary theatrical hacks. *The Battle of Life* (1847), *The Haunted Man* (1849), *The Star of the North* (1855), *The Muleteer of Toledo* (1856), *The Half-Caste; or, The Poisoned Pearl* (1856)—these followed each other rapidly, most of them for production at such popular outlying theatres as the Grecian and Surrey. Only one play, and that at the close of his twenty years' activity, seemed more ambitious than the rest: *David Garrick*, a comedy-drama which, after opening in Birmingham, arrived in 1864 at the Haymarket.

Then, in 1865, Liverpool audiences saw the first performances of *Society*; six months later, when Marie Wilton and H. J. Byron presented it at the old Prince of Wales's Theatre in Tottenham Street, its author, T. W. (Tom) Robertson, was recognized as a new and valuable dramatist. Encouraged, he went on to several plays with similarly laconic titles, *Ours* (1866), *Caste* (1867), *Play* (1868), *Home* (1869), *School* (1869), *M.P.* (1870) and others. Most of them, after Byron had left in 1867, were put on by Marie Wilton and another partner: in 1867 she married her principal actor, Squire Bancroft, but for some time he did not share in the management. Robertson's domestic plays were known as the 'teacup-and-saucer' theatre. As one critic observed, he wished to urge the public to bring their 'fireside concerns' to the Prince of Wales's, and he sought to do it by making his plots and characters and settings as realistic as he possibly could. He delighted his audiences by using not the old conventional flats in which doors were merely canvas frames with the knobs painted in, but more solidly built scenery (real knobs and all): visually and verbally, he aimed at realism.

This, of course, is a relative term, and today Robertson seems to be artificial. But he did carry realism as far as his contemporary audiences would permit, and his work keeps an appealing charm. One of his virtues was his insistence on bringing life into the theatre. While he abandoned the distressed maidens and black villains and impossibly noble heroes, he strove to avoid any doctrinaire approach. With a basic creed essentially Victorian, he took a wide view of the world around him. The loudness of the profiteer, Mr Chodd, in *Society* is no more an object of attack than the egocentric meanness of Lady Ptarmigant; the brutality of Eccles in *Caste* is not emphasized more than the thoughtlessness of Hawtree and the thoroughly obnoxious pretensions of the Marchioness.

In style, too, he was individual. Though at times we still recognize the stilted tone of the sentimental drama, at others Robertson is trying his best to make these people speak naturally. Here is the scene in *Caste* when George D'Alroy shocks his mother, the Marchioness, by telling her that he is married to Esther Eccles:

George Stay, mother. [MARCHIONESS *turns slightly away.*] Before you go [GEORGE *has raised* ESTHER *from sofa in both arms*] let me present to you Mrs George D'Alroy. *My wife!*
Marchioness Married!
George Married.
> [*The* MARCHIONESS *sinks into an easy-chair.* GEORGE *replaces* ESTHER *on sofa, but still retains her hand. Three hesitating taps*

at door are heard. GEORGE *crosses to door, opens it, discovers* ECCLES, *who enters.* GEORGE *drops down back of* MARCHIO-NESS'S *chair.*

Eccles They told us to come up. When your man came, Polly was out, so I thought I should do instead. [*Calling at door.*] Come up, Sam.

[*Enter* SAM *in his Sunday clothes, with short cane and smoking a cheroot. He nods and grins.* POLLY *points to* MARCHIONESS. SAM *takes cheroot from his mouth and quickly removes his hat.*

Sam had just called, so we three—Sam and I and your man—all came in the 'ansom cab together. Didn't we, Sam?

[ECCLES *and* SAM *go over to the girls, and* ECCLES *drops down to front of table, smilingly.*

Marchioness [*with glasses up, to* GEORGE]. Who is this?

George My wife's father.

Marchioness What is he?

George A—nothing.

Eccles I am one of nature's noblemen. Happy to see you, my lady. [*Turning to her.*] Now my daughters have told me who you are—[GEORGE *turns his back in an agony as* ECCLES *crosses to* MAR-CHIONESS]—we old folks, fathers and mothers of the young couples, ought to make friends. [*Holding out his dirty hand.*]

Marchioness [*shrinking back*]. Go away! [ECCLES *goes back to table again, disgusted.*] What's his name?

George Eccles.

Marchioness Eccles! Eccles! There never was an Eccles. He don't exist.

Eccles Don't he, though. What d'ye call this?

[*Goes up again to back of table as* SAM *drops down. He is just going to take a decanter, when* SAM *stops him.*

Marchioness No Eccles was ever born!

George He takes the liberty of breathing notwithstanding. [*Aside.*] And I wish he wouldn't!

Marchioness And who is the little man? Is he also Eccles?

[SAM *looks round.* POLLY *gets up close to him, and looks with defiant glance at the* MARCHIONESS.

George No.

Marchioness Thank goodness! What then?

George His name is Gerridge.

Marchioness Gerridge! It breaks one's teeth. Why is he here?

George He is making love to Polly, my wife's sister.

Marchioness And what is he?

George A gasman.

Marchioness He looks it. [GEORGE *goes up to* ESTHER.] And what is she—the—the sister?

[ECCLES, *who has been casting longing eyes at the decanter, edges towards it, and when he thinks no one is noticing, fills wine-glass.*

Polly [*asserting herself indignantly*]. I'm in the ballet at the Theatre Royal,

Lambeth. So was Esther. We're not ashamed of what we are! We have no cause to be.

That is a fair specimen of Robertson's dialogue. Reading it, we should remember that 'realistic' dialogue, however it may echo the speech of its day, must sound old-fashioned within a few years. Little can escape that fate. Even so, when *Caste* is revived today, that scene comes through as speakable and acceptable. One other thing. In the very full stage directions we see Robertson's keen awareness of the need to bind together words and action and of the inability of ordinary words to express what he wishes. Conscious of the realistic dramatist's constant problem, he falls back (as so many twentieth-century writers would) upon gesture and stage movement when words fail.

Though Robertson himself did not carry his work far, he deeply influenced the theatre of the seventies. If the plays that derived from him were more sentimental and artificial than his had been, we realize how he led other men to deal not simply with sensation or intrigue, but with what we can call themes. Thus, during 1868, H. J. Byron—usually in farce or burlesque—turned to write *Cyril's Success*, unimportant maybe, but an honest attempt at a 'problem' drama: a popular novelist's domestic happiness is nearly ruined by the public response to his books. Some years later, in 1875, Byron followed this with *Married in Haste*, a competent study of artistic jealousy between husband and wife.

Robertson's sentimental strain was most evident in the work of James Albery: *Two Roses* (1870), once enormously popular—Irving acted in it—began a long line of soft and pretty comedy-dramas. In general, Sydney Grundy took the same course. *A Pair of Spectacles* (1890), based on a French play, became a rather mawkish commentary on social life (but it stood up well to an Arts Theatre revival in 1949). *A Fool's Paradise*, if it had had sincerity and strength of purpose, might have been an agreeable domestic study. *Sowing the Wind* (1893) considered the problem of the illegitimate child so delicately that it failed to make any real impact. Possibly the spirit of Grundy's theatre is symbolized in the name of his most familiar work, *A Bunch of Violets* (1894): he was more contentious out of the theatre than in it.

When William Archer, then a young critic, wrote in 1882 a book called *English Dramatists of Today* he surveyed the writers he believed to be the arrived, or the coming, men of the English stage. They seem to us now to be a curious group: James

Albery—if Albery is a name still powerful in the London theatre, James is remembered only because Irving created a part in *Two Roses*—F. W. Broughton, Bronson Howard, Paul Merritt, Robert Reece, S. Theyre Smith, F. C. Burnand (editor of *Punch*), Herman C. Merivale, George R. Sims, W. G. Wills (of the Napoleonic melodrama, *A Royal Divorce*) and H. J. Byron. Most of them have vanished under what Kipling called 'the daily deepening drift' of the files. The few dramatists, among Archer's men, who would last better were Alfred Tennyson, though today his plays are an acquired taste; Sydney Grundy; W. S. Gilbert; and—most important—Arthur Wing Pinero and Henry Arthur Jones, both young and hopeful. Like Robertson, they began with trivial works and would become innovators. Pinero, who had been a serviceable actor in Irving's company, appeared as a dramatist in 1877 with a sketch called *£200 a Year*: he came to the theatre with an actor's sense of the dramatic and his own punctilious respect for technique. Before his serious work he wrote a royal flush of farces, of which three, joyfully inventive, *The Magistrate* (1885), *The Schoolmistress* (1886) and *Dandy Dick* (1887) are still played again and again. We remember from them such passages as the magistrate's narrative of his overnight escape from the law, and a line in *The Schoolmistress* when someone, blundering in from a darkened hall with a head beneath her arm, murmurs: 'It is an embarrassing thing to break a bust in the house of comparative strangers.'

In spite of its endearing seedy barrister, Dick Phenyl, the comedy of *Sweet Lavender* (1888) suggested only another Grundy; but Pinero had more serious work to do, and he triumphed in *The Second Mrs Tanqueray*, which George Alexander produced at the St James's in 1893. Acclaimed as the beginning of a dramatic revival, this is the tale of Aubrey Tanqueray's second wife Paula—that period figure, a woman with a past. It is a redoubtably planned part for a dramatic actress ('The future is only the past again, entered through another gate'), and Mrs Patrick Campbell, then unknown, seized it excitingly. The play, in which social conventions are opposed to natural instincts, was by a craftsman expert in the marshalling of his plots. It may worry us a little when Tanqueray, in the first act, finds that he has a couple of letters to finish, and his three friends take the chance to put us in the picture. But Pinero, never fumbling mistily, would always make sure that his expositions were clear to the last comma. *The Second Mrs Tanqueray* still holds the stage, though it may seem that its invention conceals a certain shallowness of emotion. It is much better than *The Notorious Mrs Ebbsmith* (1895), which mingles the pathetic with the spuriously theatrical, and depends on such a curtain as when the free-thinking heroine, after throwing a Bible into the fire, snatches it back again.

We shall hear more of Pinero in the Edwardian period. He might be a sentimentalist and often conventional; his ornate dialogue might trouble Max Beerbohm, yet he was also a pioneer who helped in the foundations of the twentieth-century realistic theatre, and who showed the virtues of the play of ideas to others who would work more boldly. He could often be surprising. *Trelawny of the 'Wells'* (1898), his last major work before the turn of the century, was an affectionate tribute to the theatre of three decades or so earlier, in which the actor-dramatist Tom Wrench can be identified as Tom Robertson. During the seventies, when Pinero was first working in the theatre, another young man, Henry Arthur Jones, began similarly to experiment in the writing of farces, comediettas and melodramas, one of them *The Silver King* (1882). Two years afterwards came *Saints and Sinners*, where Jones showed clearly his true objectives. Its background is a middle-class environment in a provincial town, and its chief persons are a ruthless small business-man and a mean little grocer of low mentality and hypocritical godliness. Against them is Letty, daughter of a pastor who symbolizes ideals and desires beyond those of the sordid world in which he lives. The play takes a double course. On the one hand, we are presented with a set of everyday problems of the provincial middle class; on the other, a somewhat melodramatic story in which Letty is betrayed by a high-born villain. The two moods are ill combined; and yet the fact that Jones is dealing with a subject which goes considerably beyond Pinero's favourite theme of the woman with a past may incline us to accept *Saints and Sinners* as a more remarkable play in 1884 than, say, *The Profligate* was in 1889. In the later *Judah* (1890); an unsuccessful verse experiment, *The Tempter* (1893); and two splendid plays, *The Triumph of the Philistines* (1895) and the short-lived *Michael and his Lost Angel* (1896) Jones insisted that, if the drama were to advance, it must get beyond themes of sex to depict, in the largest sense, man's religious faith and spiritual life.

This does not mean that he restricted himself to a single kind of play and plot. Between *The Tempter* and *The Triumph of the Philistines* appeared *The Masqueraders* (1894), about a man's all-consuming and altruistic love for a thoughtless woman. His treatment of emotional themes—in which he was more intense than Pinero—gives a special quality to another form of drama, *Mrs Dane's Defence* (1900), which exemplifies his gift for nervously written theatrical dialogue. Here is a portion of the scene in which Sir Daniel Carteret divines Mrs Dane's secret.

The examination starts quietly:

Sir Daniel Then we'll consider that episode closed, and we'll make a fresh start.

Mrs Dane Yes, ask me anything you please. I'm only too anxious to help you in getting at the truth.

Sir Daniel That ought not to be very difficult. [*Seats himself in revolving chair at writing table, takes a pen and occasionally makes notes of her answers.*] Now Felicia Hindemarsh was your cousin?

Mrs Dane Yes.

Sir Daniel Her father was the vicar of Tawhampton?

Mrs Dane Yes.

Sir Daniel And your other cousin—Annie Allen?

Mrs Dane I had no other cousin. When you asked what my cousin's first name was I couldn't say 'Felicia Hindemarsh', so I gave the first name I could think of.

Gradually the tension increases:

Sir Daniel When Felicia Hindemarsh left Tawhampton, where did she go?

Mrs Dane I don't quite know.

Sir Daniel But you had letters from her. Where did they come from?

Mrs Dane Let me think—it was some seaside place I think.

[*Pause.*

Sir Daniel You don't remember?

Mrs Dane No. I'm getting so terribly muddled, I don't know what I'm saying. I—I—you frighten me.

Sir Daniel I frighten you?

[*His manner throughout has been calm and kind but very firm.*

Mrs Dane Yes. I know you're very kind, and that I've nothing to fear, but I feel—I feel as if I were being thumb-screwed, and if you ask me one more question I must shriek out for help. [*A little pause.*] I'm sure it would be better for me to go and write it all out when I'm alone [*making a movement to go*]. Don't you think so?

Sir Daniel [*arresting her with a gesture*]. No.

Now the dialogue moves into a new pace:

Sir Daniel When was the last time you saw Felicia Hindemarsh?

Mrs Dane After the fearful scandal in Vienna she wrote to me in Montreal. She was desperate and begged us to shelter her. We had been like sisters, and I wrote to her to come out to us, and we would give her a home.

Sir Daniel And you did?

Mrs Dane Yes, till her death.

Sir Daniel When was that?

Mrs Dane About a year ago.

Sir Daniel Where?

Mrs Dane At Montreal.

Sir Daniel She lived with you in Montreal—as Felicia Hindemarsh?

Mrs Dane No; we called her Mrs Allen.

Sir Daniel Give me the names and addresses of those people who knew you in Montreal as Mrs Dane, and her as Mrs Allen.

Mrs Dane I'll write them out. Let me bring it to you this evening. What are you going to do with it?

Sir Daniel I'm going to prove that you are Lucy Dane—*if you are Lucy Dane.* [*She looks at him.*

Sir Daniel Does Risby know who you are?

Mrs Dane What do you mean?

Sir Daniel Does Risby know who you are?

Mrs Dane Yes—he knows that I am Mrs Dane.

Sir Daniel The cousin of Felicia Hindemarsh.

Mrs Dane [*after a pause*]. Yes.

Sir Daniel You told Risby, a mere acquaintance, that Felicia Hindemarsh was your cousin, and you didn't tell Lionel, you didn't tell me?

Mrs Dane I—I—[*She looks at him*] I—oh—I'll answer you no more. Believe what you please of me! I want no more of your help! Let me go!

Sir Daniel [*stopping her*]. How much does Risby know?

Mrs Dane Don't I tell you he knows I am Mrs Dane?

Sir Daniel Woman, you're lying!

Mrs Dane [*flashes out on him*]. How dare you? How dare you? [*Stands confronting him.*

Sir Daniel [*looking straight at her*]. I say you're lying! You are Felicia Hindemarsh!

This, though *Mrs Dane's Defence* is seldom acted now, has been invariably effective in performance. Yet we must admit that it occurs within a play that hardly justifies its passion, for—even when we recall the social conventions of 1900—Mrs Dane's past contained nothing strikingly terrible, and there is no dramatic necessity for her sentimental return to her son. Jones, always much in earnest, could descend, like Pinero, into facile sentimentalism. Unlike Pinero, he showed little ability to move with the times: a skilled technician, who thought seriously about the drama and helped to lay a firm base for his successors, he seemed to lose touch with his surroundings and to become a relic of the past. This was by no means so in *The Liars* (1897), which evoked the kind of laughter heard rarely in the theatre since Goldsmith and Sheridan; it revived the spirit of the comedy of manners.

In comedy we shall come later to Bernard Shaw. Another

Irishman, Oscar Fingal O'Flahertie Wills Wilde, wrote four plays that matter (or, at least, have been frequently revived): *Lady Windermere's Fan* (1892), *A Woman of No Importance* (1893), *An Ideal Husband* (1895) and *The Importance of Being Earnest* (1895). Superficially, the first three might be extensions of the now much-extended sentimental drama. Their plots and their serious dialogue are desperately melodramatic. But Wilde was primarily an epigrammatist, and if he was fond of a phrase he would thrust it in whether or not the context warranted it. With discipline he might have given much to the theatre. As it is, beyond the shimmering spun-glass cascade of the one masterpiece, his work has had far more notice than it demands. The critic Ivor Brown put it neatly once when he suggested that the serious scenes were written by Fingal O'Flahertie Wills and the comedy—transferable epigrams and all—interleaved by Oscar Wilde.

The most reasonable thing to do now is to quote this one-man partnership in both his moods. First, a passage from *Lady Windermere's Fan:*

Mrs Erlynne Lady Windermere, before heaven, your husband is guiltless of all offence towards you! And I—I tell you that had it ever occurred to me that such a monstrous suspicion would have entered your mind, I would have died rather than have crossed your life or his—oh! died, gladly died!   [*Moves away to sofa R.*

Lady Windermere You talk as if you had a heart. Women like you have no hearts. Heart is not in you. You are bought and sold.   [*Sits L.C.*

Mrs Erlynne [*starts, with a gesture of pain. Then restrains herself, and comes over to where Lady Windermere is sitting. As she speaks, she stretches out her hands towards her, but does not dare to touch her*]: Believe what you choose about me. I am not worth a moment's sorrow. But don't spoil your beautiful young life on my account! You don't know what may be in store for you, unless you leave this house at once. You don't know what it is to fall into the pit, to be despised, mocked, abandoned, sneered at—to be an outcast! to find the door shut against one, to have to creep in by hideous byways, afraid every moment lest the mask should be stripped from one's face, and all the while to hear the laughter, the horrible laughter of the world, a thing more tragic than all the tears the world has ever shed. You don't know what it is. One pays for one's sin, and then one pays again, and all one's life one pays. You must never know that.—As for me, if suffering be an expiation, then at this moment I have expiated all my faults, whatever they have been; for tonight you have made a heart in one who had it not, made it and broken it.—But let that pass. I may have wrecked my own life, but I will not let you wreck yours. You—why, you are a mere girl, you would be lost. You haven't got the kind of brain that enables a woman to get back. You have neither the wit nor the courage. You couldn't stand dishonour! No! Go back, Lady Windermere, to the husband who loves you, whom you love. You have a child, Lady Windermere. Go back to that child who even now, in pain or in joy, may be calling to you. [*Lady Windermere rises*]. God gave you that child. He will require from you that you make his life fine, that you watch over him. What answer will you make to God if his life is ruined through you? Back to your house, Lady Windermere—your husband loves you! He has never swerved for a moment from the love he bears you. But even if he had a thousand loves, you must stay with your child. If he was harsh to you, you must stay with your child. If he ill-treated you, you must stay with your child. If he abandoned you, your place is with your child.

> [*Lady Windermere bursts into tears and buries her face in her hands). (Rushing to her*]. Lady Windermere!

Lady Windermere [*holding out her hands to her, helplessly, as a child might do*]. Take me home. Take me home.

Mrs Erlynne [*is about to embrace her. Then restrains herself. There is a look of wonderful joy in her face*]. Come!

Compare that with a scene from *The Importance of Being Earnest*, the very sun-in-splendour of English farce: no one had ever said nothing in particular more wittily and with so confident an air. Here Lady Bracknell, a dowager who is like a Himalayan peak at large in and round London, and who speaks in avalanches, examines the eligibility of John (Jack) Worthing for her daughter's hand:

Lady Bracknell [*pencil and note-book in hand*]. I feel bound to tell you that you are not down on my list of eligible young men, although I have the same list as the dear Duchess of Bolton has. We work together, in fact. However, I am quite ready to enter your name, should your answers be what a really affectionate mother requires. Do you smoke?

Jack Well, yes, I must admit I smoke.

Lady Bracknell I am glad to hear it. A man should always have an occupation of some kind. There are far too many idle men in London as it is. How old are you?

Jack Twenty-nine.

Lady Bracknell A very good age to be married at. I have always been of opinion that a man who desires to get married should know either everything or nothing. Which do you know?

Jack [*after some hesitation*]: I know nothing, Lady Bracknell.

Lady Bracknell I am pleased to hear it. I do not approve of anything that tampers with natural ignorance. Ignorance is like a delicate exotic fruit; touch it and the bloom is gone. The whole theory of modern education is radically unsound. Fortunately in England, at any rate, education produces no effect whatsoever. If if did, it would prove a serious danger to the upper classes, and probably lead to acts of violence in Grosvenor Square. What is your income?

Jack Between seven and eight thousand a year.

Lady Bracknell [*makes a note in her book*]: In land, or in investments?

Jack In investments, chiefly.

Lady Bracknell That is satisfactory. What between the duties expected of one during one's lifetime, and the duties exacted from one after one's death, land has ceased to be either a profit or a pleasure. It gives one position, and prevents one from keeping it up. That's all that can be said about land.

Jack I have a country house with some land, of course, attached to it, about fifteen hundred acres, I believe; but I don't depend on that for my real income. In fact, as far as I can make out, the poachers are the only people who make anything out of it.

Lady Bracknell A country house! How many bedrooms? Well, that point can be cleared up afterwards. You have a town house, I hope? A girl with a simple, unspoiled nature, like Gwendolen, could hardly be expected to reside in the country.

Jack Well, I own a house in Belgrave Square, but it is let by the year to Lady Bloxham. Of course, I can get it back whenever I like, at six months' notice.

Lady Bracknell Lady Bloxham? I don't know her.

Jack Oh, she goes about very little. She is a lady considerably advanced in years.

Lady Bracknell Ah, nowadays that is no guarantee of respectability of character. What number in Belgrave Square?

Jack 149.

Lady Bracknell [*shaking her head*]: The unfashionable side. I thought there was something. However, that could easily be altered.

Jack Do you mean the fashion, or the side?

Lady Bracknell [*sternly*]: Both, if necessary, I presume. What are your politics?

Jack Well, I am afraid I really have none. I am a Liberal Unionist.

Lady Bracknell Oh, they count as Tories. They dine with us. Or come in the evening, at any rate. Now to minor matters. Are your parents living?

Jack I have lost both my parents.

Lady Bracknell Both? . . . That seems like carelessness. Who was your father? He was evidently a man of some wealth. Was he born in what the Radical papers call the purple of commerce, or did he rise from the ranks of the aristocracy?

Jack I am afraid I really don't know. The fact is, Lady Bracknell, I said I had lost my parents. It would be nearer the truth to say that my parents seem to have lost me. . . . I don't actually know who I am by birth. I was . . . well, I was found.

Lady Bracknell Found!

Jack The late Mr Thomas Cardew, an old gentleman of a very charitable and kindly disposition, found me, and gave me the name of Worthing, because he happened to have a first-class ticket for Worthing in his pocket at the time. Worthing is a place in Sussex. It is a seaside resort.

Lady Bracknell Where did the charitable gentleman who had a first-class ticket for this seaside resort find you?

Jack [*gravely*]: In a hand-bag.

Lady Bracknell A hand-bag?

Jack [*very seriously*]: Yes, Lady Bracknell. I was in a hand-bag—a somewhat large, black leather hand-bag, with handles to it—an ordinary hand-bag in fact.

Lady Bracknell In what locality did this Mr James, or Thomas, Cardew come across this ordinary hand-bag?

Jack In the cloak-room at Victoria Station. It was given to him in mistake for his own.

Lady Bracknell The cloak-room at Victoria Station?

Jack Yes. The Brighton line.

Lady Bracknell The line is immaterial. Mr Worthing, I confess I feel somewhat bewildered by what you have just told me. To be born, or at any rate bred, in a hand-bag, whether it had handles or not, seems to me to display a contempt for the ordinary decencies of family life that reminds one of the worst excesses of the French Revolution. And I presume you know what that unfortunate movement led to! As for the particular locality in which the hand-bag was found, a cloak-room at a railway station might serve to conceal a social indiscretion—has probably, indeed, been used for that purpose before now—but it could hardly be regarded as a natural basis for a recognized position in good society.

Jack May I ask you then what you would advise me to do? I need hardly say I would do anything in the world to ensure Gwendolen's happiness.

Lady Bracknell I would strongly advise you, Mr Worthing, to try and acquire some relations as soon as possible, and to make a definite effort to produce at any rate one parent, of either sex, before the season is quite over.

Jack Well, I don't see how I could possibly manage to do that. I can produce the hand-bag at any moment. It is in my dressing-room at home. I really think that should satisfy you, Lady Bracknell.

Lady Bracknell Me, sir! What has it to do with me? You can hardly imagine that I and Lord Bracknell would dream of allowing our only daughter—a girl brought up with the utmost care—to marry into a cloak-room, and form an alliance with a parcel. Good-morning, Mr Worthing!

[*Lady Bracknell sweeps out in majestic indignation.*

The nineteenth century is also sweeping out. Its last playgoers will find unlooked-for changes in a new century, and before long a new reign.

Seven

Drama in the Twentieth Century

Edwardian

That useful label 'Edwardian drama' covers not only the reign of Edward VII (1901–10) but also the last twelve months of Queen Victoria and the first years of George V, until the outbreak of the world war in August 1914. Theatrically, the period is as compact as the late Victorians might have found it complex. It brought the rise (or the revolt) of the Theatre of Ideas, that challenge to an enervated stage; the stirring and swell of the repertory movement; the feeling that with a new century there was a new theatre or the beginnings of one. It was only a few years since most of the London critics, and the playgoers who meekly followed suit, had scorned Henrik Ibsen, the Norwegian dramatist whose work was like a charged north-easter shattering the drawing-room windows, blowing through the hothouse of the Victorian stage. Most of the residents were angry. In 1891 a critic had written sourly, 'To conceive of the Ibsen Drama gaining an extensive or permanent foothold on the stage is hardly possible.' Henry Arthur Jones, who could usually be moved to wrath—he and Sydney Grundy were notorious—talked of the 'lobworm-symbolic drama'. But prophecy, especially in the theatre, has often been thankless; and few things were wilder than the attack on Ibsen (such resolute supporters of his as Bernard Shaw and William Archer would soon be proved right). It was indeed an odd period: consider (though this is far less significant) the choice at the turn of the century of the young Stephen Phillips as Britain's Sophocles, Dante and Milton.

The more perceptive writers and craftsmen recognized Ibsen's quality, his doctrinal realism, his insistence upon working in ideas instead of commonplaces. There were attempts, notably by Arthur Pinero, to adapt to the commercial stage Ibsen's criticism of life through drama: in fact, even as early as 1884, the angry

Henry Arthur Jones (with Henry Herman) had founded on *A Doll's House*—but, of course, with a 'happy' ending—a piece called *Breaking a Butterfly*.

In the year 1900, sunrise of a century of revolt and of a theatre that would suddenly grow up, playgoers had much else to consider. Wherever he wrote or spoke—which was most of the time—the vigorously polemical, red-bearded Irishman, Bernard Shaw ('Nothing exasperates me more than to be Georged in print') seldom failed to distil the quintessence of Ibsenism. His own apotheosis had yet to come, but he knew very well what he wanted from the theatre as 'a factory of thought, a prompter of conscience, an elucidator of social conduct, an armoury against despair and dullness, and a temple of the Ascent of Man'. The stage in general had never thought of itself as a temple and an armoury. Many classical revivals apart, it moved to the sound of the domestic dinner-gong of Pinero and Jones or to the romantic trumpet-notes of Ruritania. In the classical theatre, though a passionately single-minded zealot, William Poel, was at work in any hole or corner he could find, attacking the picture-frame stage, removing the green mould of traditional and otiose business, and insisting on a musically inflected speech of great range and suppleness, any fashionable Shakespearian revival belonged to the Decorated School of opulent realism, Roman plays in the shining marble of Alma-Tadema, rabbits scampering in the Wood near Athens, and *Twelfth Night* acted on the grassy terraces that *Punch* called 'swardy'. This was the manner of Herbert Beerbohm Tree who ruled Her (His) Majesty's Theatre, an altogether different personality from the gaunt genius Henry Irving, then in the very ebb of his Lyceum management. The inevitable Pinero and Jones governed the contemporary stage, Pinero always a little in front (he would be throughout life). Several other writers were about, such people as Grundy, R. C. Carton, Robert Marshall and Haddon Chambers (besides a young Scot, James Matthew Barrie, who seemed likely to slip out of the drawing-room), but this was in sum a solidly based world of the Theatre Theatrical, governed by methods uncompromisingly realistic and by the steadily orthodox paternalism of its actor-managers, then at their meridian. Plays moved to the comforting rumble of the four-wheeler.

There was much powerful, firm-based acting; craftsmanship in text and performance was acclaimed. Such critics as Shaw and Max Beerbohm might be sarcastic about the well-made play in the tradition of Scribe and Sardou; but W. S. Gilbert (who had a vested interest) spoke for the majority when he told William Archer (reprinted in Archer's *Real Conversations*, 1904), 'I don't like to see a thing left at a loose end. I confess to a preference for finished form.' In spite of strange premonitory stirrings, noises off, a sense that something might be ready to splinter the established pattern, turn-of-the-century playgoers were perfectly content with a theatre that usually said what they wished to hear, and in a manner familiar to them. It was so in London, with the West End stages at the centre, and in the provinces, sustained then by score upon score of touring companies, carbon copies —social drama, melodrama, farce, elaborate musical comedy— of accepted productions in the metropolis.

Those who looked for discoveries, for some new and major figure to suggest comfortably that the spirit of Shakespeare had not waned, found an answer in the romantic verse plays of Stephen Phillips. The theatre had desperately needed a return to verse, a longing repeated intermittently down the years. Though there had been little to show except a few works by Tennyson (*Becket* for one, shaped by Irving for performance) and such a turgid affair as *The Tempter* (1893) by Henry Arthur Jones, of all people—

> She's wine, enrapturing wine! I am a cup
> Brimming with richer vintage than did e'er
> An earthly summer bear to earthly sun.
> Drenched and surcharged I am, yet ache and thirst
> For draughts diviner and more secret still,
> Th'avatar, nay, the very lees and dregs
> Of very love itself!

—playgoers kept on hoping for 'enrapturing wine' from some neo-Elizabethan cellar. Then Phillips arrived, a former actor (and a distant cousin of the splendid Shakespearian, Frank Benson). Critics, even Archer, greeted him in the most hyperbolical terms, startling for verse that as a rule was limpidly forgettable. He could preserve a concentrated narrative, which was a virtue in a poetic dramatist; he could often find a resounding phrase and sometimes express ecstasy; he could bring off such lines as

> So still it is that we might almost hear
> The sigh of all the sleepers in the world
> And all the rivers running to the sea

but it was a small talent, and it soon faded. The names of *Herod*

(1900); his most substantial play, *Paolo and Francesca* (presented by George Alexander at the St James's in 1902); and *Ulysses* (1902) stay on record. Phillip is among the castaways of the theatre. As we can see if we return to those thin green-and-gold volumes with the tarnished gilt wreath, the strangest thing was that, though obviously sub-Elizabethan, he believed all the while that he was escaping from the Elizabethan manner. Thus he said to Archer:

> A deliberate rebellion against the Elizabethan tradition is the best hope for English poetic drama. That, at any rate, has always been my view, and I have tried to act up to it. But people can't, or won't, see that.

Phillips was still writing (Tree had yet to do his *Nero*) at the time the Theatre of Ideas flowered at the Court in Sloane Square. This was in the autumn of 1904, under the management of an ardent actor-dramatist-producer, Harley Granville Barker (unhyphenated in those days) and his business partner, an older man, J. E. Vedrenne. Behind them was the strong impulse of Bernard Shaw, who had said dogmatically in 1898:

> I can no longer be satisfied with fictitious morals and fictitious good conduct, shedding fictitious glory on robbery, starvation, disease, crime, drink, war, cruelty, cupidity, and all the other commonplaces of civilization which drive men to the theatre to make foolish pretences that such things are progress, science, morals, religion, patriotism, imperial supremacy, greatness, and all the other things the newspapers call them.

The venture brought its audience, the 'congregation', to a little theatre by the Underground station in Sloane Square on the Chelsea fringe. During its life—and it lasted until the summer of 1907—it gave 988 performances of thirty-two plays; 701 of these were of eleven plays of Bernard Shaw, and among the other names were such dramatists as Barker himself, John Galsworthy, St John Hankin, W. B. Yeats, John Masefield, Maurice Maeterlinck, Ibsen (a revival of *Hedda Gabler*) and Euripides—three plays in the texts by Gilbert Murray that (though a later world would be ungrateful to them, scorning the Swinburnian rhythms) did much more for Greek drama in English than any other translations have achieved. Ivor Brown was only reasonable when he said fifty years on, remembering Murray with affection, 'If Greek plays are acted now in English, the version chosen may be some bare-bones prosaic stuff which convinces you that, whatever

Greek tragedy may have been intellectually, it had no pulse of poetry, no leap of metre, no warmth of phrase.'

Those three years at the Court—the Thousand Performances, as they have been named—would have a permanent influence on the English stage, though at the time they hardly changed play-going custom. The West End theatre was as assured and competent as ever. It would have been absurd then, as now, to claim that everything in the new drama was masterly, and everything on the conventional stage in decline. Even so, after the Court, the theatre could never be quite the same again. We cannot wonder why Desmond MacCarthy chose as epigraph for his book on the season the lines from *As You Like It* 'Wast ever in court, shepherd?'—'No, truly.'—'Then thou art damned.'

The applause must have surprised Pinero. He had held candidly, in his polished-mahogany idiom, that 'not only are wealth and leisure more productive of dramatic complications than poverty and hard work, but that if you want to get a certain order of ideas expressed or questions discussed, you must go pretty well up in the social scale'. (By the 1970s such a suggestion as this would be a collector's rare primitive.) Certainly Pinero followed his own rule. Early in the century his most impressive play was *Iris* (1901), a technician's portrait, tragedy supervening, of a rash young woman who must lose a fortune if she remarries. Far better were *His House in Order* (1906), put on by Alexander at the St James's, as much the temple of the drawing-room drama as the Court was of the Theatre of Ideas; and, less commercially successful (though one ought not to use 'commercial' in a pejorative sense), another St James's play, *Mid-Channel* (1909). Each was impeccably contrived in the day's mode. Pinero would never endure the last-second revisions of a dog-eared script. Sending each act to the printer as he finished it, he would stage-manage (to-day 'direct') his final rehearsals from a definitive version: no actor could deviate by a comma. Both *His House In Order*, a narrative of domestic rebellion, the revolt of a young second wife who must withstand the hectoring dislike of her husband's family—it sounds like a parable of the Old Drama and the New—and *Mid-Channel*, tightly controlled tale of a broken marriage ended by suicide, were sturdily theatrical and fortified by a master-builder. Henry Arthur Jones, more prolific than his rival, had half a dozen plays in the brief period before the Court, none of them (the clumsily named *The Princess's Nose* and the rest) more than useful comedies of the minute. An honest, obstinate dramatist, he would rise only (*The Liars* was an exception) when, as in a later piece, *The Hypocrites* (New York, 1906; London, 1907), story of a pregnant girl forced into perjury by the provincial family whose son had seduced her, he could let his indignation bear him forward on the surge.

At the beginning of the century there was capable work by Hubert Henry Davies, a student of feminine psychology most easily remembered for two plays. One, *Mrs Gorringe's Necklace* (1903), remains because its wit is proof against the stilted serious passages and an arbitrary tragic ending: suicide—here it is an ultimate revolver-shot—could tempt the Edwardians. Four years later, a quartet-comedy, *The Mollusc*, about a woman's dictatorship from the sofa, had more pith than its too meagre successors. Alfred Sutro, most approved for *The Walls of Jericho* (1904), employed a gift for pleasant aphorism that lightened his starched-cuff dialogue.

It does not help now to name everyone in a group of efficient writers, all matched to their time, all taking an expected course along tracks that within half a century would be overgrown and disused. Three men from what today we call the Theatre of Entertainment—though one of them wears the ascription uncomfortably—stood from the ruck of the London stage. Two would still be writing after thirty years; a third died tragically before the end of Edward VII's reign. He was St John Hankin who, during his short working life, appeared to be wittier and more truthfully promising than another of the trio, William Somerset Maugham. Shaw praised Hankin's high comedy as a 'stirring and important criticism of life'. His wit, unlike far too much of Wilde's, derives from the situation and the character, as Sir Barry Jackson (who often staged *The Cassilis Engagement* (1907) at the Birmingham Repertory) would never fail to assert. Hankin's comedies should have more than the passing tribute of a sigh. Another is *The Return of the Prodigal* (1905; unluckily revived in 1948) about a prodigal son who is not ashamed of himself, and who, neatly inverting the old conventions, strikes off again as calm as when he arrived. Max Beerbohm (in *The Saturday Review*) said that Hankin set out neither to prove nor to probe anything, merely to communicate his good-natured amusement. 'Mr Shaw,' Beerbohm added, 'observing a prodigal son, would have knitted his brows, outstretched his index finger, and harangued us to the effect that the prodigal was perfectly right, as a citizen, in his refusal to work under the present conditions of labour, and that these conditions are irrational, dangerous, and ought to be abolished.'

The other writers we think of now, the young Maugham and Barrie, would increase their fame in years ahead. They were entirely dissimilar: Maugham at that hour a brisk cynic with an ear for the facile stage epigram—by which he meant looping the loop on a commonplace and coming down between the lines—and Barrie a dramatist of sound Scottish sense, for ever on the frontier (and often crossing it) of romantic fantasy. He too was a superb craftsman, a talent frequently discounted, and never more than in the 1970s. His seeming artlessness concealed a most precise art, and he had another asset. His managing Scottish Maggie in *What Every Woman Knows* says '[Charm] is a sort of bloom on a woman.' It is also a bloom on a playwright. This, coupled with his fly-by-night imagination, made of him a writer impossible to ignore. His richest Edwardian plays were *The Admirable Crichton* (1902) and *What Every Woman Knows* (1908). The first, a fantasy with a hard centre of ironical truth beneath the chocolate, shows how, during two years on a desert island in the Pacific, the social positions in a shipwrecked household are reversed. The butler (quoting 'I was a king in Babylon and you were a Christian slave') becomes, temporarily, the autocrat: in one sense the play is almost a meditation on the speech of the Shakespearian Ulysses on degree. The second piece is a portrait of a tactfully managing Scottish wife who directs her humourless politician-husband. Both *Crichton* and *What Every Woman Knows* were still in revival during the 1970s; each in its time has been turned superfluously to a 'musical'.

Another of Barrie's Edwardian plays, the children's adventure of *Peter Pan* (1904), has become a rather rubbed legend, though the best of its Never-Never Land make-believe is irresistible: little from the nursery shelf is missing. Over all are the figures of Peter himself, boy eternal, and the pirate Captain Hook, terror of the high seas and black sheep of Balliol: 'his hair dressed in long curls which look like black candles about to melt, his eyes blue as the forget-me-not and of a profound insensibility, save when he claws, at which time a red spot appears in them. He has an iron hook instead of a right hand, and it is with this he claws.' The text has a clot of embarrassing lines apparently easy to cut but in practice uncuttable: Barrie's whimsy is deeply embedded in all his work.

Somerset Maugham, whose view of the world hardly coincides with Barrie's in any particular, had been trained as a doctor, and in the theatre knew how to issue the right prescription. As a dramatist he began with a set of story-telling comedies, sardonic,

Bernard Shaw at the time of the Court seasons

A scene from Houghton's *Hindle Wakes*, Playhouse, 1912

A scene from Pinero's *Mid-Channel*, St James's, 1909

The Garden of Eden scene in Shaw's *Back to
Methuselah*, Birmingham Repertory, 1923. Set by
Paul Shelving

The Royal Shakespeare Theatre,
Stratford-upon-Avon

smart and amoral, and without any noticeable missionary design. 'The aim of drama,' he said, 'is not to instruct but to please. Its object is delight.' The early plays have come up fairly well in revival, notably *Lady Frederick* (1907). Possibly at this remove *Smith* (1909), impregnated with the class-consciousness of the Edwardians, may prove unexpectedly to be the most lasting. It is not too consciously clever; and Smith, the parlourmaid, who attracts her mistress's brother (back from the Colonies) because she cannot afford the sins of her social betters, is a thoroughly disarming portrait. In creating her Maugham for once wore his heart on his sleeve. Probably he was tired by then of a reputation like his own Blenkinsop's in *Mrs Dot*: 'When I was quite young it occurred to someone that I was a cynic, and since then I've never been able to remark that it was a fine day without being accused of odious cynicism.' There, if Blenkinsop's is the voice, Maugham is the ventriloquist.

It would have shocked the period's West End playgoers and actor-managers to realize that one day the Court Theatre in Sloane Square would dominate Edwardian stage history. In 1904–7 it was the republic of the Theatre of Ideas, and clearly the first President was Bernard Shaw. One of the Irishmen who in their time have captured the English stage, Shaw had been for three years in the 1890s a shrewdly propagandist drama critic without mercy to the routine work that then held the theatre. He began his own playwriting in 1892 with *Widowers' Houses*, assault on slum landlordism; the negligible *The Philanderer* (1893); *Mrs Warren's Profession* (1893), attacking the social conditions that encouraged and sustained prostitution; and the anti-romantic comedy of *Arms and the Man* (1894). There were other plays as well (including a trifle about the young Napoleon, *The Man of Destiny*, written in 1895) but it took the repertory work of the Court to fix Shaw in the public mind (though the Sloane Square 'congregation' had to be a minority). 'Drama', Shaw declared, 'is no mere setting up of the camera to nature; it is the presentation in parable of the conflict between man's nature and his environment; in a word, of problem.' It was his delight—and he regarded humour as an essential solvent—to startle an audience by denying the truth of an established convention: Masefield long afterwards would call him 'Erasing Shaw who made the folly die.' He enjoyed fasioning an image of himself ('My reputation is built up . . . on an impregnable basis of dogmatic reiteration') but, all said, he was deeply serious, and he added to his published texts the ancillary prefaces, tracts, sermons, encyclicals, which buttressed them: with Pinero and Jones he was quick to popularize his plays in official reading editions. Frequently capricious and tire-some—in later years curiously gullible—Shaw has nevertheless remained the major dramatist of his world, and one of the most redoubtable of all time.

His principal Edwardian play was *Man and Superman* (written 1903; Court, 1905) which develops the philosophy of the Life Force, self-knowledge through selective breeding of the Super-man. We have too often to meet a cut version without the elo-quent third-act dream scene, a 'Shavio-Socratic dialogue' in the Void near Hell. Lacking this—which is sometimes acted alone as *Don Juan in Hell*, alive with Shavian assertion on most matters between creative evolution and music ('the brandy of the damned')—the play is still a flashing comedy of feminine pursuit, durable entertainment if wanting its full intellectual volume. For Don Juan in the 'dialogue', reason must dominate:

> That is why intellect is so unpopular. But to Life, the force behind the Man, intellect is a necessity, because without it he blunders into death. Just as Life, after ages of struggle, evolved that wonderful bodily organ the eye, so that the living organism could see where it was going, and what was coming to help or threaten it, and thus avoid a thousand dangers that formerly slew it, so it is evolving today a mind's eye that shall see, not the physical world but the purpose of Life, and thereby enable the individual to work for that purpose instead of thwarting and baffling it by setting up shortsighted personal aims as at present. Even as it is, only one sort of man has ever been happy, has ever been universally respected among all the conflicts of interests and illu-sions . . . the philosophic man: he who seeks in contemplation to discover the inner will of the world, in invention to discover the means of fulfilling that will, and in action to do that will by the so-discovered means.

In most of his work Shaw was the Life Force of the theatre. Charles Edward Montague, the *Manchester Guardian* critic, said of one of his plays that he drew the spectator's mind after him 'as an express train rushing through a station draws a paper bag'. It was among his defects that the train so rarely paused. Shaw could talk excessively; he was over-fond of knockabout, verbal and physi-cal; and he would insist on his favourite jokes (the one about the typical Englishman had been a winner since another dramatist's *Hamlet*—'there the men are as mad as he'). Yet, in his own style, Shaw is unexampled. An occasional play does show its age, as did, oddly, the brief and direct *Candida* (written in 1894, published in 1898, and in the Court repertory) during its London revival in 1977. *Captain Brassbound's Conversion* (Court, 1905), a comedy on the stupidity of revenge, was not especially exciting in the original production: Ellen Terry, for whom it was designed, could not do much with the serenely managing Lady Cicely. But there are few complaints yet about *You Never Can Tell* (written, 1896; Court, 1905), a calculated fashionable comedy with a mind behind the fashion; *John Bull's Other Island* (1904), which can be taken as a diverting allegory of relations between the English and Irish and contains in the priest Keegan a figure of visionary wisdom; the copious *Major Barbara* (1905)—its text scored for cannon and tambourine—which among a good deal else is a denunciation of the crime of poverty; and *The Doctor's Dilemma* (1906), primarily a joke against a profession Shaw never ceased to worry.

All of these were in the Barker–Vedrenne programmes. After the Court came the rather blurred *Caesar and Cleopatra* (written for Forbes-Robertson as early as 1898, and staged nine years later at the Savoy), Shaw's effort 'to pay an instalment of the debt that all dramatists owe to the art of heroic acting'; the 'disquisitory' *Getting Married* (1898), examining marriage from every aspect, religious or secular, and apt to loiter on the way; *Misalliance* (1910), about parents and children and containing (not that it matters) an often wrongly attributed line, 'Who's on for a game of tennis?'; *Fanny's First Play* (1910), with its inner and topical anecdote of youthful rebellion; *Androcles and the Lion* (1913), a gentle study in religious experience; and *Pygmalion* (1914), done, remarkably, at a conservative stronghold, Sir Herbert Tree's His Majesty's Theatre. This fable of a Covent Garden flower-girl taught to speak like a duchess, a kind of Cinderella rescued by the Spirit of Phonetics, may be minor Shaw, but it is more rewarding than the amiable musical *My Fair Lady* made from it in the late 1950s.

In considering Shaw's work until 1914 we have gone chronologically beyond the confines of the Court. The simple list of Shaw's themes is enough to suggest what was happening in the hitherto calm waters of the English theatre. An orthodox playgoer, brought to Sloane Square, might have found himself crying, with the Second Gentleman in *Othello*: 'Do but stand upon the foaming shore,/The chidden billow seems to pelt the clouds.' That chidden billow, the Theatre of Ideas, was a theatre of revolt, alarming to Edwardians who found a discussion of such a matter as social degree quite disturbing enough. We must return to the Court and its dramatists, to the actor and director Granville Barker, to John Galsworthy, John Masefield and W. B. Yeats. Barker, one day to be near-canonized for his work on Shakespeare production, practical and theoretical, was handsome, Italianate and urgent, an idealist influenced by Shaw (whom he impersonated as Tanner in *Man and Superman*), but with a searching mind of his own. An early play of his, *The Marrying of Ann Leete* (staged 1902), looked back to the hypocritical conventions, the class barriers and the stirrings of social rebellion a century earlier. Entirely out of the period run, it is startling to read its laconic dialogue beside the ornamentation of a Pinero text: life lingers in it, though (as a Royal Shakespeare Company revival proved in 1975) its effects are elusive. At the Court, except for the untypical whimsy of *Prunella*, written with Laurence Housman, Barker staged only *The Voysey Inheritance* (1905)—which would be his most familiar play—on the theme of absolute honesty. Allardyce Nicoll said of it that it emphasized 'by a series of mallet tappings the sense of crushing, belittling imprisonment which he, along with other dramatists, felt in the life of his day, the seeming futility of higher ideals, the desire for freedom, the passionate spirit of revolt'. But the piece has to end in a compromise. Barker wrote more forcibly in *Waste* (1907), the tragedy of a disastrous crossing of private life and political career: in its day it was foolishly banned because of its talk of abortion. Better still, and given a full-scale revival at the new National Theatre in 1977—a decision that would have delighted Barker, always a National Theatre advocate—*The Madras House* (1910) examined feminine repression, social custom, social prejudice and gallant idealism: it rose naturally from a period progressively rebellious. In performance today it seems twenty minutes or so too long: Barker could be as unstintedly voluble as Shaw, but both in his debating power and his earnest study of character he stays as a chieftain in the record of the Theatre of Ideas. His expansive dialogue (the laconicism of *Ann Leete* was transient) is more speakably naturalistic than Pinero's carefully polished, literate, but often orotund periods.

The humanitarian John Galsworthy, then a novelist who was discovered for the theatre at the Court, had no trouble at all with his dialogue except when he sought to be amusing: the effort then could be palpable, though he seldom wasted his time in trying: no dramatist was more single-minded—he would not be deflected from his purpose. His one play at the Court, first of a long line that would extend almost to the 1930s, was *The Silver Box*

(1906)—originally drafted as *The Cigarette Box*—a drama of social injustice ('One law for the rich . . .'). There had been nothing earlier like the scene in the Magistrate's court where Jones, a charwoman's husband, is sentenced, and an MP's son, Jack Barthwick, escapes:

Magistrate [*to Jones*]: Your conduct here has been most improper. You gave the excuse that you were drunk when you stole the box. I tell you that is no excuse. If you choose to get drunk and break the law afterwards you must take the consequences. And let me tell you that men like you, who get drunk and give way to your spite or whatever it is that's in you, are—are—a *nuisance to the community*.
Jack Barthwick [*leaning from his seat*]: Dad, that's what you said to me?
[*His father hushes him.*

One or two later plays, after the Court début, would sag: we have heard little of *Joy*, or of *The Elder Son* (1912) in which Galsworthy turned, Edwardianly, but here unsparingly, to consider degree. Two masterpieces he would not match again were *Strife* (1909) and *Justice* (1910). The first, set round a South Wales tin-plate works, is an acutely poised treatise on strikes and on fanatical intransigence, that ends after useless suffering and with 'a woman dead and the two best men broken', just where it begins: 'D'you know, sir—these terms, they're the very *same* we drew up together, you and I, and put to both sides before the fight began? All this—all this—and—and—what for?' The scrupulously argued *Justice: A Tragedy*, undeviatingly 'a picture of blind justice', contained a wordless scene of solitary confinement that would lead directly to a reform in the law. At the première, after the curtain had fallen, the gallery audience, and some of those in other parts of the house, stayed in the darkened Duke of York's until half an hour before midnight, shouting 'We want Galsworthy!' until Granville Barker appeared to assure them that the author had gone. The most compassionate of men, Galsworthy would always be impartial, though (as late as 1920) the critic James Agate said of him: 'He is in himself an entire Humane Society. He sides with the fox against the man in pink, the hen-coop against the marauding fox, the chickweed against the chicken, and whatever it is the chickweed preys on against that ferocious plant.'

Also staged at the Court, John Masefield—who one day would be Poet Laureate—and W. B. Yeats were two poets represented only by brief prose plays. Masefield's *The Campden Wonder* (1907), spare and relentless, was founded on an agonizing episode in

Cotswold history. Sensitive though he was, he never held back from tragedy, as Shaw was apt to do, and he used the word in two successive titles, *The Tragedy of Nan* (1908) and *The Tragedy of Pompey the Great*, which post-dated *Nan* in performance but was written earlier. As L. A. G. Strong has said, *Nan*, dedicated to Yeats, influenced in some passages by the Irish dramatist Synge, and set by the Severn in Regency Gloucestershire, came close to that 'impassioned fusion between sordid circumstance and mystical reality' at which Masefield's work was directed. Nan, living with a devilish aunt, is an orphan whose father has been hanged for sheep-stealing; her lover is contemptibly futile; at the last she is goaded to tragic splendour. The problem is a crazed old man, the Gaffer. Though his speech can sing on the lips of an imaginative actor (H. R. Hignett, for example, in the Mercury Theatre revival of 1943), it does need the most delicate tact in delivery. A responsive voice can bring to us the picture of the high tide of Severn swirling up under a harvest moon and seizing the nets of the salmon-fishers:

> The tide 'll sweep them away. O, I've known it. It takes the nets up miles. Miles. They find 'em high up. Beyond Glorster. Beyond 'Artpury. Girt golden flag-flowers over 'em. And apple-trees a-growin' over 'em. Apples of red and apples of gold. They fall into the water. The water be still there, where the apples fall. The nets 'ave apples in them.

Nan And fish, Gaffer?
Gaffer Strange fish. Strange fish out of the sea.
Nan Yes. Strange fish indeed, Gaffer. A strange fish in the nets tomorrow. A dumb thing. Knocking agen the bridges. Something white. Something white in the water. They'd pull me out. Men would. They'd find my body. [*shuddering*] I couldn't. I couldn't.

Masefield's other important Edwardian play, one that fell into neglect—it had a minor London revival in 1920—was the movingly austere *Pompey the Great*. Most of its action is classically off-stage; it has a grand Messenger speech for a centurion; the slave Philip's song lingers in the mind ('Though we are ringed with spears, though the last hope is gone,/Romans stand firm, the Roman dead look on'); and the fourth act, on board the vessel at Pelusium, uses some daring seamen's-chanty effects. A good deal of Masefield himself appears, too, in his version, *The Witch* (1911), of an anguished Norwegian play, Hans Wiers-Jenssen's *Anne Pedersdotter*. In the theatre he was seldom acclaimed; but the poet-dramatist who loved the power of the word and the 'acted passion beautiful and swift' may well outlive much that has been the sport of temporary fashion.

The Pot of Broth (written 1904; Court, 1905), by another poet, the Irishman William Butler Yeats, was a mild, beguiling anecdote; a minor piece by a writer who tried to express 'the deeper thoughts and emotions of Ireland', and whose richest work before he became preoccupied by the symbolism of the Nō drama, the aristocratic stage of Japan, was in the incantatory verse of such plays as *The Countess Cathleen* (acted 1899), *The Shadowy Waters* (1900; acted 1904), *On Baile's Strand* (1904), *Deirdre* (1906) and *The King's Threshold*. In this (1903) the poet Seanchan cries:

> I would have all know that when all falls
> In ruin, poetry calls out in joy,
> Being the scattering hand, the bursting pod,
> The victim's joy among the holy flame,
> God's laughter at the shattering of the world.

In theatre history we may think first of Yeats as one of the founders, with Lady Gregory and others, of the Abbey in Dublin, so fortunate in its unexampled group of great native players. It was fortunate also in the drama of John Millington Synge, master of the Irish renaissance, whom Yeats encouraged to return at the age of twenty-eight from his barren years in Paris. Back in Ireland, Synge looked and listened. 'Every speech,' he said, 'should be as fully flavoured as a nut or an apple, and such speeches cannot be written by anyone who works among people who have shut their lips on poetry.' Certainly he wrote of Irish peasants in those transfiguring prose rhythms that have proved calamitous to many lesser men without the trick of, let us say, Mary Doul's speech in *The Well of the Saints*:

> For when I seen myself in them pools, I seen my hair would be grey or white, maybe, in a short while, and I seen with it that I'd a face would be a great wonder when it'll have soft white hair falling around it, the way when I'm an old woman there won't be the like of me surely in the seven counties of the east.

Synge wrote only six plays in his brief life, but their influence is enduring. *Riders to the Sea* (1904), from the period immediately preceding the Abbey, was the compressed result of his study of 'the eternal life of man, spent under sun and in rain and in rude physical effort never changed from the beginning.' The scene is a western island. At the centre is the mother, Maurya, who realizes

that her only surviving son must perish as the rest have done.
Presently his body is brought home:

Maurya [*raising her head and speaking as if she did not see the people around
her*]. They're all gone now, and there isn't anything more the sea can
do to me. . . . I'll have no call now to be up crying and praying when the
wind breaks from the south, and you can hear the surf is in the east,
and the surf is in the west, making a great stir with the two noises, and
they hitting one on the other. I'll have no call now to be going down
and getting Holy Water in the dark nights after Samhain, and I won't
care what way the sea is when the other women will be keening. [*To
Nora*] Give me the Holy Water, Nora; there's a small sup still on the
dresser.   [*Nora gives it to her.*

Maurya [*drops Michael's clothes across Bartley's feet, and sprinkles the Holy
Water over him*]. It isn't that I haven't prayed for you, Bartley, to the
Almighty God. It isn't that I haven't said prayers in the dark night
till you wouldn't know what I'd been saying; but it's a great rest
I'll have now, and it's time, surely. It's a great rest I'll have now,
and great sleeping in the long nights after Samhain, if it's only a
bit of wet flour we do have to eat, and maybe a fish that would be
stinking.

    [*She kneels down again, crossing herself, and saying prayers under
    her breath.*

Cathleen [*to an old man*]. Maybe yourself and Eamon would make a
coffin when the sun rises. We have fine white boards herself bought,
God help her, thinking Michael would be found, and I have a new
cake you can eat while you'll be working.

The Old Man [*looking at the boards*]. Are there nails with them?

Cathleen There are not, Colum; we didn't think of the nails.

Another Man It's a great wonder she wouldn't think of the nails, and all
the coffins she's seen made already.

Cathleen It's getting old she is, and broken.

        [MAURYA *stands up again very slowly and spreads out the pieces of*
        MICHAEL'S *clothes beside the body, sprinkling them with the
        last of the Holy Water.*

Nora [*in a whisper to* CATHLEEN]. She's quiet now and easy; but the day
Michael was drowned you could hear her crying out from this to the
spring well. It's fonder she was of Michael, and would anyone have
thought that?

Cathleen [*slowly and clearly*]. An old woman will be soon tired with
anything she will do, and isn't it nine days herself is after crying and
keening, and making great sorrow in the house?

Maurya [*puts the empty cup mouth downward on the table, and lays her
hands together on* BARTLEY'S *feet*]. They're all together this time, and
the end is come. May the Almighty God have mercy on Bartley's
soul, and on Michael's soul, and on the souls of Sheamus and Patch,
and Stephen and Shawn [*bending her head*]; and may He have mercy

on my soul, Nora, and on the soul of every one is left living in the world.

> [*She pauses, and the keen rises a little more loudly from the women, then sinks away.*

Maurya [*continuing*]. Michael has a clean burial in the far north, by the grace of the Almighty God. Bartley will have a fine coffin out of the white boards, and a deep grave surely. What more can we want than that? No man at all can be living for ever, and we must be satisfied.

> [*She kneels down again, and the curtain falls slowly.*

Elsewhere Synge's manner was what Yeats called 'audacious, joyous, ironical'. He wrote [*In*] *The Shadow of the Glen* (1903), which owed much to the maidservants whose folk-weave chatter he heard through the chinks of a kitchen ceiling in Wicklow; the astringent comedy of *The Well of the Saints* (1905) about blind beggars, man and wife, who, having had their sight miraculously restored, welcome renewed darkness; *The Tinker's Wedding* (1908), which he had worked at, off and on, for years without getting it entirely right; his cynical-poetic masterpiece, *The Playboy of the Western World* (1907), which for various reasons—mainly his candid view of the peasant character—myopic patriots could not endure; and the late and not fully revised *Deirdre of the Sorrows*, published after his death. *The Playboy*, perennially triumphant, is about the callow youth who comes to a country inn on the coast of Mayo, boasting that he has killed his father in 'a windy corner of high distant hills'. Whereupon he is treated as a hero until the bellicose father suddenly arrives. Yeats, tireless in praising Synge, said, 'He made his own selection of word and phrase, choosing what would express his own personality; above all, he had word and phrase dance to a very strange rhythm.' It was a bewitching rhythm, as all but the tone-deaf have found in listening to such a speech as this (by the Playboy, Christy Mahon) from the love scene:

[*With rapture*]: If the mitred bishops seen you that time, they'd be the like of the holy prophets, I'm thinking, do be straining the bars of Paradise to lay eyes on the Lady Helen of Troy, and she abroad, pacing back and forward, with a nosegay in her golden shawl.

Synge, grave and dark-haired, with the humorous mouth and the eyes 'at once smoky and kindling' (Masefield's description) died in March 1909 when he was only thirty-seven. Early one morning he said to his nurse in the Dublin hospital, 'It is no use fighting death any longer', and turned over and died.[1]

[1] See the letter from Yeats to Lady Gregory, 24 March 1909.

There were other skilled Abbey Theatre dramatists in various modes, among them Padraic Colum, T. C. Murray, Lennox Robinson (who began with a group of tragedies and whose more lasting work would come later) and the endearing and immensely prolific Lady Gregory, whose short folk-plays—such as *Spreading the News* (1904) and *The Workhouse Ward* (1908)—are safe in record. Yeats's friend, patron and collaborator, she was one of the creators of the Irish theatre. Another, in the first years of the century, was a wealthy Englishwoman, Annie (A.E.F.) Horniman, who had been a friend and helper of Yeats in London, and who was also, self-effacingly, a pioneer in the new theatre movement (she had financed the production of Shaw's *Arms and the Man* in 1894). During 1904 Miss Horniman, as she was always known, brought about the sudden efflorescence of the Abbey by buying, converting and subsidizing the building for the Irish National Theatre Society. When eventually—and, it seems, inevitably—she differed from the Dubliners she decided to take a theatre of her own in Manchester, and so to create the third historic enterprise of the Edwardian years. One had been the Vedrenne–Barker season; another the Abbey; now Miss Horniman inaugurated the provincial repertory movement, the rising in the north. (Though she hated the word 'repertory', it would establish itself.) Opening in 1907 at the Midland Hotel Theatre, the players, directed by Ben Iden Payne and including, at various times, such people as Lewis Casson (later director), Ada King, Miss Darragh, Mona Limerick, Sybil Thorndike, Charles Bibby, Esmé Percy, Herbert Lomas, occupied the Gaiety Theatre, dedicated to the best authors of all ages and with 'an especially wide open door to present-day writers who . . . have something to say worth listening to and say it in an interesting and original manner.' This meant that it both followed the Court and evolved the so-called 'Manchester school', whose plays were tough links in a Pennine chain of English drama. Here were kitchens and small sitting-rooms, rebellions in middle-class streets, a new and formidable theatre contemptuous of Pinero's assertion that one must 'go pretty well up in the social scale'. The authors were such men as Charles McEvoy (*David Ballard*), Allan Monkhouse (*Mary Broome*: can the son of the house marry a maidservant? how the Edwardians had this on their minds!), Harold Brighouse and Stanley Houghton, who died in 1913 at the age of thirty-two. He wrote two of the fighting Gaiety plays, *The Younger Generation* (1910; its title speaks for itself) and the better *Hindle Wakes* (1912), a Lancashire view of a period problem. Alan, son of a self-made millowner in the town of Hindle, goes off for a week-end with a mill-girl, Fanny, daughter of one of his father's employees. He regards it as a cheerful escapade, she as an act of defiance. Shocked, the parents insist that the two must marry. But Fanny speaks with the independent voice that was becoming so familiar, but had not been heard in quite these terms:

Alan   But you didn't ever really love me?

Fanny   Love you? Good heavens, of course not! Why on earth should I love you? You were just someone to have a bit of fun with. You were an amusement—a lark.

Alan   [*shocked*]. Fanny! Is that all you cared for me?

Fanny   How much more did you care for me?

Alan   But it's not the same. I'm a man.

Fanny   You're a man, and I was your little fancy. Well, I'm a woman, and *you* were *my* little fancy. You wouldn't prevent a woman enjoying herself as well as a man, if she takes it into her head?

Alan   But do you mean to say that you didn't care any more for me than a fellow cares for any girl he happens to pick up?

Fanny   Yes. Are you shocked?

Alan   It's a bit thick; it is really!

Fanny   You're a beauty to talk!

Alan   It sounds so jolly immoral. I never thought of a girl looking on a chap just like that! I made sure you wanted to marry me if you got the chance.

Fanny   No fear! You're not good enough for me. The chap Fanny Hawthorn weds has got to be made of different stuff from you, my lad. My husband, if ever I have one, will be a man, not a fellow who'll throw over his girl at his father's bidding. You're not man enough for me. You're a nice lad, and I'm fond of you. But I wouldn't ever marry you.

Revivals have proved that the plain statement is still sharply and rightly theatrical. 'Should Fanny marry Alan?', the famous poster for *Hindle Wakes*, might be an epigraph for the drama of its time.

The Gaiety also put on *Jane Clegg* (1913) by a young Ulsterman, St John Ervine, who later, for a brief contentious spell, would be the Abbey Theatre manager; later still, a popular London dramatist (who never matched his early ambitious work) and a blunt and respected drama critic. *Jane Clegg*, as stern as its title, is about a woman, aching for independence, who has suffered much from her mean and weak-willed husband; refusing to forgive him once more—and scorning a purely theatrical trumped-up solution—she sends him from the house. A grim little drama in various shades of grey, it has continued to command a stage.

During the spring of the Theatre of Ideas, and in a new dramatic world of independence, revolt and fervent affirmation, repertory—itself an adventure—was gaining fast. Alfred Wareing, an idealist hard to resist, founded a Scottish Repertory Theatre in Glasgow, laurelled now because it attempted Chekhov's *The Seagull* in 1909, for the first time in Britain: too soon, but a brave effort, and appropriately on an autumn night. Edwardians had begun to recognize that, apart from Ibsen and—strange companions—the routine products of the French stage, there was indeed a world elsewhere. The most valuable of the new Repertories, each of which would outlive Manchester and Glasgow, were the Playhouse in Liverpool (1911), owned by many shareholders in the city; and in particular the Birmingham Repertory, child of one of the most selfless of English theatre philanthropists, Barry Vincent Jackson (who was knighted in 1925). Like Miss Horniman, he was wealthy; a man of compelling faith, and the stage had always excited him. He wanted its history to come alive, so his Repertory was a revolving mirror that reflected the centuries. Ready for experiment, he would not yield to fleeting fashion. Among his gifts were a fastidious elegance of mind and a way of discerning talent in the young: he made of his theatre a university of the stage, and one day its graduates would be everywhere in high places. Though Birmingham ('a rather sensitive and imperious city' said Lord Morley with a certain understatement) would never be easy for Jackson, he managed in his unassuming way, and in that Station Street theatre with its narrow, steeply raked auditorium, to gain permanent fame:

Here by the glow the dazzled comers saw
Illyria, the lofty towers of Troy;
They knew the word that went from Illinois,
They knew the stinging sanity of Shaw.

Barry Jackson came to his work at an hour when the dramatist, long enslaved by convention and by his actors, began to assert himself. On one side the everyday stage, placid, assured: musical comedy from the Gaiety and Daly's; plays from the 'thinking theatre' (as Barrie's girl Ginevra put it in *Alice-Sit-by-the-Fire*), 'plays always about a lady and two men, and, alas, only one of them her husband'. On the other side, beyond the drawing-rooms and the musical-comedy backcloths, a theatre of revolt, manned by the footpads of the new drama. It was Jackson's resolve, at Birmingham, 'to enlarge and increase the aesthetic sense of the public; to give living authors an opportunity of seeing their work performed, and to learn something fresh from revivals of classics; to serve an art instead of making that art serve a commercial purpose'. Briefly, not to take the cash and let the credit go. On a spring evening in 1913 Jackson spoke the rhymed iambics of a prologue by his friend John Drinkwater, before the Repertory curtain rose on *Twelfth Night*: a prologue that pledged the theatre to 'those master-men who are our captains. Life, and life again . . . . /That shall be our care/And all shall surely follow.' Follow it did.

This *Twelfth Night* was just a few months after Granville Barker had put on the comedy at the Savoy Theatre: one of three Shakespeare revivals between the autumn of 1912 and the spring of 1914 that, in speed and freshness, would revolutionize classical production, governed then by the excessively spectacular methods of Tree. These first years of the century had brought so many innovations to the theatre at large that playgoers from the mid-1890s would have been dazed. The West End of London had had another determined repertory venture, Charles Frohman's at the Duke of York's in 1910: only 128 performances compared with the near-thousand of the Court, but one that contained new plays (all of which we have noted) by Galsworthy (*Justice*), Shaw (*Misalliance*) and Barker (*The Madras House*), as well as a wire-and-sandpaper study of suburban frustration, invitingly called *Chains*, by a new dramatist, Elizabeth Baker, and a couple of short pieces by Barrie. His *The Twelve-Pound Look*, brief comedy of a wife's rebellion—again the word—was a model of its kind. Twelve pounds, to a downtrodden wife, was the price of a typewriter and of freedom, something that must always date the play neatly.

The pioneers' disappointment was the failure of the poets' theatre to produce a lasting play. Phillips's comet had almost burned itself out. Rudolf Besier's *The Virgin Goddess* (1906), set in ancient Greece and written in expected and unexceptionable iambics, was too involved with the purple dusk of dreams and the silver spirit of the dawn. Such men as Gordon Bottomley and Lascelles Abercrombie kept to the study rather than the stage, though they would have occasional performances, and neither yielded too easily to traditional influences. The least ephemeral name would be that of James Elroy Flecker, who had been a consular official in the Near East, and who died of consumption

in Switzerland when he was thirty. He saw neither of his plays in
the theatre. Indeed, the first (and, it may be held now, the better),
Don Juan, had to wait many years for even a single performance,
and the second, *Hassan*, loyally fostered by its director, Basil
Dean, would fare poorly after it had had a first sumptuous production (Henry Ainley as Hassan; music by Delius; ballets by
Fokine) at His Majesty's in the autumn of 1923—nearly nine years
after Flecker's death.

The plays kept away from any movement of their time, though
Don Juan (1911), told in a modern English setting, could have
been said to represent the Theatre of Ideas pressing upon the
theatre of Stephen Phillips. It is a fantasy that appears to be on the
rim of sunrise. Bernard Shaw detected its quality. Absurdities
aside—and political argument has to trip up a poet—there are
magnificent passages, Juan's declamation, 'Hot leapt the dawn
from deep Plutonian fires'; the often anthologized speech for the
dying patriot, which is not lyrical but dramatic verse (the patriot,
shot on the Thames Embankment, is a Tory Prime Minister); and
the epithalamium:

> Smile then, children, hand in hand,
> Bright and white as the summer snow,
> Or that young king of the Grecian land,
> Who smiled on Thetis, long ago,
> So long ago, when, heart aflame,
> The grave and gentle Peleus came
> To the shore where the Halcyon flies,
> To wed the maiden of his devotion,
> The dancing lady with sky blue eyes,
> Thetis, the darling of Paradise,
> The daughter of old Ocean . . .

Flecker has sometimes to stretch his narrative to accommodate the
verse, and this is true also of the more famous *Hassan*. Suggested
originally by an old Turkish farce, it reached the theatre as a
full-scale and often unsparing exercise in the romantic-macabre.
Through it we hear clearly the tones of the poet of the sun, of the
Damascus gates, of the high snows over Lebanon; but the details
of the play, after it has been first heard, can slide curiously from
the memory. What do remain (as in *Don Juan*) are various
speeches of sensuous beauty unparalleled in the Edwardian
theatre, the ghazel, 'How splendid in the morning glows the lily';
Ishak's 'Thy dawn, O Master of the World, thy dawn;/The hour
the lilies open on the lawn'; and the epilogue of the golden

journey ('Sweet to ride forth at evening from the wells,/When shadows pass gigantic on the sand'). Whatever we may think now of the excessive Oriental lacquering of Flecker's theatrical prose, he was a concentrated and self-critical craftsman. J. C. Squire recorded a *Hassan* passage as it was in draft and in the final text. It is worth pondering. The first draft read:

Caliph Surely you are of gentle birth and do not know your true origin. For how should a confectioner acquire the art of verse? Wherefore should a confectioner decorate his wall with a Bokhara carpet? In gems and miniatures and broidered silks I tested you at the Palace and you were surely a connoisseur. But never have I seen a man like you for poetry and carpets. When you tread on a carpet, you drop your eyes to earth to catch the pattern, and when you hear a poem you raise your eyes to the stars to hear the tune.

Hassan No mystery, Master, attended thy servant's birth. My father was a confectioner, and his father too. It thou doubtest, look at me. Also have I the stature, the grace, the outline of nobility?

Caliph But whence your poetry—and whence your carpets? Have you had a great teacher?

Hassan Master, I have not sat at the feet of the wise nor sucked honey from the lips of philosophers. But as for Poetry, I have learnt to read and I have loved to hear.

The passage appears in the final text as, simply:

Caliph What a man you are for poetry and carpets! When you tread on a carpet, you drop your eyes to earth to catch the pattern; and when your hear a poem, you raise your eyes to heaven to hear the tune. Whoever saw a confectioner like this! When did you learn poetry, Hassan of my heart?

Hassan In that great school, the Market of Baghad.

First Interval

In August 1914 (while Flecker, at Davos in Switzerland, was in the last months of his life) the First World War broke out, and the curtain was lowered suddenly on what we have called the Edwardian period, though King Edward's reign had ended in 1910. It would be nearly five years before the theatre and its conflicting elements could recover after that frightening interval, but it managed very soon to resume the impetus that had been bearing it forward while the Edwardian dramatists showed the age and body of the time its form and pressure.

True, for a few months, the War had seemed likely to set a period to all progress. No more was done about the objections to the Censorship which had been troubling the advance-guard of Edwardian writers and had led (1909) to a Select Committee of Lords and Commons to review the matter. No cheer there, and nothing during a brief dispute in 1912 over the cutting of two speeches from a Devon drama, *The Secret Woman*, directed by Granville Barker and written, of all people, by the quiet novelist of Dartmoor, Eden Phillpotts.

For a while during the War the London stage was awash with minor revivals, and with spy plays, military melodramas, musical comedies in profusion, and the still fairly novel revues in their go-as-you-please ribboning of song and dance and sketch. In the West End there was an inevitable hint of hysteria; productions whisked on and off. In the provinces Glasgow (at once) and Manchester (later) were repertory casualties. Birmingham and Liverpool struggled on through the War, and so did one or two smaller theatres: the Plymouth Repertory was actually founded at the end of 1915, and would have twenty often surprising, if little publicized, years, latterly controlled by Bernard Copping, an excellent actor who had played Henry in *Jane Clegg* at Manchester.

No important new dramatists arrived. Only Barrie (he had been created a baronet in 1913) added any important work. His two full-length plays were *A Kiss for Cinderella* (1916) and *Dear Brutus* (1917). The first of these, which was received at the time (and we must remember what that time was, in the middle of the War) as a work of 'quaint humour and fresh pathos', has now become—its dream-scene apart—uncontrollably mawkish. This was always Barrie's danger: acutely imaginative, an exact technician trained in the Edwardian theatre, he could yield in his dialogue to the self-indulgent sentimentality that clots many of his stage directions. The second play, *Dear Brutus*, is still potent. Here Barrie disposes of the belief that a 'second chance', that cherished but empty phrase, can make all the difference to the man or woman who asks for it. One of these characters says, 'It's not Fate. Fate is something outside us. What really plays the dickens with us is something in ourselves. Something that makes us go on doing the same sort of foolish things, however many chances we get.' There the veil of charm (a word that pursued Barrie through life) drops to show the weary truth. A few dissatisfied people do get their second chance in the magical wood that grows on Midsummer Eve outside the house of Lob, who is

Shakespeare's Puck grown old: 'No garden is there now. In its place is an endless wood of great trees; the nearest of them has come close to the window. It is a sombre wood, with splashes of moonshine and of blackness standing still in it.' Most of those who enter go on doing 'the same sort of fool things'. In the words of Cassius—it is a title that, though Barrie underlines it heavily, some have found puzzling—'The fault, dear Brutus, is not in our stars,/But in ourselves, that we are underlings.' Much of the second act 'to the moon in wavering morrice moves'. Then its close when Margaret, imagined daughter of the wastrel artist who finds his true self in the Wood, fades from us, terrified, in the encroaching dark, is as piercing in performance as anything in the drama of its time. 'We begin to lose her in the shadows', and 'out of the impalpable that is carrying her away', she cries in hopeless anguish: 'Daddy, come back; I don't want to be a might-have-been.'

Shaw during the War had only a few insignificant shavings; but he was already at work on *Heartbreak House* and *Back to Methuselah*. Galsworthy, though he had written a good deal since *Justice*, did nothing that marched with his important plays: his compassionate ardour would not be entirely refuelled in the theatre until *The Skin Game* a few years ahead. In their autumn, Pinero and Jones, for so long the great twin brethren, had begun to lose touch. Jones, who had had one genuine flash of comedy in *Mary Goes First* (1913), aided by that dictator among comediennes, Marie Tempest, failed completely in *The Pacifists* (1917): political opinions are uneasy to dramatize. Pinero's *The Big Drum* (1915), a thin comedy on the vulgarity of self-advertisement, lasted for a hundred performances; his other play of the war period, *The Freaks* (1918), an 'idyll of suburbia', was negligible. Somerset Maugham's merciless comedy of American expatriates in England, *Our Betters* (1915), began its life in New York and would not reach London for eight years. He had also a supple and unexaggerated women's comedy, *Caroline* (1916), of which he said with candour, years later: 'If I were a critic I should perhaps feel it my duty to make the observation that the play really is finished by the end of the first act.' His *Love in a Cottage* (1918) which the *Times* critic regarded as an attempt to expose the demoralizing influence of the lake of Como, has long slipped into oblivion.

Verse plays were as rare as ever in a period inimical to them. Stephen Phillips made his farewell: the magniloquent *Armageddon* (1915), presented by John Martin Harvey, with a prologue in

Hell and a scene in which the spirit of Joan of Arc, appearing to a British general tempted to avenge the destruction of Rheims by reprisals against Cologne, declaimed: 'Have I not seen the very stars in heaven/Flash all together at some splendid "No"?' Phillips died in December that year, aged forty-nine; he left an estate of £5. John Masefield during the War wrote three plays which survive in the text rather than the theatre; *Good Friday* (1917) is much the most familiar, a rhymed drama of the Crucifixion, plain statement (decorated only in the speeches for a blind man) that contains another of Masefield's Messenger narrations and ends in a dying fall when the play sinks to peace beneath the Paschal moon. In a brief historical episode, *Philip the King* (1914), Philip of Spain sits at daybreak, awaiting news of the Armada, hearing in his sleep mocking and accusing voices, and at length accepting the tragedy of defeat ('Give a bruised spirit peace'). The most dramatic of Masefield's plays from this period remains neglected, *The Faithful* (1915), a snow-charged study in loyalty and revenge from the ceremonious, sinister Japan of 1701, which Jackson put on at the Birmingham Repertory. Masefield, like Yeats, had been impressed by the Japanese Nō drama.

One arrival (at the Kingsway Theatre) early in the War excited connoisseurs: scenes from the vast Napoleonic epic of *The Dynasts* upon which Thomas Hardy, in his Dorset retreat, had spent four Edwardian years: a work in an extraordinary assemblage of styles, and composed in three parts, nineteen acts and one hundred and thirty scenes, that no one had contemplated seriously in theatrical terms. Now Granville Barker—who else?—believed that its hour had come. He could give only a selective impression of a chronicle that moved bewilderingly between bathos and genius, the blankest of functional verse and the rarest achievement in threnody, rondeau, ballad and choral lyric ('Yea, the coneys are scared by the thud of hoofs'). In spite of those wonderfully evocative stage directions for the study, Hardy had never intended *The Dynasts* for what he used to call a mummery-show. None had really expected to hear it, or passages from it, in normal performance—one day it would reach its fitting stage of the imagination, on radio—and nothing could have been more daunting than the apparatus of the Overworld: such lines as 'These are the Prime Volitions,—fibrils, veins,/Will–tissues, nerves, and pulses of the Cause,/That heave throughout the Earth's compositure.' Barker chose with sympathetic care. Henry Ainley, as Reader, recited at a desk before the stage; two grey-robed women, one on each side of the proscenium arch, spoke for Chorus; and the scenes were assembled in three sections, Trafalgar, the Peninsular War, Waterloo. It was all a surprise to Hardy. Quite unpractical, he had suggested that, if his play were ever performed, there should be 'a monotonic delivery of speeches with dreamy conventional gestures, something in the manner traditionally maintained by the old Christmas mummers'.

The Dynasts lasted for a few months. During the rest of the War there was nothing comparable to it. In the record-books it is flanked by revivals of *Drake* and *The Earl and the Girl*. These were typical.

Most wartime productions were either revivals or plays that flicked out of sight and mind. Harold Brighouse, Lancashire dramatist of various solid plays of the industrial North, wrote the forthright comedy of *Hobson's Choice* (London, 1916), which has been revived again and again with its intolerably managing young woman from the Salford of 1882. St John Ervine's sternly affecting *John Ferguson* (Abbey, Dublin, 1915) would not get to London—and then only to Hammersmith—until after the War. Many other plays were merely faint scribbles. Who now remembers *Jolly Jack Tar*, *The Freedom of the Seas*, *By Pigeon Post*? Some of the musical productions would linger, *The Maid of the Mountains* (1917) for one, with a mediocre libretto by Frederick Lonsdale who blossomed into a popular dramatist, and the *Bing Boy* revues mainly because in one of these George Robey and Violet Loraine sang 'If you were the only girl in the world.' But the piece that would gum itself to the records, though its run has since been far exceeded, was Oscar Asche's 'musical tale of the East', *Chu Chin Chow* (1916), less of a play than a brand of fantastic revue with real camels, the Cobbler's Song, and 'Any time is kissing time.' It was running still when the War ended, and indeed went on—at Tree's His Majesty's (Tree had died in 1917)—until 1921, part of the mythology of the London stage. *Cairo*, a 'mosaic in music and mime', followed it. After being so involved with one kind of gorgeous East, His Majesty's would be scarcely a tactful choice for *Hassan* in 1923.

By the close of the War the theatre had had to recognize the now dangerous competition of the cinema and to know that it would never again be standing alone. One day the silent film would expand to the talking film; radio would change from mild domestic fun with a cat's-whisker primitive to a national institution; and later yet, after we had crossed the wide ravine of the Second World War, television would overwhelm the country.

Though at the armistice of November 1918 most of these things were beyond the horizon, the silent film was already a theatre-wrecker. As early as 1909 a column of notes on the music-hall had ended with the words: 'The opposition of skating-rinks and electric theatres has been felt keenly in certain quarters during the year, but the rivalry of these forms of amusement to the Variety business is hardly likely to be permanent.' In 1913 a writer on the stage had said, more anxiously than he would admit: 'The drama can never be affected by the popularity or otherwise of the kinematograph. . . . So long as it is true to itself and produces the right kind of play, all the picture palaces in the world can have no effect upon box-office receipts.' He would have been much less dogmatic in 1919 when people had begun the habit that, once started, they did not drop for some time, of going to 'the pictures' every week. Hollywood astronomers found new planets monthly; in Britain such names as Alma Taylor and Chrissie White meant more in the provinces than did those of the average West End leading actress. The music-halls, which had in any event to meet the provincial rivalry of draggle-tail revue, would suffer badly. So would the touring system, and so would the lesser repertory companies.

Always, it seemed, the old guard was battling in retreat. Once, the Theatre of Ideas had challenged the Theatre Theatrical just as the bright, sharp radiance of electricity had challenged the more romantic glow of the old gas limes on a storytellers' stage of illusion and make-believe. Now that theatre of traditional illusion would fade before the tin boxes that arrived on Mondays in town after town, with a week's entertainment in the can. Multiplying amateur companies helped gallantly to keep the living theatre alive in the stricken areas. But the days of the old-school pomping folk were numbered.

There was fresh hope for the classical stage, though in the winter of 1918 none would have speculated on the future. At the corner of Waterloo Road and The Cut, back beyond the south bank of the Thames, a redoubtable woman, Lilian Baylis, was transforming the battered house known as the Old Vic, and latterly a species of coffee-and-culture Mission, into a popular home for Shakespeare and opera. (A National Theatre, first proposed in 1848, was coming a little nearer.) The renaissance down in Stratford-upon-Avon (then far from theatrically fashionable) was on its way, even if now it needs hindsight to detect the faint glimmer. Frank Benson—knighted in 1916—had grandly pre-served across the years the spirit of annual Shakespeare festivals that had necessarily been brief and intimate. The summer festival of 1919, first under W. Bridges-Adams, would mark a change no one then realized.

Between the Wars

The theatre of the nineteen-twenties, with many of the conventions relaxed or struck away during the War, would be a furious chaos of contradictions, doubts and conflicting enthusiasms. The nineteen-thirties, crowded as they were, appear now to have been relatively jaded, depending largely upon the vigour of their classical revivals and the advent of new players.

These were fermenting decades of contradiction and paradox; of fashions that cancelled each other out and experiment that could be as wild as cakes-and-ale comedy would grow desperate. It was Shaw's noble autumn; the zenith of another Dublin genius, Sean O'Casey, with his Elizabethan union of tragedy and farce; the time of the young Coward and the older Maugham; of the foreshadowing, in two plays by T. S. Eliot, of another surge of verse drama; and of the work of the century's prime farceur, Ben Travers. It was the time of such various writers as Frederick Lonsdale, J. B. Priestley, Emlyn Williams and James Bridie, and of a few other plays (from many produced) that are likely to come again from the shelf. The actor-manager all but disappeared. The director took charge. Great acting flowered. Sybil Thorndike apostrophized the towers of burning Troy or faced her judges at Rouen; Edith Evans, voice of the Restoration, entered St James's Park, fans spread and streamers out; John Gielgud, Hamlet of his generation, spoke for the Terry line.

True, little memorable happened in 1919, hyphen between the war years and the new decade. John Drinkwater's *Abraham Lincoln*, bred at the Birmingham Repertory, reached the obscure Lyric, behind the markets at Hammersmith, that had been bought by a fastidious idealist, Nigel Playfair. In his biographical dramas Drinkwater (already among the freshest of the now undervalued Georgian poets) aimed at 'keeping in the sparest prose idiom something of the enthusiasm and poignancy of verse'; he never managed this better than in the austere and urgent *Lincoln*, with its chorus-verses for two Chroniclers that, in revival, it has been wrongly fashionable to cut. In another play new to the London of 1919, *The Lost Leader* (acted at the Court), Lennox Robinson, the Irish dramatist, suggested that, after all,

Charles Stewart Parnell did not die in 1891; he merely feigned death, allowing another to take his place: the narrative had to fade inconclusively, but its core was truly theatrical enough. It has not been revived in London.

Here we must think first of writers who led, or who would lead, the British drama between the wars. Bernard Shaw re-appeared in 1921 at an old address, the Court Theatre, with *Heartbreak House*, 'a fantasia in the Russian manner on English themes' (he used a Chekhovian technique long before Chekhov was fully regarded in England). A summary of Shavian thought and experience, the play—warning to the irresponsible and indolent—is a satirical comedy upon the heartbreak house that, ostensibly, was cultured, leisured pre-war Europe, and the leisured class that had let civilization slide to bankruptcy. Some of it is perverse; but Shotover, its railing Isaiah of an old sea-captain, can glow into incandescent prose. The poet in Shaw, usually buried many fathoms deep, does emerge in passages that sigh about the mind as fragments of a dream can do until we ask whether they, or the affairs of the waking world, are the true reality. An exchange during the third-act coda on a summer night in Sussex would never sound more apt than it did during the Second World War. 'Learn your business as an Englishman,' says Shotover. 'And what', asks Hector, 'may my business as an Englishman be?' Whereupon Shotover rakes him fore and aft: 'Navigation. Learn it and live; or leave it and be damned.'

It would be some years before *Heartbreak House* grew into the public mind; many of its early critics were dismissive. *Back to Methuselah*, which Shaw called a metabiological pentateuch, and which reached London (inevitably the Court) in 1924, had been presented at Birmingham during the previous autumn. Barry Jackson's decision was the bravest ever taken by a repertory theatre. ('Is your family provided for?' Shaw asked Jackson.) The pentateuch took four nights to present: a Shavian *Ring*, it is a full-dress festival of the dramatist's philosophy, passing from the primal innocence of Eden, at the Biblical 4004 B.C., to a world 'As Far as Thought Can Reach', established at A.D. 31,920. A vast parable of creative evolution (without the 'distractions and embellishments of *Man and Superman*') shines into radiance under the first dayspring with the Shavian Serpent ('I have willed and willed and willed'), who indoctrinates Eve under the greenwood tree. Eve, much the more compelling of our first parents, tends the flame watchfully through her long speech in Mesopotamia when she is spinning and Adam delving, and Cain, their warrior son, is first of the clanking Jingoes. Next, the sequence moves downhill towards a Hampstead symposium of the early nineteen-twenties when a bantering, thwacking Shaw, the first rapture dimmed, lampoons a pair of Liberal politicians easily identified, and allows them little but a certain resilience, a readiness to take punishment. Here we do lose sight of 'the tremendous miracle-working force of will nerved to creation by a conviction of necessity'. The debate continues, with similar farcical decorations, in *The Thing Happens* (2170) where Shaw wastes time on his favourite Britannus joke, gibing at the Anglo-Saxon attitude; comic embellishment blurs the great theme, the Shavian insistence that where there's a will there's a way, that a span of threescore years and ten is death in infancy, a mayfly-fading, and that to save the world man must wax great in years and wisdom.

Part Four, *The Tragedy of an Elderly Gentleman*, is a dust of flippancies occasionally aerated by a rallying wit. Then, in Part Five, *As Far As Thought Can Reach*, though man, tied to his 'tyrannous body', is still subject to death, Lilith, coming from the dark, looks to a day when man's will has conquered, when the last stream between flesh and the spirit has been forded, and life (world without end) is a glory of pure intellect, 'the vortex freed from matter', a 'whirlpool in pure intelligence that, when the world began, was a whirlpool in pure force'. Before the dimming of the lights, the children and the ancients—'these infants', says Lilith—have held debate in the glade beneath the hill. On the uplands the time for flippancy is passing. At the last, Shaw's prose, finding its gravest harmony, makes music for ear and mind:

> Of Life only is there no end; and though of its million starry mansions many are empty and many still unbuilt, and though its vast domain is as yet unbearably desert, my seed shall one day fill it and master its matter to its uttermost confines. And for what may be beyond, the eyesight of Lilith is too short. It is enough that there is a beyond.

Back to Methuselah is a sustained intellectual feat, though dramatically, as Ivor Brown would say, the play is 'as variable in value as our English skies are variable in weather'. It has had a few well-judged revivals, the last by the National Theatre company in two nights at the Old Vic during the summer of 1969.

Immediately after the pentateuch, in March 1924, *Saint Joan*—staged in New York three months earlier—arrived at the

New Theatre, with Sybil Thorndike as Joan, one of the major performances of the century. Shaw took a theme suggested to him by his wife, that to the old-school romantic would have meant heroics, fanfares, the pageantry of Court and conquest, and a tremendous melodramatic to-do round the stake at Rouen. (All of this very far indeed from the Shakespearian, late-Tudor, view of Joan in *Henry VI, Part I*.) Shaw was never a romantic: to him—as he would say in a Preface—Joan was simply 'the most notable warrior Saint in the Christian calendar, and the queerest fish among the eccentric worthies of the Middle Ages'. She combined 'inept youth and academic ignorance' with 'great natural capacity, push, courage, devotion, originality, and oddity'. The first London audience found a country girl stripped of the obvious theatrical blazonry and speaking with a country accent ('Where be Dauphin?') There were moments unlooked-for in Shaw, the changing of the wind on the Loire, the voices in the Cathedral bells. But, instead of the Coronation, he went straight to the ambulatory at Rheims when all the pomps had passed. Instead of the stake in Rouen market-place, to a contentious epilogue on a restless midnight of summer lightning in the year 1456. The ages kissed and commingled in the bedchamber of Charles VII; Joan, Venerable and Blessed, had the play's last word, 'O God that madest this beautiful earth, when will it be ready to receive Thy saints? How long, O Lord, how long?' Today, when *Saint Joan* is as assured a classic as any play of the century, we have come to recognize its warmth, the wit of the debate in Warwick's tent, and the power of the trial. Equally, we regret the occasional slang, the Shavian chaplain, and certain elementary jests. All said, it remains a firmly controlled episodic chronicle that, since Dame Sybil, has found a succession of Joans, among them Mary Newcombe, Wendy Hiller, Elisabeth Bergner, Celia Johnson, Siobhan McKenna, Barbara Jefford, Joan Plowright and Eileen Atkins.

After this there was a five years' gap until, at the first of the Malvern festivals (1929; Shaw as the patron saint) and, later in London, Barry Jackson—knighted by now—presented the political extravaganza of *The Apple Cart*. Its author described this King-versus-Cabinet comedy as 'a frightful bag of stage tricks as old as Sophocles', but audiences have accepted happily a rapid cut-and-thrust in which the King (Magnus of Britain) wins not by exercising his royal authority, but by threatening to resign and to go to the democratic poll. The poorest scene, an interlude with the King's 'antidote to democracy', his fluttering and swooning mistress, Orinthia, has been disproportionately applauded because of Orinthia's first player, Edith Evans, who gave to the part a false reputation.

The Apple Cart has lasted longer than any of its successors during the nineteen-thirties, though all have been revived. *Too True To Be Good* (1932) demands an animated microbe, a chambermaid-nurse-adventuress, a burglar-parson, a Bunyan-inspired sergeant, a private soldier (Meek), clearly drawn from T. E. Lawrence of Arabia—a friend of the Shaws—and a sententious anchorite. These personages join in a piece about which Shaw was thoroughly frank. People, he said, must laugh for an hour, be serio-comically entertained for the next hour, and then —when not tired of being wholly serious—receive the torrent of sermons they need. Hence *Too True To Be Good*, in effect a course of lectures on the medical profession, post-War youth, religious doubt, and any other subject that caught the dramatist's fancy. The night ends with an eloquent cry for an affirmative in a world of negatives: more eloquent than anything in the next play, *On The Rocks* (1933), though this gained renewed life at a Mermaid Theatre revival in 1975. Set in the Cabinet Room of 10 Downing Street, and filled with people called Aloysia Brollikins, Sir Broadfoot Basham, and Sir Bemrose Hotspot—Shaw, like Charles Lamb, believed wistfully in the comic name—its most persuasive person is a democrat, Hipney, from the Isle of Cats, who observes, 'All this country, or any country, has to stand between it and blue hell is the conscience of them that are capable of governing it.'

In *The Simpleton of the Unexpected Isles* (Malvern, 1935), which did not reach London for ten years, and was then seen only at a club theatre, Shaw returns to creative evolution. Intermittently dramatic, it is a fable now of polygamy in the Pacific, now of a herald angel, testily genial, who wings from the empyrean to sound the Last Trump. The Shavian Judgment Day has no apocalyptic voices, thunder and lightning, merely a heavenly staff-officer to explain that the drones, those who have neither use nor purpose, will be extinguished for ever; for those who survive the judgment there will be an eternity of surprise and wonder. Shaw is inexplicit about the method of selection. We gather that usefulness and adaptability are two of the major virtues, but what are the others?

He had three more full-length plays during the Thirties: *The Millionairess* (1936), which is negligible; *Geneva* (1938), topical satire soon out of date but worth revival for the sake of its comic portraits of the dictators, Mussolini as Bombardone and Hitler as Battler; and *In Good King Charles's Golden Days* (1939), acted at the Malvern Festival when Shaw was eighty-three. This comedy, mingling figures from the Restoration (King Charles, Isaac Newton, George Fox, Nell Gwyn and so on), and set in Newton's house at Cambridge, dispenses with action almost entirely. Once manœuvred into sight, the people are left to talk; the last act is a duologue between King Charles and his Queen, Catherine of Braganza. It is 'a true history that never happened', a wise, oddly serene play in perfectly cadenced rhythms.

Still writing at the outset of the Second World War in 1939, Shaw was the last of the theatre's elder statesmen, from twenty years earlier, in full production. Pinero, Jones, Barrie and Galsworthy had died. Yeats, who died in the summer of 1939, had added a few pieces of myth and ritual and two brief and startling plays, one in prose, *The Words Upon the Window-Pane* (1934) which brings to a Dublin séance the tortured voices of Jonathan Swift and Vanessa, and the even shorter *Purgatory* (1939) in verse: this is set outside a ruined house where ghosts 'must re-live their transgressions . . .' not once but many times. Maugham, having announced typically that he had finished his work for the stage, just as typically kept his vow. Of the Barker–Vedrenne dramatists, neither Granville-Barker himself (hyphenated now) nor Masefield was writing much for the public stage. Masefield had a few verse plays; Granville-Barker, with his second wife Helen, an American—his first had been the actress Lillah McCarthy—had contented himself with translating some minor comedies from the Spanish; two original plays, *The Secret Life* and *His Majesty*, were apparently designed for the study. Laurence Housman, who long before had collaborated with him in the fantasy of *Prunella*, had a belated success with *Victoria Regina*, his 'scenes from a biography', done at a club theatre, the Gate, in 1935, and in Coronation year (1937) permitted at last its full West End caparison.

Between the wars Pinero and Jones, regal from the eighteen-nineties and the Edwardian world, had all but abdicated. Twice, and each time unluckily, Pinero returned. In *The Enchanted Cottage* (1922) he tried to show how, through love, beauty is born. A young, war-broken man and an unattractive woman, who have married only as a formal gesture 'for mutual consolation', find true love under the spell of an enchanted cottage; while their love is constant they must remain 'fair and bonny' to each other. The play seems, incredibly, to be Pinero under the influence of Barrie;

it has gone into the darkness, and so has the tired, ghost-like comedy of *A Cold June* with which a great dramatist ended his career: he left two plays unproduced in London, *Dr Harmer's Holidays*, a Jekyll-and-Hyde variant (tried in New York) and *Child Man*. Henry Arthur Jones, for long his friend and rival, had one final success, *The Lie*, written ten years before its London appearance in 1923: a sturdily old-fashioned melodrama with a third-act curtain when a betrayed woman (Sybil Thorndike at her most forcible) rushed upon her betrayer, crying 'Judas sister! Judas sister!'

John Galsworthy died in 1933. As a novelist he had continued a stately progress. As a dramatist his work was a sierra. After his death an over-zealous manager endangered his reputation by reviving the plays in unwanted 'festivals'. Later, almost totally eclipsed in the theatre—even *Justice*, not ideally cast, failed in 1968—he had posthumous fame on television, especially with the elaborate serial version of his group of novels, *The Forsyte Saga*: one of the few television productions remembered in what so far has been a transient medium, the talk of a day or so, forgotten in a week. During the nineteen-twenties Galsworthy had his most prolific theatre decade with a dozen plays, none without its quality, though after a lapse of time several can appear to be bloodless.

'A drama', he wrote early in his career, 'must be sharpened so as to have a spire of meaning.' Determined to be judicial, he lost at times the theatrical drive, the fierce impulse of a partisan piece in which right must be right and there can be no contrary argument. Yet he could usually create a conflict, as he did invigoratingly in the pride-and-prejudice dramas of *The Skin Game* (1920) and *Loyalties* (1922). The first, and better, reports the battle between the Hillcrists and the Hornblowers, the county's old order and the thrusting new-rich. 'All life's a struggle', Hillcrist says to his daughter, 'between people at different stages of development in different positions, with different amounts of social influence and property. And the only thing to do is to have rules of the game and keep them.' Shamelessly, Mrs Hillcrist ignores the rules to defeat the intruders. Her husband, the scrupulous squire, mourns in the last words of the play:

What is it that gets loose when you begin a fight, and makes you what you think you're not? What blinding evil? Begin as you may, it ends in this—skin game! Skin game! . . .

Mrs Hillcrist I don't understand.

Hillcrist When we began this fight we had clean hands—are they clean now? What's gentility worth if it can't stand fire?

Loyalties, in its time a flash of social realism, considers caste warfare in Britain. A Jewish newcomer, aflame with racial pride, is in the right when snobbishness has deemed that he should be wrong. Only at the play's end, as Eric Gillett has said, does the author's intention become fully clear. 'Loyalty is not enough. There must also be understanding and charity, and that is a point Galsworthy continued to make throughout his working life.' Of his other post-War plays, *Windows, The Forest, The Show* and the rest, which usefully stiffened the London theatre of the nineteen-twenties, we need name only two. In *Escape* (1926) the problem, in its simplest form, is this: what would you do if you met an escaped convict? The convict, formerly Captain Matt Denant, has reached Dartmoor Prison through one of the typical accidents that haunt Galsworthy's people. From the first he is doomed, but the dramatist makes an exciting thing of the hare-and-hounds chase across the moor, though some of the figures encountered are cardboard. There is less cardboard in *The Roof*, Galsworthy's final play (1929), a group of episodes in a French hotel imperilled by fire. Much of the writing is just and precise: the play's flat failure, which kept its author from working again for the stage, was a small tragedy of the period. Galsworthy will come again. Now we can remember his affirmation: 'A good plot is that sure edifice which rises out of the interplay of circumstances on temperament, or of temperament on circumstances, within the enclosing atmosphere of an idea.'

Barrie, for whom this would have been over-explicit, wrote only two other important plays apart from a dinner-table anecdote, *Shall We Join the Ladies?* (1921–2), designed simply to tease, and put on for a run as a curtain-raiser (for such bonuses still existed) to *Loyalties*. Denis Mackail said it was unfinished because Barrie could not finish it: 'Nobody really minded who the murderer was, and if the author had been quite certain himself, and had gone on to tell them, it might easily have been a much flatter affair.' Sixteen years elapsed between *Mary Rose* (1920) and *The Boy David*. The first, a ghost-play about a girl who vanishes on a Hebridean isle-that-likes to-be-visited and returns, unchanged, after twenty-five years, has uncomfortably whimsical passages. During others we feel the shiver, the helpless terror, of the second-act curtain of *Dear Brutus*. In 1920 *Mary Rose* trembled immediately into success; it had in it something to console many whom the War had bereaved; today its best scenes bear revival, though listeners have to choose which side they are on when they hear the line (again Barrie's lifelong obsession with motherhood, perceptible in so many of his plays): 'The loveliest time will be when my baby is a man and takes me on his knee instead of my putting him on mine.' *The Boy David* (1936) was an unlucky failure in performance, a much-pondered Biblical play, a fragile, elusive invention based upon the First Book of Samuel, designed for the Austrian actress Elisabeth Bergner, and calling (as Barrie admitted) for 'an adroitness in stage effect that is beyond the author's skill who knows what he wants but not how to get it'. Unexpectedly defective in structure (the third-act Visions are clumsy), the piece had its admirers, among them Granville-Barker (who had by then become the theatre's elder statesman) and since Barrie's death it has gained support in more direct and less costly productions than the first. The trouble with his work must always be its self-indulgent sweetness which at times can only remind us of what Polly, in *Caste*, felt about redcurrant jam, 'at the first taste, sweet; and afterwards, shuddery'. Barrie, we may feel, knew. One of the last stage directions in the closing David-and-Jonathan scene is, simply: 'They are not sentimental.'

Somerset Maugham's dialogue, except in one late play of barren experiment, *The Sacred Flame*, was seldom shuddery. Four of his dozen-odd plays in London between the wars should live, most notably *The Circle*, a show-piece of twentieth-century comedy relishing in narration, precise in dialogue, character relentlessly observed, wit both verbal and vital. It is the tale of a deplorable prig and his wife who yearns for escape; of his father, a 'downy old bird', who ponders epigrams in a cottage in the grounds; and an ultimate elopement, without rope-ladder and conscious moon, but with a car in the drive and two veterans of thirty years' experience to speed the departure: there the wheel spins full circle. As A. V. Cookman, one of the most searching drama critics of his period, said after a revival, a brief speech, enormously effective in its place, completely exposes the comedy's serious purpose without exposing the smallest rumple in its texture:

> My dear, I don't know that in life it matters so much what you do as what you are. No one can learn by the experience of another because no circumstances are quite the same. If we made rather a hash of things, perhaps it was because we were rather trivial people. You can do anything in this world if you're prepared to take the consequences, as consequences depend on character.

It is curious that, on the first night of *The Circle* (1921) the Haymarket gallery was what the young Daisy Ashford would call 'sneery'. No trouble at all at the London première of *Our Betters* (1923), just eight years after it had been acted in New York. The play begins with an ironical moment often overlooked, the sound, on the pavement below the Mayfair drawing-room, of the simple chant, 'Won't you buy my sweet lavender? . . . sweet-scented lavender.' What follows is a merciless comedy that needs merciless playing, the exposure of a gang of selfish, amoral American expatriates. Maugham's interest is in those he is racking and flaying; they are thoroughly alive under torture, whereas the more respectable characters are the only ones to remain rigid on the page, and do not move in the theatre with any comfort. The amoralists, lit by their phosphorescent marsh-fires, are buoyantly active, and witty without ceasing. 'I have plenty of heart', says one of these pilgrim-daughters, 'but it beats for people of my own class'.

In such a survey as this we can suggest merely which of a dramatist's plays may survive. Critics seldom consider what the too often unwarily applauded work of their own period may be like thirty years on. Kipling was wise:

> You've a better chance to guess
> At the meaning of success
> (Which is greatness—*vide* Press)
> When you've seen it in perspective in the Files.

The Constant Wife (1926; London 1927), and certainly Maugham's last play but one, *For Services Rendered* (1932), appear to be marked for survival; not *The Sacred Flame* (1929), metallic and bewilderingly prolix (he tried, unhappily, a 'greater elaboration of dialogue than he had been in the habit of using'); or the ultimate *Sheppey* (1933), sardonic and uneasily symbolic; or even *The Breadwinner* (1930), a satirical masculine parallel to *A Doll's House*. This anecdote of a stockbroker who stamps on his silk hat and prepares to go out of the life of the 'engaging and delightful' family (Maugham's phrase) that has bored him unutterably, does need a major performance to keep us alert. *The Constant Wife*, neo-Restoration comedy of marital manœuvring, has a cheerful artificial raillery. *For Services Rendered* seems to grow with the years, a picture of post-War chaos represented by life in a country solicitor's house in Kent that a critic, James Agate, referring to Iago's comment (*Othello*, I. iii. 350) on the bitter drug, called the

Villa Coloquintida. They are just as they were, says a blinded man about 'the incompetent fools who ruled the nations':

> I know that we were sacrificed to their vanity, their greed, and their stupidity. And the worst of it is that as far as I can tell they haven't learnt a thing. They're just as vain, they're just as greedy, they're just as stupid as ever they were. They muddle on, muddle on, and one of these days they'll muddle us all into another war.

The play is written in a stripped, wintry prose. Maugham had nothing left for the Theatre of Entertainment. Presently, after *Sheppey* was over, and according to plan, he left the theatre, deciding that there was autumn in the air, tiring of stage conventions, and sighing for the liberty of fiction. He had been a sovereign wit, he had known always how to tell a story in terms of the theatre, and he had written at least one masterpiece.

So to the new dramatists, with a last word on John Masefield for the sake of a single play, the now remote *Melloney Holtspur* (1922). It had a few matinées in the summer of 1922, and some listeners may still remember an expert radio production thirty years later. A fantasy of the haunters and the haunted, a shadowed-spring and midnight-moon linking of two generations, the ghosts of the past woven into the fortunes of the future, it has always stayed in shadow; through the years directors and readers should rediscover it and its use of the watching ghosts in a way the Elizabethans might have understood.

Among the new dramatists there would be the Irish genius, Sean O'Casey; the popular, likeable, extremely professional and later much revived Noël Coward who, in a long working life of fifty years (towards the end of which he was knighted) would write perhaps three plays for posterity; the prolific and glossy Frederick Lonsdale, who had already had a career in musical-play libretti; the Scot, James Bridie; the Welshman, Emlyn Williams; and the Yorkshireman, J. B. Priestley (their territorial designations would be reflected in their work). Ben Travers proved himself to be the century's high master of farce, known in his time as 'Aldwych farce'; and several dramatists wrote one or two plays that would last. Indeed, between the wars there was fully as much, if not more, important work than there would be later in the century, from the so-called revolution of 1956 onwards. The difference was that plays by the earlier dramatists were disciplined in a form that would become outmoded (not at all the same thing as saying that it was false or inferior).

Above the newcomers were the first few plays of the Irishman, Sean O'Casey (Shaun O'Cathasaigh, though that was a name for Dublin usage only). After a bleak period during the nineteen-thirties he would never fully recover his public, but four of his plays—two of them in particular—have moved into history. The first three, *The Shadow of a Gunman* (1922; London, 1927), *Juno and the Paycock* (Dublin, 1924; London, 1925) and *The Plough and the Stars* (1926) were bred at the Abbey Theatre. There he was praised often for being a naturalistic dramatist; Granville-Barker would speak one day of 'spontaneous realism'. But little is photographic in O'Casey's work. The dialogue is heightened, richly cadenced; the action has the Elizabethan juxtaposition of tragedy and farce. O'Casey was a man of the Dublin tenements, a labourer and a rebel; he knew he could write, and he wrote. When Dublin, in traditional fashion, opposed him, he came to London; later, after W. B. Yeats had myopically refused *The Silver Tassie* for the Abbey, he fought his way with insistent courage, aided by his loyal wife Eileen and a multitude of friends. He was over forty when the Abbey staged *The Shadow of a Gunman*, a two-act tragedy set in 1920 during the struggle in Dublin between the rebels and the Black-and-Tans. It is the tale of a vain tenement poet who has no objection to being thought a gunman if it helps him with an admiring girl; the play darkens to black tragedy. Thereafter came the two unassailable masterpieces. *Juno and the Paycock* is a tragi-comedy of a Dublin tenement during the troubles of 1922; its 'Paycock' is 'Captain' Boyle, a slow-strutting waster of the taproom who, though he had been only once on the water, and then in a collier from Dublin to Liverpool, can talk in this way with Joxer Daly, his jackal and man of quotations, with a face like 'a bundle of crinkled paper':

Joxer God be with the young days when you were steppin' the deck of a manly ship, with the win' blowin' a hurricane through the masts, and the only sound you'd hear was 'Port your helm!', an' the only answer, 'Port it is, sir!'

Boyle Them was days, Joxer, them was days. Nothin' was too hot or too heavy for me then. Sailin' from the Gulf of Mexico to the Antanarctic Ocean, I seen things, I seen things, Joxer, that no mortal man should speak about that knows his catechism. Ofen, an' ofen, when I was fixed to the wheel with a marlinspike, an' the win's blowin' fierce, an' the waves lashin' and lashin', till you'd think every minute was goin' to be your last, an' it blowed an' blowed—blew is the right word, Joxer, but blowed is what the sailors use . . .

Joxer Aw, it's a daarlin' word, a daarlin' word.

Plenty of gusto there, not much 'photographic realism'. Juno is the Paycock's wife (nothing to do with 'Homer's glorious story of ancient gods and heroes') who reaches ineffable tragedy in her last mourning. No one who saw the first London performance will have forgotten Sara Allgood's cry, or Arthur Sinclair cocking a grave eye, coaxing a phrase, observing that the whole world's in a 'state o'chassis', or Sydney Morgan's Joxer saying in his ingratiating drone: 'I've met many a Wicklow man in me time, but I never met wan that was any good.'

Like *Juno*, *The Plough and the Stars*, second of the great twin brethren, is compact of the darkest tragedy and the most exuberant farce, written in a rushing tumble of words, rich in the unexpected epithet, and lit always by a poetic fire. Both plays move on a full, free tide of speech. *The Plough*, compassionate tragedy of a disrupted people, is in the Dublin of 1915–16: rioters during its first Abbey production in 1926 said foolishly that it defamed the men of Easter Week. There were no more interruptions after the fifth night when Yeats, appearing on the Abbey stage, an offended deity, asked: 'Is this going to be a recurring celebration of Irish genius? Synge first and then O'Casey; Dublin has once more rocked the cradle of a reputation . . . The fame of O'Casey is born here tonight. This is apotheosis.' *The Plough and the Stars*, once experienced, dwells in the mind from the moment when the charwoman Mrs Gogan begins her chatter, to the final anguish and the soldiers' chorus of 'Keep the Home Fires Burning' above the night of grief: 'The glare in the sky seen through the window flares into a fuller and a deeper red.'

With these plays O'Casey established himself among the major British dramatists. *The Silver Tassie* (written 1928; London, 1929) seemed to be blocked when Yeats insensitively refused it for the Abbey—his argument makes no sense today—but C. B. Cochran, ever an adventurous manager, staged it in Shaftesbury Avenue. It had the imprimatur of Shaw ('literally a hell of a play') and, in years ahead, of Granville-Barker, who said that O'Casey,

broke loose . . . into that remarkable second act of *The Silver Tassie*, where he employs symbolism of scene and character, choric rhythms of speech and movement, the insistence of rhyme, the dignity of ritual, every transcendental means available, in his endeavour to give us, seated in our comfortable little theatre, some sense of the chaos of war. At the centre of the play is a Dublin footballer who returns from Flanders paralysed from the waist downwards: there is a fierce contrast between the first act and the third and fourth. But the key scene is in the second act in the war zone, by "the jagged and lacerated ruin of what was once a monastery", all dominated by the shape of a great howitzer: there O'Casey moves into the chanted choruses, the haunting terrors, the wild humours, the invocation to the gun ('Guardian of our love and hate and fear,/Speak for us to the inner ear of God'), and the final cry, "Every man born of woman to the guns, to the guns."

Though the *Tassie*, unsparing portrait of war's horror and its aftermath, will never be acclaimed as the earlier plays are, it is grimly, harshly affecting: more so than the anti-realistic *Within the Gates* (1933), with four Hyde Park scenes, on a spring morning, a summer noon, an autumn evening and a winter night, that can hardly carry their apparatus of the poetic-symbolic.

Noël Coward, a dramatist to whom O'Casey was by no means sympathetic, began his career in 1920—before then he had been a young actor—and through half a century conducted his own Theatre of Entertainment. He had (his own phrase) a talent to amuse. He was also a technician who knew just how to time and present his clipped dialogue: he could write as laconically as another, and entirely different, dramatist of a succeeding period, Harold Pinter. The trouble would be that he wrote so rarely in permanent ink: in trying most types of play except verse drama, he preserved an unvaried cast of mind and outlook. His people used a swift, brittle, ephemeral wit, 'tapping like typewriters', Mrs Patrick Campbell said (she did not add that the ribbon could be faint). Though his plays have been revived more often than those of any of the century's dramatists except Shaw, most of them—with remarkable exceptions—come like shadows, so depart. He has long been an amusing cult; his best writing deserves all that has been said of it, but a generation will grow which may leave everything on the shelf but *Hay Fever* (1925), *Private Lives* (1930) and *Blithe Spirit* (1941)—or, possibly, *Present Laughter* (1947). His work during the nineteen-twenties included a competent juvenile comedy, *The Young Idea* (1921), with a pair of twins deriving, as he knew—and as Shaw knew—from *You Never Can Tell*; and a feverish comedy-drama, *The Vortex*, called 'hectic' at the time (1924) and banging away, complete with variation on the Closet scene in *Hamlet*, at the follies of Mayfair, the sins of society. As it happened, the success of *The Vortex* and its near-hysterical third act would make the name of a born writer of comedy. Later, he would do a great deal in numerous genres, including the self-conscious patriotic panorama of *Cavalcade* (Drury Lane, 1931): this, among other things, ruined a summoning word which spread like a stain on watered silk until it was used for even 'a cavalcade of sideboards': not many words—'nostalgia' is another—have been so sorely treated.

For all his versatility, in musical plays (the romantic operetta of *Bitter Sweet*) and in diverse revues, as well as much in the straight theatre; for all his untroubled panache, and for all his alert and economical craftsmanship, we return again and again to the four principal comedies. Two of these were between the wars. *Hay Fever*, diversion on the river-bank of Bohemia, is about a far from quiet week-end in the Thames-side house of a famous actress who has never retired but who acts her head off in private life. A passage between two house-party guests, a diplomatist and a shy young girl, is Coward at his most accomplished, dialogue that would have astonished Pinero and Jones:

Jackie Have you travelled a lot?
Richard [*modestly*] A good deal.
Jackie How lovely!

[*A pause*

Richard Spain is very beautiful.
Jackie Yes, I've always heard Spain was awfully nice.

[*Pause*

Richard Except for the bull-fights. No one who ever really loved horses could enjoy a bull-fight.
Jackie Nor anyone who loved bulls either.
Richard Exactly.
Jackie Italy's awfully nice, isn't it?
Richard Oh, yes, charming.
Jackie I've always wanted to go to Italy.

[*Pause*

Richard Rome is a beautiful city.
Jackie Yes, I've always heard Rome was lovely.
Richard And Naples and Capri—Capri's enchanting.
Jackie It must be.

[*Pause*

Richard Have you ever been abroad at all?
Jackie Oh, yes; I went to Dieppe once—we had a house there for the summer.
Richard [*kindly*] Dear little place, Dieppe.
Jackie Yes, it was lovely.
Richard *Russia* used to be a wonderful country before the war.
Jackie It must have been . . .

There is also a cunning last scene when which the week-end guests, worn out by the entire business, steal off silently while the Bliss family, at its late breakfast-table, is arguing about the topography of Paris. This is endearing and unforced comedy; with reason the National Theatre chose the play for revival in 1965. As for *Private Lives*, which Coward described as a play of 'two violent acids bubbling together', it can remind us of a sophisticated fairy-tale, the equivalent of romps in a powder-magazine: an entire act is given over to a bickering duologue of flash and outbreak and recovery, a pattern repeated with crafty variations until a last wrestling bout among the broken records and overthrown chairs. Here Coward whisks the sun into our dazzled eyes; when we can see again the comedy is over. *Private Lives* exemplifies what Coward would make one of his characters say in a later piece: 'Learn from the ground up how plays are constructed, and what is actable and what not.'

Other writers of comedy, in contrasting moods, were Frederick Lonsdale and the superb farceur Ben Travers. Lonsdale spent his time in the stage Dukeries (every peer, it was suggested, but Southend), freely conferring titles and earl-and-the-girl witticisms. His work (in a Hardy line, 'mirrors meant to glass the opulent') has been much revived, for epigrams, eighteen-carat or rolled gold, must always have their place in the theatre; Lonsdale was a far better craftsman than Wilde (*The Importance of Being Earnest* apart). Still, we must doubt how much of his work will be durable. It includes *Aren't We All?* (1923); *Spring Cleaning* (1925), in which a husband, to teach his rebellious young wife a lesson, brings a prostitute to her dinner-party; *The Last of Mrs Cheyney* (1925), a mesh of artifice with a celebrated third-act breakfast scene on the loggia; and *On Approval*, an adroit quartet-comedy, a dance for two couples. This may outlast its fellows even if we feel that the slanging-match in a Scottish country-house is less triumphant than it appeared to be during the nineteen-twenties.

The work of Ben Travers should last longer. There have been few really important British farce-writers. Travers, Lord of Misrule, is unquestionably the century's master and has been ever since the sequence (1925–33) when he wrote nine plays for the partnership of Tom Walls and Ralph Lynn at the Aldwych Theatre—hence the label 'Aldwych farce', that was a little awkward after 1960 when the theatre had become the London address of the Royal Shakespeare Company. A devotee of Pinero, and believing in the firmest construction, Travers always insisted that his plays should rise from a strong launching-base of realism. Once realism had been established, he said, the characters could take-off. In brief, never let the balloon go up without preparation; remember that the best farces soar out of some intricate plot. The endless zest and wit of the Travers farces might have confuted Leigh Hunt, who dismissed the form as 'an un-ambitious, undignified, and most unworthy compilation of pun, equivoque, and claptrap'. Travers devised them for what was almost a stock company, led by the quicksilver Ralph Lynn: in *A Cuckoo in the Nest* (1925) he tied himself into lugubrious reef-knots as he attempted to sleep under a washstand. Travers had mur-dered sleep; the actor might have bedded himself down on a fakir's trough of nails. Much else: *Rookery Nook* (1926), very like its name, and with a stage direction, 'Juddy turns away upstage disgusted, swearing in Chinese'; *Thark* (1927), in a haunted Nor-folk manor ('I'll come after you with the sheets,' says the butler called Death); *Plunder* (1929), which the National Theatre revived in 1976, with a cunning Scotland Yard examination scene; and so forward to *A Bit of a Test* (1933), with Lynn as the captain of an English cricket eleven in unlooked-for Australian difficulties. Away from the Aldwych, *Banana Ridge*, a farce beginning in London, moving to Malaya, and depending upon an ingenious problem of paternity, arrived in 1938 (with Alfred Drayton and the former victim of the Aldwych plays, Robertson Hare, now a leading actor in his own right); it had a long London revival in 1976–7 during Travers's renaissance as grand master of his craft.

It is fruitless to trace any pattern through the inter-war decades. Until their last few years the verse drama was weary, though wistful playgoers had not forgotten *Hassan*:

Caliph If there shall ever arise a nation whose people have forgotten poetry, or whose poets have forgotten the people, though they send their ships round Taprobane and their armies across the hills of Hin-dustan, though their city be greater than Babylon of old, though they mine a league into earth or mount to the stars on wings—what of them?
Hassan They will be a dark patch upon the world.

No student of Flecker, reading this, will forget the earlier lines, 'To a Poet A Thousand Years Hence':

> I who am dead a thousand years,
>   And wrote this sweet archaic song,
> Send you my words for messengers
>   The way I shall not pass along.

Yeats, seeking 'not a theatre but the theatre's anti-self', came through only in *The Words Upon the Window-Pane* and *Purgatory*;

W. H. Auden and Christopher Isherwood were so determined during the nineteen-thirties not to be versifiers in an outmoded style that they forgot to write dramatic poetry at all (their likeliest play, 1936, was *The Ascent of F6*, often symbolic, about a demon-haunted Himalayan mountain); Humbert Wolfe could not make himself felt on the stage; and Dorothy L. Sayers's *The Zeal of Thy House* (1937) and *The Devil To Pay* (1939) were mild transients.

One dramatist did emerge, the already influential poet Thomas Stearns Eliot (who had previously experimented). His *Murder in the Cathedral*[2] (1935), a Canterbury Festival play, proved there and in London, as directed by E. Martin Browne, to be the most surprising production of its period: a noble exposition of the nature of saintliness, with Thomas Becket at its heart. Its verse forms were as varied as its use of a chorus was commanding. Eliot explained:

> The rhythm of regular blank verse had become too remote from the movement of modern speech. Therefore what I kept in mind was the versification of *Everyman*, hoping that anything unusual in the sound of it would be, on the whole, advantageous. The avoidance of too much iambic, some use of alliteration, and occasional unexpected rhyme, helped to distinguish the versification from that of the nineteenth century.

The result, as we have it now, is a play that in text and performance still grows into the mind after many revivals and is starred with such lines as:

> From where the western seas gnaw at the coast of Iona
> To the death in the desert, the prayer in forgotten places by
> the broken imperial column.

Robert Speaight was the first Becket; Robert Donat played the part in 1953, his last stage appearance on an affecting night at the Old Vic; and Richard Pasco did so for the Royal Shakespeare Company in 1972.

Another play by Eliot, *The Family Reunion* (1939), has a contemporary setting and a structure of classical myth. Though at first we have to be aware of the author testing and observing rhythms and of his typical insistence on the definite article, the play (founded on the Furies' pursuit of Orestes) does grow progressively richer, developing its tale of sin and expiation in stylized naturalism (with the choral voices of conscience and prophecy).

---

[2] Henzie Raeburn, the actress, suggested the title.

There was nothing like this in the plays of James Bridie and J. B. Priestley, though Priestley was never more resolutely imaginative than in *Johnson Over Jordan* (also 1939), and, with both dramatists, the Theatre Theatrical and the Theatre of Ideas moved amicably side by side and frequently overlapping. Bridie was the pseudonym of a Scottish doctor, a philosopher and a wit, Osborne Henry Mavor. It was modish to call him the Scottish Shaw, but he was like no one but himself, and had not Shaw's compulsive force. It was equally modish to say that he could not write third acts; that he had no conception of what Mr Curdle elsewhere calls 'a kind of universal dovetailedness, a sort of general oneness'. This was exaggeration; but it is true that Bridie's last acts seldom satisfy. He wrote with a taking enthusiasm and speed; he was adventurously discursive; he had humanity and a healing good humour. When challenged on his last acts, he said: 'Only God can write last acts, and He seldom does. You should go out of the theatre with your head whirling with speculations. You should be lovingly selecting infinite possibilities for the characters you have seen on the stage.' His friend Ivor Brown—not the most copious drama critic of the time, but the best of them—said after Bridie's death in 1951, 'We shall continue to be deliciously plagued with the questions he raised and the answers that he did not give.'

During the nineteen-thirties, when first known to the theatre in general, he did answer most of the questions: in *The Anatomist* (London, 1931) about the Edinburgh surgeon John Knox, who trafficked with the resurrection-men Burke and Hare; in *Tobias and the Angel* (London, 1932), a serenely fantastic ramble in the gardens of the Apocrypha, with Raphael himself, disguised, to look after the diffident little Tobias, who becomes a hero; in *A Sleeping Clergyman*, a too copious episodic drama of heredity which seeks to prove that we cannot breed genius by eugenics; and in *The King of Nowhere* (1938), seen at the Old Vic with Laurence Olivier as an actor suffering from persecution mania.

J. B. (John Boynton) Priestley, even more adaptable, also began to take over the London theatre in the nineteen-thirties, writing in this period everything between allegory (*Johnson Over Jordan*) and Yorkshire farce (*When We Are Married*, 1938). Immensely fluent and resourceful, he had written seventeen or so plays by the end of the decade; a dramatist of uncompromising sense, he could sail away on strange seas of thought, even though, as a rule, critics liked him best as a direct storyteller. People who tell stories as well as he does are uncommonly rare; moreover, he has a passionate interest in life and character, and a speculative, searching mind. 'My plays,' he said once, 'are meant to be *acted*, not read. They are not literary . . . but at their best intensely and triumphantly theatrical. . . . Though my plays have ideas in them, I have never regarded the theatre as a medium for ideas—the plays and the actors are there to move people.' Gareth Lloyd Evans, who quotes this letter in his admirable *J. B. Priestley—the Dramatist* (1964), comments:

> He claims no more than to be an accomplished workman, but it is extraordinary how so often we find ourselves expecting that we should get more than this from him. This is because the best of Priestley is so very often the best of anything that can be found of its time.

His truest play between the wars, and one of the finest he would ever write, is that small miracle of quietism, *Eden End* (1934): a doctor's house in a Yorkshire village during 1912: two or three hours stolen from time and fixed indelibly. It reappeared in a National Theatre revival (1974). During the decade Priestley was closely occupied with theories of time. In the early *Dangerous Corner* (1932) he showed that certain moments can hold many different possibilities: a chance remark may lead to misery. Here the characters take one line, return to their starting-place, and finally take another line; it is an absorbing piece of plotting. *Time and the Conways*, which held a Duchess Theatre audience rapt on a hot summer night in 1937, demonstrates Dunne's theory of serialism, repetitive time. Midway in the piece we see the people of the first act, a fairly typical middle-class provincial family on an autumn night of 1919, as they will appear nearly two decades on. It is the vision of a girl we have watched at her coming-of-age party; she sees now what must happen far ahead, the wreck of plans and hopes. The third act returns us to the first autumn night where, with our prevision, all that passes must be strange and disturbing: 'There are so many things to do.' Priestley created a family as real as, in another decade, the Lindens would be. 'The point about *Time and the Conways*', A. V. Cookman said rightly, 'is not time but the Conways': they stay unblurred. A less impressive time-play (also 1937) is *I Have Been Here Before*, illustrating 'circular time', and with an idea of 'modified recurrence', as stated by Ouspensky, that apparently excited Priestley more than his persons did.

His last play before the War, and after the curiously clotted *Music At Night* (Malvern, 1938), was his contentious *Johnson Over*

Jordan (1939), a morality that is an elaborate experiment in form, evoking the life and nature of an Everyman who is in the state of Bardo. This, according to Tibetan belief, comes immediately after death. Prolonged and dream-like, it is in 'what may be called the fourth dimension of space, filled with hallucinatory visions'. Using everything, masks, ballet, music, heightened speech, Priestley succeeds fully only in the simplicities of his last act, the Inn at the World's End, and the final passage when Johnson bids farewell to this life before moving out against the rim of space, a blue void lit by a single star. The play has not yet been revived; it will be. By the time the decade had ended we knew that Priestley was a whole regiment of dramatists, prepared for anything.

Emlyn Williams, speaking for Wales, spoke potently for the Theatre Theatrical. He has always been original and compassionate, quickened by his Celtic enthusiasm and his pleasure in plotting. We mourn for *Spring 1600* (the Shakespearian spring), its loveliness never surely realized either in 1934 or a rewritten version eleven years later. Some of his earliest work is still the most expert: *Night Must Fall* (1935), a psychological murder drama, and *The Corn Is Green* (1938): semi-autobiographical, this is governed by a single-minded village schoolmistress (created in the theatre by Sybil Thorndike) who discovers in a boy's essay something more than a spark of mere talent.

So many writers of talent and imagination arrived between the wars (and frequently vanished again) that it would be superfluous and clouding to call the roll. Some must be named. R. C. (Robert Cedric) Sherriff, who would continue in the theatre for three decades, was a Thames Valley insurance agent of thirty-two when he wrote *Journey's End* (1928; staged for a run in 1929), the simplest and most tingling war play we have yet had. Allan Monkhouse (in one scene of *The Conquering Hero*, 1924), Reginald Berkeley and Hubert Griffith were other dramatists who evoked the Western Front, but *Journey's End* is still sovereign. Within a claustrophobic dug-out 'before St Quentin on the eve of the March offensive of 1918', Sherriff, haunted by his own memories of the Front, tells a plain tale plainly. O'Casey, in the second act of *The Silver Tassie*, would give in deliberately unrealistic terms perhaps the bitterest impression of the 1914–18 war that we know. Sherriff uses no comparable dramatic guile, yet his chosen episode and its treatment summon so sharply the years of grief, futility and heroism that *Journey's End* must stir an audience with any kind of feeling. (It did so on its London revival in 1972 before many to whom that remote war before last meant only a few pages of history.) Sherriff's other memorable play of the nineteen-thirties—he wrote it with the actress Jeanne de Casalis—was another form of journey's end, *St Helena*: Napoleon caged in his Longwood exile, ten or a dozen scenes of slow disintegration precisely imagined and expressed.

Any choice from the welter of London plays between 1919 and 1939 must seem to be arbitrary. One new young dramatist, Terence Rattigan, whose *French Without Tears*, a light comedy of a 'cramming' establishment on the Biscay coast of France, ran for more than 1,000 performances, would be a force later on, and with more substantial work. Several writers renowned in their time are now almost irretrievably obscured. Thus by the nineteen-seventies—except for *Toad of Toad Hall*, a potted version of Grahame's *The Wind in the Willows*—no one was reviving or thinking of A. A. Milne: skilled in gentle comedy but usually putting grace before meat, his most engaging persiflage was in *Mr Pim Passes By* (1920); the first act of *The Truth About Blayds* (1921) promised much, but the night crumbled. C. K. Munro, pseudonym of a distinguished civil servant, C. K. MacMullan, is also lost today. For a while, in *At Mrs Beam's* (1921), he glorified that depressed area, the stage boarding-house; his ambitious, thoughtful and verbose political plays have been neglected. Clemence Dane (Winifred Ashton), first among the women dramatists—others of varying merit were 'Gordon Daviot', Lesley Storm and Margaret Kennedy, did create a persuasive Queen Elizabeth I, not just a Tudor in a tantrum, in her highly coloured 'invention', *Will Shakespeare* (1921). Among the few verse plays of its period, and hampered by an infinitely improbable plot (Shakespeare accidentally stabbing Marlowe to death at Deptford), its speeches for Elizabeth can still come from the page. *A Bill of Divorcement* (also 1921), in spare, speakable prose, is a period piece, an unflinching drama that we can respect long after the reform it urged (lunacy as a just ground for divorce) has been conceded. *Wild Decembers* (1932) continues to be the most plausible of the Brontë chronicles. A second and extremely popular woman dramatist, Dodie Smith, the teacup-storm to Clemence Dane's tempest, wrote half a dozen plays during the nineteen-thirties—the family party of *Dear Octopus* (1938) in particular—that had the right fingering for their time.

Names, and more names. John van Druten, copious, naturalistic and competent, went in the end to America. Originally extolled for a sympathetic school play, *Young Woodley* (1928), a boy in love with his housemaster's wife, he continued to write a good deal that, useful at its hour—*London Wall* (1931), for example—has since been put aside. Clifford Bax, primarily a historical dramatist, was as fastidious and graceful as any contemporary: we recall him now for *The Rose Without a Thorn* (1932), the story of Henry VIII and Katheryn Howard. His *Socrates* (1930), seldom performed, has the tranquillity of a long summer afternoon that falls unwillingly to night. Bax is a miniaturist; in painting, Nicholas Hilliard might be his counterpart.

Various dramatists who tried to navigate the period's choppy sea, its turmoil of cross-currents, were no less effective at the moment than their rebellious successors would be in thirty or forty years. The now absurdly disregarded John Drinkwater, though he seldom recovered the spirit of *Abraham Lincoln*, left some biographical plays (*Robert E. Lee, Mary Stuart, Oliver Cromwell*) of unfaltering dignity; his Cotswold comedy, *Bird in Hand* (London, 1928) was shaped by a writer who, like the craftsman of his own poem, 'moved in comely thought'. Eden Phillpotts, a novelist practised in the theatre—his share in the Censorship quarrel of 1912 had been forgotten—was newly honoured for a sequence of rustic Devon comedies: no dramatist babbled better of green fields. Prized by the public, they were under-prized by critics weary of one generous high tea after another; but *The Farmer's Wife* (written 1916; London, 1924) had a fruitful run and would live. Of two Irish dramatists, Lennox Robinson, whose most recognizable work now is *The White Headed Boy* (1916; London, 1920) was always an astute character-builder; Denis Johnston's tragi-comedy, *The Moon in the Yellow River* (1934), is a study of Irish fanaticism and playboyism, with one frightening theatrical stroke.

The West End of London benefited in diverse ways from the efficiency of H. M. Harwood (*The Grain of Mustard Seed*, 1920), Benn Levy (*This Woman Business*, 1925); Rodney Ackland who, as in *Strange Orchestra* (1931), explored the map of the day's Bohemia; Ashley Dukes, whose romantic Regency narrative, *The Man with a Load of Mischief* (1924), retains its ivory gloss; and St John Ervine, far now from the dramatist of *Jane Clegg* and *John Ferguson*, who contented himself with a trinity of popular successes: most accomplished were *The First Mrs Fraser* (1929) and *Robert's Wife* (1937). We must note also Rudolf Besier's *The Barretts of Wimpole Street* (1930)—a last play by the author of *The Virgin Goddess* a quarter of a century before—which captured both the thunder-light of Elizabeth Barrett's home and the tension of her elopement; Ronald Mackenzie's *Musical Chairs* (1931), set in a

Galician oilfield and written in the Chekhovian spirit without too obvious a scatter of pupil-mannerisms; Charles Morgan's *The Flashing Stream* (1938), a drama critic's intellectual melodrama; and Sutton Vane's *Outward Bound* (1923), a modern morality of the ship of the dead with a still uncanny first act on the edge of the unknown.

Ephemeral musical plays and revues proliferated (revue had at least one master, unmatched yet, the far from ephemeral Herbert Farjeon, who was restored in a Mermaid Theatre anthology, 1975); the music-hall had lost much of its cherished rowdy gusto, and the noisier dance-bands ate into its programmes. Without break, the 'thriller', or puzzle-play, in all its complicated manifestations—wildest in two American imports, *The Bat* and *The Cat and the Canary* (both 1922)—kept the decades furnished with shots in the dark, screams in the twilight and cats among the pigeons. In this world of the sliding panel a *Hassan* speech might have been regarded as topical: Rafi's 'Did someone ask me why this house is called the House of the Moving Walls?' A few of the less preposterous plays were by Edgar Wallace. But many other dramatists, crafty on occasion, might have remembered Robin Oakapple's suggestion to old Adam in Gilbert's *Ruddigore*: 'How would it be, do you think, were I . . . by making hideous faces at him, to curdle the heart-blood in his arteries and freeze the very marrow in his bones?' To which Adam replies tersely: 'It would be simply rude—nothing more.' This was the kind of play a critic, towards the end of the Twenties, tried hopefully to describe:

> It seemed fairly clear that either Hilda or her degenerate brother had something to do with the death of their uncle, who had thus disinherited them completely in favour of Edna. They meet with some success in a plot designed to estrange Miss Darling from her Canadian lover by placing her in a compromising position, and in déshabillé, with Harry, whose attempt to maltreat her is stopped in an amazing manner, presumably by Burton's confederate, just as he is half-throttled and doped with morphia from a hypodermic syringe when he is trying to hold up the Yokel, taking from the shelf a sheet of old Harding's diary bearing the bloodstained finger-prints of the murderer.

We cannot charge Patrick Hamilton with this kind of nonsense. Two of his psychological thrillers, *Rope* (1929), the narrative of a murder for excitement's sake (suggested by the notorious Loeb–Leopold case in America), and the late Victorian *Gas Light* (1939) have survived with little loss.

When at length the sirens sounded at the beginning of the Second World War in September 1939, the theatre had no particular obsession of the moment; it was offering the usual 'mingled yarn, good and ill together, English plays and foreign, classics and ephemera, and none could have played with much profit the modish game called 'looking for trends'. The West End might not have been fiercely sociological, though a daily-newspaper critic who praised the theatre of 1977 for 'exploring racial and sexual discrimination, class divisions, worker solidarity', and so forth could have remembered that there had been a world elsewhere. We cannot lightly underrate years when Shaw and O'Casey were at their meridian, when Galsworthy produced two of his best plays, when Maugham was ending his career and Coward beginning, when (to be eclectic) Eliot wrote *Murder in the Cathedral*, Priestley wrote *Eden End* and *Time and the Conways*, Travers wrote nine Aldwych farces, Bridie was a new voice from the north, and neither the Theatre Theatrical nor the Theatre of Ideas lacked its ammunition. (How many now remember a strangely prophetic drama, *The Right to Strike*, written in 1920 by a young dramatist, Ernest Hutchinson, who died in the following Year?)[3]

Suddenly, as they had done in 1914, the lights went out. Again there would be a prolonged stage wait.

Second Interval

At first, as during the other war, managers chose revivals, even *Chu Chin Chow* and *By Pigeon Post*, a spy thriller of 1918. There were new plays as well, but it was not an hour for the dramatist, and the theatre was again disrupted for a time when the heavy bombing of London began in the summer of 1940.

When, after nearly five years, recorders surveyed the lists, they found that comedy had dominated, though on a higher level than in 1914–18. Coward, only just over forty and already an elder stateman, wrote *Blithe Spirit* (1941), with a husband plagued by the clashing of two wives, the quick and the dead (she must have caused unimaginable havoc on the shores of Styx); *Present Laugh-*

---

[3] This was about a railwaymen's strike in Lancashire. A group of local doctors organized a motor-lorry relief service, and one of them was killed by a wire stretched across the road. His friend acted at once. 'I will not attend any railwayman,' he said, 'or any railwayman's family while this strike continues, nor will any doctor in Valleyhead, nor in the whole country when the facts are known.'

ter (1942), some of his more sustained moonshine concentrated upon an egocentric actor to whom all the world's a stage; and the embarrassing Cockney-family play, *This Happy Breed* (also 1942). Terence Rattigan, who before the War had evaded diplomacy as a career—to the lasting benefit of the theatre—followed the frivol of *French Without Tears*, and some other forgotten pieces, with a well-made sentimental drama about the Royal Air Force, *Flare Path* (1942); an equally well-organized farce, *While the Sun Shines* (1943), which had over 1,000 performances; and, for Alfred Lunt and Lynn Fontanne, a neatly plotted comedy, *Love in Idleness* (1944), which in New York became *O Mistress Mine*. Peter Ustinov was another fresh name, happiest, it appears now, with the regression of *The Banbury Nose*, which moves backward across sixty years as it rails against ancestor-worship and (here in the military caste) the tyranny of custom.

Priestley, writing a comedy as well, was more serious in *They Came to a City* (1943), established outside a great city wall; the audience, barred from entering, discovers how various types respond to the Utopian wonders within—either with infinite delight or finding the place a hell. Emphatically sincere and thoughtful as it is, it seems wordy now. *Desert Highway* (1944)—two acts in the desert war and an interlude 2,000 years earlier—is a parable, stimulating in its day, on the brotherhood of man. Bridie was amusing in *Mr Bolfry* (1943) which for once ends as admirably as it begins, and contrives to raise in the West Highlands a devil in the shape of a clergyman. In retrospect, the most durable of three plays by Emlyn Williams—though we might not have said so then—was *The Wind of Heaven* (1945), an intense tale of a Second Coming, the wonder that befell a bereaved Welsh mountain village in the eighteen-fifties.

The strongest stage excitements during the War were in classical revival. Thus, since the Old Vic Theatre had been bombed in 1940, a Vic company began to operate at the New—now the Albery—in the autumn of 1944 with some of the most celebrated productions of the century. Here Laurence Olivier, as a Red King, one raised in blood and one by blood established, was a stunning Richard III; and Ralph Richardson ruled *Peer Gynt*. At the same time, John Gielgud, still the Hamlet of his generation, touching the part to a music unknown since Forbes-Robertson, was leading a repertory at the Haymarket. The provinces, often areas that had not known the living theatre for years, were served by several companies ('pomping folk', the Cornish would call them) sent out by the new Council for the Encouragement of Music and the Arts: later, and less cumbrously, the Arts Council. Thanks to CEMA, the refurbished green-and-gold casket of the Royal at Bristol, built in 1776, became the first State-subsidized theatre in Britain.

After the War

The new Arts Council of Great Britain, which received its Royal Charter in 1946, was, in Robert Speaight's words,

> The official agency through which is expressed the national responsibility for maintaining the standard of the arts and making them available to the whole population.

Born in wartime emergency, it would be of the first importance in helping an art whose only subsidies had been from such private philanthropists as Miss Horniman and Barry Jackson.

From the end of the War until the early summer of 1956 there were eleven years in which (as we look back now) the British stage, subsidized or unsubsidized, seemed to be waiting for revelation. At the time this was not obvious, but a few lines from John Whiting's *Saint's Day* (1951)—a play that arrived prematurely—are a possible analogy to events of what would be the anarchic nineteen-fifties:

> Careful! We are approaching the point of deviation. At one moment there is laughter and conversation and a progression; people move and speak smoothly and casually, their breathing is controlled, and they know what they do. Then there occurs a call from another room, the realisation that a member of the assembly is missing, the sudden shout into the dream and the waking to find the body with the failing heart lying in the corridor—with the twisted limbs at the foot of the stairs—the man hanging from the beam, or the child floating drowned in the garden pool. Careful! be careful! We are approaching that point. The moment of the call from another room.

There had been no thought of this immediately after the War ended. The theatre was too closely occupied in discovering itself. The Arts Council had helped many areas where the stage had been wiped out during the nineteen-thirties; even touring revue, beset by the talking films and the radio, had long ebbed into the sand. Repertory was finding fresh force, and would generate more. London's small experimental theatres—far fewer than there would be in another generation—began to work at full pitch. Even so, for a while revivals would dominate. It was a period of superb acting, but new writers were reticent at the daybreak of peace. When they did speak we heard the poet's voice of Christopher Fry. The theatre of revolt would overtake him in mid-career, but Fry has always been a dramatist for the future, a man whose work will stay when most of the rebel writers, post-1956, are hardly more than names in an index.

Another post-War excitement was the renaissance of Stratford-upon-Avon. First, through three seasons of dramatic change (1946–8), Sir Barry Jackson transformed the Shakespeare Memorial Theatre,[4] which (mainly because of the Governors' complacency) had been allowed to run down during the years after W. Bridges-Adams left Stratford, and further (and inevitably) declined during the War. Upon Jackson's base—for he, over all, was the inspiration—a new Stratford would rise. In London there were more rumours of a National Theatre, but this, if no longer a mirage, would still be some time ahead.

In the passage of readjustment and recovery between 1945 and 1950 the senior British dramatists were Bernard Shaw, in the last embers of his sunset; Priestley and Bridie, in full production; T. S. Eliot, with a new form of serious comedy; Noël Coward, pausing a little; Frederick Lonsdale, his skills outmoded; and Sean O'Casey, with at least two plays that renewed our hope. Among their juniors Terence Rattigan and Peter Ustinov were exploring; and Wynyard Browne, whose picture of a vicarage household, *The Holly and the Ivy*, was subtly restrained, and William Douglas Home, with a prison play, *Now Barabbas . . .* and the light comedy of *The Chiltern Hundreds*, were men to watch. Triumphantly, it seemed, there was Christopher Fry.

Shaw first. In 1949, when he was ninety-three, a revived Malvern Festival (it did not continue) presented *Buoyant Billions*, a 'comedy of no manners' with an unexpected springiness and zest: its only noticeable message to the world appeared to be the observation of a Chinese priest (in Belgrave Square), 'The future is for the learners.' There can be no room for the complacent, for those who fail to recognize the virtues of humility. Wayward, extravagant, and endearing, it could hold a Malvern audience;

---

[4] The old Memorial Theatre, which had stood since 1879, was destroyed by an unexplained fire in March 1926. For six seasons W. Bridges-Adams bravely conducted the 'festivals', as they were known then, in a local cinema; and the present theatre, designed by Elisabeth Scott—it became the Royal Shakespeare nearly thirty years later—was opened in 1932.

that autumn it had five cold weeks in a London theatre inimical to it, and if it returns it can be only as a curio. Shaw's last work, *Far-Fetched Fables* (1950), was insignificant, but he went on creatively evolving until the end, which came just before daybreak on 2 November 1950. Masefield, four years earlier, had saluted 'the bright mind ever young'. Shaw's position in the British theatre was unassailable; no dramatist of the century has been more freely revived. At his death a critic suggested that the only thing to be said was in the words of Shaw's own Hesione Hushabye: 'Well, we've had a very exciting evening. Everything will be an anti-climax after it.'

Not everything. Between 1945 and 1950 Priestley had written two uncommon plays, *An Inspector Calls* (staged by the Old Vic company during its term at the New Theatre) and *The Linden Tree*. The first of these (1946) is set in the year 1913, a world that is tottering blindly to its fall. There comes to a prosperous and complacent North Midland family a so-called Inspector, his identity never known. He is an embodiment of conscience, and his warning is clear: 'We don't live alone. We are members of one body. We are responsible for each other.' The sermon on selfishness, guilt, lack of social conscience, shoots its question-marks as a porcupine its quills. Priestley keeps expectation at stretch; his first act might be from some doctrinal play of the Manchester school in the Gaiety's typical mood. *An Inspector Calls* was revived expertly at the Mermaid Theatre in 1973; but *The Linden Tree* (1947) awaits a major revival. Priestley at his wisest, it is an affirmation of faith. On the surface the tale of a veteran professor's fight against enforced retirement, the conflict is also a symbol of the nation's fight; not content to be one of the passengers on a stormy voyage, Linden will work with the crew while strength remains. A political play, *Home Is Tomorrow* (1948), is earnest and verbose; *Summer Day's Dream* (1949) an enrichingly mellow vision of an England a quarter of a century on—the period will have to be extended a bit—when the atomic war and 'great emigration' are over; those left in a denuded island have found peace in bringing the land again to blossom in the slow content of the primeval Eden.

Bridie kept pace with Priestley, play for play: failing in the whimsical fantasy of *The Forrigan Reel* (London, 1945), though we treasure its first sentence, 'Was ever an unfortunate country gentleman and timber merchant so bamboozled and bitten by a gallimaufry of such untoward circumstances?'; at ease with *Dr Angelus* (1947), a *danse macabre* in which the exploits of a murderous criminal of the 1860s are shifted to the Glasgow of 1920; enjoying a go-as-you-please Highland-village comedy, *Gog and MacGog* (1948) about an 'itinerant poet' of McGonagall quality; and reaching meridian in the first and second acts of *Daphne Laureola* (1949), a character study of a lonely and unhappy woman. This, which ran for nearly a year, seems to be inseparable from the original bravura performance by Edith Evans, but its hour will return, though the last act is one of Bridie's minor thirds.

Noël Coward had a poor few years in which his work—best, no doubt, in the metallic melodrama of *Peace in Our Time* (1947)—was shallow and unresourceful. But Terence Rattigan, some now faded matters apart, wrote two of the plays that have always burnished his name. One (1946) is *The Winslow Boy*, recalling the notorious Archer–Shee case of 1908. A young cadet, expelled from the Royal Naval College at Osborne on a charge of petty theft (a five-shilling postal order) is vindicated after a Parliamentary and legal flare. Vigorously wedding drama and doctrine, the play is in effect a petition of right, a plea for the liberty of the individual; it contained one of the strongest characters Rattigan would create, the barrister—light of the Bar and the Opposition Front Bench—who wins the case for the boy: Emlyn Williams acted him on the stage, Robert Donat on the screen. This is the kind of assured writing in which the dramatist is unashamedly (and properly) a partisan. His other fine play was *The Browning Version* (1948), presented as half of a double bill—the other half is practically forgotten—and proving to be as compressed and searching a psychological portrait as the stage had known in years. The figure is a schoolmaster, a failure in his profession and in his marriage: grey, tired and unlovable, his time is spent either in grappling with insensitive schoolboys or at home with the evil woman (at the limit of her resources) who is his wife. This would be Rattigan's most important gift to the theatre. Emlyn Williams revised the tantalizing *Spring 1600*, always on the rim of success and never crossing it; and there were numerous plays unlikely to survive but with much sound, grained-oak craftsmanship: two by R. C. Sherriff (*Miss Mabel* and *Home at Seven*), never patronizing the small-town and suburban people of whom he wrote; Lonsdale's *The Way Things Go* (1950), the same old ducal family breathing in epigrams; some Irish work by Paul Vincent Carroll, which could have the flick of an angry stinging-nettle; and Joan Temple's *No Room at the Inn* (1945), about the plight of wartime evacuees, urgent as drama and a form of social indictment of which post-War dramatists would claim a monopoly. Peter Ustinov wrote *The Indifferent Shepherd* (1948), an intellect at work but life and the theatre seldom coming together.

The period's surprise was the renewed shining of the verse play, brief enough before the clouds masked it again but heartening while it lasted. Sean O'Casey, never an explicit verse dramatist but with an instinctive poetic quality, included in his extremely personal *Red Roses For Me* (1943; London, 1946) a haunting third act when a Dublin bridge across the Liffey turns to a bridge of vision, tired slum-folk regain their youth and vigour in a few transfiguring moments, and we hear such a speech as 'A gold-speckled candle, white as snow, was Dublin once; yellowish now, leanin' sideways, and gutherin' down to a last shaky glimmer in the wind o' life.' The political side of the play means less than the garnish of phrase. In *Purple Dust* (staged in Liverpool, 1945, but not in London for several years) it is again the language that rules a surge of farcical fantasy in a remote Irish village and the shell of a crumbling mansion; O'Casey wrote during the wearing to dust of old and cherished tradition, and the green waters of the river that tumbles into the room at the final curtain are those of the river of Time. O'Casey is always aware of the texture of the language, the sway and lift of a sentence. So too in the much inferior *Oak Leaves and Lavender* (1945; London, 1946), a personal tribute to Britain in the years of peril: its dialogue, passionately charged and ready with the unexpected word, the metaphorical meteor, is hindered throughout by a rickety plot. The London production was so drearily botched that we have never had a chance to appreciate *Oak Leaves* in performance. *Cock-a-Doodle-Dandy* (1949), a capricious genius's own favourite play, would take ten years to reach London, a comedy of the rightful joy of life, its exhilaration shadowed a little by O'Casey's obsessive views on the Catholic Church, but again and again breaking out: 'It isn't here you should be, lost among th' rough stones, th' twisty grass, and th' moody misery of th' brown bog; but it's lyin' laughin' you should be where th' palms are tall, an' wherever a foot is planted, a scarlet flower is crushed; where there's levity living its life, an' not loneliness dyin' as it is here.'

True verse drama appeared in three plays presented at the Mercury Theatre in London by E. Martin Browne: Norman Nicholson's *The Old Man of the Mountains* (1945), retelling in a Cumbrian setting the tale of Elijah and Ahab; Anne Ridler's *The Shadow Factory* (also 1945); and in the same year, and most adventurous, Ronald Duncan's *This Way to the Tomb!* told in a masque and anti-masque with many stanzaic subtleties. Still, the poets most discussed in those years were T. S. Eliot and Christopher Fry. Arnold Bennett had written in his journal during 1924 that Eliot 'wanted to write a drama of modern life (furnished flat sort of people) in a rhythmic prose'. In 1949, at the Edinburgh Festival (then in its third year) Eliot arrived as the dramatist of *The Cocktail Party*, framed as a fashionable comedy of manners (few people discerned the source of the story in the Euripidean *Alcestis*) but, in its concern with spiritual guardianship and with self-sacrifice, exploring the deeper reaches of the human soul. Its medium is a stylized verse, close to familiar conversation, that enables Eliot to pass from the most urgent utterance to the most relaxed dialogue. He would write three plays in this method, all directed by Martin Browne. *The Cocktail Party*, a perennial theme for argument and revived in many places, is rooted firmly in the century's record.

Where Eliot's verse was more and more retiring, Christopher Fry's, rich and copious, caused dramatic poetry to dance again. No dramatist has made less fuss about the durable work he has added to theatre history. Though he had had much stage experience, and before the War had written for Sussex village amateurs his gentle *The Boy With a Cart*, about Cuthman, one of the county's saints, he first set a London audience cheering with *A Phœnix Too Frequent* (Mercury, 1946). A one-act comedy, founded on an old tale (as far back as Petronius) of an Ephesian woman (widow of 'a coming man untimely gone'), it is set in a tomb near Ephesus. After deciding to die of grief (with maid in attendance), quietly inurn'd, she is perfectly ready to become the wife of a visiting centurion. Throughout Fry never says the expected thing, and the unexpected he says with a freshness and wit that are magnified in the full-length *The Lady's Not For Burning* (1948), first of his four mood-plays of the seasons. In this it is spring in a market-town called Cool Clary, and in '1400 either more or less or exactly'. Here, both at the Arts (with Alec Clunes) and in the following year (with John Gielgud) in the West End, the language, flashing like a heliograph in sunlight, captivated playgoers who had never listened, in the fullest sense, to any verse apart from the classics. In effect—we do not remember the play for its narrative—it is about a man who wants to be hanged and a woman, accused of supernatural soliciting, who does not want to be burned. In a preface to the text Fry speaks of it as 'human intelligences in a dance together. . . . The comedy is a climate, of damp and dry, of spirit and matter, playing April with each

other, and the climate is the comedy.' The people can talk like
this:

> Nothing can be seen
> In the thistle-down, but the rough-head thistle comes.
> Rest in that riddle. I can pass to you
> Generations of roses in this wrinkled berry.
> There: now you hold in your hand a race
> Of summer gardens, it fades under centuries
> Of petals. What is not, you have in your palm.
> Rest in the riddle, rest; why not? This evening
> Is a ridiculous wisp of down
> Blowing in the air as disconsolately as dust.
> And you have your own damnable mystery too,
> Which at the moment I could well do without.

Later, for the Canterbury Festival, Fry wrote *Thor With Angels*,
and its lovely lines that welcome to Britain St Augustine and the
spring. In 1950 Laurence Olivier appeared, at the St James's, in
the autumn comedy of *Venus Observed*, at heart about loneliness,
solitude, ageing, with a depth no recital of the plot can suggest. In
1950 Fry adapted and enriched an Anouilh comedy which he
entitled *Ring Round the Moon*, and Peter Brook directed: we can
merely note his services across thirty years as a translator and
adapter of work by Giraudoux, Anouilh, Ibsen and Rostand. It
has been a custom to consider his own plays simply in terms of
his language ('looping and threading, turning and entwining';
'Phrase in linking phrase, with commas falling as airily as lime-
flowers'), and to ignore the thought that fuels them. He is a man
piercingly observant, warmly compassionate and intuitive; the
fact that he abhors the violence and the rancid diction modish in
the nineteen-sixties and seventies is a reason for a passing neglect
that later generations may not understand.

Towards Rebellion

Fry and his fellow-judges of an Arts Theatre competition to mark
the Festival of Britain in 1951 awarded the first prize to John
Whiting's then esoteric *Saint's Day*: it had had as glum a reception
from the drama critics (or most of them) as any play within
memory. Six years later their action would have been bewildering. Whiting was out of his time. He did not wait for the 'point of
deviation' in the speech we have already quoted; in the favourite

analogy of the nineteen-fifties, his play came before what so many would call the new wave. It might have been the first premonitory trembling, the lift, the swell far out. Actually Whiting had written it as far back as 1947; when it was revived at the Birmingham Repertory in 1962 Fry, in a message to the director, John Harrison, spoke of 'a personal view of modern life which was almost unknown until Whiting wrote his play: it conveys most memorably the apocalyptic atmosphere which is never far distant from our times'.

The theme of *Saint's Day* is self-destruction. Inexorably pessimistic, a wild landscape of the mind, it has a fine and sombre first act. Later it tails off, but it will long be a show-piece for expositors and exegetists who ask why the old poet and philosopher met in the first act should end in the third, hanged upon one of his own trees. In 1951 the play and its reception brought to the public mind a strange, powerful dramatist who would always stand apart. Earlier in the same year his first produced play, *A Penny for a Song*—it would return in a revised text, 1962—had been a charming, innocent caprice written at a time of great personal happiness. The scene is Dorset, a hot summer day in 1804 with Napoleon's fleet likely to arrive at any hour. According to its author, the play expresses the idea of Christian charity; most people, taking it as a gentle Regency frolic, have found it out of key with Whiting's other work. *Marching Song* (1954) reverted to self-destruction. A general of a defeated nation, released after long imprisonment when the occupying forces have gone, may be tried as a scapegoat for defeat; the Prime Minister, knowing this will harm the country's reputation, allow the man (who is weary of the world) thirty-six hours to take the alternative of suicide; though, transiently, a young girl, hard and honest, draws him back, he chooses death. Technically more accomplished than *Saint's Day*, it is less disturbing: Whiting is playing with ideas rather than people.

During the first half of the nineteen-fifties the theatre had new leaders. Shaw and Bridie had gone. Priestley did relatively little: *The Scandalous Affair of Mr Kettle and Mrs Moon* (1955) is amiably over-stated comedy, better received on the Continent. O'Casey's *The Bishop's Bonfire*, 'a sad play within the tune of a polka' (1955), which brought him back to the Dublin stage and would not arrive in England for some time, changes its mood from comedy and farce to melodrama in the Boucicault manner. Eliot's *The Confidential Clerk* (1953), with its intricate problem of paternity —reminiscent of Gilbert or Wilde, but taking a hint from the

Ion of Euripides—is the least of his three later plays; W. A. Darlington, holding it to be technically his best, added that 'only an occasional heightened phrase reminds us that Mr Eliot's medium, after all, is still verse'. Noël Coward held to comedy: *Relative Values* (1951), a country-house gambol unafraid of the irrelevances that mean more in the theatre than the text; and *Quadrille* (1952), full of lovers' meetings and partings and elopements (period 1873–4). Written for Alfred Lunt and Lynn Fontanne, without them it does seem all dressed up and nowhere to go.

Among new dramatists, Denis Cannan had poor luck after a promisingly shrewd comedy, *Captain Carvallo* (1950). Roger MacDougall (who had undergone the testing disciplines of a screenwriter) had four plays without family resemblance: the most enjoyable, a triviality called *To Dorothy A Son* (1950); the most ambitious, *Escapade* (1953), suggesting that a child's vision is clearer than an adult's. A writer of potential authority, crippling illness would take him from the theatre. Graham Greene, the novelist, wrote *The Living Room* (1953), a rather arid discussion of the problem of human inadequacy. N. C. (Norman Charles) Hunter, author of several earlier and forgettable plays, suddenly found himself—but not the harsher critics, unable to forgive two redoubtable Haymarket Theatre successes—with *Waters of the Moon* (1951; revived, 1977) and *A Day by the Sea* (1953), too glibly and unkindly dismissed as sub-Chekhovian. Hunter was a wistful impressionist, able to create sharply pondered upper middle-class parts—this also would be held against him—for some of the day's principal players.

Major work before 1956 was by Ustinov, Rattigan and Fry. Samuel Beckett too, possibly, though few guessed what an influence he would be: as much of one as the German anti-heroic dramatist, Bertolt Brecht, never generally popular in Britain in spite of determined efforts to stage everything he wrote. Beckett, who had been James Joyce's secretary, is an acquired taste. Allardyce Nicoll could not acquire it. In the last edition of this book he described *Waiting for Godot* as 'somewhat repetitively boring' and quotes a student of the so-called Theatre of the Absurd (Martin Esslin christened it): 'The dramatic idea of *Godot* is that the drama is no longer possible.' We gather that during the late summer of 1955, when the young Peter Hall staged at the Arts this not immediately lucid allegory of the nature of existence—first written in French, 1952—director and cast were not entirely sure what it meant. Reporting the cross-talk of a pair of tramps on a country road, it could be mistaken for intellectual vaudeville; critics in 1955 were variously dogmatic about its obliquity and symbolism and it became the day's table-talk, either to be scorned as a hoax or accepted as a moving parable of life. Its value is highly arguable, but it established a cult. 'Perhaps the play's main meaning', a critic has said, 'is that life has no meaning.' A thought, maybe.

Peter Ustinov, never a cult, produced two acceptable plays, each staged in 1951. *The Love of Four Colonels*, which ran a dozen times as long as the other, begins with the untrue opening line, 'We seem to have run out of conversation': it is a group of sketches set in and by a German castle where the Sleeping Beauty wakes; the Colonels, a four-Power commission on love and man's view of woman, find themselves wooing their ideal beauty as the lovers they imagine themselves to be. Hence four playlets after Marivaux, Shakespeare, Saroyan (possibly) and Chekhov. Though the piece rambles, it does box the compass inventively. In his second play, *The Moment of Truth*, Ustinov wants us to accept a senile Marshal of a partitioned republic, a scapegoat for political contrivers, as another Lear: the parallel can be hampering, and the play belongs less to the old man than to the shifty Prime Minister who says, 'To me this is a phase in an endless manœuvre.' Dynamic with ideas, and aiming at heart and mind, the piece could be twice as impressive if it were half its length.

Terence Rattigan had four plays, two of them (*Who is Sylvia?* and *The Sleeping Prince*) run-of-the-mill, a third, *The Deep Blue Sea* (1952), the best he would ever write, precisely constructed and delicately ruthless, and a fourth, *Separate Tables* (1954), a closely linked double bill. *The Deep Blue Sea* is the near-tragedy of a woman who suffers from an insatiable physical desire desperately at war with her middle-class propriety and her clear understanding of her lover. At first she seeks an easy way out. Found unconscious at curtain-rise—her attempt to gas herself has failed—she must go through with the day, and during that day Rattigan exposes what has brought Hester to the end of hope and patience. She has left her kindly, troubled husband, a High Court judge, for a shabby flat in Ladbroke Grove where she lives with a former test-pilot, careless and uncomprehending, who must have our grudging sympathy. To him Hester is part of an existence compact of high-powered cars and 'good chaps'; to her husband she is a deeply valued possession; neither can give her what she needs so obsessively. Rattigan, in a courageous development, does not take the obvious course; though traditionally well-made, it is by no means an easy or obvious play, and it is never at fault in movement or character. *Separate Tables*, on the whole theatrically valid when revived in 1977, is a double bill of events in a seaside hotel; the second half has always been more touching than the first. Rattigan then was at the crest of his power as an expert story-teller who never believed the stage to be a place for polemics. It was unlucky that he chose, in a preface to a volume of his work, to invent as a typical playgoer the middle-class, well-to-do Aunt Edna, from Kensington, whose tastes deserved as much attention as those of the avant-garde. He was promptly and acrimoniously attacked—attacks, long continued, from the newer anarchic dramatists who were themselves ruled by a demanding symbolic figure, Aunt Elsie from Hoxton. Neither of the abstractions matters; still, the business would haunt Rattigan to the end of his career.

Christopher Fry, also independent, would suffer even more. Within a year or two the theatre's epigraph would be 'Absent thee from felicity awhile.' No world for the author of *The Firstborn* (written in 1945; revised version, London, 1952), *A Sleep of Prisoners* (1951) and *The Dark Is Light Enough* (1954). The earliest of these is an Old Testament drama of the prelude to the Deliverance, the plagues of Egypt and their end in the death of the firstborn; the narrative is never sacrificed to the verse which reports urgently from the scene itself—never from a remote distance—and, in particular, establishes the conflict between Moses and his foster-brother the Pharaoh. *A Sleep of Prisoners*, with relatively few of the verbal enrichments that endeared him to the theatre at an hour grey and dusty of speech, employs Fry's most austere eloquence. Thus:

> Good has no fear;
> Good is itself, whatever comes,
> It grows, and makes, and bravely
> Persuades, beyond all tilt of wrong;
> Stronger than anger, wiser than strategy,
> Enough to subdue cities and men
> If we believe it with a long courage of truth.

The four men of the play are prisoners, held in a church. Through their past in a sequence of Biblical dreams—prompted by debate and conflict in waking hours—they find the courage to trust in the power of good over evil. Now, if the world will recognize it, must be the time to take 'the longest stride of soul man ever took'. In *The Dark Is Light Enough* (a title deriving from Fabre on the

tortuous flight of the butterflies in stormy weather),[5] Fry defied
the contemporary sins that he called the fear of language and the
fear that no audience could be adult (a word with various theatrical meanings). His language in this winter play is less luxuriant
than in those of spring and autumn: it has the spare beauty of
branch and twig in the anatomized traceries of December. The
period is 1848, time of the abortive Hungarian revolution against
the Austro–Hungarian empire. A country house, that of the
Countess Rosmarin Ostenburg, is in the direct path of the rebel
troops along roads 'sour with men marching'. The rising must
affect the Countess and all concerned with her. But she has only a
week to live. When she dies on a stormy evening we realize how
she has kept her course through a world she has loved, upon 'an
earth which has entertained me'. She has been wayward, her
sense of direction eccentric; but through winter and rough
weather, she reaches the end with faith untarnished.

Little more than two years after this the stage would reach its
point of deviation, the 'sudden shout into the dream . . . the
moment of the call from another room'.

Rebellion and After

'Insurrection, with one accord, banded itself and woke.' It did not
declare itself until the night of 8 May 1956, theatrically as impressive a date, in its extremely restricted context, as the opening of
the French Revolution. The English Stage Company had just
begun a season of 'contemporary repertory' at a 'writers' theatre'
which happened—and we might say as usual—to be the Royal
Court in Sloane Square. After two productions, one mild
enough, the other Arthur Miller's American witch-hunt, *The
Crucible*, the company found suddenly that it was detonating
high explosive: a play by a 26-year-old actor, John Osborne,
called *Look Back in Anger*. Osborne would be the first of what the
Court's alert press agent, George Fearon, dubbed 'the angry
young men' (by no means confined to Sloane Square). No
dramatist could hope to repeat the shattering impact of that first

[5] Fabre: 'It was across this mass of leafage and in absolute darkness, that the
butterflies had to find their way in order to attain the end of their pilgrimage.
Under such conditions the screech-owl would not dare to forsake its olive-tree.
The butterfly . . . goes forward without hesitation . . . So well it directs its tortuous
flight that, in spite of all the obstacles to be evaded, it arrives in a state of perfect
freshness, its great wings intact . . . The darkness is light enough.'

play. Apparently, discontented youth had been waiting to hear, in public, the kind of impetuous white-hot invective against an older generation and contemporary life in general that Osborne's anti-hero expressed so readily. There could have been a more reasonable mouthpiece than this resentful and self-pitying Jimmy Porter who had married above him, and who kept a sweet-stall in a Midland town (Derby, perhaps, not that it matters); but young audiences—and a critic who said, rather touchingly, that he could never love anybody who did not love *Look Back in Anger*—took it all as the word from Sinai. So, and in effect, inadvertently, the new English drama was born. It was a time in which infinitely more alarming and important things would be happening in the world—the Hungarian rising, the Suez affair. 1956, indeed, would be a boiling-point year, a year of protest (and deep insecurity); and 'theatre of protest' was one of the many labels used for a revolt that derived simply from an attic box-set and a play fashioned in the traditional manner with a far from traditionally outspoken protagonist. Probably as much as anything it was a class rebellion, a punitive expedition bent upon wrecking the drawing-rooms and country-houses of the West End stage, and organized by what A. P. Herbert called gently 'the less contented young'. He added:

I am not one of those who moan and mourn
'It was without our leave that we were born!'
And therefore claim the right to sit and wince
At almost everything that's happened since.

In the circumstances it was strange that a play produced just a month before *Look Back in Anger* should have shown in the West End the style and elegance that mark the best British high comedy. This was Enid Bagnold's fastidious *The Chalk Garden*, something that later, in the theatre's changed climate, would never have the fullest critical appreciation (as distinct from public response, a long run and a profitable revival). It opened, as by right, at the Haymarket. Front-rank woman dramatists have been scarce—neither of those early prominent in the new order, Ann Jellicoe and Shelagh Delaney, seem to have stayed the course—but Enid Bagnold, an independent spirit and defiantly patrician, will have her niche in the twentieth-century theatre for at least two plays, this and, after nearly a decade, *The Chinese Prime Minister* (1965), damaged in London by its miscasting. *The Chalk Garden*, in its Sussex manor-house, with *grande dame* and enigmatic companion, is designed for page and stage: again and again we recognize an acute wit securely in the situation and never wandering into transferable epigram from a Wildean scene. Here any given line belongs to its speaker, and to no one else: it is dialogue framed to withstand the exacting usage of the years: the dramatist's sound is her own, and so is the lighting; radiance can fall from an unexpected quarter.

It was a form of playwriting that appeared likely to be doomed. In this spring and early summer of 1956 the central London stage found itself harried from both west and east: on one side, the Court, on the other the Royal at Stratford East (Stratford-atte-Bowe) where Joan Littlewood and her Theatre Workshop company trained their guns upon tradition. They had just discovered a robust, hard-drinking garrulous Dublin dramatist, Brendan Behan, author of *The Quare Fellow* (May 1956), set in an Irish gaol twenty-four hours before an execution. In another two years he would provide *The Hostage*, a fantastic tragi-comedy in which a young Cockney soldier is held as an IRA hostage in a Dublin lodging-house. Behan was lucky to have his work shaped by Joan Littlewood; so was the nineteen-year-old Salford girl Shelagh Delaney, who after seeing a play by Terence Rattigan, decided that she could do better and turned up with the affectingly sincere little piece *A Taste of Honey* (1959), aided immeasurably by the directness of its production. Joan Littlewood's vigorous, no-nonsense company could do this sort of thing, and it had a way too with rambling Cockney musicals that had an air of near-improvisation. But in general the Workshop, which originated in North Country touring after the War, could be over-valued. Eventually it lost its first careless rapture, though its influence on a particular form of community theatre was potent in its day, and is legendary yet: everything matter-of-fact, apparently spontaneous, often over-stated. 'I do not believe in the supremacy of the director, designer, actor, or even the writer,' Joan Littlewood said in 1961. 'It is through collaboration that this knockabout art of the theatre survives and kicks.'

Stratford East, which ceased to kick after a while—though something is usually afoot there—was always secondary to the Royal Court, power-house 'born out of passion and enthusiasm', still the home of the English Stage Company, still the theatre that exercises what one of its founders, George Devine, called 'the right to fail', and has much to its credit as well. Its record has been a switchback, but it has produced John Osborne, Arnold Wesker, N. F. Simpson and David Storey, it has given hospitality to many young writers of diverse merit (Christopher Hampton, Edward Bond, David Hare, Mary O'Malley), and it has looked far and unexpectedly for its revivals (*A Cuckoo in the Nest, The Changeling*). Towards the end of the nineteen-sixties, remarkably, it rediscovered for the stage three almost forgotten plays by D. H. Lawrence, *A Collier's Friday Night, The Daughter-in-Law* and *The Widowing of Mrs Holroyd*, bold ventures (school of kitchen-realism) in a medium that suited Lawrence less than any other.

Back to the point of deviation. 'There is laughter and conversation and a progression; people move and speak smoothly and casually; their breathing is controlled . . . Then there occurs a call from another room.' It had been a call to arms. Presently it would be wrong, in the judgment of a voluble minority, to write plays according to the set rules of battle, anything that respected an old order. As time passed, everything and anything could happen in the name of social realism. Dramatists, mostly working-class, began to do more or less what they liked—though, except in club theatres until the autumn of 1968, they could not say it as demotically as they liked—and, as if to accommodate them and their increasingly fragmented plays, stages were altered physically: the curtained proscenium arch yielded to platform stages, thrust stages, more rarely theatres-in-the-round, anything to prove that the time was free and older techniques were cobwebbed. Directors (in the words of Tyrone Guthrie, who had been pining for this for some time) could use 'a more highly plastic method of choreography'. Hence the open stages, the exiguous sets, the rejection of drawing-room naturalism, the mocking of plaster swags, poised caryatids and velvet curtains, the whole familiar framework of the Theatre Theatrical. Sets would not always be exiguous; frequently directors and designers would revert, a shade guiltily, to older ways, but once the theatre adopted the trick of exposing the mechanics of a production in (say) lighting and scene-shifting, it would never lose the habit.

The trouble over the years has been to discover for these surroundings plays that are more than ephemeral. By the mid-1970s the experimental drama, or Other Theatre, was in a blind alley of its own making. The Fringe (as it was also called; there were plenty of other names) spent itself on minority studio-projects fed by its own dramatists, watched by its own coterie audiences, confined in a world apart. Meantime, as it had done since 1956, the solid core of the West End's commercial theatre ('commercial' was illogically pejorative) remained stoically constant, beleaguered but indomitable, hardly aware of the test-tube groups that at heart would have given much for one of those central addresses, swags, caryatids and all.

What, at the end of 1977, is roughly the pattern created during the twenty-odd years since 1956? Television had been a pressing danger; but its growth until a set became apparently as necessary to a home as chairs and tables imperilled the cinema more than the theatre; at the same time, in a television-governed age, it has become vital for the theatre to recruit its future playgoers.

By 1977 the National Theatre, under its lately-knighted director, Sir Peter Hall, was established at last on the south bank of the Thames, only a few arrow-flights from Shakespeare's Bankside. Suggested first in 1848, it had been for over a century the shadow of a dream. True, at one period between the wars, a place had been prepared for it in South Kensington; but at heart few could have believed that this would be its ultimate home. At length, compared with the century's slow dragging of feet, all seemed to happen at once: the arrival of theatre subsidies, the passage through Parliament (1949) of a National Theatre Bill and the Royal laying of a foundation-stone on a summer day in 1951, some distance from the present site. It was then that Dame Sybil Thorndike spoke the Masefield ode with its lines, hardly fitted to the coming revolt, 'Making joy daily bread and beauty known' and 'Man's passions made a plaything and sublime.' The great complex by Waterloo Bridge was opened formally in 1976; there had been a period from 1963 when the company, for most of the time directed by Sir Laurence (Lord) Olivier, occupied the Old Vic which the Shakespearians of the Lilian Baylis foundation had left after nearly half a century. The new, heavily subsidized National was in itself the British theatre in microcosm, with three auditoria, the proscenium-stage Lyttelton, the open-stage Olivier and the rectangular box of the Cottesloe which was primarily a show-case for the Fringe (it could move between such pleasures as David Pownall's *Motocar* and Julian Mitchell's *Half-Life*, witty in a manner uncommonly alert and civilized).

The other major subsidized company is the Royal Shakespeare, which received its title in 1961. Since then it has divided its forces between the theatre at Stratford-upon-Avon and the Aldwych in London, a previous all-purposes house which will be its metropolitan home until a new theatre at the Barbican in the City. Shakespeare revivals have proliferated, wisely and helpfully as a rule, occasionally in superfluous caprice. Directors, the ruling power, have a trick of saying what they think Shakespeare should have meant: a dubious introduction for new playgoers.

However, many ideas—in Peter Brook's productions for example, as renowned as contentious—have been theatrically valid. Certainly the RSC, guardian of another national theatre, has become internationally famous, brow-bound with the oak. As a whole, the British classical stage has never been peopled better than by such players—a choice from riches—as Sir Laurence Olivier, Dame Peggy Ashcroft, Sir John Gielgud, Sir Ralph Richardson, Sir Alec Guinness, Dorothy Tutin, Judi Dench, Barbara Jefford, Paul Scofield, Ian Richardson, Richard Pasco and Alan Howard.

The so-called 'commercial' theatres of the unsubsidized West End, forty or so—a number that keeps fairly stable—have themselves long worked together as an unofficial, corporate and old-established National. Outside London, throughout the regions—provinces is an outmoded word—the widening system of repertory theatres, with varying Arts Council grants vital to life, keeps the living stage warmly animated and has contributed a good deal to the West End. Music-halls in the old sense have practically vanished, but their work goes on in numerous 'clubs', especially in the North.

In 1968, twelve years after the storm, a second sharp change in the theatre removed the Censorship, the end of a sustained battle and of innumerable, sometimes comic, attempts at evasion. Though by then it was merely a matter of opening the stable door wider, partisans promptly tore down the door, cast it on the flames and danced round the bonfire: another defeat for 'middle-class morality' and anything left over from a primeval existence. Since that time almost anything once taboo has been openly discussed or represented. Certain inevitable absurdities aside—for children are always ready to sack the nursery—the theatre has gradually settled. Its main flaws now are the simulation of wanton violence and sadism and the loss of control over language. Again and again this is debased by uninhibited coarseness, an apparently obligatory bravado. One director retorted that anybody could hear the same thing at any morning on a building-site; but it is doubtful whether many visit the theatre for that particular amenity. Objectors are told they are 'genteel', another word that is misused at an hour when, in Galsworthy's phrase, gentility has to be 'standing fire'. Just as the Edwardian drama lived in sitting-rooms, so many of the proudly proletarian writers after 1956 went to the kitchen (and usual offices). Hence the 'kitchen sink' label that added to the clustering clichés of the period (Theatre of Cruelty, Theatre of Menace, Theatre of the

Absurd and so forth), phrases from a muddled world on which we can impose no very persuasive pattern. Curiously, there has been a reactionary wistfulness for the security of those near-mythical Edwardians.

When all is said, the theatre is emerging safely from its twenty years' strife. There is ample talent, and there will be more when younger writers cease to talk to themselves; when they realize that free debate on sex and religion does not necessarily mean undisciplined self-communion in a studio, and that unselective 'reports from the front line', as a hopeful critic called them, must slip swiftly into oblivion. One writer (*The Times*, 11 November 1977) could say of a certain piece, throwing up his hands: 'Presumably the actors are consenting adults and have accepted their parts without compulsion. . . . It is a turgid, offensive, and meaningless indulgence cloaked in the guise of social relevance.' The last two words have shrivelled into meaningless patter.

Into the Future

Writers at any time are always, and naturally, anxious, for the good name of their own period. Yet, as this book has shown, the theatre did not rise fully armed from the mists of last Tuesday week. Kipling (now being rediscovered) wrote of the season's daffodil that never hears

> What change, what chance, what chill,
>   Cut down last year's;
> But with bold countenance
>   And knowledge small
> Esteems her seven days' continuance
>   To be perpetual.

We know that only a few dramatists from any given time can endure. Thus we have seen the fate of William Archer's choices when he was discussing in 1882 the arrived or coming men of the London stage. The list would soon be curled at the edges. Seventy years on, when only a few of these dramatists were names, another book by another critic looked briskly to the future; his choices too would be sunk beneath the drift of the files. So again, after yet another decade: names that had seemed permanent would quickly dim. They were Broughtons or Merritts or Howards. That is why we cannot afford to be easily hyperbolical about a newcomer on too slender evidence.

Eliot's *Murder in the Cathedral*, Canterbury
Cathedral, 1970

The interior of the Olivier Theatre, part of the
National Theatre complex

The National Theatre, South Bank

Sir Ralph Richardson and Sir John Gielgud in the
National Company's production of Pinter's *No
Man's Land*, 1975

A scene from the RSC production of Stoppard's
Travesties, Aldwych, 1974

Now, before considering the dramatists who headed the theatre at Christmas 1977, we should see what happened to the leaders early in 1956, all working in forms that would soon be branded as conventional. Terence Rattigan (knighted in 1971) continued to write until his death; at that time (November 1977) his *Cause Célèbre*, founded on a notorious murder case of the mid-1930s, was running in London: there, deserting his customary practice, he used skilfully a near-television technique, a mosaic of quick episodes and flashbacks. Though for a long while before this he had produced nothing to match *The Deep Blue Sea* or *The Browning Version*, such plays as *Ross* (1960)—a treatment of the enigmatic and histrionic introvert Lawrence of Arabia—and the cumulatively affecting *After Lydia*, at first (1973) part of a double bill, did honour to a man steadily unswayed by the confusion round him. Rattigan was not a writer for the more heated polemics. As far back as 1953 he said of his plays, asserting his belief in strength of character and narrative: 'If these are not what are called plays of ideas, the reason is not that ideas do not sometimes occur to me . . . I really don't think the theatre is the proper place to express them.'

Noël Coward (knighted 1970), who kept at work during the decade 1956–66, acted himself in the last autumnal trio, collectively entitled *Suite in Three Keys*. Though his technique was unscratched, not much from those years may exist for the future except a comedy of a home for old actresses, *Waiting in the Wings* (1960): battered by the critics, to Coward's grief, it had a preservative gentleness and kindness. The once comparably prolific J. B. Priestley added little fresh. *A Severed Head* (1963), which he dramatized with Iris Murdoch from her novel, had over a thousand performances, but for Priestley it had to be a by-path. Round his eightieth birthday, managements were beginning to revive his work—*An Inspector Calls*; at the National, *Eden End*—and we could speculate again on the concealed depths and the half-stifled poetic sense of an allegedly plain-man dramatist.

Of three writers with entirely different approaches to the stage, John Whiting had the most resolute and least comfortable play, *The Devils* (RSC, 1961). Founded on a book by Aldous Huxley, it told the true story of an early seventeenth-century scandal in the French provincial town of Loudun: home of a libertine priest persecuted by a frustrated Mother Superior and her nuns, brought to trial, tortured and executed. Obsessed by the power of evil, Whiting allows the play after its early scenes to dwindle to an assemblage of horrors. An endearing wit, Peter Ustinov, has yet to write his masterpiece. *Romanoff and Juliet* (1956; ten days after *Look Back in Anger*) is topical fantasy, its lovers caught in the cold war, East–West, Russia–America, between the embassies in 'the smallest country in Europe' (for critics it was Ustinovia). *The Unknown Soldier and His Wife* (1968), 'two acts of war separated by a truce', is more expansive: it slides back to the Romans, lunges forward across the centuries, and looks to the future, putting into Ustinov's own terms the ancient cry, 'Would ye be wise, ye cities, fly from war.' N. C. Hunter, who died in 1971, had an unpretentiously first-rate play, *The Tulip Tree* (1962), basically about middle age and containing one unexpected outbreak against Nature. It was acted at the Haymarket, among the most civilized of West End theatres but to the faction-fighters always a citadel of reaction, a kind of massive and eternal drawing-room.

Quietest of English dramatists, R. C. Sherriff (who died in 1975, aged seventy-nine) did have one *succès d'estime* that, like *Journey's End*, may appear in the theatre of the future. Acted at the Birmingham Repertory in 1955, *The Long Sunset* reached London, at the Mermaid, only in 1961. Yet another journey's end, it is at the close of the Roman occupation of Britain early in the fifth century, Sir Mortimer Wheeler's 'age of *crépuscule* and quicksand', a slipping into the dark, a sudden chaos in the ordered realm between Vectis and the Wall. Fixed ineffaceably in the imagination, the piece is on three levels; the Rome that was, the Roman province that is ceasing to be and the Britain that will emerge.

William Douglas Home, out on his own as a confirmed West End dramatist, and inventive enough for three men, is both abundant and apparently unself-critical, the author of some forty plays in three decades. A few (*Aunt Edwina, The Cigarette Girl, In the Red*) can be dismissed outright; but enough is left—consider the style and assurance of *The Reluctant Debutante* (1955), *The Secretary Bird* (1968), *Lloyd George Knew My Father* (1972) and *The Kingfisher* (1977)—to suggest that, like the clipped tones of the early Coward, this agreeable voice from the Right will be heard in some later theatre. Undoubtedly Ben Travers's will be heard: no one from Right, Left or middle complains about a thoroughgoing professional from the blood royal of British farce. He had always wanted to write a comedy, apart from his Aldwych riots; and in 1975, when he was eighty-nine, he had probably the triumph of his life, *The Bed Before Yesterday*. Here the title is the key: the comedy is set in the early nineteen-thirties when a mature woman realizes delightedly what sex can be: the writing is lovable and frankly exuberant.

These are, or were, the principal revenants from another world except for Graham Greene, an occasional dramatist most telling in *The Complaisant Lover* (1959), modulating from the edge of farce to the edge of tragedy; the two verse dramatists whose names have to chime together, Eliot and Fry; and Sean O'Casey, poet without portfolio. Explicit verse plays seemed to have become the pariahs of the theatre. But T. S. Eliot's *The Elder Statesman* (1958), directed, as his other plays were, by E. Martin Browne, had an uncommon third act in which, as A. V. Cookman said, an apparent 'memory from Sophocles is used with characteristic elusiveness to let fall on a realistic psychological drama of self-revelation a gleam of extra-mundane meaning'. The basic structure here is that of *Oedipus at Colonus*. Regarded as the least of the final trio, it may be more lasting—notably its final scene—than some of the first critics ('ancient verities typically re-stated') sought to prophesy. Christopher Fry, whose two plays were staged with a wide gap between them, *Curtmantle* (1962) and the summer comedy, last of the seasonal quartet, *A Yard of Sun* (1970), was not aided by a mediocre Royal Shakespeare production of the first, an interpretation of Henry II's reign and its conflicting personages. It had the misfortune also to arrive soon after a highly theatrical, but shallow, piece on the same theme, *Becket* by the French dramatist Jean Anouilh. In *Curtmantle* we consider Henry's life, as William Marshal does, in memory: 'time and place become fluid, as they do in our thoughts', and, unimpeded, we pass across thirty years, watching the development of a difficult character and a difficult reign. Allardyce Nicoll commented here that Fry's verse was growing more intimately related to current speech patterns while still leaving himself the opportunity of moving to richer forms. The summer comedy *A Yard of Sun*, set in Siena after the War, and with a central theme of renewal, radiates warmth and goodwill ('You hear the ground under you purring again, warm like a cat's back').

Sean O'Casey, with Shaw, his friend and fellow-Dubliner, one of the century's two greatest dramatists, died at his Devon home in mid-September 1964; he was eighty-four and almost blind, but six days earlier he sent to New York an essay critical of 'the present-day trend in the theatre living now among the shadows where naught but dark things happen; to me life couldn't have achieved so much were it always busy destroying itself'. He had

had the delight in 1959 of seeing *Cock-a-Doodle Dandy* on the stage at last, in a Devine production at the Royal Court (1959), and he went on to write four other plays, none yet performed in London; at full-length, *The Drums of Father Ned* (published 1960), a cheerful joke about a Tostál, or festival of plays of music, in the town of 'Doonavale'; and, in single acts (1961), *Behind the Green Curtain* attacking religious bigotry; *Figuro in the Night*; and the good-tempered sketch *The Moon Shines on Kylenamoe*. This was about an English peer arriving by night at a tiny Irish station at the back of beyond: 'Stoppin', says the Guard, 'at Killcolm, Ballyfunbarr, Kylenamoe, Kylenatorf, Killcormac, an' all the rest of them, depositin' eager passengers without fear or threpidation!'

No eager passengers for the verse play. Only two, besides those of Fry and Eliot, have mattered in the theatre over the last twenty years. One, Dylan Thomas's *Under Milk Wood* (1956), was the poet's-eye view of a Welsh coastal village between one midnight and the next. It was originally designed for radio, but its sensuous vermicular speeches translated easily to the stage:

First Voice She comes in her smock frock and clogs.
Mary Ann Away from the cool scrubbed cobbled kitchen with the Sunday-school pictures on the whitewashed wall and the farmers' almanac hung above the settle and the sides of bacon on the ceiling hooks, and goes down the cockleshelled paths of that applepie kitchen garden, ducking under the gippo's clothespegs, catching her apron on the blackcurrant bushes, past beanrows and onion-bed and tomatoes ripening on the wall towards the old man playing the harmonium in the orchard, and sits down on the grass at his side and shells the green peas that grow up through the lap of her frock that brushes the dew.

There have been many revivals, most successfully those by James Roose-Evans[6] who broke away from the complicated realism of the first staging to a sympathetic stylized production that relied entirely upon the orchestration of the Welsh voices. Thomas finished *Under Milk Wood* in a hurry, and it tails off; until then it sings in the mind. The other verse play, a superb achievement but harshly criticized (except by such men as Cookman and Eric Keown) was Jonathan Griffin's *The Hidden King* at the Edinburgh Festival of 1957. Griffin, sensitive poet and one of the country's most accomplished translators, wrote here a chronicle, under the

[6] Roose-Evans also founded one of London's most important Fringe theatres, at Hampstead. Among several others, at the end of 1977, were those at Greenwich, Shepherd's Bush (the Bush) and Chalk Farm (the vast auditorium of the Round House).

rifted sky of the late Renaissance, in which, like his King, he said 'noble things as if he had a right to say them'. It is an evocation of Dom Sebastian, King of Portugal, thought to have been killed in 1578 at Alcazar during the sanguinary battle with the Moors. Twenty years have passed, and there is a Stranger in Venice: has he been 'fording a river twenty years wide'? As Robert Speaight, who acted in it on the open stage of the Assembly Hall at Edinburgh, with Robert Eddison as the King, has declared, it is 'exceptional in the alliance of intellectual rigour with tragic passion and romantic trappings'. The future will recover it.

Griffin's play was written before 1956 but staged after it. Since *The Hidden King* he has kept to translation, including so testing an achievement as Heinrich von Kleist's *The Prince of Homburg*, produced (1976) at the Royal Exchange in Manchester, the country's biggest theatre-in-the-round and certainly an arena for adventure. By 1977 the repertory theatres at Bristol, Nottingham, Manchester and Leeds were as exhilarating as any in the regiment that now kept guard over the stage beyond London.

We have spoken of dramatists who in the main kept outside the new order. What of the challengers? Retrospectively, it is fairly clear now that, with one major exception, dramatists of the late nineteen-sixties have overtaken the group from an earlier decade. John Osborne, who unwittingly started it all in 1956, has not (we can hazard) written much, in a large output, to raise the spirits of future generations. But he is an artist, if a touchy one, who has used his actor's intuition; his dialogue is as judged as it is fluent; and he can build detailed and demanding characters: George in *Epitaph for George Dillon* (presented 1957; a collaboration with Anthony Creighton); Archie Rice in *The Entertainer* (1957); Luther ('an animal rubbed to the bone with doubt') in the portrait-play of that name (1961); the savagely imagined, self-reproachful, guilt-oppressed solicitor in *Inadmissible Evidence* (1964); the old man in the angrily elegiac *West of Suez* (1971). One of his less-regarded works, *The Hotel in Amsterdam* (1968), a group portrait dominated by an absentee, grips the memory. The problem is that too often Osborne is simply in low spirits; like Mrs Gummidge, he feels it more than other people. His second success (immediately after *Look Back in Anger*), a semi-allegorical play, *The Entertainer*, owed a lot to the tingling veracity with which Laurence Olivier acted the third-rate comedian, dead behind the eyes. It has been blurred in revival.

The less vehement Arnold Wesker, also fostered at the Court, is a Jewish writer from the East End with an experience (remembered in his plays) of many diverse jobs: furniture-maker's apprentice, farm labourer's seed-sorter, kitchen porter, pastry-cook, and so on. He began with a trilogy more of ideas than of narrative progression. *Chicken Soup with Barley* (1958) and the relatively tame *I'm Talking About Jerusalem* (1960) dramatize the efforts of two Jewish working-class families, from the nineteen-thirties to the nineteen-fifties, to keep and practise their Socialist ideals; between them is *Roots* (1959), only tenuously attached: there a girl who has got away from her ignorant rural relations realizes suddenly that she is thinking for herself ('It's happening to me, I can feel it's happened'). A fervent, propagandist, idealistic, now and then (like some contemporaries) oddly elegiac dramatist, rich in unstereotyped character—though there can be unexpected relapses to cardboard—Arnold Wesker has not had a consistent theatrical response. *Chips With Everything* (1962), from an RAF training camp, is the most efficient, if not the most persuasive, of several other plays. Generously sincere (*The Friends, The Old Ones*), he has lost his first glow.

John Arden, at the Court in its early years, has been another ready and (in style) unusually flexible writer, moving in theme from Yorkshire slum folk and the welfare state (*Live Like Pigs*, 1958) to old age and its troubles (*The Happy Haven*, 1960), and even Arthurian legend (*Island of the Mighty*, RSC 1972, with his wife, Margaretta D'Arcy). He has almost a Galsworthian way—though neither of these very different men might agree—of stating a problem and letting us judge. One of his plays is of permanent value, *Serjeant Musgrave's Dance* (1959), a startling atmospheric piece about the nature of violence, set in a winter-bound Northern town about 1880; John Russell Taylor has called it 'a subtle and complex demonstration of the inextricability of pacifism and violence'. Though it does exhaust itself, much of the play is like a strong and brooding woodcut, and Musgrave, 'wild-wood mad', is a figure memorably possessed. *Armstrong's Last Goodnight* (Chichester Festival and National Theatre, 1965), a mid-sixteenth-century duel between practised diplomatist and buccaneering Border chief, is Arden's other uncommon work, composed in a carefully judged dialect. Later plays, though copious, have been unhelpful. He is an incalculable dramatist, battling and verbose, but the edge of his writing seems to be momentarily dulled.

This has to be said too of a man so different, and so remote from the young dramatists of his period, that we wondered at his arrival during the flourish of revolt. Critics have a passion for discovering and tracing 'influences', and N. F. (Norman Frederick) Simpson has been pigeonholed as a man from the Theatre of the Absurd (Ionesco and the rest). Actually he is in the mainstream of English nonsense, and he is quite prepared, with a gleam in his eye, to explain that his plays are about life as he sees it: 'Like most Englishmen, I have a love of order tempered by a deep and abiding respect for anarchy, and what I would one day like to bring about is that perfect balance between the two which I believe it to be peculiarly in the nature of English genius to arrive at.' He said of his farce, *One Way Pendulum* (1959), that, 'with its turrets and high pointed gables, it should have a particular appeal for anyone approaching it for the first time with a lasso': a Simpsonian phrase by a dramatist who lives in the world of the non-sequitur governed by absolute logic, and whose stage in his best play is occupied for most of the night by a replica of an Old Bailey court put together by a suburban enthusiast with a do-it-yourself set. Presently it acquires a judge, though not a jury ('They are here in spirit, m'lord') and this kind of cross-examination:

Prosecuting Counsel You were not, I imagine, in Reykjavik. . . ?
Mr Groomkirby I couldn't say for sure where that is, sir.
Counsel Yet you absented yourself from it?
Mr Groomkirby As far as I know, I did, yes . . .
Counsel And Chengtu, and Farafangana, and Pocatello?
Mr Groomkirby I'm afraid I'm not all that much good at geography.
Counsel Not much good at geography, Mr Groomkirby, yet you want the Court to believe that in order to be present in Chester-le-Street you absented yourself from a whole host of places which only an expert geographer could possibly be expected to have heard of.

Simpson's nonsense is grandly wreathing, as indeed it is in *The Cresta Run* (1965), a second play, this time presumably about international espionage, which sank with barely a trace.

The Theatre of the Absurd, into which classifiers rushed to deposit Simpson, is a fairly vague term coined for the dramatists who (like the prolific Romanian in Paris, Eugène Ionesco) have written plays that in form and matter reflect humanity's lack of purpose. The Parisian Irishman Samuel Beckett's wildly influential *Waiting for Godot* (*En attendant Godot*), a metaphor for what, in another of the day's labels, is called 'the human condition', is this kind of play. So is his shatteringly glum *Endgame* (1957), from a dead world, with its relish in despair, its blind dictator and his slave-son, and (much parodied) the legless parents in dustbins.

Beckett has written many plays, each briefer than the last, and dwindling to repetitive gabble by heads in urns (*Play*, 1964) to feverish monologues—one for a spotlit mouth—or even spasmodic gasps. *That Time* (1976) ends with a note for the actor, 'After three seconds eyes open. After five seconds smile, toothless for preference.' Obviously he says much to his devotees ('precisely worded parables in which the characters are concrete universals, moving through time'); others find it a dubious gift. Time must be the arbiter.

It is true that Harold Pinter, also linked with the Absurdists and influenced by Beckett, has developed since the late nineteen-fifties into one of the most regarded British dramatists of his time. With him is a younger man, Tom Stoppard, whose plays appear to contain fifty words for every one of Pinter's. It is the difference between the cascade of Niagara and a precisely channelled stream, though as a rule we have no idea where Pinter's stream springs or where at length it will flow. Formerly, like Osborne, a professional actor out of London, he is, like Wesker, a Jew from the East End and he has produced a formidable list of works for the theatre, television, film and radio. His first full-length piece, *The Birthday Party* (1958), about two men from the unknown who carry off a third into the unknown from the banal surroundings of a seaside boarding-house, lasted for a week in London at the old Lyric Theatre, Hammersmith. It has now its place in the canon, labelled with what the late Hilton Brown, in another context, called 'imperishable gum', as a Comedy of Menace. A critic in *The Birmingham Post*, while *The Birthday Party* was at Wolverhampton on its pre-London tour, found the first two acts disturbing and the third disastrous; the piece as a whole reminded him of Thomas Rymer on *Othello*: 'Some burlesque, some horrors, a ramble of comical wit, and some mimicry to divert the spectators.' Now we know more of Pinter, admirers (of all three acts) have rallied. He went on to spectacular improvement with *The Caretaker* (1960), which could be about loneliness and survival, and is in fact an absorbing anecdote of two strange brothers, a cluttered room in a West London suburb, and a comically evasive, pathetically cunning tramp who may or may not lose his expected haven. The end, however obvious it seems, is inconclusive. Pinter is the master of ambiguity: his audiences go out arguing. A character in *The Caretaker* says: 'I can take nothing you say at face value; every word you speak is open to any number of interpretations.' More books have been written on his work than upon any other contemporary, and they solve little, for

Pinter shows us what he wishes to show and leaves us to decide.

His dialogue can be either the most laconic stichomythia or detailed and rhythmical. No one has a more exact ear—it is like a tape-recorder. No one makes a more astute use of silences. The flaw is that these people can be spectral. In memory several of the plays melt into each other: their titles, *The Collection* (1962), *Landscape* (1969), *Old Times* (1971), convey as little to anyone but a fascinated specialist as the names of the characters do. *The Caretaker*, *The Homecoming* (1965), which Pinter defines as a play about love and the lack of love, and *No Man's Land* (1975), stand from the haunted haze: if he had written nothing else, Pinter would be secure among the century's dramatists. He is not one of the rebels, not a coterie man; whatever his prefatory debt to Samuel Beckett, he is an original. Not much marks so surely the change in the drama over seventy years as a successive reading of Pinero's *His House In Order* and Pinter's *No Man's Land*. This, presented at the National with two extraordinary performances by Sir Ralph Richardson as the owner of an opulent house by Hampstead Heath, and Sir John Gielgud as an equally puzzling, and splendidly articulate, parasite, seems to be about the limbo between reality and illusion, a no man's land of the mind, something 'which never moves, which never changes but which remains forever, icy and silent'.

Neither Pinter, though he had an early double bill transferred there, nor Tom Stoppard, at the head of the newest group of dramatists, is Royal Court-bred. Stoppard, of Czech descent, formerly a Bristol journalist, and the most volubly eloquent talker in the modern theatre, was honoured first as the author of *Rosencrantz and Guildenstern Are Dead* (1966), concentrating on those two attendant lords from *Hamlet* propelled to their fate on the fringes of a tragedy they never understand. Beckett again, maybe; possibly we should value him for the hints that other writers have transformed. So far Stoppard has succeeded most thoroughly with *Jumpers* (National company, 1972) and *Travesties* (RSC, 1974). *Jumpers*, which begins with the murder of a logical positivist who is also a gymnast ('the close association between gymnastics and philosophy is I believe unique to this university'), depends for most of the night on a professor of moral philosophy who, in performance, resembles a windmill ambitious to be Senior Wrangler, and who is actively engaged in metaphysical speculation. Somehow the moon is involved as well as a dead hare, a detective named Bones, a tortoise and a former musical comedy star: it is all, said a critic, 'blithely and celestially funny', and this (whatever may be hidden beneath the farce) is what audiences will salute first.

Travesties, even better, is—the author speaking—'a work of fiction that makes use, and misuse, of history. . . . Real people and imaginary people are brought together without ceremony; and events which took place months, or even years, apart are presented as synchronous.' Actually the affair, as hilarious as erudite, is an exuberant inflation of a question-mark. Having realized that Lenin, James Joyce and Tristan Tzara, the Dadaist poet, were living at the same time during the First World War in 'the pacific civilian haven of Zurich', Stoppard brings them together. Finding too that Joyce acted as business manager for *The Importance of Being Earnest* by an English-speaking cast—an insignificant British consular official as Algy—he uses this Henry Carr, another man from the margin, as his storm-centre. We first meet Carr as a seedy cynic in later middle age, his wits cloudy about him as he hazily evokes wartime Zurich in a smother of loose ascription and fuzzy recollection. From this we slide into an extravaganza that could be called *Carr in Wonderland*, governed by the man's younger self at the centre of a Walter Mittyish exercise: everything and everybody mixed madly in the wrong proportions which, theatrically, are the right ones. A brief scene is written entirely in Shakespeare quotations; another, and longer, in limericks; *The Importance of Being Earnest* is required reading; and Carr is always likely to say such things as:

> It is this complete absence of bellicosity, coupled with an ostentatious punctuality of public clocks, that gives the place its reassuring air of permanence. Switzerland, one instinctively feels, will not go away . . . Desperate men who have heard the clocks strike thirteen in Alsace, in Trieste, in Serbia and in Montenegro, who have felt the ground shift beneath them in Estonia, Austro–Hungary, and the Ottoman Empire, arrive in Switzerland and after a few deep breaths find that the ringing and buzzing in their ears has regulated itself into a soothing tick-tock, and that the ground beneath their feet, while inevitably sloping, is as steady as an alp.

Unlike too many current dramatists, Stoppard, whose ideas glitter like the Milky Way, prizes the language and does not scatter it with gratuitous obscenities. At the close of 1977 he was one of the theatre's main and idiosyncratic hopes.

It is time-wasting to hunt for any grand design among the new writers. Professionally adroit, they have accomodated themselves to any demands (and these are considerable) that the theatre can make. There are such men among them as Simon Gray, who in *Butley* (1971) has precisely defined a waspishly exhibitionist don, and in *Otherwise Engaged* (1975) a self-sufficient publisher—call him a solipsist—assailed during his evening at home by a covey of intruders; Christopher Hampton, whose 'bourgeois comedy', *The Philanthropist* (1970), might be inter-leaved with Gray's work, but whose *Savages* (1973) is an intensely felt, if diffuse, play prompted by the genocide of South American Indians; and Trevor Griffiths, whose home ground is political, but whose amplest work, *Comedians* (1975), is a dissection of laughter and its sources. Frank Marcus, invigorating as drama critic and dramatist (his meridian so far is *The Killing of Sister George*, 1965), has said that his plays are 'about illusion and reality, the impossibility of living either with or without illu-sions'. Alan Bennett can be both uncannily a parodist—consider his allegorical school play, *Forty Years On* (1968)—and as touch-ing as in *The Old Country* (1977): this, though its humours are real as well, turns quietly into a wistful portrait of a political exile.

There are many other writers at various levels, in or out of the West End. An obsession with violence can vitiate the work of Edward Bond, a concentrated, clinical Royal Court dramatist (*Saved, Lear, Bingo*): he is most rewarding in *The Sea* (1973) and in passages of *The Fool* (1975), a picture of the poet John Clare. Charles Wood, whose chief and bitter theme has been military life, wrote for the National a panoramic piece called *H: Being Monologues in Front of Burning Cities* (1969): flashing up the Indian Mutiny—'H' is General Havelock—its verbal and visual powers have been underrated. Peter Terson, most noticeably as a supple craftsman in semi-documentary material; the thoughtful John Bowen (*After the Rain*, 1966), preoccupied, as he says, with myth; David Mercer, Dennis Cannan, David Rudkin, Willis Hall and Keith Waterhouse (often collaborating), the veteran Ronald Gow, John Mortimer: all of these have added at least one notable play to the theatre's intricate fabric. The roll could be extended. The late Agatha Christie looked after the puzzle-play (to such startling effect that *The Mousetrap*, 1952, has lasted through more than a quarter of a century). Two new woman dramatists have appeared: Pam Gems, whose *Dusa, Fish, Stas, and Vi* (1976) is entirely feminine, a group study of four flat-mates; and Mary O'Malley, who offered in *Once A Catholic* (1977) her impression of a Harlesden convent school twenty years ago (not surprisingly, she was herself at school in Harlesden just then). Though anything that underestimates faith in an age with too little can be perilous, the piece bubbles with amusement, and does speak seriously about the lack of understanding between teacher and pupil. Orthodox religion has had a poor showing in the modern theatre: in fairness, one critic said gently, we need a farce about agnosticism. Still, a Religious Drama Society (Radius) exists and prospers; its headquarters are at the 'actors' church', St Paul's, Covent Garden.

Now, at the end of our period, we can take a last group of prominent writers, linked (however theorists may search) by nothing but craftsmanship. Humour, as we know from Trevor Griffiths, is so personal a thing that admirers of the late Joe Orton's hyperbolically discussed comedies (*Loot*, 1966, for one: outrageous in theme, sub-Wildean in dialogue) probably find it easy to resist the civilized ingenuities of Alan Ayckbourn. Least derivative and assertive of writers, he has the privilege of testing his own plays in repertory at Scarborough. Expert at putting them together from carefully considered trifles, he is fond of choosing an insoluble stage problem and solving it there and then. In his typically confident trilogy *The Norman Conquests* (1974) he presents a single situation, during a country week-end, from three points of view: one play in the sitting-room, a second in the dining-room, a third in the garden: the interlocking grip never slackens. Ayckbourn may sometimes have to avoid stretching his technique for the sake of the exercise—as in the legerdemain of *How the Other Half Loves* (1969), or the ultimately jarring *Absent Friends* (1975)—but his range, within a few years, has been heartening for British comedy. In *Bedroom Farce* (National, 1977) he sets side by side three bedrooms in different houses without using for a moment the kind of situation the title might suggest; he is too an alchemist with the apparent leaden commonplaces of domestic badinage. *Just Between Ourselves* (1977) alarmed pigeonholing writers by its logically distressing development: the nervous breakdown of a woman who is left helpless in profound emotional shock. Ayckbourn is far more than a reliable light entertainer.

A graver dramatist, Robert Bolt, has belonged (as Ayckbourn has) almost entirely to the West End theatre. His first play, *Flowering Cherry* (1957), was a rather ordinary study of futility and self-deception. In *The Tiger and the Horse* (1960), 'unnaturally articulate', he said, but also gracefully literate, a man who has shunned controversy realizes that, in the stock phrase, he can no longer remain uncommitted; and *A Man for All Seasons* (1960, and also concerned with the individual and his social conscience) is a portrait of Sir Thomas More, who died for his honesty, refusing to 'incline to the King's pleasure'. Bolt tells this with controlled passion; the contentious feature is the use as chorus of a functionary called the Common Man to bind the narrative. A fantasy, *Gentle Jack* (1963), was an error; but *Vivat! Vivat Regina!* (1970) illustrates Bolt's method of bringing to the theatre an intricate historical progress—here the relations between Elizabeth I and Mary Queen of Scots—without either losing his way or minimizing his characters. He has been similarly accomplished in *State of Revolution* (National, 1977), a selective record of the Russian Revolution, with Lenin of the overwhelming will at its heart.

David Storey, novelist and dramatist, has been faithfully a Royal Court man, though several of his plays have gone on to the West End. He has written nine in ten years, most of them solidly naturalistic (e.g. *In Celebration*, 1969; *The Contractor*, 1969; *The Changing Room*, 1971; *The Farm*, 1973). One, *Home* (1970) is a movingly subdued impression of patients on the terrace of what proves to be a mental home; and, unlooked-for and indifferently received, *Cromwell* (1971) is an inexplicit, eerie piece from a country (presumably seventeenth-century Ireland) where ignorant armies clash by night. There have been other plays, among them the first and difficult *The Restoration of Arnold Middleton* (1967), with its psychological tensions, and the last a rowdy black comedy, *Mother's Day* (1976), that could have been signed by Orton. That is negligible; but at his most governing, while exploring the fissures in family life (*In Celebration*), chronicling Saturday afternoon under the stand of a Northern League Rugby club (*The Changing Room*), reporting the elliptical dialogue, pierced by silences, of *Home*—this was performed definitively by Ralph Richardson and John Gielgud—or crossing the river in *Cromwell* ('Its shoals, its rocks, its crevices . . . its gleams'), Storey is a dramatist consistently and excitingly adaptable. It is as superfluous to evolve any theory about him as about the work of Peter Nichols. Like Storey, he is a clear observer, a frequently astringent writer. Also like him (and others: Wesker the prime example) Nichols's work can be autobiographical. His mark is the wry, understanding humour that has allowed him to create (from experience) the parents of a spastic child in *A Day in the Death of Joe Egg* (1967), and in *The National Health; or, Nurse Norton's Affair* (1969), to cross-cut an unsparing hospital documentary with a parody of popular nurse-and-doctor fiction. The best of his other plays have been the swift montage of *Forget-Me-Not Lane* (1971) and—appreciated by any pedestrian—the comic-sinister prophecy of *The Freeway* (1974); the worst is a dragging farce about a military concert-party in Malaya, *Privates on Parade* (RSC, 1977).

So, at length, to Peter Shaffer. His twin brother, Anthony, wrote *Sleuth* (1970), on its day the most brow-creasing of the theatre's intentional puzzles; but the Shaffer we usually mean is the author, always refusing to repeat himself ('Labels,' he has said, 'are not for playwrights'), of such entirely disparate and compelling work as *The Royal Hunt of the Sun* (1964); the blind man's buff of *Black Comedy* (1965) with its reversal of light and darkness, an enchantingly imaginative farce where the dark is light enough; and the strange and not instantly summoning psychiatric dilemma of *Equus* (1973). All of these were acted at the Old Vic during the National Theatre's tenancy. *Equus*, in particular, has gone round the world; but it is *The Royal Hunt* that lingers now, the Spanish expedition to the lands of the Inca, Pizarro's capture of the remote, god-like Atahuallpa, god of the earth and sky, and the ensuing rapprochement and most damnable of treacheries. In this play of conquest, heroism, brutality and cupidity, the dramatist wished to create (and did so) 'by means both austere and rich—means always disciplined by a central aesthetic—an experience that was entirely and only theatrical'.

A Play Tonight

Here now, looking towards the two last decades of the most turbulent and changeable century in the history of the British drama, we have no cause to believe that the theatre will fail in spirit or achievement. It had no competition at all when the century was young and Edwardians, brought up to the rule of actor-managements and an unshakeable West End tradition, were going, some almost furtively, to Sloane Square to see what the anarchists were about. Today, in the most competitive world it has known and one that financially has altered out of all knowledge, it is holding its place. Structurally, it represents a triple alliance: the two national companies and the Repertories that between them compose a National Theatre of the regions; the West End's phalanx; and the unbiddable and fertile Fringe, compact of companies often oddly christened and preserving a raging enthusiasm. The Dickensian Mrs Badger reported the words of her late husband, Captain Swosser. 'If you have only to swab a plank,' he said, 'you should swab it as if Davy Jones were after you'; and this is what the Fringe does, in London swabbing away at lunch-time as well as at night: something Edwardians would find inexplicable.

Much else would puzzle them, brought up as they were on the doctrine of degree ('Untune that string, and hark, what discord follows!') and upon Pinero's judgment: 'Is it not true . . . that we are not greatly stirred by the sorrows of those in humble condition?' Pinero said also, 'A serious political play is impossible.' How would he have received a director who explained in 1964 that *Hamlet* was about 'the problems of commitment in life and politics'?

In general, except at the Court, the Edwardian theatre interpreted social problems as the problems of aristocratic society. After two wars, and in a welfare (and Trade Union) state, many dramatists come direct from the working class, old values are dispersed, conventions smothered. Snobbery remains, as it always will, but it is inverted snobbery. To seek any obvious pattern in the ever-shifting record since 1956 and 1958 is superfluous. We can think of the theatre, in the words of A. V. Cookman years ago, as a crystal over which searchlights play, each finding its mark, resting upon it illuminatingly, and fading to make room for another at a different level. Dramatists write about everything. Within weeks, it would seem, newspaper headlines are in a play. It is a topical theatre, an argumentative theatre, a theatre that (in spite of Jimmy Porter) is never short of 'causes'; it is also—and calmly among the din—a theatre of entertainment.

Of course, various writers have been influenced from one source or another. Brecht, Beckett, Ionesco: the names and the categories and the labels recur. Some derivations are plain; some are not. There will be other influences as fashion moves. The stage now is never still. In the mid-1960s directors were saying, 'It is enormously important to have a theatre where one can take risks,' and 'We want to be in a world of experiment.' The risks are taken; the experiments continue. Inevitably, there is nonsense; there is also a great deal of vigorous talent. We have the players, capable always of what Masefield called 'the acted passion beautiful and swift'; many evenings in the theatre can be acronychal, that pleasant astronomer's word for a rising of stars at nightfall.

What the time (and with it the drama) lacks as much as anything is an unflawed faith, the kind of faith that moved

> the northern Guildsmen, these
> That were the makers of our Mysteries.

We cannot perpetually believe in disbelief. We need, too, the rediscovery of a certain symmetry and grace; of language that can lift heart and mind. 'Music would unground us best,' wrote Christopher Fry, 'As a tide in the dark comes to boats at anchor,/And they begin to dance.'

That full tide will return. Meanwhile the British theatre is enduring. Tonight we'll hear a play.

Bibliography

Play-lists and General Reference Books

Lists of English plays are provided in *The Mediæval Stage* by Sir E. K. Chambers (2 vols., 1903) and *The Elizabethan Stage* (4 vols., 1923), G. E. Bentley's *The Jacobean and Caroline Stage* (5 vols., 1941–56) and Allardyce Nicoll's *History of English Drama, 1660–1900* (6 vols., 1952–9; also a seventh volume, *English Drama, 1900–1930: The Beginnings of the Modern Period*, published in 1973). For the period to 1700, A. Harbage's *Annals of English Drama* (new edition, revised by S. Schoenbaum, 1964) is a useful handbook; and (to 1660) Sir Walter Greg's massive *Bibliography of English Printed Drama to the Restoration* (1939–59), an invaluable detailed study. *The Oxford Companion to the Theatre* (edited by Phyllis Hartnoll, 3rd edition, 1967, with list of theatre books compiled by D. M. Moore) contains numerous entries on theatres, dramatists and actors; for dramatists see also *The Reader's Encyclopaedia of World Drama*, edited by John Gassner and Edward Quinn (1970) and Myron Matlaw's *Modern World Drama: An Encyclopaedia* (1972). Allardyce Nicoll's *World Drama* (second edition, revised and enlarged, 1976) is important. So, for British drama, is *The Irresistible Theatre: From the Conquest to the Commonwealth* by W. Bridges-Adams (1957). *A Dictionary of the Drama* by W. Davenport Adams (one volume only, A-G., 1904) is informative within its tantalizing alphabetical limits.

English Theatrical Literature, 1599–1900 is a remarkable bibliography by James Fullarton Arnott and John William Robinson (1970) that incorporates Robert W. Lowe's *A Bibliographical Account of English Theatrical Literature*.

The catalogue of the 'Larpent' plays executed by D. Macmillan (1939) is supplemented by the British Museum's *Plays Submitted to the Lord Chamberlain, 1824–1851* (1964).

The Middle Ages and Early Tudor Period

The two volumes of *The Mediæval Stage* by Sir E. K. Chambers remain a standard authority. This is supplemented now by Karl Young's *The Drama of the Mediæval Church* (2 vols., 1933), Hardin Craig's *English Religious Drama of the Middle Ages* (1955), M. D. Anderson's *Drama and Imagery in English Mediæval Churches* (1963), which introduces much fresh material, and various specialized studies. All the extant English manuscript plays have been edited. Peter Happé edited *English Mystery Plays: A Selection* (1975). For staging, R. Southern's *The Mediæval Theatre in the Round* (1957), G. R. Kernodle's *From Art to Theatre* (1944) and Glynne Wickham's four volumes, *Early English Stages* (1959–71) present much detailed information. Folk drama is dealt with by Sir E. K. Chambers in *The English Folk Play* (1933) and R. J. E. Tiddy in *The Mummers' Play* (1923).

The Tudor moralities and interludes, after long neglect, are attracting more attention. Most of the plays are included in the Malone Society series and J. S. Farmer's Tudor Facsimile Texts. Among important critical contributions are A. P. Rossiter's *English Drama from Early Times to the Elizabethans* (1950), T. W. Craik's *The Tudor Interlude* (1958), Bernard Spivak's *Shakespeare and the Allegory of Evil* (1958), D. M. Bevington's *From Mankind to Marlowe* (1962), and Anne Righter's *Shakespeare and the Idea of the Play* (1962) which studies the relationship between playwright and spectators from mediæval times to the later years of the sixteenth century.

The Elizabethan, Jacobean and Caroline Period

Prime authorities are Sir E. K. Chambers and G. E. Bentley. The form of the Elizabethan stage has been much discussed, and certain of its features are still controversial; among later studies are *The Globe Playhouse: Its Design and Equipment* by J. C. Adams (1942; second edition, 1961); *the Globe Restored* (1953; second edition, 1968) by C. Walter Hodges; Leslie Hotson's *Shakespeare's Wooden O* (1959); Irwin Smith's *Shakespeare's Globe Playhouse: A Modern Reconstruction* (1956); *Theatre of the World* by Frances A. Yates (1969); and *Shakespearean Staging, 1599–1642* by T. J. King (1971). Related subjects are considered in Alfred Harbage's *Shakespeare's Audience* (1941) and *Shakespeare and the Rival Tradi-*

tions (1952), B. L. Joseph's *Elizabethan Acting* (1951; second edition, 1964); and Muriel C. Bradbrook's *The Rise of the Common Player: A Study of Actor and Society in Shakespeare's England* (1962). The staging of the Court masque is discussed in A. Reyher's *Les masques anglais* (1909), Allardyce Nicoll's *Stuart Masques and the Renaissance Stage* (1937), Enid Welsford's *The Court Masque* (1927), Lily B. Campbell's *Scenes and Machines on the English Stage during the Renaissance* (1923; reprinted, 1960), and S. Orgel's *The Jonsonian Masque* (1965). Many of the original Inigo Jones designs are reproduced in *Designs for Masques and Plays at Court* (1924), a catalogue prepared by P. Simpson and E. F. Bell. Sir Walter Greg, in *Dramatic Documents from the Elizabethan Playhouses* (2 vols., 1931) gives the texts of, and analyses, the surviving prompt-books and associated material.

Most of the plays are now available and well edited, some printed separately, and others in collections. General studies abound; many volumes examine individual dramatists, and others particular dramatic forms. We have such works as *Elizabethan and Jacobean Playwrights* by H. W. Wells (1939), Una Ellis-Fermor's *The Jacobean Drama* (1936; revised, 1965), and A. Harbage's *The Cavalier Drama* (1936). Elizabethan tragedy has been much discussed in general and special aspects; for example, Willard Farnham's *The Mediæval Heritage of Elizabethan Tragedy* (1956), W. Clemen's *English Tragedy Before Shakespeare* (1961), Muriel C. Bradbrook's *Themes and Conventions of Elizabethan Tragedy* (1935), *Seneca and Elizabethan Tragedy* by F. L. Lucas (1922), *Elizabethan Revenge Tragedy* by Fredson Bowers (1940), and *English Domestic or Homiletic Tragedy* by H. H. Adams (1943). Irving Ribner surveys comprehensively *The English History Play in the Age of Shakespeare* (1957). Comedy is dealt with in Muriel C. Bradbrook's *The Growth and Structure of Elizabethan Comedy* (1955), tragi-comedy by E. M. Waith (1952) and M. T. Herrick (1955), pastoral drama by Sir Walter Greg (1906), and the 'jig' by C. R. Baskerville (1929). Principles underlying the period's dramatic practice are explored by Madeleine Doran in *Endeavours of Art* (1954) and by Mary C. Hyde in *Playwriting for Elizabethans, 1600–1605* (1945). L. C. Knights discusses the social background of the early seventeenth century stage in *Drama and Society in the Age of Jonson* (1937). H. N. Hillebrand has described *The Child Actors: A Chapter in Elizabethan Stage History* (1926), and Michael Shapiro's *Children of the Revels* (1976) is also devoted to the boy companies and their plays.

Those who are interested in the question of collaborative

authorship during the period should note Cyrus Hoy's series of articles published in *Studies in Bibliography* between 1956 and 1961, as well as S. Schoenbaum's historical survey of *Internal Evidence and Elizabethan Dramatic Authorship* (1966).

So much has been written about Shakespeare that we have to be extremely selective. The best compact bibliographical guide is *Shakespeare* (1973), edited by Stanley Wells. For the life, there are *William Shakespeare: A Study of Facts and Problems* (2 vols., 1930) by E. K. Chambers; Edgar I. Fripp's *Shakespeare, Man and Artist* (2 vols., 1938); Peter Alexander's *Shakespeare* (1964) and S. Schoenbaum's *Shakespeare's Lives* (1970) and *William Shakespeare: A Documentary Life* (1975). Texts include the one-volume editions of Peter Alexander (1957) and (the Riverside Edition, 1974) of G. Blakemore Evans; and, in separate plays, the New Cambridge, New Arden, and New Penguin editions. On various themes there are *A New Companion to Shakespeare Studies*, edited by Kenneth Muir and S. Schoenbaum (1971); *The Reader's Encyclopædia of Shakespeare*, edited by O. J. Campbell and E. J. Quinn (1966), Geoffrey Bullough's *Narrative and Dramatic Sources of Shakespeare* (8 vols., 1957–75), Charlton Hinman's *The Printing and Proofreading of the First Folio of Shakespeare* (2 vols., 1965), *Shakespeare's Imagery and What it Tells Us* by Caroline F. E. Spurgeon (1935); Arthur Colby Sprague's *Shakespeare and the Actors: The Stage Business in His Plays, 1660–1905* (1944; reprinted, 1963) and *Shakespeare's Histories: Plays for the Stage* (1964); Harley Granville-Barker's *Prefaces to Shakespeare* (4 vols. from 1927; also 4 vols. of an illustrated paper-back edition, edited by M. St Clare Byrne, 1963); and J. L. Styan's *The Shakespeare Revolution* (1977). *Shakespeare Survey*, edited by Allardyce Nicoll and later by Kenneth Muir, has been published annually since 1948.

Marlowe's achievement, both in general and particular, has found many interpreters, notably Una Ellis-Fermor in *Christopher Marlowe* (1927); C. F. Tucker Brooke in *The Life of Marlowe and The Tragedy of Dido Queen of Carthage* (1930); Frederick S. Boas in *Christopher Marlowe: A Biographical and Critical Study* (1940); John Bakeless in *The Tragicall History of Christopher Marlowe* (2 vols., 1942); Paul H. Kocher in *Christopher Marlowe: A Study of his Thought, Learning, and Character* (1946); F. P. Wilson in *Marlowe and the Early Shakespeare* (1954); J. B. Steane in *Marlowe: A Critical Study* (1964); and Judith Weil in *Christopher Marlowe: Merlin's Prophet* (1977). Irving Ribner edited *The Complete Plays* (1963).

Ben Jonson too has been closely studied; there is invaluable critical material in the eleven-volume edition of the *Works*, begun in 1925 and edited at first by C. H. Herford and Percy Simpson, and later by P. and E. M. Simpson. Eric Linklater's *Ben Jonson and King James* (1931) is an affectionate portrait.

The Restoration Period

A general survey appears in the first volume (1660–1700) of Allardyce Nicoll's *A History of English Drama 1660–1900*. Leslie Hotson's *The Commonwealth and Restoration Stage* (1928; revised edition, 1964) presents valuable material on the fate of the theatre during the time (1642–60) when the drama was officially banned. Montague Summers has written on *the Restoration Theatre* (1934) and *The Playhouse of Pepys* (1935); the period is covered in the first volume of G. C. D. Odell's *Shakespeare from Betterton to Irving* (2 vols., 1920); and other books include A. Thaler's *Shakspere to Sheridan* (1922) on theatrical conditions and the staging of plays; Eleanore Boswell's *The Restoration Court Stage* (1932), and Bonamy Dobrée's critical study of *Restoration Tragedy* (1929). Naturally, the comedies of the time have received most attention, as in Bonamy Dobrée's *Restoration Comedy* (1924), Ten Eyck Perry's *The Comic Spirit in Restoration Drama* (1925), Kathleen M. Lynch's *The Social Mode of Restoration Comedy* (1926), L. I. Bredvold's *The Intellectual Milieu of John Dryden* (1934), J. H. Smith's *The Gay Couple in Restoration Comedy* (1948), D. Underwood's *Etherege and the Seventeenth Century Comedy of Manners* (1957), and N. N. Holland's *The First Modern Comedies* (1959). Several of the main dramatists have been specifically studied, and all have had their work recently edited in collected editions. Several scholars contribute to a symposium on *William Congreve*, edited by Brian Morris (1972; Mermaid Critical Commentaries).

The Eighteenth Century

A general survey of the theatre of the period is contained in the second and third volumes of Allardyce Nicoll's *History of English Drama, 1660–1900* (1959).

For many years John Genest's ten-volume *Some Account of the English Stage* (1832) was the standard season-by-season record of performances; this is supplanted now by the eleven volumes of *The London Stage, 1660–1800* (1960–5), edited by E. L. Avery, C. Beecher Hogan and others; and it is supplemented by D. Mac-

Millan's *Drury Lane Calendar, 1747–1776* (1936) and C. Beecher Hogan's *Shakespeare in the Theatre: A Record of Performances in London, 1701–1800* (2 vols., 1952–7).

Kalman A. Burnim, in his *David Garrick, Director* (1961), ranges over theatrical matters during the later part of this period. Richard Southern's *The Georgian Playhouse* (1948) and *Changeable Scenery* (1952) should be consulted, with D. F. Smith's *Plays about the Theatre in England* (1936) and *Critics in the Audience* (1953). Colley Cibber's *Apology* (1740; ed. R. W. Lowe, 1889) is a revealing record, and much other material appears in the lives and autobiographies of later actors: note Carola Oman's *David Garrick* (1958). There have been several books on Sheridan, including Madeleine Bingham's *Sheridan: The Track of a Comet* (1972). *The Wandering Patentee* by Tate Wilkinson, famous manager of the York circuit (originally published in four vols., 1795), was reissued (2 vols.) in 1973. Sybil Rosenfeld's *Strolling Players and Drama in the Provinces* (1939) and *The Theatre of the London Fairs* (1960) contain much information about performances away from the major London houses.

F. W. Bateson deals with *English Comic Drama, 1700–1750* (1929). The origins and development of the sentimental drama are traced in, for example, J. W. Krutch's *Comedy and Conscience After the Restoration* (1924) and in wider surveys by F. O. Nolte (1935) and A. Sherbo (1957); ballad-opera is examined by E. M. Gagey (1937) and W. E. Schultz (1923), and farce by L. Hughes (1956).

The Nineteenth Century

Allardyce Nicoll surveys nineteenth-century drama in the fourth and fifth volumes of *A History of English Drama, 1660–1900*. E. B. Watson's *Sheridan to Robertson: A Study of the 19th Century London Stage* (1926), *Drury Lane Journal: Selections from James Winston's Diaries 1819–1827*, edited by A. L. Nelson and G. B. Cross (1974); C. Rice's *London Theatre in the Eighteen-Thirties*, edited by A. C. Sprague and B. Shuttleworth (1950), William Archer's *English Dramatists of Today* (1882), *The Victorian Theatre: A Survey* by George Rowell (1956) and Rowell's selection of *Victorian Dramatic Criticism* (1971) are all helpful. Other drama criticism includes the work of Hazlitt (e.g. *A View of the English Stage*, 1818) and Leigh Hunt (e.g. *Critical Essays*, 1807) in various editions; Bernard Shaw's *Our Theatres in the Nineties* (3 vols., 1931); Clement Scott's

From 'The Bells' to 'King Arthur' (1897), which deals with Irving's work at the Lyceum; *Theatrical Notes* by Joseph Knight (1893), G. H. Lewes, *On Actors and the Art of Acting* (1875); Henry Morley's *The Journal of a London Playgoer from 1852 to 1866* (1891), and A. B. Walkley's *Playhouse Impressions* (1892).

Among players' biographies are J. Boaden's *Memoir of Mrs Siddons* (2 vols., 1827; variously reprinted), Yvonne French's *Mrs Siddons, Tragic Actress* (1836), H. N. Hillebrand's *Edmund Kean* (1933), Giles Playfair's *Kean: The Life and Paradox of the Great Actor* (1950 edition), J. C. Trewin's *Mr Macready: A 19th Century Tragedian and his Theatre* (1955) and *Benson and the Bensonians* (1960), Alan Downer's *The Eminent Tragedian: William Charles Macready* (1966), *The Life and Life-Work of Samuel Phelps* by W. May Phelps and John Forbes-Robertson (1886), John William Cole's *The Life and Theatrical Times of Charles Kean, FSA* (1959), Gordon Craig's *Ellen Terry and Her Secret Self* (1931), Laurence Irving's *Henry Irving* (1951). Sir F. edited Macready's *Reminiscences and Selections from his Diaries and Letters* (2 vols., 1875); the *Diaries, 1833–1851*, were edited by William Toynbee (2 vols., 1912), and edited and abridged by J. C. Trewin as *The Journals of William Charles Macready 1832–1851* (1967). Players', dramatists', managers' and critics' autobiographies include Sir Squire and Lady Bancroft's *The Bancrofts: Recollections of Sixty Years* (1909), the *Memoirs* of Charles Mathews (4 vols., 1838–9), *Recollections and Reflections* of James Robinson Planché (1872), Alfred Bunn's *The Stage: Both Before and Behind the Curtain* (3 vols., 1840), *Thirty-Five Years of a Dramatic Author's Life* by Edward Fitzball (1859), and Clement Scott's *The Drama of Yesterday and Today* (2 vols., 1899).

Much has been written on the history of the Gilbert and Sullivan Operas, notably Reginald Allen's *The First Night Gilbert and Sullivan* (with complete texts; revised edition, 1975), Audrey Williamson's *Gilbert and Sullivan Opera* (1955), and Leslie Baily's *Gilbert and Sullivan and Their World* (1973). The popular 19th century stage is discussed by F. J. Harvey Darton in *Vincent Crummles* (1926), M. Willson Disher in *Blood and Thunder* (1949), and A. E. Wilson in *East End Entertainment* (1954).

The Twentieth Century

Among the many books on the drama since 1900 are Allardyce Nicoll's detailed *English Drama 1900–1930: the Beginnings of the Modern Period* (1973); *The Collected Letters of Sir Arthur Pinero*, edited by J. P. Wearing (1974); Una Ellis-Fermor's *The Irish Dramatic Movement* (2nd edition, 1954); William Archer's *Real Conversations* (1904; particularly the talks with Pinero, Gilbert and Stephen Phillips); three volumes of Max Beerbohm's collected criticism, *Around Theatres* (new edition, 1953), *More Theatres* (1969), *Last Theatres* (1970), all edited by Rupert Hart-Davis; Desmond MacCarthy's *The Court Theatre, 1904–7* (1907); J. C. Trewin's *The Edwardian Theatre* (1976); Robert Speaight's *William Poel and the Elizabethan Revival* (1954); St John Ervine's *Bernard Shaw: His Life, Work, and Friends* (1956); M. M. Morgan's *A Drama of Political Man: A Study in the Plays of Harley Granville-Barker* (1961); *Modern Dramatists* (1912) and *The Youngest Drama* (1923) by Ashley Dukes; F. Vernon's *The Twentieth-Century Theatre* (1924); Ivor Brown's *Parties of the Play* (1928); James Agate's volumes of drama criticism, notably *First Nights* (1934); Norman Marshall's *The Other Theatre* (1947); E. Martin Browne's *The Making of T. S. Eliot's Plays* (1969); Richard Findlater's *Banned! A Study of Theatrical Censorship in Britain* (1967) and *Lilian Baylis* (1975); J. C. Trewin's *The Theatre Since 1900* (1951) and *Shakespeare on the English Stage 1900–1964* (1964); *A Bridges-Adams Letter Book* edited by Robert Speaight (1971); *Drama from Ibsen to Eliot* by R. W. Williams (1952); *J. B. Priestley—The Dramatist* (1964) by Gareth Lloyd Evans; Edward Gordon Craig's *On the Art of the Theatre* (1911; reissued, 1956); Derek Stanford's *Christopher Fry* (1951); David Krause's *Sean O'Casey: The Man and His Work* (1960); Eileen O'Casey's *Sean* (1971); W. A. Darlington's *6001 Nights: Forty Years a Critic* (1960); Peter Brook's *The Empty Space* (1968); John Russell Taylor's *Anger and After: A Guide to the New British Drama* (revised, 1969) and *The Second Wave: British Drama for the Seventies* (1971); Martin Esslin's *The Theatre of the Absurd* (1962) and *Pinter: A Study of His Plays* (third expanded edition, 1977); *Contemporary Dramatists*, edited by James Vinson (2nd edition, 1977); Oleg Kerensky's *The New British Drama: Fourteen Playwrights Since Osborne and Pinter* (1977); Irving Wardle's *The Theatres of George Devine* (1978); and John Elsom and Nicholas Tomalin's *The History of the National Theatre* (1978).

Index